The Great Social Laboratory

THE GREAT SOCIAL LABORATORY

Subjects of Knowledge

in Colonial and

Postcolonial Egypt

Omnia El Shakry

STANFORD UNIVERSITY PRESS
STANFORD, CALIFORNIA

Stanford University Press
Stanford, California
©2007 by the Board of Trustees of the Leland Stanford Junior University.
All rights reserved.
No part of this book may be reproduced or transmitted in any form or by any means, electronic or mechanical, including photocopying and recording, or in any information storage or retrieval system without the prior written permission of Stanford University Press.
Printed in the United States of America on acid-free, archival-quality paper

Library of Congress Cataloging-in-Publication Data
El Shakry, Omnia S.
The great social laboratory : subjects of knowledge in colonial and postcolonial Egypt / Omnia El Shakry.
   p. cm.
Includes bibliographical references and index.
  ISBN 978-0-8047-5567-2 (cloth : alk. paper)
  ISBN 978-0-8047-9331-5 (paper : alk. paper)
  1. Social sciences—Study and teaching—Egypt—History—19th century. 2. Social sciences—Study and teaching—Egypt—History—20th century. 3. Social sciences—Research—Egypt. 4. Egypt—Intellectual life—19th century. 5. Egypt—Intellectual life—20th century. I. Title.
H62.5.E3E4 2007
304.60962'0904—dc22
2007012976

ISBN 978-0-8047-8192-3 (electronic)

Typeset by Bruce Lundquist in 10/13 Sabon and Stone Sans display

In memory of Zaynab Shahata
(1911–98)

Contents

Acknowledgments ix
Note on Transliteration and Translation xiii

Introduction: Colonialism, Nationalism,
and Knowledge Production 1

PART I The Anthropology of the Modern Egyptians:
From the Fin-de-Siècle to the Second World War

1 The Ethnographic Moment 23

2 Anthropology's Indigenous Interlocutors:
Race and Egyptian Nationalism 55

PART II From Ethnographic Realism to Social Engineering:
The Problem of the Peasantry, 1925–1945

3 The Painting of Rural Life 89

4 Rural Reconstruction:
The "Road to a New Sanitary Life" 113

PART III The Problem of Population, 1925–1945

5 Barren Land and Fecund Bodies: The Emergence
of Population Discourse in Interwar Egypt 145

6 Body Politics: Gender, Reproduction, and Modernity 165

PART IV The Revolutionary Moment

7 Etatism: Theorizing Egypt's 1952 Revolution 197

Conclusion 219

Notes 223
Bibliography 291
Index 319

Acknowledgments

First books are rarely the product purely of their authors, and there are many individuals and institutions without whom this book would never have been completed. The research and writing for this book were made possible by the generous support of the American Research Center in Egypt; the Fulbright Traditional Scholar Program; the University of California President's Research Fellowship; and a Chancellor's Postdoctoral Fellowship at the University of California, Berkeley.

While I was researching in Cairo, the staff at Dar al-Kutub, Dar al-Watha'iq al-Qawmiyya (Madame Nadia and Madame Nagwa in particular), and Dar al-Hikma were exceptionally accommodating. Joyce Tovell, the archivist of the Rare Books and Special Collections Library at the American University in Cairo, and an old acquaintance, was kind enough to allow me to examine the Hassan Fathy Archives before they were even formally catalogued. Steve Urgola graciously permitted me to revisit the archives. In Egypt, the staff at the Fulbright Office made my stay in Cairo pleasant and productive. I especially thank Safaa Abadi, as well as Nevine Gad El Mawla, Sally Salama, Hind El-Rasmy, Hanan El-Rihany, and Maggie William.

This project first took shape while I was a graduate student at New York University, where I was fortunate enough to be surrounded by outstanding scholars and mentors. I am above all grateful to the individuals who initiated me into the study of the Middle East, Lila Abu-Lughod, Samira Haj, and Timothy Mitchell. I have benefited beyond measure from their scholarship, their criticisms, and the generosity of their time. Timothy Mitchell guided me through this project in many of its phases, from its initial conception to its latest incarnation, and I have learned much from his very unique style of writing history while generating theory. Ahmed Ferhadi, also of N.Y.U., enabled me to make my Arabic better than I had thought possible. At Princeton University I found an intellectual bedrock for the comparative study of colonialism and European intellectual history, under the erudite guidance of Gyan Prakash and Suzanne Marchand. My work has been much enriched by their intellectual provocations and the vast expanse of their knowledge. I wish to express my profound gratitude to my advisor, Bob Tignor, who has supported me and this project unequivocally, continuously pushing me to articulate my arguments, and, above all, to think world-historically.

During my Fulbright year in Cairo, where I did my final research and writing, I enjoyed the company of Mahmood Ibrahim, Donald and Barbara Reid, Fakhri Haggani, and Hamdy El Gazzar; they proved that laughter and knowledge need not be mutually exclusive. Hoda ElSadda, Laila Galal Rizk, Ra'uf 'Abbas, Muhammad 'Ali, and 'Asim al-Disuqi all provided much helpful advice and guidance for my Cairo travails. At the University of California, Davis, Suad Joseph took me under her wing almost immediately upon my arrival; her scholarly and personal support have been truly outstanding. The History Department and the Middle East/South Asia Group at Davis have been tremendous resources. The dean of social sciences, Steven Sheffrin, two department chairs, the late Dan Brower and Susan Mann, and my mentors, Joan Cadden, Sally McKee, and Clarence Walker, have seen this project through to fruition. My students at Davis, both graduate and undergraduate, have vastly enriched my intellectual life, continuously challenging me to articulate the contours of colonial and postcolonial history.

I have benefited greatly from meetings and other opportunities to present my work, in particular, at the Davis Center of Princeton University, the Humanities Center of Stanford University, and the Women and Memory Forum in Cairo. Special thanks go to the many individuals who have read, heard, and commented on various parts of this work: Lila Abu-Lughod, Nadia Abu El-Haj, Rifa'at Abouel Haj, Amy Aisen, Paul Amar, Talal Asad, Beth Baron, Joel Beinin, Dan Brower, Joan Cadden, Chris Chekuri, Alice Conklin, Robert Crews, Hoda ElSadda, Marwa Elshakry, Khaled Fahmy, Michael Gasper, Gayatri Gopinath, Peter Gran, Fakhri Haggani, Nadeem Haj, Samira Haj, Suad Joseph, Adeeb Khalid, Ussama Makdisi, Suzanne Marchand, Mark Mazower, Barbara Metcalf, Timothy Mitchell, Gyan Prakash, Donald Reid, Martina Rieker, Joshua Schreier, Sudipta Sen, Stephen Sheehi, Dana Sherry, Diane Singerman, Baki Tezcan, Robert Tignor, Helen Tilley, Peter Van der Veer, Bob Vitalis, Lisa Wedeen, Lisa Wynn and Maha Yahya.

My editor, Kate Wahl, has thoroughly demystified the process of publishing, providing helpful criticism and guidance all along the way. I would also like to thank Kirsten Oster for her assistance. Anna Eberhard Friedlander was a fastidious copyeditor, and I am grateful for her keen editorial eye. I especially thank Dana Sherry, who provided invaluable research and editorial assistance. The three anonymous reviewers for Stanford University Press were models of collegiality, offering exacting and constructive criticism. I am especially thankful for their efforts, and hope that I have responded with due diligence, while acknowledging that all oversights and errors are my own.

Chapter 5 was published in a slightly modified form as "Barren Land and Fecund Bodies: The Emergence of Population Discourse in Interwar Egypt," *International Journal of Middle East Studies*, 37, no. 3 (2005): 351–72. A segment of Chapter 7 was published in "Cairo as Capital of Socialist Revolution?" in *Cairo Cosmopolitan: Politics, Culture, and Urban Space in the New Middle East*, edited by Diane Singerman and Paul Amar (Cairo: American University in Cairo Press, 2006). I thank Cambridge University Press and the American University in Cairo Press for permission to reprint.

The complex calligraphic piece, "Parsing sentences," that adorns the cover of this book was originally conceptualized as a wall painting in the form of notebook paper—a light-gray rectangle interrupted with faint blue lines and one intersecting red line defining a margin. Upon each line is a procession of imagined marks resembling Arabic, with only one word legible to those who read the language. These "words" promise meaning yet deliver none, they taunt and frustrate the viewer who believes that they can be read, but cannot read them. This frustration is akin to what is felt by the exile, the colonized intellectual, or the immigrant, who speaks two languages, inhabiting both yet possessing neither fully. The alienation of the viewer is thus created by an effect of language that renders it alien and familiar at the same time. I thank Leila El Shakry for permission to use the piece.

I have been fortunate to be surrounded by friends at times far removed from the world of academia but supportive of my work in countless ways. In New York City, Wail Khalid, Uzma Wahhab, Raysa Villalona, and Mark Gilmer were always willing to enjoy wonderful dinners and hear about my trials and tribulations. To Dr. Jennifer Nash I owe a special debt that I know I will never be able to repay. In Oakland, California, Louise Paige and Mark Chediak welcomed me into their home and hearts and listened patiently as a recalcitrant New Yorker adjusted to the Bay Area. My bicoastal friends Elizabeth Merchant and Emily Wittman helped me bridge the gap between East and West. Josh Kelly, Matt Salata, Jessica Thayer, and the lovely Claire

Salata (a.k.a. the "bear") have been a source of friendship, support, and inspiration, helping turn California into a home.

My entire extended family in Egypt has been a tremendous and constant source of joy and laughter. My second family, Feryal Nawar, Abd al-Aziz al-Assar, and Reem Samir, have always provided me with a home and a sense of place and belonging in Cairo. Mushira El Shakry, the late Ahmed El-Gaddawi, Amr and Ussama El-Gaddawi, and Hanan Badr have fed me so very many times amidst raucous laughter and pointed discussions about politics, cinema, and literature.

I am eternally grateful to my parents, Aida Nawar and Sayed El Shakry, for their tireless support and encouragement, and for instructing me in the habits of translation quite early on. In ways that perhaps I myself am not yet aware of, they have contributed greatly to my desire to become a scholar. Above all else, it is they who taught me that all labor is ennobling. Throughout my life, my younger sisters, Hoda and Leila—one now a literature scholar, the other a visual artist, have provided me with a sense of wonder at the creativity and vitality of youth, and their constant support has underlined all that I do. Samira Haj has been a continuous presence in my personal and intellectual life, providing me with an example in her intellectual honesty and integrity. Mark Mazower has been a tireless supporter of my work, approaching everything with intellectual verve and curiosity, and more importantly a true brother.

To my sister Marwa I owe an immeasurable debt of love and gratitude—from our earliest years we have shared our ideas, memories, and hopes. It is rare that one can find true intellectual companionship—even rarer when that person is a sibling. Each of these pages is marked by that companionship. To Nadeem Haj, my beloved fellow traveler, I owe my love and admiration. With forbearance he read every page of this book, several times over. Neither this book nor my life would have been the same without his presence. I dedicate this book to my late maternal grandmother Zaynab Shahata (1911–98), whose own difficult life and memories traversed the parameters of this book and whose unbounded love fashioned me into who I am. I hope that this volume will honor her memory.

Note on Transliteration and Translation

Arabic words and names have been transliterated into the Latin alphabet according to a simplified system based on the *International Journal of Middle East Studies*. To facilitate reading for the non-specialist, all diacritical marks have been omitted except for the 'ayn (') and hamza ('). Arabic words in common usage in English, such as Nasser and fellah, remain in the common form. Arabic names of authors who wrote primarily in English or French have not been changed (e.g., Hassan Fathy, not Hasan Fathi). For authors who published in both Arabic and French or English, alternate spellings of their names may occur (e.g., Taha Husayn and Taha Hussein), but the standard Arabic transliteration has been retained in the notes and bibliography for their Arabic works.

All translations from Arabic and French, unless otherwise noted, are my own.

The Great Social Laboratory

Introduction
*Colonialism, Nationalism, and
Knowledge Production*

In 1917 Egypt's premier literary intellectual, Taha Husayn, wrote his doctoral thesis on the social philosophy of Ibn Khaldun, under the supervision of Émile Durkheim at the Sorbonne.[1] The blind scholar from a humble rural background was initially inspired by Durkheim's stimulating lectures on sociology.[2] Only a few years earlier Husayn's friend, writer and philosopher Mansur Fahmi, had written his controversial thesis *La condition de la femme dans le tradition et l'évolution de l'Islamisme* under the tutelage of the anthropologically inclined philosopher Lucien Lévy-Bruhl.[3] Both thinkers were heavily influenced by the intellectual climate of the Sorbonne—immersed in the writings of Auguste Comte, Georg Simmel, and Émile Durkheim—yet chose topics that reflected an interest in the historical specificity of their own cultural milieu. Asserting that Ibn Khaldun was the first thinker to take society as an object of study sui generis, Husayn nevertheless hesitated to confer the title of "sociologue" upon the esteemed fourteenth-century philosopher.[4] Husayn's thesis demonstrated the range and erudition of Khaldunian social philosophy, while maintaining a privileged place for the modern science of society—as understood by luminaries such as Durkheim—as a distinct and autonomous science concerned with social facts while utilizing an experimental method.[5]

The complex intellectual formation and trajectory of individuals such as Taha Husayn and Mansur Fahmi belies conventional narratives of the "internationalization of the social sciences" in several ways.[6] First, although the history of the social-scientific disciplines has traditionally been written as a European field of knowledge imposed upon non-Europeans, non-Europeans were, in fact, actively involved in the development and transformation of the social sciences.[7] Nor was European knowledge simply transplanted into the colonies; rather, forms of knowledge, such as positivism, were refracted, deflected, or reconfigured in colonial contexts.[8] Second, social science itself emerged as an authoritative field of expertise in an imperial age. Scholars have unraveled the colonial genealogy of knowledge in fields with clear connections to empire—namely, anthropology and geography—as well as in disciplines with less obvious colonial associations, such as economics and psychology.[9] Thus, both Durkheimian sociology and Lévy-Bruhl's philosophical thought were critical in the development of French ethnology, demonstrating the role of ethnology in understanding, and developing, "peoples of inferior civilization."[10] Social science was thus implicated in a larger process of categorizing societies, cultures, and races within a hierarchical gradation of humanity.

Indeed, the story of the rise of the authority of social science to manage populations is by now familiar. Histories of social-scientific inquiry in Germany, England, and France have demonstrated the interconnectedness of knowledge production, empire or nation-state building projects, and the governance of populations.[11] Yet such concerns were hardly unique to Europe. A smaller, but now growing, body of literature has addressed the history and development of social science within non-Western and, specifically, colonial contexts.[12] For example, Andrew Barshay has demonstrated the interplay between unifying and particularizing impulses in Japanese social science that sought to retain a "national essence" in the face of Western influence, and Partha Chatterjee has shown how the introduction of the "modern science of politics" in colonial Bengal was tempered by indigenous notions of *dharma* (structured around religion as a form of virtue or political ethics).[13]

Yet very few studies have addressed the nature of social-scientific research within Middle Eastern societies. Rather than simply trying to fill a lacuna in Middle East scholarship, however, I argue that the story of social science in Egypt is distinctive and significant for comparative colonial and postcolonial history. Although it can be argued that the theoretical literature on subaltern studies has canonized the experience of nineteenth- and twentieth-century British India as the paradigmatic example of colonialism, it is important to ask ourselves what other historical trajectories can tell us about the development of modern forms of statecraft, political governance, and knowledge production under the pressures of European global hegemony.[14] For example, Selim Deringil and Ussama Makdisi have demonstrated that imperial Ottoman efforts at modernization in the nineteenth century were as much a local reaction to European representations of Ottoman backwardness as they were a response to perceived European military and technological superiority—a process that some have referred to in other historical contexts, such as Tianjin China, as "semicolonialism."[15]

Egypt presents an interesting historical example that spans from the semicolonial to the classically colonial. As a semi-autonomous Ottoman province that often experienced transformations in statecraft and governance in tandem with the Ottoman imperial center, Egypt was the first Arabic-speaking country to be colonized by a European power—with Napoleon Bonaparte's so-called scientific expedition of 1798.[16] Even the self-styled "founder of modern Egypt," Mehmed 'Ali Pasha (r. 1805–48), was nominally a servant of the Ottoman sultan while nevertheless pursuing his own imperial ambitions in the region.[17] British colonial rule in Egypt (1882–1936) was relatively short lived, but scholars have demonstrated the extent to which British colonialism in Egypt inaugurated widespread transformations that ranged from the recasting of the country's legal system and juridical practices to the reordering of rural space.[18] Although the story of the 1882 British presence in Egypt is perhaps the best known of the country's occupations, the lasting effects of the "long shadow of Napoleon" and the concomitant influence of Francophone culture on the development of fields of study such as geography and anthropology is also important.[19] Egypt thus experienced what we might refer to as a series of multiple or "nested" colonialisms—Ottoman, French, and British. Further complicating the received binaries of colonizer and colonized is the story of Egypt's own colonization of the Sudan and its imperial aspirations (often in emulation of the European powers) in sub-Saharan Africa.[20] An understanding of the rise of social science in Egypt thus highlights the twentieth-century history of globalized and interconnected forms of knowledge production between Europe and the Arab world under asymmetrical conditions of power, in which Egypt functioned at once as both colonizer and colonized.

The Particularity of Social Science

This book traces the development of the social sciences—anthropology, human geography, and demography—in Egypt during the late nineteenth and twentieth centuries. The aim is not to write a comprehensive history of the social-scientific disciplines, but rather to trace the development of a mode of social-scientific inquiry in colonial and postcolonial settings. Intellectuals and social reformers working within the burgeoning scientific and social associations that emerged in Egypt in the late nineteenth century formulated social science through a broad range of texts and cultural artifacts, ranging from the ethnographic museum to architectural designs to that pinnacle of social-scientific research, "the article." In this way they attempted to develop a unified science of society, based on the observation of social facts, the formulation and testing of theories, and the eventual application of scientific principles to the social world. In the process, they converted social-scientific ideas into concrete social engineering projects.

Egyptian intellectuals, many of whom were equally conversant in Western and Arab intellectual traditions, grappled with the tension between a commitment to a universal mode of knowledge production and a commitment to the specificity of local difference—a uniquely charged dilemma in the colonial context and one faced by intellectuals in regions as far flung as Bengal, Martinique, and Senegal.[21] Egyptian social scientists grounded their sociology of knowledge in the particular and the local. Such a foundation was not a simple valorization of the local over the universal; it was, rather, the registering of a more radical epistemological difference from the West—a difference based on the rejection of universal anthropocentric (or secular) history and universal taxonomies of civilization.[22]

Encyclopedist European social thought was based upon the post-Enlightenment project of creating an epistemology founded on universal rationality (conceived of as ahistorical and independent from social and cultural particularity), practiced by self-constituted, autonomous agents freed from the fetters of tradition.[23] This corpus of ideas would become central to defining both what it meant it to be a rational, moral, and autonomous agent freed from the constraints of tradition and prejudice, and the meaning of progress itself.[24]

It can be argued that modern European colonial projects were marked by the desire to transform the world into their own image in the name of the good of the other—an image based upon Enlightenment ideals, themselves contingent upon the distinction between civilized and barbaric life. In the words of Britain's agent and consul general in Cairo, Sir Evelyn Baring, the "moral and material improvement" of subject races was best accomplished by Englishmen whose "special aptitude . . . in the government of Oriental races pointed to England as the most effective and beneficent instrument for the gradual introduction of European civilization into Egypt."[25] Civilization as such referred always and only to European civilization. It is this story, of the *particularity* of European history and civilization *masquerading as the universal*, that constitutes the fundamental plot of colonialism.[26]

Colonial rule was premised upon the purported moral and material improvement of the colonized native population. The paradox of the "rule of colonial difference," according to Partha Chatterjee, lay in its insisting on the legitimacy and universality of modern regimes of power (when social regulations become "an aspect of the self-disciplining of normalized individuals, power is made more productive, effective, and humane"), while simultaneously denying the universality of those principles in the colonial context.[27] The production of the "empirical truth of colonial difference," typically understood within the colonial context as racial difference, was often embodied in colonial positivist social science with its relentless emphasis upon taxonomy and classification, in which natives functioned as representatives of their race. The language and ideology of improvement were, therefore, belied by the practices of knowledge production about the native population, which aimed at the elaboration and exploitation of difference rather than the uplift of the indigenous population.[28]

Yet the story told here is of a different order. It is the story of the Egyptian nationalist intelligentsia, who in resisting the totalizing and racialized nature of European claims to progress, reason, and the nation-state, staked the claims of social science on the particularity of local difference—as in, for example, the attempt to create an "Arab social science." In attempting to argue, however, that as non-Westerners Egyptians had internal indigenous sources of progress, indigenous reformers inadvertently accepted many of the very premises central to Western categories of thought (progress, reason, the nation-state).

Anticolonial nationalists claimed the moral and material improvement of the demographic masses as their primary object. In fact, it is my contention that the continuous moral and material improvement of the population, governed through flexible modern forms of power—the cornerstone of the colonial project—is continued within the context of the modern nation-state.[29] It is in the continuation of strategies of governance such as the development of instrumentalist knowledge, statistical languages, the logic of rational planning, the systematic targeting of subaltern populations for improvement and social uplift, and the internalization of a notion of backwardness—indeed the project of the modernizing, industrializing nation-state itself—that the colonial legacy continues. However, rather than view the colonial state as a "bad copy" of a supposedly uniform and coherent European model of modernity, I am more interested in exploring the ways in which Egyptian intellectuals and social reformers attempted to render models of modernity intelligible through the grid of indigenous social and cultural values and practices, and through reformulation or critique.

A central argument of this book is that within colonial social-scientific enterprises, "natives" functioned as passive objects of observation, taxonomy, and classification ("specimens"), that is, individual or collective representatives of their race, embedded within a hierarchical discourse of civilizational progress. The indigenous nationalist elite, in contrast, inaugurated its own social-scientific program, in which both the uniqueness (a precondition for nationalism) and educability (a precondition for progress) of the collective national subject (e.g., the peasant, the village, the family) could be demonstrated through ethnographies, field experiments, and social-engineering projects—which would remedy the imputed stagnation of Egyptian society.

Such projects were inextricably linked to the sciences of land (geography and agriculture) and the sciences of labor (human geography and demography), and geared toward the social welfare of the demographic masses. The same amount of effort expended by colonialists on the production of the empirical truth of colonial difference (racial inferiority) was expended by nationalists on the educability of the collective national subject. They thus borrowed much of the language and many categories of colonial rule—notions of backwardness, improvement, progress—but in contrast to the colonial state, they staked the decisive claims of social science on the social welfare of the demographic masses.

Social welfare, of course, should not be understood solely as an idealistic, benevolent process whereby the state and social scientists guide citizens towards their own welfare. Rather, it refers quite specifically to the social and political process of reproducing particular social relations—often premised on violence and coercion—such as those between the city and the countryside, in order to ensure the successful reproduction of labor power and to minimize class antagonisms.[30] Within a social-welfare framework, Egyptian social scientists and social reformers targeted women and the peasantry (those responsible for the reproduction of labor power and the extraction of wealth from the land) for "reformed" social practices (health, hygiene, and labor) to allow for a healthy, productive, and efficient population—appropriate to the progress of the modern world. This led to the development of new modes of governance, expertise, and social knowledge—all of which entailed subtle translations and subversions of the categories of Western thought.

Translations

This book concerns itself with the problematic of knowledge production by Egyptian intellectuals within a colonial context. The social and cultural disciplines present the most pressing methodological problem in the awareness of cultural difference, "to carve out spaces that would be no less 'disciplinized' but where national identity would be implicated by defining the position of the scientist."³¹ To formulate a nationalist project of modernity, the indigenous elite often translated (that is, adopted and transformed) colonial social-scientific methodologies (such as ethnographic or statistical techniques), while simultaneously linking their arguments to nationalist claims, such as Arabism. I do not mean to insinuate that the formation of Egyptian social science owed its existence to Western forms of knowledge, or that nationalism simply replaced Orientalism. Rather, I am arguing that in the context of Egypt during the colonial and postcolonial periods the two forms of knowledge production were dialectically intertwined.

Turn-of-the-century anticolonial nationalists and pan-Islamists in Egypt often drew stark distinctions between Western and Arab or Islamic modes of thought and practice (terms such as "Western," "European," and "foreign" were often used interchangeably in Arabic writings of the early twentieth century). Yet this should not blind us to the contradictions, ambiguities, and overlaps that often existed between colonial and nationalist forms of knowledge production—distinctions between the two were complex and nebulous in practice.³² Nevertheless, "colonial" and "nationalist," function as heuristic categories necessary to understanding the ideological and political contours of intellectual debates in the social sciences, between and amongst Europeans and Egyptians. Thus, although colonial and nationalist social-scientific methods and epistemological orientations often overlapped, the larger ideological projects within which they were embedded remained fundamentally distinct.

Egyptian social scientists were often able to draw from two contending traditions of social scientific inquiry: a Western-based literature of positivism (including works by scholars such as Auguste Comte and Émile Durkheim) on the one hand, and an Arabic-language tradition of sociology (as originated by Ibn Khaldun) and annals history (for instance, works by Abd al-Rahman al-Jabarti).³³ The intellectual engagement of Arab thinkers with the fourteenth-century thinker Ibn Khaldun is in sharp contrast to Dipesh Chakrabarty's claim that "few, if any Indian social scientists or social scientists of India would argue seriously with" premodern South Asian intellectual traditions (as opposed to their engagement with the universalist European social science of, say, Marx and Weber).³⁴

Although sociology was not taught as such in Egypt until 1925, when the Egyptian University was transformed into a state institution, new branches of social inquiry were developing during the first quarter of the twentieth century, prior to the professionalization of the disciplines. Novel and relatively undefined fields such as human geography and population studies, which began emerging in Egypt in the middle of the 1920s, entailed the integration of social observation, experimentation, analysis, and planning in the constitution of a "great social laboratory where theories can be formulated and general laws deduced on human inter-relationships."[35] Indeed, it can be argued that the interwar period marks the formulation of "society" itself as an entity—an object of scientific study, social control and management.[36] This is reflected in the fact that the modern Arabic term for "society," *mujtama'*, did not come into common usage until around 1930; before then, a variety of compound phrases were used to denote social life (*al-hay'a al-mujtama'iyya, nizam al-ijtima', majmu'at al-umma, al-intizam al-'umrani, al-jama'iyya al-muntazima*).[37]

The metaphor of society as a "great social laboratory" demonstrates the authority of the language of positivism as a tool for understanding social phenomena. As Gyan Prakash has argued, the colonies were laboratories for modernity.[38] The authority of science as universal reason, he argues, was instantiated by the elite reformulation of the language of reason as an idiom of power.[39] If the "colonies constituted a laboratory of experimentation for the new arts of government capable of bringing a modern and healthy society into being," as Paul Rabinow claims[40]—if they were sites for the elaboration, experimentation, and refinement of "norms and forms" developed in the metropole—were the colonized simply dependent variables or passive objects?

To say that the colonies were laboratories of and for modernity, however, should not be to imply that they were a setting for modernity and not a site in which modernity was fashioned. As Timothy Mitchell has noted, modernity itself is best conceived of as something staged, or produced, *across* the space of cultural and historical difference.[41] In colonial Egypt, the modern (*al-hadith*) often came to mean a specific set of attributes and interlinked projects—moral and material progress, scientific and social-scientific inquiry, and the management of health, hygiene, and social welfare—that increasingly relied on new technologies of knowledge production and produced new experiences of space and time.[42] Indeed, it would be a mistake to assume that modernity is simply a category of contemporary postcolonial analysis, rather than a historically specific and local category of thought and experience.[43] The proliferation of fin-de-siècle articles discussing the reasons for Arab or Muslim backwardness (*takhaluf*), stagnation (*jumud*), and decline (*inhitat*), and the means towards progress (*tatawwur*), and of interwar discussions of modern civilization belies that assumption.[44] This book tries to redress the metropole-centered vision of a colonial modernity produced out of pressures or forces generated solely from Europe. Thus, it emphasizes the ways in which an Egyptian modernity was produced through a dialectical engagement with the epistemological and ethical domains of social science.⁴⁵

In thinking about projects of modernity, scholars have noted the heuristic value in the notion of translation (in contrast to adaptation), implying, as it does, creativity, contingency, improvisation, and the irreducible heterogeneity of identities.⁴⁶ In Chakrabarty's eloquent phrasing, "what translation produces out of seeming 'incommensurabilities' is neither an absence of relationship between dominant and dominating forms of knowledge nor equivalents that successfully mediate between differences, but precisely the partly opaque relationship we call 'difference.'"⁴⁷ Thus, rather than viewing the colonial experience as merely an incomplete version of a European model of modernity, we can explore the ways in which cultural translations sought to negotiate *other* speaking positions from which to formulate the national modern. Yet the concept of translation has, perhaps, suffered from an imprecise usage in contemporary sociological and literary writings.

To elaborate the sense in which I am using the term *translation*, I will draw upon examples from the modern Arabic literary language.⁴⁸ Thus, for example, the Royal Academy of Arabic Language, founded in Cairo in 1932, heatedly debated the validity of forming new words, whether based on classical analogical derivation; compound words; or the assimilation of foreign words or foreign modes of expression. The work of the academy in the vibrant interwar period consisted of the incorporation of new vocabularies (scientific, technological, and literary) into the already overwhelming lexical wealth of the Arabic language. Although earlier such attempts had been undertaken (beginning with the translation schools of Mehmed 'Ali), the unification and codification of such linguistic innovations through the academy was peculiarly modern. Needless to say, literary attempts at linguistic innovation both predated and coexisted with the academy's efforts, as, for example, with the literati of the *nahda*, whose language ranged from linguistic experimentation to stylistic purity.⁴⁹

This so-called modernization of the Arabic language was accomplished through the classical system of derivation from Arabic roots (*ishtiqaq*) based on various principles, but most notably analogy (*qiyas*). Such derivations were often based upon the semantic expansion of already-existing linguistic molds (*qawalib*). Thus a term such as *majmaʿ* (from the molds designating locality) originally meant a "place of gathering," but by semantic extension came to mean academy.⁵⁰ Further, certain neologisms operate through the "displacement of the object with respect to its classical meaning," as with *istaʿmara* (to colonize, as a place) which replaced the classical meaning of "to make someone inhabit, cultivate (a place)."⁵¹ These few examples—

derived from the world of language—should serve to illustrate the sense in which the work of translation was and is always a creative endeavor, but, more importantly, relies upon an already existent grammar of lexical understanding. It is in a similar sense, then, that I refer to the translation of social science and projects of modernity in the context of colonial and postcolonial Egypt.

The Intellectual Setting: Epistemological Foundations, Ideological Effects

The twentieth-century Egyptian intellectual elite was committed to the application of positivist thought and method to the problems of interwar social reform. As Anson Rabinbach has noted, the "impact of positivism on social knowledge and on the nineteenth-century ideal of reform politics has somehow escaped the scrutiny of historians."[52] Despite commonplace assumptions that positivism had become defunct in twentieth-century social-scientific inquiry, scholars have demonstrated its viability well into the twentieth century.[53] In the Egyptian colonial setting, both positivism and the politics of reform were intimately linked to the apparatus of the colonial state. Yet positivism never achieved complete dominance over social inquiry, as strains of romanticism and links to an indigenous tradition of sociological inquiry and annals history pervaded social investigations.

The epistemological grounding of social-scientific inquiry in late-nineteenth- and twentieth-century Egypt thus incorporated two major strands of thought: positivism and romanticism. The Egyptian attempt to ground the social sciences in positivism was rooted in Comtean positivism and based on the inheritance of a Saint Simonian legacy in Egypt during the early nineteenth century.[54] Comte's positivism has been characterized as "an approach which rejects as illegitimate all that cannot be directly observed in the investigation and study of any subject."[55] Positivist sociology was to become part of a unified science in which a positive language of society was created, based on the observation of social facts, the formulation and testing of theories, and the eventual application of scientific principles to the social world. Statements regarding society were proposed and corrected, and predictions were made. Sociologists were to "discover laws that govern human behavior on a large scale, and the ways in which institutions and norms operate together in a complex yet ultimately predictable system."[56] The aim was to formulate empirically grounded general laws and predictions of human behavior, based on observation and the determination of regularities. Methodologically speaking, such an approach often demanded induction and statistical correlation. For many of those working in the sciences of demography and geography (and its branches of economic, human, and historical geography), the framework of positivism enabled the progression and advancement of science through the accretion of an ever-increasing corpus of sociological facts. Further, positivist social research was often translated into concrete social engineering projects, such as the experiments in rural reconstruction sponsored by the Royal Agricultural Society in the 1930s. Indeed, in a truly Comtean spirit, the epistemological stance of positivism was ideally suited to the ideological orientation of social welfare and engineering.

The second strand of thought was the more romantic tradition of the human sciences.[57] Romantic themes such as the search for (national) origins, the overvaluation of the experience of nature, and even the notion of the social reformer as creative catalyst of social change were particularly pronounced in writings on the peasantry. This was often the position of the more anthropologically inclined, whose research on the *mentalité* of the peasantry included the representation of their everyday life, manners, and customs, and the collection of folkloric material. For these thinkers, social science was culturally specific. It should proceed from the premise of understanding the "essence" of society as a total social whole, with its specific cultural and historical antecedents. Such an approach was rooted in metaphysical constructs ("culture," *mentalité*, "personality"), and was deductive and explanatory in method. At its extreme, this position led to an ahistorical romanticism—in the imaginative attempt to capture the "cultural essence" of the peasantry, for example. Such attempts foregrounded the specificity of place, such as, for example, the location of the peasantry in the countryside, and above all their proximity to and intercourse with nature.[58] Such dichotomies as positivism and romanticism, however, continuously broke down in practice as tensions between the ideas of social reform as a positive scientific project and as a culturally specific moral project of social uplift became apparent.[59]

It must be noted that the embrace of Western positivism by middle-class intellectuals and reformers in Egypt from the turn of the century was itself riddled with difficulties. To reformulate the social and cultural disciplines while acknowledging the specificity of cultural difference was the dilemma that faced the anticolonial nationalist intelligentsia. In the Egyptian setting the liberal nationalist agenda was infused with the rhetoric of anticolonial nationalism. Thus, often enough the nationalist critique of colonialism also enabled various critiques of Western positivism, in the attempt to create an indigenous form of social-scientific knowledge. This may be related to what various Arab intellectuals have referred to as the crisis of Arab modernism.[60]

One of the central problematics of Arab intellectual thought in the nineteenth and twentieth centuries was how to be modern while maintaining the historical specificity of cultural identity—a process that Anouar Abdel-Malek has referred to as "the reconquest of identity."[61] "How can one act to remain oneself in a world dominated by the 'other'?" asks Abdel-Malek.[62] For Abdel-Malek, the history of contemporary Arab thought is best thought of as a dialectical (both cultural-ideological and political-economic) struggle for the reconquest of identity in the face of self-alienation. The question of Arab modernism—itself a profoundly colonial question—thus condensed the issues of identity (*huwiyya*), cultural heritage (*turath*), authenticity (*asala*), and modernity (*hadatha*) itself, according to Egypt's leading Marxist literary critic and theoretician, Mahmud Amin al-'Alim. According to al-'Alim, it is in the dialectic between "the backward Arab self and the civilized European other" under the constraints of colonial hegemony that the ideological battle of modernity is waged.[63] The question is how, and from what enunciatory position, can we speak as ourselves, and be sure that it is we who are speaking? Nationalism's answer to that question, according to Partha Chatterjee, was as follows:

> By my reading, anticolonial nationalism creates its own domain of sovereignty within colonial society well before it begins its political battle with the imperial power. It does this by dividing the world of social institutions and practices into two domains—the material and the spiritual. The material is the domain of the "outside," of the economy, statecraft, science and technology, a domain where the West had proved its superiority and the East had succumbed. In this domain, then, the Western superiority had to be acknowledged, studied and replicated. The spiritual, on the other hand, is an "inner" domain bearing the "essential" marks of cultural identity.[64]

This splitting of the realm of culture into two spheres- the inner and outer- provided a formulation for the selective appropriation of Western modernity.[65] The inner or spiritual was seen as the true and "essential" self, while the outer/material was deemed merely external and ultimately unimportant.

Chatterjee's discussion, although heuristically useful, proves more problematic in historical actuality, demonstrating the difficulties of generalizing across colonial histories.[66] Thus, in the case of Egypt it can be shown that the theoretical inner/outer (moral/ material) distinction was far more interconnected and fractured in practice. For instance, although Egyptian nationalist discourse clearly sought to uphold women (the quintessential "inner" domain) as a source of cultural integrity, it also localized them as an arena for the social, political, and cultural progress of the nation. That is to say, the advancement of the nation in the "material" fields of law, administration, economy, and statecraft (the "outer domain"), was positioned such that progress for the community could not be achieved independently of progress in the domain of women, and more specifically mothers. Further, the outer "material" domain could also serve as an arena for the assertion of cultural specificity and difference, as in the Nasserist attempt to create a postcolonial and post-exploitative industrialized economy marked by its *essential* difference from Western capitalist practices.

Nevertheless, anticolonial nationalism was a deeply contradictory endeavor. As a contestatory discourse fully implicated in the political quest for independence, nationalist discourse regarded colonialism as the root evil of a current backwardness. It was imperialism, so the narrative goes, that retarded national development and progress towards modernization. Yet the nationalist opposition to colonialism was often couched in terms predicated upon the very identity posited by colonialist discourse between reason and the nation-state as the culmination of history.[67] It often reaffirmed the various projects of modernity—unilinear progressive temporality, scientific progress, the nation-state as the culmination of history—while it attempted to contest them. Nationalism thus found itself in a double bind, in the process of formulating a modernity that claimed to emancipate the colonized self from its bonds of colonization, but that was already structured by many of the same values it claimed to oppose.[68]

For many thinkers in the Arab world, the contradictory enterprise of anticolonial nationalism, known as the crisis of Arab modernism, led to a schism between liberal secular (modern) and Islamist (traditional) thought. By contrast, this study regards both sets of intellectuals as modern.[69] Thus, both liberal secular and Islamist intellectuals attempted to formulate positivist scientific research agendas that would address the relative stagnation of Arab ideas, institutions, and populations. Indeed, the historical record defies such simple categorizations as traditional and modern—oppositions themselves borne directly out of the colonial experience.[70]

Thus, for example, future Islamist martyr and Muslim Brother Sayyid Qutb began his career as a writer, educator, and social commentator. Qutb's deep familiarity with the epistemological traditions of the West enabled his formulation of an Islamic modern that rejected Western idealism, materialism, and positivism as distorted theologies.[71] Qutb's oeuvre focused on the development of specifically Islamic conceptions and methodologies, which would actualize Islam as a total system (*nizam islami, manhaj islami*). The application of Islamic principles would enable the development of a postcolonial modernity freed from the fetters of the West (secularism, atheism, nationalism) and compatible with the modern ideals of social justice and equity.[72] Qutb's was one among an array of possible responses to the range of historical negations created by the colonial experience. Egyptian nationalist reformers sought to address what they perceived as ossified traditions, racial lethargy, and civilizational backwardness, restoring to the East its golden age.

Intellectuals in Society

This study is an exploration of what Gramsci termed the "organic relations between State or political society and 'civil society,'" and in particular of "the birth of new parties of dominant groups, intended to conserve the assent of the subaltern groups and maintain control over them."[73] Historians have long taken up Gramsci's call to view the role of intellectuals as "hegemonic deputies" of the state. It is therefore important to outline the relationship between the institutional structures underpinning knowledge production in colonial and postcolonial Egypt and state sponsorship of such knowledge production. Educational institutions, educational reform, and the state were closely intertwined in nineteenth- and early-twentieth-century Egypt. Modern state-sponsored education in Egypt led to the formation of a new class of intellectuals and technocrats who were well versed in the new social and cultural sciences of the West, but who were also actively involved in the nationalist movement. The tensions between the adoption of Western-oriented educational practices and the assertion of a cultural and intellectual identity distinct from the West produced a variety of intellectual responses on the part of the intelligentsia.[74] The exploration of those responses (the content of disciplinary differences) forms the bulk of this book; this section provides an outline of the institutional structures within which the new social sciences were transmitted, providing the larger context for their appropriation by indigenous elites.

A landmark in the history of modern education in Egypt was the founding in 1908 of the first private university, the Egyptian University (now Cairo University), under the direction of future King Fu'ad I (r. 1917–36).[75] The university idea was itself an indigenous project, as British support for educational reform in Egypt under the direction of the Earl of Cromer was notoriously nonexistent—approximately 1 percent of the national budget was devoted to education. It would not be until nominal independence was attained in 1922 that the government would invest more rigorously in education. In 1925 the institution was chartered as a state university, the only one existent in Egypt until 1942. Although the idea of an Egyptian national university had compelling nationalist links, in its early years the university retained a strong European presence, with many Europeans serving on the university council as deans and as lecturing faculty. For example, the renowned French Egyptologist Gaston Maspero sat on the council, French Orientalist Louis Massignon taught "History of the Philosophic Schools;" and famed British social anthropologist Evans-Pritchard taught sociology in the 1930s. Initially, French and Italian academic influences were the most dominant, although Italy's 1911 invasion of Libya dampened the Italian presence. Until Egypt's complete independence after the 1952 revolution, Anglo-French rivalries over cultural hegemony in Egypt played out in the university as the two groups competed over the language of instruction and the nationalities of deans and instructors.

Seven core subjects—geography, philosophy, Islamic history, Ancient history, Arabic, English and French Literature—were taught at the Egyptian University to a diverse student body of Europeans and Egyptians drawn from the state educational system as well as from the more traditional religious institutions. At the turn of the century four higher schools existed: law, medicine, engineering, and the *Dar al-'Ulum*, or Higher Teachers College. The university project was itself part of a long-standing pattern of royal patronage of cultural and educational institutions. Indeed, educational reforms in Egypt have a long lineage, beginning with the early-nineteenth-century reforms of Ottoman viceroy Mehmed 'Ali Pasha. During his reign, a multitude of Western-style educational institutes and professional schools, ranging from language to military schools, were founded. In addition, numerous educational missions were sent to Europe throughout his reign, including the mission that took the renowned scholar Shaykh Rifa'a Rafi' al-Tahtawi to France. The practice of sending Egyptians abroad to Europe on missions to be educated in the worldly sciences of the West continued under 'Ali's descendants, 'Abbas (r. 1849–54), Sa'id (r. 1854–63), Isma'il (r. 1863–79), Tawfiq (r. 1879–92), and 'Abbas II (r. 1892–1914). But it was under Mehmed 'Ali's grandson Isma'il that the court-sponsored revival of educational and cultural projects reached its peak. Under the guidance of 'Ali Pasha Mubarak, director of the *Diwan al-Madaris*, educational missions abroad continued, new schools opened, and older institutions were reorganized.[76]

Educational missions continued under Fu'ad, and because of the dearth of qualified Egyptian personnel several educational missions to Europe were dispatched by the Egyptian University itself between 1908–25, in the hope that returning Egyptians with doctorates would teach at the University.[77] The School of Law appointed its first Egyptian dean in 1927, and the School of Medicine followed suit in 1929. Europeans would remain dominant in the majority of departments until 1945, however. Among the university's first Egyptian professors were Taha Husayn, Mansur Fahmi, Arabic scholar Ahmad Amin, who taught as early as 1926 and eventually served as dean of the Faculty of Arts in 1939, and pioneer historian Shafiq Ghurbal.

Taha Husayn, who began teaching at the Egyptian University in 1919, was a strong presence and impetus for the indigenization of the university. Husayn had received a traditional *kuttab* and *Azhari* education, and had then attended the Egyptian University, where he was the first Egyptian to receive a doctorate, with a thesis on the medieval poet al-Ma'ari. Sent to France on an educational mission in 1914, he completed a second doctorate at the Sorbonne. In 1919 he returned from his mission to a salaried professorship, teaching "History of the Ancient East" and "Philosophy of History." He later became the first Egyptian dean of arts at the university, in 1930.

By the time that Egyptians were holding prominent positions at the university, opportunities for upward mobility through education were increasing in the 1930s and 1940s. Egyptians educated in the state educational system and the Egyptian University came to form a new category within the middle class—referred to as the *effendiyya*—that "included secondary and university students, teachers, lawyers, journalists and other professionals, white-collar employees, and lower and mid-level government functionaries."[78] Indeed, throughout the twentieth century the opportunities afforded by a state education came to overshadow the benefits of the traditional religious *Azhari* education. The propensity of the *effendiyya* for political involvement led to their centrality in national political, intellectual, and social life. The university itself became a hotbed of anticolonial nationalism and student activism and demonstrations in the turbulent 1930s and 1940s. It was these strata, it was claimed in the early 1930s, that "molded public opinion and led the nation in times of crisis, set up its ideals and stamped it with its particular character."[79] As a group the *effendiyya* were essential to the development of Egyptian nationalism and actively engaged in literary and journalistic culture as patrons and as producers of ideas.[80]

The relationship between the educated intelligentsia and the state was also solidified through the employment of many university officials in prominent governmental positions. For example, Taha Husayn served as minister of education. 'Abbas Mustafa 'Ammar, a scholar whose research included anthropology, demography, and village studies, served as minister of social affairs. 'Ammar was originally from the rural Delta province of Menufiyya. Trained under the tutelage of Mustafa 'Amir and Muhammad 'Awad as a geographer at Fu'ad I University, he received his doctorate in 1941—the first geography student at the university to be awarded that degree—and his *People of Sharqiya* was the first full-length ethnographic monograph on Egypt written by an Egyptian.[81] 'Ammar's middle-class rural background and upward mobility were not uncommon among Egyptian intellectuals of his generation.

'Ammar's intellectual trajectory unifies all the fields of study addressed in this book. Starting from a base in geography and physical anthropology, 'Ammar's research and writing covered everything from racial history to rural sociology to demography. For 'Ammar, however, the exigencies of social-scientific research within a nation-state aspiring to complete political independence from the colonial powers were pressing. As a nationalist and a social reformer, 'Ammar set out to formulate a clear and comprehensive view of the conditions of life in the province of Sharqiya, in order that standards of living in the countryside might be improved. 'Ammar was able to mobilize concepts such as race—which in the colonial context signaled native inferiority and the rule of colonial difference—for the political purposes of the nationalist movement. As a reformer who was able to make the transition into the Nasser government, 'Ammar was well placed in various ministerial positions in which he was able to make use of the social-scientific knowledge he had generated in forming national policies and programs for modernization—such as his population policies.

Discussion of the middle-class status of the intellectuals in question brings us back to Gramsci's observation regarding "the birth of new parties of dominant groups, intended to conserve the assent of the subaltern groups and maintain control over them."[82] It is a key argument of this book that the social-scientific agendas of the Egyptian nationalist intelligentsia revolved around the *educability* of the collective national subject through field experiments and social engineering projects. Such projects were inextricably linked to the sciences of land and labor, and embodied two sets of debates that dominated public intellectual discourse in Egypt during the interwar period and up until the end of World War II: the problem of the peasantry and the problem of population.[83] Social welfare provided an idiom through which social scientists and reformers could claim to speak in the name of the demographic masses and their well-being, in contradistinction to the colonial state. Within a social-welfare framework, social reformers focused on "reforming" social practices of women and the peasantry as the way to a healthy, productive, and efficient population—appropriate to the progress of the modern world.

. . .

Part I of this book contrasts the development of a colonial mode and an indigenous mode of knowledge production in the anthropology of the modern Egyptians in the late nineteenth and twentieth centuries. This first set of chapters addresses the vexed relationship of colonialism and nationalism with discourses of *race* and *identity*. Colonial anthropology (be it ethnographic or anthropometric in method) concerned itself with the categorization of the native population, perceived as individual or collective representatives of their race, within a hierarchical notion of a graded humanity; nationalist anthropologists, on the other hand, inaugurated their own social scientific program that was never a simple reflection of that of their colonial counterparts. As nationalists they based their research not on the assumption of "colonial difference" between the European and the colonized, but on the premise of the uniqueness of the collective national subject.

The second part of the book explores the writings of Egyptian and, to a lesser extent, European intellectuals concerned with the problem of the peasantry in interwar Egypt. Through this exploration I address the centrality of the peasantry to discourses of *class*. A dialectic of modernist versus romantic thought on the peasantry inaugurated, on the one hand, a positivist project of formulating a science of the countryside (in which the peasantry became an object of social-scientific intervention and engineering), and, on the other, an anthropological and romantic process of recounting and describing the peasantry as cultural artifacts of national identity. I explore three significant bodies of writing dealing with the peasantry in interwar Egypt: studies of the culture and *mentalité* of the peasant (*'aqliyyat al-fellah*); writings broadly categorized as human geography (those branches of geography concerned with the relationship between human activity and geographical phenomena); and writings centered on the social reform of the countryside.

Part III explores the constitution of "population" as an object of knowledge and social intervention and engineering. Population debates were discussed in interwar Egypt as the problem of the quantity versus the quality of the nation's inhabitants. The question of quantity centered on the debate over neo-Malthusian reduction of the birth rate, a concern that generated a flurry of statistical studies on historical demography, and debates as to whether Egypt was in fact overpopulated. The question of quality centered on the improvement of the characteristics of the population through either the encouragement and enhancement of "types" or the elimination of "defectives" through social welfare and eugenics (*tahsin al-nasl*). "Quality" included the social uplift of women in particular, often through social-hygiene and welfare projects that focused on the family—a new site of regulatory controls in the interwar period. This part of the book thus introduces the significance of discourses of *gender* in social-scientific discourses.

Taken together, Parts II and III seek to uncover the new modes of governance, expertise, and social knowledge that defined a distinctive era of nationalist politics in the interwar period in Egypt, whereas Part I explores the discursive field mapped out by colonial and nationalist discourses on the racial identity of the modern Egyptians. I thus map out the colonial and postcolonial Egyptian modern at the intersection of discourses of identity (race, *mentalité*, national "character") and discourses of governance (social hygiene, social welfare, architectural modernism, and neo-Malthusianism). Each section explores the complex imperatives and complexities of race, class, and gender within the colonial and postcolonial Egyptian contexts.[84]

The chapters that follow address the array of responses to the range of historical negations created by the colonial experience. Reformers sought to address what they perceived as ossified traditions, racial lethargy, and civilizational backwardness, restoring to the East its golden age. Identifications of the national "locus of backwardness" ranged from social and economic realities (overpopulation), to populations (peasants and women) to culture itself (superstitions, festivals). Indigenous social scientists sought to refashion the colonial project of "the moral and material improvement of the native population" in a nationalist mode. To do so they turned to a battery of epistemological orientations, disciplines, methodologies, and objects of study. Far from being a straightforward transplantation of Western ideas and methods, the versions of social scientific knowledge produced in the Egyptian colonial and postcolonial settings entailed subtle subversions and ironic historical reversals of colonial forms of knowledge.

I   *The Anthropology of the Modern Egyptians:*
    From the Fin-de-Siècle to the Second World War

1   The Ethnographic Moment

In an 1869 letter to Khedive Isma'il (r. 1863–79), renowned for his desire to recreate Cairo as a "Paris of the East," archaeologist, savant, and medical doctor Gaillardot Bey put forward a proposition: the creation of a scientific institution for geographical explorations, along with an attendant framework of museums, libraries, and educational programs.[1] The importance of this project, stressed Gaillardot, was in its reformist and civilizing spirit, a continuation of the reforms initiated by the modernizing Ottoman viceroy Mehmed 'Ali himself. Gaillardot pointed out that the establishment of such an institution would be the first of its kind in the Orient (and would rectify the relative absence of scholarly societies in Egypt), thereby placing Isma'il at the head of scientific innovations as well as moral and intellectual progress. Nor did he hesitate to remind Isma'il of the excitement created by his personal appearance at and Egypt's participation in the 1867 Exposition Universelle in Paris, which inspired the admiration not only of savants, but of the "ignorant" public as well. Attached to Gaillardot's letter was a report detailing the process of establishing the proposed scientific institution and emphasizing the need to conduct studies that would expound the country's natural resources, in view of profit, as well as its moral order, in the view of progress.[2]

A mere six years later, in 1875, the Royal Geographic Society of Egypt was founded, part of a larger cultural revival sponsored by the Egyptian court. As Gaillardot Bey's letter intimated, Khedive Isma'il was actively involved in the representation of Egypt to the Western world, or what Timothy Mitchell has referred to as the "exhibitionary order" of nineteenth-century Europe.[3] It was not only Europeans, therefore, who desired to represent

Egypt on a Western stage to a Western audience. For example, Egypt's pavilions at the 1867 Exposition Universelle were designed by French Egyptologist August Mariette; Isma'il's extravagant celebration of the opening of the Suez Canal in November of 1869 replicated key elements of the world's fairs; and Isma'il himself commissioned Verdi's masterpiece Orientalist opera, Aïda.[4] This complicity of colonial forms of knowledge production (world's fairs and Orientalist art) and Egyptian state institutions complicates our understanding of the production of knowledge in colonial contexts. Individuals who were involved in state-sponsored knowledge production—for example, those working in the Royal Geographic Society of Egypt—participated in a wider shared culture of scientific expeditions (often with their own imperial aspirations in sub-Saharan Africa), museums, and ethnographies, all of which contributed to the formulation of a colonial modernity in late nineteenth century Egypt. As Mauricio Tenorio Trillo has observed with respect to Mexico, "Mexico joined the world's fair circuit in order to learn, imitate, and publicize its own possession of the universal truths of progress, science, and industry."[5] Yet, these universal truths were invariably inflected with the specificity of locale, "Mexican sciences, Mexican art, Mexican nationhood."[6] Or as Zeynep Çelik has noted in comparing the Egyptian khedive Isma'il with the Ottoman sultan Abdülaziz, who also attended the 1867 Paris Exposition amid much fanfare, "[w]orld's fairs were idealized platforms where cultures could be encapsulated visually—through artifacts and arts but also, more prominently, through architecture."[7]

The Royal Geographic Society in Egypt (which exemplified the porous boundaries between anthropology and geography) provides an excellent case study of this culture shared by Europeans and non-Europeans who engaged anthropological and geographical ideas, practices, and debates surrounding the modern Egyptians. The foundation of the society was a crucial moment in the authorization, and transformation, of European social-scientific knowledge in Egypt. Scholars have begun to explore the ways in which authoritative disciplinized knowledge, such as nineteenth-century European geography, was formed through the "effacement of alternative subject-positions and the appropriation of other ways of knowing," for example the knowledge of central Africans.[8] By paying attention to "the historical processes that condemned certain knowledges, meanings and subjects to a place outside the field of what was considered, intelligible, rational, and disciplined scientific discourse," these studies contribute much to our understanding of the constitution of scientific knowledge in its colonial manifestation.[9] Nevertheless, although indigenous actors (in their role as "informants") appear in these accounts as coauthors of geographical knowledge, these studies do not directly address the scientific production of local geographical or anthropological knowledge by indigenous authors themselves. Curiously, very few histories of non-European attempts to produce and disseminate geographical and anthropological knowledge exist.[10]

We can address this gap by foregrounding the site of knowledge production in Egypt, and its co-production by Europeans and non-Europeans. This is not to be understood in the postmodern sense of a critique of ethnographic authority—such critiques emerge from within the disciplinary boundaries and epistemological commitments of anthropology itself.[11] Thus, rather than emphasizing the importance of these anthropological ideas for European anthropology (the formation of British social anthropology) or European classicism (the question of the origins of the Ancient Egyptians), or even the history of colonialism (how debates on the ethnic and racial classification of the modern Egyptians fed into the larger political and social context of the "long" nineteenth-century European colonization of Egypt), I instead view anthropological ideas and practices as crucial to the development of a *social-scientific mode of thought* in Egypt.[12] In this mode of thought, Egyptians were to become authors as well as subjects of knowledge. In contrasting the development of a colonial and an incipient local, or Egyptian, mode of knowledge production in the anthropology of the modern Egyptians, I argue that although a shared culture of anthropology and geography existed, subtle differences began to emerge, particularly in the heated anticolonial climate of the interwar period as political conditions transformed intellectual production.

Institutional Foundations:
The Royal Geographic Society of Egypt

The Royal Geographic Society of Egypt (RGS) was founded on May 19, 1875, under the auspices of Khedive Isma'il.[13] Its aim was to place Egypt—already at the crossroads of voyages of exploration—at the center of geographical travel to and from Africa, and to encourage the development of geography as a science, thereby stimulating industrial and commercial interests in the country.[14] Cairo, "la plus grande porte de l'Afrique," was ideally situated as the meeting place for explorers to banish "blank spots" from the map of Africa.[15] European explorers, travelers, and scholars would often pass through Cairo; among the more prestigious who spoke at the society were Georg August Schweinfurth,[16] Henry Morton Stanley,[17] Richard Francis Burton,[18] Ferdinand de Lesseps,[19] August Mariette Pasha,[20] and Francis Galton.[21]

Khedive Isma'il's imperial ambitions in the interior of Africa and the Sudan (especially from 1863 to 1885), although ultimately unsuccessful, provided much of the impetus for the African focus of the RGS's early years.[22] Perhaps nothing speaks more poignantly of Egypt's African colonial ambitions than a memorandum written by the quartermaster-general of the Egyptian army in November of 1876. Noting the September 1876 Geographical Congress held at the Royal Palace in Brussels, under the tutelage of King Leopold II, and the intensification of European interest in the fertile lands of central Africa, the quartermaster-general encouraged the Khedive to emphasize not only the exploration, but also the exploitation of equatorial Africa.[23]

The society was founded at a time when Khedive Isma'il was building upon the institutional innovations of Ottoman viceroy Mehmed 'Ali (the proverbial "founder of modern Egypt"), and establishing many of Egypt's major cultural and literary institutions, such as the National Library, *Dar al-'Ulum* Teachers College, and the national opera; Egypt's journalistic culture was also blossoming.[24] As an institution, the RGS endeavored to explore all the various branches of geography (physical, human, economic, historical, biological), as well as to encourage the development of geographical and ethnographic studies in Egypt.[25] Among its members were literati, amateur scholars of geography, geology, archaeology, anthropology, antiquity, museum curators, and "gentleman" explorers.[26] Far from being concerned solely with the exploration of Africa, the Society had as its goal nothing short of contributing to Egypt's modernization, through the production and dissemination of geographical knowledge. The khedive not only donated the building premises, a palace located on Qasr al-'Ayni Street, as well as 2,500 volumes to begin the library's collection, but he also underwrote an annual government subsidy to the society.[27]

Although the RGS had a brief hiatus shortly after its inception in which meetings and publications ceased (during Egypt's severe financial and economic crises in the late 1870s), the society quickly regained its momentum by regularizing its finances, and by 1881 it was able to send Egyptian delegates to the Third International Geographical Congress and Exhibition at Venice—the only African country represented at the congress.[28] In fact, by 1890 the president of the RGS, Abbate Pasha, could assert that the society had taken an active part in the reconnaissance of the geographical world, established congenial relations with savants and explorers, and demonstrated Egypt's continued contribution to geography.[29]

As Egypt's independence was bending under the weight of British financial and military hegemony, its former focus during the reign of Khedive

Isma'il, that of grand discoveries, was quickly shifting. Khedive Isma'il's attempts to extend his dominion into the hinterlands of southern Sudan, Equatoria, and Abyssinia between 1869–79 ended in unqualified failure. By the time of the outbreak of the Mahdist revolt in 1881 Egyptian administration in its African principalities was severely weakened. For instance, the Egyptian administration of Dar Fur, which had been formally annexed in 1874, collapsed in 1883. By that time, Khedive Isma'il had been deposed (in 1879) and his son, Tawfiq Pasha, (r. 1879–92) instated. With the 1882 invasion of Egypt by the British, Egypt's rule in the Sudan was wholly circumscribed by British policy.[30] By the time of General Charles Gordon's beheading in 1885, Egypt's involvement in Sudan was attenuated, although Egyptian teachers, soldiers, and administrators continued a strong involvement in Sudan well into the twentieth century.[31]

As Egypt's African colonial ambitions waned, the Royal Geographic Society reoriented itself geographically closer to home—toward Egypt and Sudan—and thematically toward ethnography and folklore, beginning an ethnographic collection for Sudan by 1898.[32] A critical moment in this process was the establishment of a small ethnographic museum, which was basically a more permanent version of Egypt's pavilion at the Venice Exposition of 1881. In December of 1898, Khedive Abbas Hilmi II (r. 1892–1914) inaugurated the geographical and ethnographic museum (*Le Musée de Géographie et d'Ethnographie*) of the Royal Geographic Society.[33] Although the RGS initially encountered difficulties in obtaining funding to secure objects, Frédéric Bonola Bey (with the aid of Onofrio Abbate Pasha) persisted in soliciting voyagers and friends of the society to donate some of the objects collected on their journeys; his efforts were successful, and it was primarily his vision that made possible the realization of the ethnographic museum.[34] In 1891 Bonola Bey secured a promissory loan from the government to build a museum building adjacent to the society itself, but it was not until January 1898 that construction was completed.[35]

Bonola Bey and Abbate Pasha, both Italians, were prominent figures in the Royal Geographic Society from 1885 until World War I, so much so that Donald Reid categorizes their tenure (1885–1915) as the "Italian phase" of the society.[36] Bonola Bey served as the society's general secretary, and Abbate Pasha, an ophthalmologist who was court physician to Sa'id, Isma'il, Tawfiq, and 'Abbas II, as its president. In his speech at the museum's inauguration, Abbate Pasha emphasized the importance of having created an Ethnographic Museum, one that could preserve the material culture of interior Africa prior to its prolonged contact with European civilization, as well as represent the "tableau vivant" of Egypt and its neighboring regions, its geological constitution, its flora and fauna, and the ethnography of its diverse races.[37] The museum was to be a tribute to the moral and material progress of Egypt, and was to maintain a collection of rare and historic maps and a display of portraits of "the great voyagers and savants who will make up, with time, the Pantheon of Modern Egypt," thus contributing to the natural laws of progress and civilization.[38]

At the entrance to the museum stood two statues, representing Africa and Asia. The first hall contained a rather heterogeneous collection: botanical collections of Kurdufan and Dar Fur collected between 1874–77 by one Dr. Pfund, while he was attached to a reconnaissance mission of the Egyptian government; rock specimens from the western desert, Somalia, Kurdufan, and Dar Fur; petrified trees collected by Abbate Pasha from the Libyan desert; colored earth from the Dakhleh oasis; glass specimens, plates and pottery, and salts and natrons from Egypt; fishing and hunting instruments collected from among the Dinka and Niam-Niam; photographs of Mecca, Medina, and their saints taken by Muhammad Sadiq Pasha; a granite grinder taken by Richard Francis Burton from Medina; a bird's-eye view of Cairo; a stamp from 1671; and portraits of Mehmed 'Ali Pasha and Ferdinand de Lesseps.[39]

Upon entering the second hall one encountered a 1867 panoramic relief map of the Valley of Egypt. The principal collection of this hall, more thematically unified than the first, was a series of twenty-five historic maps, beginning with a reproduction of the celebrated Papyrus of Turin, and ending with a 1897 administrative map of domains from Upper Egypt. The hall also contained a series of portraits of Egyptian sovereigns, savants of Egypt, and eminent voyagers who had explored the Nile Valley region and neighboring nations (Isma'il Pasha, Sa'id Pasha, Mahmud Pasha al-Falaki, Richard Burton, Georg Schweinfurth, General Gordon, and others), autographs, and historical souvenirs brought by delegates who had attended the opening of the Suez Canal.[40]

Rare ethnographic objects could also be found in the second hall—some taken during military expeditions, such as the Abyssinian war, others collected by Romolo Gessi; and another set collected by Schweinfurth among the Niam-Niam and in Uganda, Kurdufan, and Dar Fur. The hall also also contained a collection of rare photographs—already considered historical documents—taken by Buchta when he accompanied General Gessi to Sudan; these included images of Khartoum, the governor's palace, the spot where General Gordon was assassinated, Egyptian stations along the Nile, and a series of "scenes and types" of diverse tribes, indigenous groups, and villages of ethnographic interest.[41]

This hall also housed collections related to Egypt itself: natural specimens—such as sycamore, ebony, gums, henna, ostrich feathers, and varieties of cotton—as well as ethnographic objects such as metal items, jewelry, pottery, and furniture. Bonola Bey was particularly insistent on the importance of maintaining ethnographic collections from Egypt. The ethnographic study of the Egyptian nation, including its material culture and all aspects of ordinary quotidian life, would be collected in order to preserve the manifestations of the "race," thus helping to define its national character. Photographic reproduction of the popular life of the "race"—picturesque scenes of Egyptian life and the tribes of Nubia and the Sudan—was to be encouraged for the same reason. Bonola advocated the recording and conservation of traditional customs and objects before their eradication by modern civilization. It was hoped that in the future the society would be able to present a complete tableau of the native inhabitants of Egypt, in all the manifestations of individual and social life—a complete expression of the ethnic character of the people united by the khediviate.[42]

The Ethnographic Museum of the Royal Geographic Society encapsulated several aspects of colonial anthropology. The collection—an array of seemingly innocuous ethnographic and geographic artifacts, along with a hagiographical panorama of portraits—concealed the colonial pedigree of the objects themselves, the individuals who procured them, and the conditions under which they were obtained. For example, the specimens from Kurdufan, Dar Fur, and Abyssinia had been obtained as a direct result of violent attempts at the colonization and annexation of those territories by Anglo-Egyptian forces. Indeed, until the later part of the twentieth century, Egyptian geographers often looked upon Egypt's colonial aspirations in Africa quite favorably, asserting that Egyptian exploration of the Horn of Africa in the 1870s and 1880s had done much to further science and civilization. In the words of one of Egypt's first professional geographers, Mustafa 'Amir, "In all these expeditions scientific investigations went hand in hand with military operations and with peaceful penetration; and the geographical section of the Egyptian army was untiring in its efforts to make a name for Egypt in the world of science and to help civilization to find new fields for expansion."[43]

The maintenance of an ethnographic collection for Egypt and colonial Africa in order to "preserve the characteristics of the race" was itself part of a larger anthropological project of cataloging, typifying, and preserving the culture of native inhabitants prior to the intrusion of modern civilization. This peculiarly imperial view of geography as a set of empirical yet inert objects was itself a component of the colonization of space through geography and ethnology. During the 1798 French invasion of Egypt, a similar process had been undertaken by Napoleon's geographers, whose work was characterized by the "ability to *measure* the value of the peoples and culture they were invading" and bestow the benefits of a "universal scientific culture" and, subsequently, social happiness and human progress.[44] Yet, crucially, this trend in anthropology was also part of the work of Egyptian state-sponsored cultural institutions, undertaken by a local cosmopolitan elite—including Ottoman Egyptians, native Egyptians, Italians, and other Europeans. The reign of Khedive Isma'il, in particular, was one in which the internalization of a colonial project of the exhibition and display of native things and peoples was at its zenith. As Zeynep Çelik notes, in the Ottoman imperial context "exposition fever carried East" as Orientalized forms of architectural and ethnographic self-representation gained credence in the late nineteenth century.[45]

Analogies of Being: Abbate Pasha and Studies in Native Physiology and Psychology

Orientalist forms and practices were localized on native bodies as well as being entombed in museum culture. Within colonial social-scientific endeavors, "natives" often functioned as objects of observation, taxonomy, and classification, that is, as specimens: individual or collective representatives of their race, embedded within a hierarchical discourse of civilizational progress. The Orientalist fascination with the non-European remained encyclopedist in scope, but as Peter Pels has argued, it transformed from an earlier textually based Orientalist body of knowledge (of which the 1798 French expedition was an example) to an ethnological form of knowledge localized on native bodies.[46] This signaled the dissemination of Orientalist knowledge into the social-scientific disciplines, in which the study of the native "other" became an empirical and objective enterprise. The production of the empirical "truth of the colonial difference,"[47] understood within the colonial context as race, relied therefore on an armature of social-scientific disciplinary knowledge. Traditional Orientalism, as Edward Said has argued, was characterized by the impulse

> to divide, deploy, schematize, tabulate, index, and record everything in sight (and out of sight); to make out of every observable detail a generalization and out of every generalization an immutable law about the Oriental nature, temperament, mentality, custom, or type; and above all, to transmute living reality into the stuff of texts.[48]

Said's emphasis on Orientalism's textuality is two-fold: on the one hand is the process of transforming the living reality of the Orient into texts, and on the other is the very citationary nature of Orientalism itself (that is, the continuous reproduction of *idées reçues* about the Orient through a long lineage of Orientalist texts). As both Said and Timothy Mitchell have noted, Orientalism needed to move from the level of empirical particularities to the level of abstraction and generalization. This could be accomplished through the study of Oriental culture and *mentalité*, or the collective mind.[49] In the nineteenth century, through the scientific study of society, Orientalism became wedded to social science through a number of disciplines, most notably ethnology, sociology, and the comparative study of religion. For example, Peter Pels has tracked the transformation of classical Orientalism into ethnology through the institutionalization of science and statistics within nineteenth-century India; Nicholas Dirks has charted the relationship between Orientalist knowledge, ethnography, and the reification of caste in colonial India; and Anne Godlewska has examined the development of French geography, with its techniques of map, text and image, in late-eighteenth-century Egypt as an example of the interconnection between imperial aggression and cultural domination.[50]

What ethnological studies came to share in common with earlier Orientalist discourse was the ontological and epistemological distinction between a European self and an Oriental other. "What Orientalism offered was not just a technical knowledge of Oriental languages, religious beliefs and methods of government, but a series of absolute differences according to which the Oriental could be understood as the negative of the European."[51] One of the ways in which the fixing of difference between the European and the non-European could be scientifically established was through the experimental sciences of physiology and psychology. The oeuvre of Onofrio Abbate Pasha provides us with a unique glimpse into the transition from a textually based Orientalism concerned with collection and commentary to an experimental and clinical science of native difference. Abbate Pasha mobilized a biological paradigm in which the languages of physiology, psychology, and comparative anatomy, rather than the classical emphasis on Oriental philology and religion, were the new markers of native difference. In the words of Nicholas Dirks, the colonized subject was "first and foremost a body," and the colonized body itself served as an ethnographic text.[52]

Onofrio Abbate Pasha, born in the first quarter of the nineteenth century, had a long and colorful career in the service of the Egyptian royal court. Abbate is interesting because he was a complex and in many ways a marginal figure. He was not a colonialist in the strictest sense, being a southern Italian and a long-standing resident of Egypt. An ophthalmologist by training but an encyclopedist at heart, Abbate was well versed in history, geography, archaeology, medicine, and anatomy. As a student of the University of Palermo, Abbate was advised by a Neapolitan doctor to establish himself in Egypt, where he arrived in 1845 to enter the Egyptian government service; thus began his illustrious career as a physician, scientist, and scholar. In 1852 Abbate was transferred from Cairo to Alexandria, and soon was placed as a medical doctor on the naval fleet commissioned to the Crimea by Viceroy Sa'id Pasha (r.1854–63). Soon after, Abbate began his personal service to the khedivial family, as the private physician to the khedivial harem and to the vice-reine herself. At the beginning of Khedive Isma'il's reign, Abbate was appointed sanitary inspector of Lower and Upper Egypt; he was later appointed chief surgeon of the Government Hospital, then director of Cairo's Department of Health Service, and subsequently reassigned as medical doctor to the harem.Eventually he was attached to Tawfiq Pasha as personal medical consultant and confidant, which he remained from 1880 to 1887.

A greatly accomplished man known for his scientific rigor and humanistic devotion, Abbate had by the time of his death been an active surgeon; treated victims of Egypt's 1848 cholera epidemic; established the first ophthalmology journal in Egypt in 1852; toured Sudan with Khedive Sa'id and Ferdinand de Lesseps in 1856; served as the Egyptian delegate to the First International Congress of Medicine held in Paris in 1862; served as vice president of the Institut Egyptien; served as president of the RGS from 1890 until his death in 1915; served as president of the Société Khediviale de Medicine in 1902; and was involved with the Anarchist Free Popular University in Alexandria.[53] The bulk of Abbate's writings were published in Cairo in 1909 as a collection of articles, under the title *Aegyptiaca* (*Misriyyat*); the volume is dedicated, appropriately, to the khedivial family that supported Abbate for more than half a century, and to Khedive Isma'il in particular, in honor of his ideas of a rapprochement with Europe.[54]

Abbate's research and writings on native physiology and psychology revolved around two central themes: the scientific determination of physiological, structural, and organic differences between Egyptian natives and Europeans; and the attempt to explain certain manners and customs (such as the use of hashish), or the belief in certain supernatural practices (such as magical divination) through scientific induction and explanation. Abbate's work may be categorized with other studies of native physiology and psychology—such as A. C. Haddon's writings about the turn-of-the-century Cambridge Torres Straits expedition.[55] But unlike many other late nineteenth- and early-twentieth-century colonial anthropologists, Abbate was a longtime resident of Egypt, having spent seventy years of his life there, much of it in the service of the khedivial family. Immersed as he was in the European and Francophone communities of Egypt, Abbate belonged to a local cosmopolitan elite composed of Ottomans, Egyptians, Greeks, and Italians.[56] Abbate was not a colonial administrator, nor did his work involve the "practical" anthropology behind much nineteenth-century colonial statecraft, as has been detailed for the cases of the British in India and Africa.[57] Rather, Abbate was a far more interstitial figure, one who belonged to the world of European residents in the service of khedivial Egypt and the Ottoman Empire. For instance, the Antiquities Service (1858) and the Institut Égyptien (1859) were founded under Sa'id by Europeans, and Abbate served as vice president of the latter.[58] Under the reign of Isma'il, especially, Europeans in the service of the khedive were viewed as facilitators and harbingers of modern European civilization, and were involved in a wide array of activities, in particular the dissemination of Western intellectual institutions, techniques, and ideas. Abbate was thus part of a larger community of European scholars and technocrats in Ottoman Egypt involved in state-initiated reforms that sought to modernize the organization of the state and society.[59]

Nevertheless, Abbate did share an Orientalist and colonial worldview with his nineteenth-century European counterparts in the sciences of geography and anthropology. For example, he viewed the colonizing mission as an indispensable component of the *rapprochement* of moral and material distances. The conquests of geography and science, he argued, were necessary levers to the progress of civilization and its dissemination throughout the non-Western world. To overcome the natural and geographic barriers that separated the diverse peoples of the world, a precise and exact knowledge of geography (as well as a perfection of means of transportation) was indispensable. This view was laid out in an article written in response to an 1888 criticism of the coeval pursuit of "grand geographical enigmas" and the acquisition of territories, in which Abbate asserted the scientific value of studies conducted in the spirit of a *réel positivisme* and the "sincere and loyal sentiments of colonizers." According to his argument, it was in the pursuit of such pragmatic goals as commercial exploitation that much of the geographical progress (particularly in Africa) of the late nineteenth century had been made. In an era in which the vanguard of civilization was based on profit and utility—rather than the pursuit of "pure science" or aesthetics—the conquest of space and the progress of exact science had become inseparable.[60] This is a sentiment echoed in much geographical writing of the late nineteenth century.[61]

Well versed in the writings of his own generation of intellectual luminaries, Abbate Pasha had an intellectual frame of reference that spanned the new sciences of evolutionary biology, anthropometry, psycho-physiology (especially French), and studies of biological and psychological pathology. Two principal intellectual contexts, both thoroughly embedded within the colonial context, can best help us to understand the work of Abbate. First is the nineteenth-century anthropological preoccupation with the classification and taxonomical organization of the human race into different categories or races—the impulse behind sciences such as anthropometry, phrenology, and physiognomy. The other is the then-emerging study of the biological bases of human behavior and thought, which underlay the science of psycho-physiology (the physiology of the sense organs and motor functions), the science of labor power, and the study of medical and psychological pathology. Abbate's work lay at the intersection of these two dominant trends in nineteenth-century European thought.

Nineteenth-century anthropological taxonomies were derivative of earlier Enlightenment ideas regarding the "ordering of mankind." As detailed by Ivan Hannaford, the "first stage in the development of an idea of race" congealed between 1684 and 1815, and was characterized by a methodological shift from a metaphysical "order of things" to a more descriptive and classificatory organization of knowledge based on positivist empiricism; the establishment of new relationships among body structure, bodily endowment, and mind (often known as "national character'); and a revival of the Aristotelian writings on physiognomy and art.[62] The eighteenth century was characterized by the emergence of a corpus of writings that detailed the importance of place, climate, language and race—whether in the writings of Hobbes and the discussion of the right of conquest; Montesquieu and the importance of climate as a determining feature of the "temper of the mind"; Hume and the idea that "the character of a nation will much depend on moral causes"; Kant and the characterization of different races and national characters in terms of temperaments, physiognomy, and even their ability to appreciate the beautiful and the sublime; or Fichte and the relationship between language, purity of blood, and the notion of Volk.[63]

However, it was with the appearance of a more methodic science of man—anthropology—and the writings of Swedish botanist Carolus Linneaus, French naturalist Georges-Louis Leclerc (Comte de Buffon), and the German "founder of biological anthropology," Johann Friedrich Blumenbach, that humankind was divided into distinct natural racial categories on the basis of differences in morphology, facial types, psychological temperament, and mental abilities. Further developments in comparative anatomy, based on the biological advances of Jean-Baptiste Lamarck and Georges Cuvier, led to a series of competing theories, such as monogenesis, polygenesis, environmentalism, and transformism, that lent ever more momentum to the comparative study of different races.[64] Once the categorization of the races came to include differences in anatomical structures, and mental and mechanical aptitudes and faculties (memory, reason, imagination, aesthetics), the scientific study of racial differences in anatomy, psychology and physiology followed suit. As Ivan Hannaford has argued, race only became "real" once it had the "power to biologically rank" the races into superior and inferior categories.[65] This power to biologically rank the races was produced by and within the imperial context, as Ann Stoler and others have shown.[66]

Similarly, numerous historians of Europe have argued for the importance of understanding the natural-scientific, and specifically medical, languages of the mid- to late nineteenth century as critical matrices for the study of the individual and society. Fields of study as varied as anthropology, sociology, criminology, psychology, and psychiatry increasingly began to rely on medicalized models of health and pathology, and many detailed histories exist of the nineteenth-century development of the social sciences.[67] Such scientific models for understanding the social order coincided with developments in evolutionary biology, most notably in Darwinist thought. In his lucid study of the culture, politics, and language of degeneration that emerged in the middle of the nineteenth century, Daniel Pick argues that the European concern with degeneration, atavism, and regression was enveloped in the language of late-nineteenth-century progressive evolutionary naturalism.[68] Just as Pick details the ways in which degeneration became an "object of scientific and medical investigation," Anson Rabinbach has scrutinized the manner in which the study of human labor power became the object of a rigorous scientific program in the last quarter of the nineteenth century. Dominated by the image of the body as the human motor, studies of human labor owed their intellectual genesis to developments in physics—namely, Hermann von Helmholtz's discovery of the law of thermodynamics and Clasius's law of entropy. "The great discoveries of nineteenth-century physics led, therefore, not only to the assumption of a universal energy, but also to the inevitability of decline, dissolution, and exhaustion."[69] As both Pick and Rabinbach note, the "internal" concerns with degeneration and fatigue were crosshatched with European imperial and racial notions of the inferiority of colonial subject races.

Abbate's research and writings on native physiology and psychology centered on the scientific determination of biological differences between Egyptian natives and Europeans, and the description of analogies of being, or what Goethe once referred to as *l'être en activité*. By observing Egyptians at work and performing experimental researches in his laboratory or home, and through his direct access to cadavers as a medical doctor, Abbate Pasha accumulated a varied array of data on the Egyptian "organism," richly infused with Orientalist *idées reçues*. Drawing directly and heavily on both of the traditions of European thought outlined above—the anthropological preoccupation with classification and taxonomical organization of the human race and the emerging study of the biological bases of human behavior and thought—Abbate's work offers us a rich insight into the workings of a nineteenth-century scholar preoccupied with comprehensive study of the native population.

According to Abbate, the Egyptian race, and the fellah in particular, retained an aptitude for mechanical and imitative tasks—part of the psychological heritage of the ancient Egyptians.[70] A firm believer in the importance of ethnography for the study of the intellectual and physical qualities of a people, Abbate recounted a visit to the Suarès sugar refineries in an Upper Egyptian village south of Giza. Noting the characteristics of the indigenous laborers that lent themselves to industrial endeavors (their patience, sobriety, and diligence), Abbate reflected on his own observation of an adroit young male Egyptian worker in the factory. He asked,

> What muscular force is expended by this young Arab to utilize in a period of a few hours the enormous quantity of paper ready to envelop the sugar loafs in cylindrical form? And secondly, from whence is this difficult, mechanical aptitude derived? One, I would say, that is almost impossible to find in other races.[71]

Influenced by the research and writings of Helmholtz and of Jules Marey, Abbate tried to ascertain the physiological bases of the young Arab's rapid and regular movements—with muscle rotations on average every 15 seconds—were these mechanical, unconscious, and involuntary movements?[72]

Elaborating on the direct opposition between the mechanical exercise of active force (a response to a direct stimulus), and the higher mental functions (which are not triggered by external stimuli), Abbate asserted the inferiority of the former as activities devoid of intellectualization, that is to say primitive or instinctive in nature. Furthermore, the habitual and repetitive movements of workers produced a sort of mechanical intoxication (*ivresse mécanique*).[73] But it was among the Egyptians, in particular, that workers in the manual arts and handicrafts were incontestably agile and patient, endowed with an ability for uniform and prolonged mechanical actions, and a total absorption in physical labor. Egyptian peasants, too, exhibited similar regularized and identical movements—monotonous, somnolent, and unconscious.

Abbate linked this "mechanical aptitude" to the history of the Egyptians, and in particular to the conquest and assimilation of Egypt into the Arab empire, and concomitantly into a Semitic sphere of influence.[74] In characteristically Orientalist fashion, he characterized the Arabs as a race gifted with ardent and exaggerated imaginations, and advanced faculties of mechanism and reproduction (in contrast to the Western capacity for invention attributed to speculation, reason, and intelligence). The identification of imitation, repetition, and lack of imagination, invention or originality, as Arab or Oriental traits was an Orientalist theme common in both the eighteenth and nineteenth centuries, and found in the works of thinkers such as Montesquieu and Kant.[75] According to Abbate, these imitative and mechanistic faculties were visible in Arabs' habitual reproduction of artistic forms and motifs; their use of formulas and proofs (rather than methods) in the sciences; and in their architecture, monuments, and ornamentation, which were seen as conformist and lacking in artistic spirit, originality, and thought (the repetition of geometrical patterns, the privileging of form over sentiment). This atavistic aptitude, argued Abbate, was especially evident in the Egyptians: "visit the École des Arts et Métiers . . . you will see uniform lines and perfect reproductions rigorously executed, admirable at first glance, but, ultimately, mechanical."[76] Nor was this present only in the creative arts—in more intellectual spheres one found the same mechanical faculty: the rote repetition of facts, the existence of prodigious memories (indeed "phonographic memory," as Abbate called it), and the mechanical reproduction of arguments.

If Egyptian males were characterized by a mechanical aptitude, then Egyptian females were especially marked by a "static equilibrium."[77] Abbate queried the peculiar aptitude of Egyptian women to carry heavy objects on their heads while maintaining perfect balance. Was it the result of habituation, the influence of an atavism in the race, or the result of perfect bone structure and regular muscle development?[78] Abbate proceeded to discuss the center of gravity of human beings in motion and the effects of gravitational displacement while supporting an additional weight.[79] In the case of Egyptian women, he found that they adapted to the additional weight in such a manner as to have the center of the line of gravity pass through the vertex of the skull and the spinal column, in a straight and continuous line. It was his hypothesis that the large and regular nature of the pelvis, the normal formation of bones, and the accentuated development of the muscles of Egyptian women all contributed to their load-balancing aptitude, enabling a perfect adaptation to the laws of static mechanics. Further, those who visited the museum of Giza had commented on the habitual equilibrium of Egyptians in general, which could be seen in the epoch of the pyramids among male and female laborers carrying objects on their head. How could one explain the persistence of this aptitude over 10,000 years? Drawing on social Darwinist thought (particularly Spencer and Schopenhauer), he argued that this organic adaptation of the species to its particular conditions of existence, was, in essence a form of atavism.[80]

Indeed, it was Abbate's contention that the Egyptian woman, as an organism, was singularly developed and suited to her environment—a true reproduction of the type that pharaonic artists had engraved on their monuments.[81] The female fellahin were characterized by a static equilibrium since late antiquity, "an equilibrium in perfect rapport with the particular skeleton of the race."[82] This equilibrium was part of their ancestral heredity (from an anatomical and physiological point of view) and the fixity of the race over time. By "heredity" Abbate meant the faculties and acquired characteristics transmitted by living beings to subsequent generations, thereby establishing a general permanence of characteristics across species. Such racial "fixity" was due to the permanence of certain essential traits, but also to the transmission of particular habitual modes, and the repetition of individual characteristics across generations. Modifications of form or structure, in accordance with Owen's law, were among the essential characters of a race. Such an *habitude hereditaire* could be externally visible, as in physiognomy, facial expressions, and cranial structure, or less visible, as in skeletal development. It was through skeletal development that Abbate addressed the issue of racial heredity.[83]

Among the race of Egyptian women, he argued, there was an exact correspondence between the skull and pelvis, that is to say, an analogical parallel between the masses and surface areas of the pelvis and skull. The fixity of the female Egyptian, in terms of skeletal structure and anatomical characteristics, was thought by Abbate to be quite remarkable, especially the largeness of the pelvis, the regular form of the vertebral column, and the large amount of phosphate contained in femurs and all other bones.[84] Basing his evidence on comparisons between the archaeological remains of skeletons from J. de Morgan's research at the Necropolis of Kawamil and modern skeletons deposited at the School of Medicine at Qasr al-'Ayni Hospital, Abbate concluded that the peculiar anatomical feature of the Egyptian female—the correspondence between pelvis and cranium—was indeed present in both the ancient and modern skeletons. It was this prehistorical evidence that enabled him to confirm his hypothesis regarding the fixity of the Egyptian female, considered as generally homogeneous (due to the long history of similar conditions of existence within the Nile Valley), despite racial admixture.[85]

Abbate thus demonstrated the importance of evolutionary adaptation, the transmission of acquired traits, *habitude hereditaire*, and atavism. Mobilizing the sciences of comparative anatomy and physiology, he established several of the bases of Egyptian ethnological difference, such as mechanical aptitude and static equilibrium—both features that, he argued, illustrated the fixity of the Egyptian race since antiquity. His research provided scientific corroboration for enduring Orientalist themes, namely the mechanical and imitative proclivities of Orientals and their primitive and instinctive agility—ideal attributes for manual and physical labor.

The second component of Abbate's research addressed a second Orientalist theme: the "superstitious and irrational" manners and customs of the modern-day Egyptians. Relying, in part, on the literary genre of the "manners and customs" literature of the nineteenth century, Abbate conducted a series of studies attempting to explain, through scientific methods, "Oriental" practices such as the use of hashish, or the belief in certain supernatural practices (such as magical divination and snake charming).[86] In researching the phenomena of magical divination referred to by Lane as the *darb el-mendel*, and by Abbate as the *Fataa-el-Mandel*, true to the citationary nature of Orientalism, Abbate Pasha begins with Edward Lane's well-known text *Account of the Manners and Customs of the Modern Egyptians*.[87] Lane uses the example of a well-known diviner, 'Abd al-Qadir al-Maghribi, whom he had commissioned to perform various acts of divination for himself and for several British visitors, to detail the "Magic Square and Mirror of Ink" experiment in his chapter on "Magic, Astrology, and Alchymy."[88] A relatively complex act of magic, the "magic square" entailed the summoning of persons absent or dead. According to Lane, although he witnessed many false or inaccurate descriptions, the relative success of many of the performances was a "mystery" neither he nor others could "penetrate."[89] It was this mystery—the art and science of divination—that Abbate Pasha tried to explicate with the aid of several psycho-physiological theories of hypnosis, suggestibility, and hallucination.

Noting various historical and literary examples of divination, the summoning of spirits, hallucinations, and their relation to altered states produced by beverages, inhaled gases, or substances, Abbate maintained that the faculties of sight and hearing possessed immense subtlety.[90] The importance of the role of imagination, the soporific state induced by hypnosis, the use of melancholic, sanguine, nervous, or impressionable subjects by charlatans, and the prevalence of superstitious beliefs among ignorant peoples—all could help to explain the success of such practices.[91] But, in the same vein as the scientific research on hypnotism conducted by various nineteenth-century figures, including Charcot and Richet, Abbate aimed to provide a scientifically valid explanation for the magic square. Abbate utilized a general psycho-physiological framework to discuss different individual levels of susceptibility to hypnosis (hysterics, neurotics, and the feeble-minded), as well as the physiological and psychological state induced by hypnosis (excitation of the central nervous system, loss of voluntarism, suggestibility, hallucination, and automatism).[92]

The magic square was a practice in which the diviner would draw a "magic square and mirror of ink" (an ink blot in the center of a subdivided square) on the subject's right hand, all the while pronouncing invocations and summoning spirits. According to Abbate, whose knowledge of the practice was based only on Lane's description, the forms, objects, and spirits summoned during the magic square were suggested to subjects in a manner specifically intended to evoke a hallucination. The hallucinations themselves were induced in the subject through the excitation of their sense of vision, the richness of their imagination, and their previous associations with the suggested hallucinations. Given his premise—that ideas or mental representations were not detached from organs—Abbate drew on experimental research that demonstrated the persistence of visual impressions and images (e.g., the reproduction of complementary colors on the retina, the retention of older images when successive objects were shown). Hallucinatory objects themselves, then, were simply the persistence of older visual impressions on the retina, that is to say, the weakened retention of older sensations spawned in this instance by the suggestion of the magician. Finally, the burning of coal, incense, or other substances during the "magic square" excited vertigo and drowsiness, and eventually led to a hypnotic state. In combination with the ink blot which they were meant to focus upon, this rendered subjects susceptible to the active suggestion of the magician. Thus, it was the modification of the individuals' mental and physical state (through hypnosis, suggestion, and imagination) that produced the excitation of thought and visual sensations.[93]

Abbate's extensive study of practices such as the magic square and snake charmers was distinct from earlier Orientalist typifications of magical practices as indicative of the superstitious nature or "character" of Arabs in general and Egyptians in particular. Lane's *Manners and Customs* presented the Arab propensity toward superstitious beliefs as a component of Oriental religion—sanctioned by religious texts and prophetic utterances (*Qur'an* and *ahadith*, respectively). Abbate, in contrast, did not base his discussion on the words or writings of indigenous informants, but rather on his personal observations and scientific inductions, thus providing scientific and physiological explanations for "irrational" practices and primitive psychology. Furthermore, Abbate aimed at nothing less than eradicating such vulgar beliefs in the superstitious, the illusory, and the supernatural. As a scientist, he continually emphasized the deceptive nature of "illusions of the imagination," apparitions, human spirits, and phantoms as phenomena that exist only in the imagination—nothing more than "the specter of one's own retina."

Convinced that the "conquest of geography and science" was the catalyst of progress and civilization, Abbate sought to create a bridging of the "moral and material distances" between the peoples of Europe and the "Muslim Orient."[94] Part of that bridging entailed the eradication of cruel and barbarous customs, such as enuchism, within the Ottoman Empire, a longstanding concern for Abbate.[95] Many of Abbate's arguments about indigenous cultural practices (rather than religion) being the cause of certain barbarous practices were common to colonial critiques of native customs that offended European moral sensibilities. In India, the British relied upon similar styles of argumentation—the juxtaposition of Oriental fanaticism with Western notions of liberty, justice, and corporeal integrity—to refute the religious validity of native practices such as sati and hook-swinging.[96]

Abbate viewed his work as being in many ways the continuation of the project started by the Napoleonic expedition—a project embodied in the Institut d'Égypte and the Institut Égyptien revived in Cairo under Khedive Sa'id in 1859.[97] His own work aimed at ascertaining the scientific contours of native difference, although no longer textually based, retained the encyclopedist nature of classical Orientalism but signaled the transformation to an ethnological and embodied basis of empirical knowledge about Orientals. Abbate undertook detailed cataloging and classification of Egyptian history and civilization, and the collection of both natural and cultural artifacts. In so doing, he combined elements of classical Orientalist ideas regarding Egyptian civilization with newer psycho-physiological research to categorize the Ancient and modern-day Egyptians, loosely understood as both a civilizational and a racial unit. His natural-history model is evident in his diverse discussions of botany, zoology, and pharaonic history, and in his favorable view of the accomplishments of Bonaparte's expedition in uncovering the mysteries of Egyptian nature, art, and history, and his hagiographical praise for the members of the expedition. The drive to collect, classify, categorize, and comment was taken up by Egyptians themselves in ethnographic and folklore studies—itself one of the defining domains of the Royal Geographic Society, to which I now return.

Studies in Ethnography

What types of studies did Egyptian members of the Geographic Society carry out during its early tenure? It was, in particular, the European "gentlemanly" tradition of scientific expeditions that was emulated in Egypt in the nineteenth century, by such figures as engineer Muhammad Sadiq Pasha, who mapped routes to the Hijaz in 1861, well before Richard Burton, and Lieutenant-Colonel Muhammad Mukhtar Bey, who conducted military-scientific expeditions in east Africa (Harrar and the Somali coast) in the 1870s and early 1880s, producing the first "correct" cartographic maps of the region.[98] In the twentieth century Ahmed Hasanayn Bey, second chamberlain to King Fu'ad, presented his 1923 explorations in Libya to the Royal Geographic Society with much fanfare.[99] In 1928 the society awarded its gold medal to Hasanayn for his explorations in the Libyan Desert.[100] His memoirs of the journey were published in Arabic as *Fi Sahara' Libya* and later translated into English as *The Lost Oases* (which influenced Michael Ondaatje's novel *The English Patient*).[101] Hasanayn was commissioned to facilitate negotiations with Italy over the Libyan border, and was later to play an important if behind the scenes role in the Egyptian royal cabinet.[102] As Donald Reid notes, even King Fu'ad "could not resist a desert adventure," crossing the desert into Siwa in 1930.[103] Nor was adventure the only impetus behind such "gentlemanly" travels. In December of 1911, during the Turco-Italian war, Hafiz Afifi headed a Red Crescent mission to Cyrenaica, enjoying the company of the grand Sanusi (Sidi Ahmad al-Sharif, the head of the Islamic Sanusiyya order in Libya-Cyrenaica) himself.[104] The concerns of less glamorous twentieth-century geographers and anthropologists, however, focused on developing local ethnographic studies on a scientific basis.

By the early twentieth century, the Egyptian Royal Geographic Society was calling for detailed ethnographic studies on various populations within Egypt, signaling a reorientation away from equatorial Africa and closer to home. In 1915 the Royal Geographic Society received fresh impetus under the leadership of Prince Fu'ad (who reigned as King Fu'ad from 1917 to 1936), in his attempt to "revive court-sponsored culture," and the society began to be considered one of the premier scientific institutions of the country.[105] In the political space created by the 1922 declaration of unilateral independence and the end of the British protectorate, Fu'ad I strove to place Egypt at the forefront of advances in the sciences, arts, and letters, through his patronage of associations such as the Royal Geographical Society, the Royal Society of Political Economy, Statistics and Legislation, and the Institut d'Hydrobiologie.[106] As under Khedive Isma'il, during Fu'ad's reign significant progress was made in higher education, including the founding of the Egyptian University and the hosting of numerous international scientific congresses in Cairo, including the eleventh International Geographic Congress, in April 1925, the seventeenth session of the International Statistical Institute, in 1927, and the International Congress of Medicine, in 1928.[107] In the interwar period, Fu'ad commissioned Sorbonne geography professor Augustin Bernard to oversee a project in Egyptian history and geography, within which European historians Georges Douin, Angelo Sammarco, and Edouard Driault generated their well-known histories of the Mehmed 'Ali dynasty.[108] In this way Fu'ad continued the use of European scholars and technocrats to further the state's projects of modernization. Fu'ad also recommended the reorganization of the Ethnographic Museum on the basis of scientific classificatory schemes of the sort used in modern museums, such as that of the Musée Belge du Congo or Tervuren—the example of Tervuren was itself indicative of the colonial pedigree, and aspirations of, museum culture.[109]

The RGS benefited greatly from such royal patronage, and by 1919 it was publishing its bulletin in four fascicules and a series of memoirs annually. Its emphasis on the development of local Egyptian studies continued. In its 1918 statement of a "Programme of Work," the society called for an extension of its sphere of action to include local ethnographic studies.[110] Focusing on the study of the Nile Valley and its dependencies, this program proposed that the society's energies be directed into scientific inquiries, publications of memoirs and bulletins, and lectures, as well as the development of aids to scientific study, namely, libraries, maps, ethnographic museums, and archives.[111]

> There are many well-informed men, belonging to the administrations, to the army, or to the legal, medical, architectural professions, etc., who, being bound to live in Egypt or the Sudan, would be able to gather extremely interesting information on a particular craft, habit or object, and would probably do so as soon as they received the necessary inducement. It is therefore specially for them that we publish these few indications in regard to an important part of our programme.[112]

The document went on to suggest that scientific research be undertaken in the following branches of geography: physical geography, anthropology, ethnography, economic geography, and historical geography.[113] Ethnographic studies were particularly emphasized:

> This [ethnography] is a province in which we will come in competition with no other science represented in Cairo; it *ought therefore to call for our special attention*.

> Everybody knows the great extension that these researches have reached in all countries and their importance for the history of civilisation. It is none too soon to gather and place on record in Egypt and the Sudan the very curious documents which are about to disappear in Egypt and are undergoing rapid evolution in the Sudan.[114]

The first proposed practical applications of ethnography were studies of the Siwa Oasis, of the gypsies of Egypt, of irrigation devices, and of basket making.[115]

The interwar years represented a crucial moment in the authorization, and transformation, of European social-scientific knowledge in Egypt, with the reorientation of the RGS toward Egyptian ethnography. Egyptians, under royal patronage, participated in the ethnographic recording and cataloging of their own culture and civilization, and in the collection and classification of cultural artifacts. This is a process Clive Barnett has referred to in the European colonial context as the "archivalization of knowledges."[116] Often methodologically eclectic, these studies marked the beginnings of the transformation from an older nineteenth-century conception of civilizations to an anthropological notion of culture as a principal unit of analysis.

Egyptian members of the RGS were in the numerical minority until 1928, but, nonetheless, the interwar period did see an increase in Egyptian activity within the society.[117] Mustafa Maher was one of several Egyptians who began to take part in the anthropological study of Egypt. A member of the RGS and later minister of public education and president of the Egyptian Commission on Rural Habitat (discussed in Chapter 3), Maher published in 1919 a lengthy article titled "L'Oasis de Siouah."[118] Explicitly in accordance with the Society's *Programme of Work*, this was a monographic study of Siwa (an isolated oasis located in the Western Desert), with, as Maher put it, no scientific pretensions. Maher comprehensively cataloged various facets of Siwan geography and history, in particular the local residents' long-standing resistance to centralized authority, which was of great interest to him, as he was part of an administrative mission to reorganize the town. In his cursory ethnographic study of Siwa, Maher focused most closely on the abject nature of Siwan life (poor health, education, and housing) and morality. With regard to the latter, Maher emphasized the fact that despite their religiosity and devotion, religion had not had an edifying effect upon the Siwans, whom he portrayed as fierce traditionalists, resistant to any form of progress.[119] Indeed, the purpose of his mission was to emphasize the importance of good government and proper instruction in elevating the morals and social conditions of the inhabitants.[120] This marked a shift from previous governmental policies toward Siwa, which had been based solely on taxation and tribute. "To ensure that the population of this most interesting oasis attain moral and material improvement, it is incumbent on the government to institute modern public education, ameliorate the morality of the new generation and guarantee a system of public hygiene."[121] Maher's focus on Siwans' lives thus embodied the reorientation of the RGS both in the direction of Egyptian ethnology (albeit of a subaltern group, the oasis dwellers) and toward a focus on educability and social reform.

Indeed, the interwar period saw a marked increase in interest in Egyptian ethnology within Egypt. For example, many argued that the RGS had suffered from a lack of systematic attention to the collection of Egyptian artifacts from the present day. G. A. Wainwright, in a 1929 article entitled, "Ethnology in Egypt," urged the society to take stock of what special form of knowledge it could contribute to the advancement of science, concluding that, "she must specialize in her own culture of the present day . . . and this introduces the peculiarly important position held by Egypt in the history of the world's culture."[122] Indeed, "exhibiting the permanence of culture is Egypt's primary duty to Ethnology," particularly of the ignorant, "that class which it has been Egypt's special mission to preserve to the world—the permanence of civilization."[123] But convincing the natives of the value of quotidian elements of their own culture was not so simple a task, and Wainwright recounted the difficulty (if not impossibility) he encountered in collecting such simple artifacts as letters, bracelets, or toys.

Nevertheless, during this period the desire to render the ethnography of the Nile Valley on a rational and scientific basis provided the momentum necessary for the reorganization of the Ethnographic Museum. In fact, in 1927 a Jesuit father and teacher at the College de la Sainte-Famille by the name of Paul Bovier-Lapierre proposed the creation of an Egyptian section of ethnography for the Ethnographic Museum, and petitioned the society for funds to begin collecting Egyptian artifacts for the museum.[124] Collection was begun immediately, and the 250 objects soon collected under Bovier-Lapierre's direction included weaving looms, instruments for sewing and masonry, cooking and eating utensils, toiletries, kohl, rings, bracelets, combs, amulets, and pottery.[125] Yet by 1934, the Egyptian section of the Ethnographic Museum was still in an embryonic state, particularly in comparison to the museum's African section, which had been painstakingly prepared by Frédéric Bonola Bey at the turn of the century.[126]

However, Lapierre's efforts were not in vain. In the words of Charles Bachatly, secretary-general of the Société d'Archaéologie Copte,

> Bovier-Lapierre has given a new impetus to the Geographic Society by suggesting the creation of a section of Egyptian ethnography, he has also encouraged me to

conduct some studies on the folklore and ethnography of the Nile Valley. Studies which would be difficult for European savants with their imperfect knowledge of Arabic dialects, and the impossibility of their mixing with the Egyptian population. Being arrested in my work, however, due to my imperfect bibliographic knowledge of this subject, I have attempted to compile a bibliography of the ethnographic studies on Egypt dispersed throughout various publications.[127]

Charles Bachatly did indeed write extensively on issues relating to local Egyptian ethnography. In a series of pieces published in the Society's *Bulletin*, Bachatly explored various facets of Egyptian folklore, with a focus on the origins and significance of the superstitious beliefs of the popular classes.[128] Bachatly's work maintained the overarching continuity of Egyptian civilization, as manifested in the general survival of ancient customs, but his most interesting contribution was to overturn the classically Orientalist conception of an uninterrupted link between contemporary superstitions and ancient pharaonic customs. For example, he contested Egyptologist Flinders Petrie's contention that *khemsah wa khemesah* (the round blue talisman used to ward off the evil eye) was a direct descendant of the sacred eye of Horus of ancient Egypt; Bachatly demonstrated, instead, how in its modern form the talisman integrated aspects of the Mediterranean "hand" meant to ward off the evil eye.[129] This emphasis on the Mediterranean heritage and the assimilation of "newer" elements into an essentially pharaonic template illustrates the historicity of social customs—a point Bachatly does not himself make, but that we may also infer from his reliance on the writings of medieval Arab historians, such as the fourteenth-century Al-Buni.

Abbas Bayoumi (chief inspector of antiquities in Upper Egypt), who argued that methodical research among Egyptian peasants showed that the practices of ancient Egypt were perpetuated in the present, also invoked medieval Arab histories in his work. Using examples from practical medicine (such as fertility practices) Bayoumi drew textual parallels between ancient Egypt and such medieval texts as Ibn Kamal Pasha's *Rujuʻ al-Shaykh ila Sabah*, Jalal al-Din Al-Suyuti's *Kitab al-Rahma fi al-Tibb wal Hikma*, Ahmed Ibn Muhammad Ibn Iyas's *Nushq Al-Azhar fi Ajaʼib al Amsar*, and *Badiʼ al-Zuhur fi waqaʼi al-thuhur*.[130] The use of the medieval Arab historians and writers points to the desire to bestow upon indigenous knowledge an epistemological value often denied it by colonial disciplines such as geography and anthropology.[131] Such valuations extended to the knowledge received through interactions with Egyptians, as Bachatly and Bayoumi indicated. Knowledge, furthermore, that was "difficult for European savants" to acquire given the "impossibility of their mixing with the Egyptian population." Indeed, as for Bachatly and Bayoumi, the question of survivals was of great interest to Egyptian ethnologists, Egyptologists (who sought connections between ancient and modern Egypt), and Africanists (who sought connections between ancient Egypt and modern Africa) alike, for a variety of reasons.[132]

Folklore and Primitive "Survivals"

Scholars began collecting Egyptian folkloric material—with particular interest in the survival of pharaonic and pre-Islamic customs—around the turn of the century. Canonical foreign-language texts in this field were those of the eminent French Egyptologist Gaston Maspero, whose collections of ancient Egyptian stories and songs inspired comparisons with those of the modern Egyptians.[133] Other turn-of-the-century works concentrated on the direct and verbatim collection and translation of contemporary popular songs and legends, such as Yacoub Artin Pasha's 1895 *Contes Populaires inedits de la Vallée du Nil*, and Georges Legrain's (Director of Antiquities at Karnak) 1914 text *Louqsor sans les pharaons*.[134]

In 1919 the Geographic Society's president, George Foucart, a colorful figure "accused of spying for the British and taking liberties with Muslim women,"[135] published his detailed questionnaire *Introductory Questions on African Ethnology*. Foucart, who had studied Egyptology and was particularly concerned with the comparative study of religions, underscored the urgency of the ethnographic study of "non-civilized" peoples, as their disappearance was imminent.[136]

> The greater the barbarism presented by the forms of individual or collective life, the better we shall be able to understand the struggle in other peoples to escape from it, and the more clearly we shall appreciate the victory of Man over hostile Nature. We must lose no time in using so valuable a method of enquiry. Of the still distinct characteristics of primitive societies, many are disappearing more and more rapidly. They must be collected without delay, for they are often already in the stage of mere survivals, or dependent upon the evidence of the last survivors. In a few years, it will be too late, and many a question on the origins of societies or religions will remain finally undecipherable.[137]

Again and again, Foucart emphasized the importance of recording survivals, of questioning the aged, of being at once an ethnographer, a historian, and an archaeologist. To detect and collect such "survivals"—for instance, of pharaonic or Greco-Roman customs in modern Egypt—required the ethnographer's judgment.[138]

An important early anthropological study of survivals was Winifred Blackman's 1927 *The Fellahin of Upper Egypt: Their Religious, Social and*

Industrial Life To-Day with Special Reference to Survivals from Ancient Times. Based on anthropological fieldwork among the peasants of Upper Egypt and intended to be descriptive of customs and traditions, folklore and magic, and religious and social life, this volume is classically ethnographic, although it was also meant to shed light on issues in Egyptology.[139] The goal of Blackman's work (avowedly semi-popular) was to document the "old customs and beliefs" before their extinction, or elimination by the upper classes through the spread of education. Blackman, who studied social anthropology at Oxford with Robert Ranulph Marett (Edward Tylor's successor), was a member of the Royal Anthropological Institute and the Royal Asiatic Society, and director of the Percy Sladen Expedition to Egypt between 1922 and 1926. Blackman's younger brother Aylward Manley Blackman was an Egyptologist affiliated with the Egypt Exploration Fund; he wrote numerous books, including one on the literature of the Ancient Egyptians, and assisted Winifred Blackman with the Egyptology side of the "ancient analogies" with modern customs and beliefs.[140]

During her fieldwork, Blackman became known as the "mistress of healing," as she administered analgesics, dressed wounds, provided charms for fertility, and provided various other medical services, sometimes to hundreds of patients a day.[141] Blackman's focus on beliefs and practices such as spirit possession, the *zar*, sorcery, the evil eye, and the cult of saints and shaykhs, was to become common practice for the anthropological study of Egypt and the Middle East generally. Her discussion of "survivals," too, was among the first of its kind. In the chapter on ancient Egyptian analogies in *The Fellahin of Upper Egypt* she tackles the "resemblances of the modern to the ancient magico-medical prescriptions," setting aside the survivals associated with the cult of saints (for which she anticipated writing another book). With little explicit theoretical orientation, other than the unstated positivist evolutionism implicit in the doctrine of survivals, Blackman simply noted those similarities in housing, dress, ceremonies of birth and death, and supernatural beliefs and practices that she had observed to exist.[142]

Robert Marett, Blackman's former professor and mentor and a pioneer in social anthropology, had been a principal transmitter of the French sociological (Durkheimian) tradition to England. His interests, which included folklore, magic, and pre-animistic beliefs in the supernatural, were strongly reflected in Blackman's work. In particular, it was Marett's critique of Frazerian evolutionary rationalism, as well as his emphasis on the importance of studying the impact of "lower" cultural forms on "high" culture, that was reflected in Blackman's work.[143] In his foreword to Blackman's book, Marett underscored the age-old self-identity of the Egyptians, the enduring stability of their character, and the importance of the ethnic psychology of the folk—the "non-literary and largely inarticulate classes" who do so much to shape a country's destiny—"which alone is the key to genuine history."[144] According to Marett, "the time is doubtless coming when more Egyptians will come forward as investigators duly educated in the critical use of evidence; and they will be welcome."[145] Blackman concurred, noting that she was "most anxious that educated Egyptians should recognize the importance of the anthropology and folklore of their country."[146]

From the viewpoint of Marett and Blackman, the importance of anthropological and folkloric collections was their contribution to the study of "savage" religious beliefs. Although still working within an evolutionary framework, Marett formulated a critique of Frazerian evolutionary rationalism. Frazer's interpretation of the development of religion was teleological and rationalist—primitive religion or magic was seen as the "savage equivalent of our natural science."[147] Instead, Marett combined elements of Durkheimian social psychology with William James's voluntaristic empiricism, focusing on primitive magico-religious beliefs as "imperative willing," as with the case of magical spells.[148] Blackman's emphasis upon survivals, which entailed the use of charms, talismans, spells, and magic, underscored the belief in the primitive (and not Islamic) supernatural aspects of social life in the Egyptian village. Both Marett and Blackman, then, were firmly situated within the intellectual and social domain of British social anthropology. Their desire that Egyptians themselves come forward to engage in anthropological inquiry was soon to be realized, however.

Muhammad Ghallab was one Egyptian who did so. This Upper Egyptian wrote his doctoral thesis, titled "Les survivances de l'Égypte antique dans le folklore Égyptien moderne," at the University of Lyon; the first dissertation written by an Egyptian addressing the question of the pharaonic legacy of modern Egyptian folklore, it was published in 1929 under the same title.[149] This text, in effect a comparative study of ancient and modern popular traditions, was divided into four parts, discussing popular literature, general psychology, society, and the supernatural. Ghallab relied heavily on sources such as Gaston Maspero's and Artin Pasha's collections of folklore (predominantly popular lyric songs) in tracing the existence of ancient survivals in modern Egyptian folklore. In this regard, Ghallab was much like his Greek counterparts, who sought to connect ancient and modern Greece in developing an ideologically motivated field of national folklore studies.[150]

Ghallab's work must be understood in the context of the upheavals that rocked Egypt in the aftermath of the 1919 revolution. Although subject to numerous varying interpretations (which I discuss in depth in Chapter 3), the revolution of 1919 is generally taken to mark the emergence of a coherent anticolonial nationalist discourse and political movement. The larger context of Ghallab's arguments was the development of pharaonicism (*al-fir'awniyya*) within Egyptian nationalist discourse (discussed in Chapter 2). An intellectual trend that "may be defined as that body of opinion which postulated the unique and durable Egyptian national essence persisting from the Pharaonic era to the present," pharaonicism took its mature shape in the period after World War I and the 1919 revolution.[151] In fact, in a 1926 article Muhammad Husayn Haykal called upon nationalist intellectuals to help establish concrete links between the modern Egyptians and their pharaonic ancestors through the comparative study of literature, rituals, customs, and religion—the exact intellectual agenda that Muhammad Ghallab had set out in his dissertation.[152] Indeed, given the increasing interest of the Egyptian literate public in Egyptology, as well as the flurry of literary texts with pharaonic themes in the 1920s, Ghallab's thesis topic was well chosen.

The aim of Ghallab's dissertation had been to contest the assumption, prevalent in the West but even more so in Egypt, that Egyptian civilization—its manners, customs, traditions, and culture—was Arab and Islamic in origin. Instead he sought, through a study of collective psychology (*les caractères essentials du type Égyptien*) as demonstrated in folklore, to prove the existence of traces of beliefs and practices more or less evolved from antiquity.[153] Ghallab's technique was primarily literary and comparative, but it was also anthropological insofar as he relied upon his own knowledge of the manners and customs of the modern Egyptians, and in particular of the inhabitants of his village.[154]

Ghallab's thesis was published only two years after Blackman's, and there is no reason to believe he would have read her text. The only descriptive account of the modern Egyptians cited by Ghallab was Edward Lane's *Manners and Customs of the Modern Egyptians*. Given Ghallab's primarily literary method, he employed neither positivist nor historical-aesthetic criteria. Unlike many later folklorists or anthropologists, he did not attempt to classify folklore by region, nor did he attempt to trace the "origins" of folklore or trace its historical evolution in type (for example, as culminating in lyric narrative). In fact, Ghallab did not analyze the theoretical import of survivals at all—whether in terms of a synchronic analysis of social function (e.g., a Durkheimian conception of cohesion) or a diachronic reconstruction of the evolution of particular popular traditions. His concern was of a different order, related to the uniqueness and uninterrupted continuity of the civilization of the Nile Valley. I will return to the nationalist context of Ghallab's writings, but let us first look at the substance of his work.

At the core of Ghallab's argument was his assertion that the folk songs and legends that circulated in the countryside were pregnant with ancient and ancestral traditions, and it was these recurring "primitive" themes that could be found in the contemporary oral traditions he set out to investigate. Ghallab viewed this unity of themes as the manifestation of an underlying collective Egyptian psychology.[155] Thus, he argued, popular heroes of old could be adapted to modern times without appearing anachronistic.

It was the peasantry in particular that, more than any other social class, had preserved their ancient type, despite the multiple colonial invasions Egypt had endured. It was among the peasantry that one found the longest unbroken historical continuity of the Egyptian type. According to Ghallab, the peasantry were characterized by improvidence, an intense attachment to the land they cultivated, gaiety, and superb oratory capabilities; yet they continued to echo the complaints of their ancestors.[156] The rhythms of work and punishment, pain and resignation, repeated themselves across the centuries, as illustrated by folk songs.[157]

What were some of these ancient survivals? According to Ghallab, it was above all in the realm of the supernatural (religion and magic) where the continuity with Egypt's ancient past was seen best.[158] For Ghallab, the continued vitality of totemism and animism, belief in spirit possession (*zar*), belief in the evil eye, astrology and divination, concepts of fate, the horror of absolute nothingness, funeral offerings to the dead, the special role of magic, the cult of trees, the cult of saints—all attested to the survival of ancient customs. Ancient divinities, he argued, could be seen to have evolved into modern saints; the cult of saints itself was not of orthodox origin (neither Muslim nor Coptic). Ancient religious beliefs that were thought to have disappeared had in fact left their mark on the practices of the peasantry, but were ascribed an orthodox monotheistic source. Even the most orthodox of Islamic concepts—the power of the word (and name) of God as divinely revealed in the Qur'an—could be seen to have an ancient origin.

Ghallab's text was filled with anecdotal evidence. For example, in discussing the so-called cult of trees, he noted the reverence with which the peasants in his village viewed a particular tree in which a Coptic saint was thought to reside. Not knowing this, he scandalized the villagers by suggesting in January of 1922, a particularly cold winter, that they cut down the old acacia for firewood. That same year there was an influenza epidemic to which he fell victim—a just punishment for his transgression.[159] Another example he cited of a survival was that of a well-known lawyer who, as a sign of mourning over the exile of the nationalist leader Sa'd Zaghlul, stopped cutting his hair—a practice included in ancient funereal rites.[160]

The offhand reference to Zaghlul betrays the nationalist underpinnings of Ghallab's text, which relied upon the idea of survivals to posit an unbroken historical continuity in *la nation Égyptienne*. Zaghlul had been exiled to Malta in 1919 by the British after his delegation pressed its demands for independence at the Paris Peace Conference, following the outbreak of rioting in Cairo and the provinces known as the 1919 revolution. Ghallab's thesis was meant to corroborate the idea of a unique and uninterrupted Nile Valley civilization—one with roots much older than the Islamic conquest of Egypt and developed upon ancient Egyptian foundations. He concluded that, as shown by the transmission of a core nucleus of themes in orally transmitted primitive traditions, the character of the inhabitants of the Nile Valley had remained unmodified, its social life perpetuated.[161]

The assertion of ethnological uniqueness was always premised on an exclusionary logic. In the late 1920s and early 1930s Ghallab published articles in the Arabic journal *al-Siyasa al-Usbu'iyya* in which he voiced decidedly negative views of the Arab mentality as being "inferior," "primitive," "narrow-minded," and "short on imagination."[162] As Gershoni and Jankowski have noted, it was through the science of Egyptology that Ghallab's writings attempted to affiliate Egypt with the Hellenic-Mediterranean and Western worlds rather than the Arab-Semitic and, I would add, African worlds. "Egypt is a nation which emerged on the banks of her Nile and among her mountains surrounding it. There is nothing to link her with the Asians, nor a common nexus tying her to the Nubians, nor strands of kinship connecting her to the North Africans."[163]

Both Winifred Blackman and Muhammad Ghallab addressed the anthropological study of survivals, emphasizing the "primitive" (rather than Islamic) components of contemporary Egyptian culture. Blackman's work was part of the so-called salvage work of early-twentieth-century British social anthropology, whereas Ghallab's assertion of the historical continuity of Egyptian civilization from pharaonic times to the present (pharaonicism) came from within Egyptian nationalist discourse. Ghallab thus represented a particular phase of post-1919 Egyptian nationalist thought—one that attempted to assimilate Egyptian history and civilization into an older heritage highly valued by the West: that of pharaonic Egypt and the Hellenic-Mediterranean world.

. . .

The shifting terrain that I trace within the anthropology of the modern Egyptians ranged from the development of Orientalist ethnography (Abbate Pasha) to "gentlemanly" anthropology (Hasanayn Bey) to the development of ethnography as a scientific genre (Bachatly, Bayoumi), and finally to the development of anthropological monographs (Ghallab). It is essential to bear in mind, however, that the formation of Egyptian social-scientific practices was inherently tied up with colonial practices. The foundation of the Royal Geographical Society itself exemplifies the complicity of colonial forms of knowledge and the indigenous state-sponsorship of knowledge production in nineteenth- and twentieth-century Egypt. Thus, the early work of the RGS was premised on Isma'il's lofty ambitions to establish an "African empire." Indeed, the epistemological value of Egyptian geographical knowledge was initially established in the violent context of the colonization of the Sudan and other parts of Africa.

To establish themselves as local producers of geographical and anthropological knowledge, Egyptian social scientists had to bestow epistemological value upon local knowledge (oral, folkloric, written, and historical) and to endow it with a historical pedigree (medieval Arab historians were thus figured as producers of anthropo-geographical knowledge, Ibn Khaldun as the first human geographer). In this way they ensured Egypt's status as a legitimate producer and disseminator of scientific knowledge. For example, Egyptians did indeed take up British social anthropology's invitation to study "the folk" as sources of indigenous culture and tradition, viewing the popular classes as the distilled essence of nationhood and identity.

For European anthropologists such as Winifred Blackman and R. R. Marett, the existence of anthropological survivals was evidence of the continued importance of the "primitive" in Egyptian culture. The collection of such survivals before their extinction may be seen as part and parcel of the anthropological constitution of Egypt as premodern constituting "an*other* time" (in Johannes Fabian's words) or the "contemporaneity of the noncontemporaneous" (in Reinhart Koselleck's phrasing).[164] In contrast, Egyptian nationalist Muhammad Ghallab claimed anthropological survivals as part of the here and now. Questioning the anthropological denial of coevality, Ghallab asserted Egyptian nationhood as thoroughly modern yet permeated by antique folk presences. Overcoming anthropology's teleological vision and fixation with primitive ontologies thus entailed an epistemological shift toward an understanding of "the folk" as a crucial aspect of modern national culture and personality.[165]

2 Anthropology's Indigenous Interlocutors
Race and Egyptian Nationalism

> Know that all peoples—in the East, West, South and North—although of one origin are distinguished by three things: morals, appearance, and language.
>
> —*Abu Qasim Sa'd bin Ahmed Al-Andalusi, Tabaqat al-Umam (eleventh century)*

In 1935, Egyptian intellectual Salama Musa published his *Misr asl al-hadara (Egypt, the Origin of Civilization)*, in which he argued that the origins of civilization itself could be found in Egypt.[1] Loosely following anatomist and paleo-anthropologist Sir Grafton Elliot Smith's framework of cultural diffusionism, Musa endeavored to inspire in his readers both a sense of pride in Egypt's antiquity, and, more importantly, an open-ended sense of possibility for enlightened contemporary social reform. Musa was an avowed Fabian with eclectic intellectual predilections, and his retelling of the diffusionist tale contained familiar themes, interesting omissions, and unusual elaborations. He chastised his Egyptian contemporaries for neglecting to take a scholarly interest in their pharaonic heritage—thereby leaving its study to European colonizers and Orientalists—and for their assumption that modern Egypt no longer retained any organic connection with its pharaonic ancestors. Arguing that all Egyptians (Muslim and Coptic), and particularly the peasantry, were the lineal descendents of the ancient Egyptians, Musa presented an impressionistic account based on archeological evidence and conjectural history, as well as cultural evidence, of ancient Egyptian "survivals" in modern culture. In arguing for Egypt as the origin of civilization, Musa relied predominantly on archaeological and cultural, rather than racial, evidence of ancient Egypt's worldwide influence.

Indeed, it could be argued that for indigenous scholars the utility of the idea of "race" was eventually discarded in the interwar era in favor of more unifying ethnological conceptions of a common Egyptian history and culture. However, that would elide the complexities and nuances embedded in the concepts of culture (*thaqafa*) and civilization (*hadara*) as they were defined throughout the twentieth century, as well as the emergence of new concepts such as national personality (*shukhsiyyat al-umma*). Many of these terms came to embody the ineffable quality of national character and identity (*huwiyya*), but the discourses surrounding them often carried racialist undertones with nebulous biological associations.

The Arabic terms *thaqafa* and *hadara* contain the same ambiguity as their English counterparts, denoting civility, education, and refinement, and also the anthropological idea of culture and the historical concept of civilization (in its moral and material senses). Indeed, Salama Musa claimed to have been the first to popularize the term *thaqafa* in its European sense, using it to refer to the mental aspects of a society or its accumulated body of knowledge (science, literature and the arts), whereas *hadara* referred to the material aspects of human life (material culture, labor, institutions).[2] An exploration of the transformations in the terms *thaqafa* and *hadara* in Arabic would surely require a discussion of Salama Musa, as well as of Egypt's premier twentieth-century intellectual, Taha Husayn, whose 1938 *Mustaqbal al-thaqafa fi Misr* argued for the Hellenic-Mediterranean basis of Egyptian culture and its cultural affiliation with Europe, rather than with the "backward" nations of the East.[3] It would also require a discussion of Egyptian geographer 'Abbas Mustafa 'Ammar, whose discussion of the Arab-Islamic heritage and unity of the Nile Valley overturned European racial taxonomies and may be seen as the dialectical negation of Musa's and Husayn's arguments, as well as of the pharaonicist impulses they embodied.

As Egyptian anthropology emerged, it sought to fashion for itself a particular role within the context of British colonialism in Egypt and the Anglo-Egyptian Sudan. In contrast to turn-of-the-century European social anthropology, which sought to place Egypt within the taxonomic classification of the human races, Egyptian nationalist anthropology sought to demonstrate the ethnological uniqueness of the Egyptian culture, race, and history. As nationalists, Egyptian anthropologists premised their research not on an assumption of the "colonial difference" between the European and the colonized, but on the premise of the uniqueness of the collective national subject. There was no coherent and singular nationalist ideological agenda regarding the foundations of Egyptian identity, however. At least two competing views of the ethnological basis of Egyptian identity existed throughout the interwar period: pharaonicism and Arabism, both of which I will explore in this chapter.

Nor was the emphasis on the ethnological unity and uniqueness of Egypt and the Nile Valley indicative of the "the growing self-awareness or imagination of a collective subject . . . that produces the meaning of the nation."[4] Rather, as Timothy Mitchell has argued, nationalism entailed the complex and indeterminate process of producing the national self through an oftentimes violent process of "making-other." Stated simply, ethnological uniqueness is always premised on an exclusionary logic that defines what the nation is not. In the context of Middle Eastern nationalism, few scholars have noted the extent to which this process was itself racialized. As Eve Troutt Powell rightly notes, "writers and nationalists were acutely aware of the discourse on race being conducted in western Europe. . . . [A]nalysts of race and nationalism should take care not to assume that nationalists in Egypt were deaf and blind to the very charged issue of race in the late nineteenth and early twentieth centuries."[5]

Taking the example of Zanzibari twentieth-century intellectual nationalist discourses on race, Jonathan Glassman has pointed out the need to rethink distinctions between race and ethnicity, particularly the notion that race was an imported colonial European ideology, whereas ethnicity belonged to indigenous ideology.[6] He argues, instead, that there are myriad cultural discourses that divide humanity on the basis of difference into constituent groups, usually on the foundation of metaphors of descent. Thus, he asks, "what happens if we abandon the fixation on scientific doctrines and instead recognize racial thought as a shifting field of discourse, a general set of assumptions that humankind is divided among constituent categories, each of which is distinguished by inherited traits and characteristics?"[7] This line of thought leads us to productively question the analytic divide between race and ethnicity and between nationalism and other forms of ethnic thought, and to reconstruct, as Glassman does, the "precise conversations and debates from which racial thought emerged," for example in the history of the "intelligentsia's rhetoric of history and civilization."[8]

In the Egyptian context, this entails an exploration of the nationalist proponents of pharaonicism and Arabism—those who engaged with colonial and anthropological understandings of race and culture, translating, critiquing, transforming, and mobilizing such ideas to the political purpose of the nationalist movement. In this exploration we must attend not only to the ways in which nationalist discourses on race and culture marked out their difference from European colonial accounts by focusing on ethnological uniqueness; we must also examine the ways in which the emphasis on uniqueness disembedded Egypt from its African context and heritage, thereby contributing to an indigenous discourse of race.

Popularizations of Race

European scientific discourses on race were widely disseminated (and locally transformed) in the nineteenth and twentieth centuries throughout the non-Western world, from Latin America to the Middle East.[9] At the turn of the nineteenth century, the Arabic popular literary-scientific journal *Al-Muqtataf* began to address the field of anthropology, informing its audience of the scholarly topics that constituted the domain of this newly established science.[10] From its inception in 1876, *Al-Muqtataf* popularized anthropological accounts of the study of mankind, along with biological and social studies popular in Europe at the time. Between 1876 and the start of World War II, the journal published and translated the works of such thinkers as Huxley, Pasteur, Bastian, Lubbock, Wallace, Spencer, and Tylor.[11] For example, in 1892 the journal reprinted a Max Müller lecture on philology and anthropology, which highlighted the separation between studies of language and of race.[12] The journal's "Question and Answer" column received and responded to questions about the scientific study of man and the latest developments in anthropology, such as an 1897 request for recommended reading in anthropology, to which the editors responded by suggesting E. B. Tylor's *Anthropology*.[13] The column titled "Al-'ilm fi al-'amm al-madi" (Science in the past year) contained occasional updates on anthropological inquiry; in the February 1912 issue, for example, the column gave an overview of developments in a section titled "Al-anthropolojiyya ay 'ilm al-insan" (Anthropology or the science of man), and covered the 1911 Universal Races Congress in London, which was described as addressing relations between white and nonwhite peoples (*shu'ub*).[14] This column also reported discoveries of the "oldest human remains," as in its 1913 and 1914 issues.[15]

Al-Muqtataf was not the only journal to participate in the dissemination and popularization of anthropological knowledge. Jurji Zaydan's widely circulated periodical *Al-Hilal* responded to questions regarding skin color, and published updates on topics such as the effects of long- and round-headedness, in 1898 and 1899 respectively.[16] For example, in the 1900 article "Asnaf al-bashar" (The races of man), the journal's editors addressed a question about the reasons for the racial differences.[17] Their response to this relatively complex question, regarding not only differences in skin color, stature, and strength, but also manners, customs, and language; relied on a concept of regional differences. Taking monogenesis to be relatively consensual, they argued that regional environmental differences (including temperature, water, soil, topography) were the foundational basis for human differences.[18] Further, they argued, since the cumulative effects of region, as well as of the general laws of evolution (*namus al-irtiqa' al-'amm*) were exceedingly slow, differences between indigenous and transplanted populations (for example between black Africans and black Americans) were not always immediately visible.

The journal addressed the thorny question of monogenesis versus polygenesis on other occasions, taking up the question of *asl al-insan* in 1912, and of *al-sulalat al-bashariyya* in 1929.[19] In the latter article, differences among men were presented as the result of internal anatomical and physiological differences, following the writings of Sir Arthur Keith, Scottish anatomist and physical anthropologist, on what the journal described as the evolution of physical or racial types (*tatawwur al-anwa'*). The belief in the accuracy of anthropological methods was such that by 1938 *Al-Muqtataf* was touting anthropological advances in determining the age, gender and racial type of human remains in forensic or criminal anthropology.[20]

In 1912 *Al-Hilal*'s, editor Jurji Zaydan, published a full-length text titled the *Races of Man* (*Tabaqat al-umam*).[21] A study of the origins of human stocks and their subsequent differentiation into various nations and tribes, Zaydan's text elaborated the physical, mental, religious, cultural and moral differences between human groups. The title of Zaydan's text was taken from the text of an eleventh-century Muslim jurist, Sa'd al-Andalusi, whose *Tabaqat al-umam* divided nations (*umam*) not on the basis of racial categories but on the basis of the presence or absence of the arts of knowledge (*funun al-ma'arif*). Al-Andalusi's first group, those with the arts of knowledge, included Indians, Persians, Greeks, Romans, Israelites, Egyptians, and Arabs; and those without knowledge were (among others) Africans, Berbers, Russians, Turks, and Chinese. Al-Andalusi devoted the entirety of his text to the nations with the arts of knowledge, elucidating their various contributions to knowledge and outlining authors and texts in fields such as philosophy, language, medicine, astronomy, mathematics, natural science, architecture, and the theological sciences. As Zaydan pointed out in the introduction to his own book, al-Andalusi's notion of human difference relied solely on the criteria of knowledge accumulation, whereas his 1912 text integrated the new sciences of ethnology and anthropology.

The older knowledge of the medieval Arab geographers and travelers was based on imagination and exaggeration, but the sciences of ethnology and anthropology, according to Zaydan, were based on observation and experimentation. Comparative ethnology was thus a branch of natural science that attempted to elucidate the general laws of evolution. Ethnology was equally important to the philosophy of history—that is, to determining the reasons for the decline and renaissance of nations. Zaydan's text was based on A. H. Keane's *The World's Peoples* (1908), which was organized according to the ladder of evolution as follows: Africans, Mongols, Amerindians, and Caucasians.[22] Zaydan's text proceeded to outline in detail the various nations and tribes that constituted these major racial groupings.

Throughout this period, the numerous terms used to designate what we would now refer to as "race" included *al-ajnas al-bashariyya* (human varieties), *al-sulalat al-bashariyya* (human stocks), *al-asnaf al-bashariyya* (human types), *al-anwa' al-bashariyya* (human species), *al-'anasir al-bashariyya* (human elements), *tabaqat al-umum* (national groups), and even *shu'ub* (people)—all of which indicate the ambiguity if not malleability of notions of human difference.[23] Salama Musa, that scion of nineteenth-century European thought, avidly took up issues of European racial science, consistently using the term *al-sulalat al-bashariyya* to refer to the various racial "families." Musa laid out these various racial types in his *Misr asl al-hadara*. Musa began his discussion with an anecdote in which anatomist Grafton Elliot Smith laid out before him an ancient Egyptian and a modern Englishman's skulls and pointed out the homology between these two races. Musa, echoing European ideas, claimed that Egyptians were of Mediterranean stock, as were Italians, Spaniards, North Africans, Ethiopians, Arabs, Mesopotamians, southern French, and some Britons (especially the Welsh)—all being characterized by dolichocephalism (long-headed features: *al-ru's al-istitala*).[24]

Indeed, Musa, relying roughly on Smith's categorization, separated human races (*sulalat al-naw' al-bashari*) into six groups. First came the aboriginal Australians, a hirsute race unaware of agriculture, building, or weaving, but familiar with embalming. Next were black Africans (*al-Zanuj*) from central and south Africa, such as the Shilluk of the Sudan and the Bushmen of the Kalahari. Characterized by corkscrew hair, broad noses, and wide lips, most Africans, according to Musa, were savages (*mutawahishun*), although their barbarism had been ameliorated by the transmission of Egyptian civilization to sub-Saharan Africa. Despite this they had not advanced (*taqaddum*), but were arrested in their development, and at times had even regressed (*taqahaqur*). Musa's third category was the Mediterranean race, of which Egypt was a part. The fourth group, the Alpine race, encompassed the inhabitants of central Europe, extending to the border of western China, and was characterized by broad-headedness. Included in the Alpine race were Armenians, Turks and Syrians, French, Swiss, northern Italians, Hungarians, and Macedonians. Following was the Nordic race, located in Northern Europe—Germany, England, Denmark, Norway, and Sweden—and characteristically tall and fair-skinned. The final category was the Mongol race, which included the Chinese, Tatars, Amerindians, and Eskimos—a round- or broad-headed race, like the Alpine race, but with less body hair, wider noses, and prominent foreheads.[25]

Musa was quick to point out that within the various human races each *umma*, or community, developed its own linguistic, religious, and social particularities, such that each *umma* became a *sulalat* (stock) in its own right. Thus one could distinguish a Yemeni from an Egyptian, on the one hand, and a Swiss person from a Syrian, on the other, although both groups in each pair belonged to the same racial category. In this way Musa formulated a notion of national particularity (or personality) that was akin to a unique racial stock. Hence, "just as every individual has a personality which is the composite of his biological and social heritage, so too does every *umma* have a personality composed of its history and its cultural and social heritage."[26] Musa even used the term Egyptian personality (*"al-shukhsiyya al-misriyya"*) to refer to this Egyptian essence. In effect, Salama Musa demonstrated how biological notions such as *al-sulalat al-bashariyya* (or racial stocks) were transformed into the more innocuous sounding "national personality" (how *sulalat* became *shukhsiyya*). Thus, Egypt, a country of Mediterranean (and not African) stock, under the influence of thousands of years of history and civilization, attained a specificity all its own.

The Land of the Pharaohs

As with its Mediterranean neighbors to the north who sought to trace a spiritual connection between ancient and modern Greece, Egyptian nationalists argued for "the unique and durable Egyptian national essence persisting from the Pharaonic era to the present," an ideology referred to as pharaonicism (*al-fir'awniyya*).[27] Pharaonicism took its mature shape in the period after World War I and the 1919 revolution. In particular, it was the concurrence of Egypt's formal independence from the British and the discovery of King Tutankhamun's tomb in 1922 that gave pharaonicism its greatest impetus.[28] Several different strands of argumentation were components of pharaonicism: the idea of a biological and racial continuity between the ancient and modern, the idea of shared social norms and cultural practices, and the idea of a *mentalité* common to both the ancient and modern Egyptians.[29] In a 1926 article, for example, Muhammad Husayn Haykal called upon nationalist intellectuals to help establish concrete links between the modern Egyptians and their pharaonic predecessors, through the comparative study of literature, rituals, customs, and religion.[30]

Arguably, pharaonicism made the greatest impact on literary discourse, as can be seen in works from the late 1920s and early 1930s such as Tawfiq al-Hakim's novel *Return of the Soul* (*'Awdat al-ruh*), Ahmad Sabri's play *The High Priest Amon: A Pharaonic drama* (*Kahin Amun*), and Ahmed Abu Shadi's poetry collection *The Land of the Pharaohs* (*Watan al-fara'ina*).[31] Egypt's "prince of poets," Ahmed Shawqi, published in *Al-Muqtataf* a *qasida* in praise of Tutankhamun and the civilization of his era, along with several other poems.[32] In the early 1920s, the popular journal *Al-Hilal*, then under the editorship of Émile Zaydan, decorated its cover with pharaonic imagery,[33] and images of the discovery of Tutankhamun's tomb littered the monthly press. In the sciences, pharaonicism's most immediate manifestation was in the development of Egyptology by indigenous scholars, led principally, if not exclusively, by Ahmad Kamal, who struggled to gain entry into a largely colonial field.[34] Despite its relative marginality to Egyptian academic disciplines, Egyptology remained relevant to Egyptian public discourse. Thinkers such as Salama Musa, Marcus Simaika, Muhammad Husayn Haykal, and Ahmad Husayn went so far as to claim a biological or racial link between the ancient pharaohs and the modern Egyptians.[35]

It was in Salama Musa in particular that pharaonicism found its most ardent advocate. Born in Zaqaziq to a Coptic family of modest but sufficient means, Musa attended government secondary schools, graduating from the Khedivial College in 1907. An avid reader with a voracious (if unfocused) intellectual appetite, he left Egypt for Europe during various periods between 1907 and 1913. Musa stayed in Paris and London, where he eagerly imbibed the ideas of Spencer, Darwin, Shaw, Wells, and the other major intellectual figures of his day. Musa's ideas were a curious combination of social Darwinism, Fabianism, and Spencerian biology. His career as a journalist in Egypt spanned some forty years replete with controversies, government censorship, and acrimonious journalistic rivalries; by the 1920s Musa was one of the best-known writers in Egypt.[36] Indeed, Musa was so well known a figure in Egypt's cultural and intellectual landscape that Najib Mahfuz modeled a character after him in the last volume of his *Palace Walk* trilogy.[37]

As an Egyptian who had lived in the West, Musa was keenly aware of, and embarrassed by, Egyptian ignorance (including his own) of pharaonic history. Upon his return from France, Musa immediately signed up for a Cook's tour of Upper Egypt, "I traveled for two months studying the Egyptian antiquities; the rather painful, even shameful motive for this trip was that whenever I had made somebody's acquaintance in Europe, he had at once started asking me questions about the Pharaohs, to which I knew no answers."³⁸ Musa was acutely attuned to the political ramifications of his nascent pharaonicism. In his autobiography he recounts the

> subjects to which I gave a good deal of attention in my political struggle. One was the greatness of Egyptian civilization in Pharaonic times and the use a study of its history could have for stimulating national pride. I became convinced of the propagandistic value of this historic approach by what I learned in Europe, and more particularly in Britain, about Egypt having sent the first waves of civilization to other parts of the world, thus causing man to emerge from the stone age into the age of agriculture. This theme is set forth in my book, *Egypt, the cradle of civilization*.³⁹

Musa's personal recounting of the rationale for his pharaonicism—as pure nationalist propaganda—was very much the product of his belated re-narration of his own intellectual history, colored, as it were, by his post–World War II antipathy toward the Western imperialist nations.⁴⁰ In fact, at the time that Musa was most vigorously espousing his ideas on the affinity of the ancient and modern Egyptians, his impetus was the establishment of a parallel between Egypt and the Western nations, convinced as he was of the superiority of European culture.

According to Vernon Egger, Musa's early objective was "to help Egypt dissociate from her past and be remade in the image of Europe."⁴¹ Throughout the 1920s Musa addressed, as did many intellectuals within Egypt, the problem of Egypt's cultural identity. He developed his pharaonicism in contradistinction to competing ideologies of Easternism, which he viewed as backward-looking and reactionary, holding up, as they did, models of classical Arabic literature, science, and philosophy.⁴² Unsurprisingly, the literary writers whom Salama Musa considered to be at the vanguard of Egyptian literature ('Abd al-Qadir Hamza, 'Abbas Mahmud al-'Aqqad, Ibrahim al-Mazini, and Taha Husayn) were inspired by pharaonicist themes. Yet even writers whom Musa would have considered retrogressive in outlook, particularly proponents of neo-classicism such as Ahmed Shawqi, had espoused pharaonicist impulses.⁴³

At the crux of Musa's rejection of Easternism as an ideology lay the problem of progress, modernity, and European advancement in science, industry, and technology. Musa associated the East with agriculture and literature, rather than with industrialism and science and hence progress.⁴⁴ Indeed, Musa felt that he needed to resolve the issue of the cultural and racial identity of the Egyptians in order to provide Egypt with an appropriate historical heritage and future trajectory so that it could align its fate with the progress of the Western nations. The work of Grafton Elliot Smith provided the perfect solution.⁴⁵ Much of Musa's self-education in the history of ancient Egypt was gleaned from the works of Smith, a well-known anatomist and paleo-anthropologist (widely referred to by his contemporaries as Elliot Smith) who had taught at the Qasr Al-'Ayni Medical School from 1900 to 1909 and pioneered the controversial idea of cultural diffusion.

In brief, Smith's cultural-diffusion theory held that the ancient Egyptians had invented civilization, devising its fundamental arts and crafts as well as its scientific doctrines, and thus the development of neolithic culture had originated in ancient Egypt. According to Smith, this was evidenced by the widespread distribution of megalithic and other stone monuments (mastabas, rock-cut tombs, pyramids), spiritual beliefs and practices (the worship of "givers of life"), and customs (circumcision, burial patterns, mummification), all of which could be found in places as far flung as Polynesia, the Malay archipelago, the British Isles, and Japan. Smith argued that the spread of such beliefs, customs, and practices—"master-themes"—could not be explained as independent inventions exhibiting the psychic unity of mankind (the evolutionists' explanation), but that they were the product of the migration of people, culture, and ideas.[46]

Not only did Smith's cultural-diffusion theory fly in the face of orthodox evolutionary theory, but in positing "the paramount importance of Egypt as the source of a world-wide spread of distinctive beliefs and practices," it was a blatant refutation of several long-held European theories regarding ancient Egypt and the development of civilization.[47] Smith argued that Egyptian civilization was autochthonous and not imported, and that ancient Egypt (and not Greece) was the source of civilization itself (and hence of European civilization); finally, by positing the emergence of the Archaic civilization in Egypt alone, he overturned social-evolutionary theories that held that civilizational advances were not the purview of any one single civilization, but had evolved simultaneously all over the globe. Rather than something "exotic and alien to European culture," Smith posited the Egyptians as the very wellspring from which European civilization emerged.[48] Indeed, at his most radical he asserted, "Egypt was, in fact, the creator of civilization."[49] In this way, Smith assimilated the history of Egypt into the history of the West, and his ideas were thus a natural fit with Salama Musa's ideological agenda.

While in Egypt, Smith had won the admiration of his Egyptian medical students, to whom he sought to teach the principles of anatomy as well as the "natural differences between peoples."[50] However, his diffusionist ideas and Egyptological endeavors remained relatively unknown to the Egyptian public until in the late 1920s Salama Musa began publishing a series of articles on Smith.[51] In his 1935 text *Misr asl al-hadara,* Musa advanced Smith's diffusionist thesis, advocating a place for Egyptology (*al-misrulujiyya*) in national culture. Lamenting the prevalence of Europeans in Egyptology, Musa argued that once Egyptians acknowledged an organic link between the ancient and modern Egyptians, they might take more seriously the study of ancient culture. Such an organicism ("the blood of the Pharaohs runs through our veins collectively"), bolstered Musa's claim that all Egyptians, Muslim and Coptic, were the lineal descendants of the pharaohs. Musa thus tried to overturn commonplace assertions that the Copts were the only pure descendants of the pharaohs. He argued that the ruling classes (rather than the Copts as such) were the most miscegenated, having mixed with Greeks, Arabs, and Turco-Circassians, whereas the ordinary workers and peasants (predominantly Muslim) who comprised the bulk of the population remained racially unadulterated.[52] In the interest of establishing a unifying ethnological nationalism, then, Musa deftly argued that, in effect, the Muslim population of Egypt, because of its larger working class population, was closer to the pharaohs than the Copts.

Musa acknowledged Smith's racial classification scheme and Egypt's place within it as a Mediterranean race (following Sergi), but he emphasized the archaeological and cultural aspects of the diffusionist thesis over the racial evidence.[53] In particular, Musa was intent on arguing the homology between the ancient Egyptians and the Neolithic Europeans, as such a homology helped support Musa's contention that Egypt needed to look to Europe for cultural guidance. Thus, Europe could be viewed as an *affine* of ancient Egypt rather than as an alien and external entity, and the adaptation of its culture as a reclaiming of an ancient heritage rather than as a nationalist betrayal.[54] Indeed, Vernon Egger argues that although by 1930 Pharaonicism had become defunct,[55] Musa continued to advocate a pharaonic identity for Egypt, hoping to "instill within Egyptians a pride in their national heritage," "to convince the Egyptian public Egypt's golden age was the Pharaonic period" and "to establish a direct link between this remote Egyptian past and the world-conquering modern European civilization."[56] Further, Egypt's illustrious heritage could serve as an impetus to social reform and historical becoming, a hope evident in Musa's frequent, and poignant, formulation of the problematic: "We who invented civilization . . . should not be reduced to barbarism."[57]

Musa was a vocal proponent of Westernization, but perhaps the most renowned advocate of a non-Easternist identity for Egypt was Taha Husayn, whose 1938 text *The Future of Culture in Egypt* (*Mustaqbal al-thaqafa fi Misr*) advanced the thesis that Egypt was, culturally speaking, a part of the West and not of the East. Taha Husayn, claims Louis Awad, "represents in the twentieth century what Rifa'a al-Tahtawi represented in the nineteenth, the greatest single intellectual and cultural influence on the literature of his period."[58] Several features of Husayn's text are noteworthy: his characterization of Egyptian culture as the inheritor of an ancient Greco-Aegean civilization (including philosophy, law, art, political geography, and monotheistic morality); his contestation of the notion that the East was spiritual whereas the West was material; and his modernist conception of culture and education.[59] Husayn viewed culture both as an ineffable and indelible "soul, a spiritual principle" (in Renan's phrasing), and as a body of artistic, literary, linguistic, politico-juridical, and scientific production, transmitted through education and the media.[60] By positing culture as a trajectory, a path from the past up through the present that bears its traces and which impels one toward the future, Husayn considered the viability of Egyptian culture to be premised upon the selective appropriation of Western ideals, ideals that were already embedded in Egypt's ancient history. Scholars such as Salama Musa and Taha Husayn thus represented one phase of post-1919 Egyptian nationalist thought—one that attempted to assimilate Egyptian history and civilization into an older heritage highly valued by Western scholars—that of pharaonic Egypt and the Hellenic-Mediterranean world.

Toward an Indigenous Anthropology: 'Abbas Mustafa 'Ammar

British colonial anthropology, observed Egyptian geographer and anthropologist 'Abbas Mustafa 'Ammar, aimed to typify, classify, categorize, and otherwise objectify the native population.[61] 'Ammar—the first graduate of the Egyptian University in geography to be awarded a Ph.D. and author of the first full-length ethnographic monograph to be written by an Egyptian—reformulated British social anthropology, critically reworking concepts of race for the political purposes of the nationalist movement. Rather than being a straightforward transplantation of European knowledge, 'Ammar's oeuvre demonstrates the historic subversions and ironic reversals implicit in the complex process of translation. 'Ammar's work and life embody in many ways the development of local social-scientific research agendas in Egypt. At the vanguard of social science (he was trained by Egypt's first geographers and later sent on an educational mission to England), 'Ammar was very much the product of Egypt's state educational system, and provides insight into the types of research agendas that Egypt's first generation of state-educated scholars were exploring. 'Ammar was also the product of Egyptian nationalism, part of the so-called generation of 1919, and wrote as a "loyal son of Egypt"; he was thus acutely aware of the obligations of social science to the service of the nation-state. Indeed, 'Ammar was in many ways typical of a later phase of Egyptian nationalism, which sought to demonstrate the ethnological basis of the unity of Egypt and the Nile Valley, focusing on the region's specifically Arab and Islamic heritage. This Arab-Islamic emphasis represented the dialectical negation of Taha Husayn's thesis that Egypt was the inheritor of Hellenic and Mediterranean culture. 'Ammar's work may be seen in opposition to two distinct bodies of literature—twentieth-century Egyptian nationalist writings that emphasized Egypt's pharaonic heritage, such as those of Salama Musa; and the long history of European writings on Egypt (in archaeology, Egyptology, and anthropology) that emphasized its pharaonic heritage and incorporated that heritage as an integral part of European history and civilization.[62] Thus, for example, the foremost concern of much British anthropology and archaeology at the turn of the century had been the determination of the "non-Negro" racial origins of the ancient and modern-day Egyptians, and the identification of Egypt as the source of European civilization, thereby assimilating the history of Egypt into the history of the West, and removing it from its African context.[63]

Geographical Foundations

'Abbas Mustafa 'Ammar, originally from the Delta province of Menufiyya, was trained as a geographer under the tutelage of Mustafa 'Amir and Muhammad 'Awad Muhammad at Fu'ad I University, where he received his M.A. in 1936.[64] He was then sent on an educational mission from 1937 to 1941, to obtain his Ph.D. at the University of Manchester's Department of Geography and Anthropology. He eventually held positions such as director-general of the Fellah Department in the Ministry of Social Affairs; minister of social affairs; and chairman of the National Commission for Population Problems. 'Ammar was also a member of the Arab States Fundamental Education Center, at Sirs al-Layyan, Menufiyya in Egypt—a research center devoted to multifaceted study and reform of rural society, and among the first of its kind.

'Ammar's mentors were, as he phrased it "the spiritual fathers of geographical studies in the Egyptian field"—Mustafa 'Amir and Muhammad 'Awad were the first two professional Egyptian geographers. Although geography was among the seven core subjects taught to students of the Egyptian University, the development of geographical studies in Egypt did not begin in earnest until 1925, with the formation of a joint department of history and geography in the College of Arts that offered a unified program of instruction. Two years later instruction shifted from French to Arabic. Finally, in 1930 geography split off from history, and became its own department. All aspects of human geography (racial, social, historical, economic, political, regional) and natural geography were covered, and particular emphasis was placed on Egypt and the Nile Valley.[65]

As Mustafa 'Amir noted, the study of modern geography did not involve simply the study of the natural world (the way in which his audience understood "classical" or physical geography), but rather the study of the interrelationship between human activity and the natural world (*al-nahiyya al-tabʿiyya wa al-nahiya al-bashariyya, al-makan wa al-insan*). The new geography thus differed from the old in its emphasis on global interconnections, and as such, could lead to increased cooperation among nations. 'Amir was particularly proud of the congenial academic relations that had been established between the Egyptian University and universities in Liverpool and Manchester, with Egyptian students pursuing higher studies in England, and the geography departments of various institutions embarking on joint expeditions in the Arab world. He considered Egypt's participation in the study of modern geography a prerequisite for nationalism and national identification, as evidenced by his claim that scholars now believed Egyptian civilization to be autochthonous, "born of the Egyptian environment" rather than an alien or Western import.[66] With a conception of geography that was expansive enough to include the study of archaeology, prehistory, and the study of race, 'Amir viewed the field as a prerequisite for Egypt's entry into the modern world as a producer of modern scientific knowledge, participating in conferences, expeditions, and the like. Mustafa 'Amir was appointed assistant professor of geography at the Egyptian University in 1927, after having graduated from the Higher Teachers College in 1917 and having earned a master's degree from the University of Liverpool in 1921, working under P. M. Roxby. At various points in his career 'Amir also served as rector of Faruq I University in Alexandria and as dean and vice rector at Fu'ad I University in Cairo.[67]

Muhammad 'Awad was a native of the Delta town of Mansura. Like 'Amir, he was a graduate of the Higher Teachers College (1920), and went on to receive his B.A. and M.A. from the University of Liverpool in 1924 and 1926, followed by a Ph.D. from the University of London. Among his classic writings in geography were the 1936 *Nahr al-nil* (*River Nile*) and *Al-Istiʿmar wa al-mathahib al-istaʿmiriyya* (*Colonialism and Colonial Schools of Thought*), but he also maintained an interest in literature, translating Goethe's *Faust* and composing fiction.[68] In 1947 'Awad was chosen to head the Institute for Sudan Studies at Fu'ad I University. He attended the 1937 Cairo Conference on Birth Control (discussed in Chapter 6), and was later a member, along with 'Abbas Mustafa 'Ammar, of the 1953 National Population Commission. Together, Mustafa 'Amir and Muhammad 'Awad had played a critical role in the formation at the Egyptian University of the geography department, with its orientation toward historical geography.[69] 'Ammar maintained his mentors' predilection for historical geography in his monograph of an Egyptian province (*The People of Sharqiya*) with his lengthy introduction detailing the various historical waves of Arab migration into the province. Prior to his study of Sharqiya, 'Ammar had conducted a field study of the Sinai between 1933 and 1934 (published as *Some Aspects of the Human Geography of the Peninsula of Sinai*), and Sharqiya was meant to serve as a point of comparison.[70]

Anthropological Investigations

Committed to in-depth local studies, 'Abbas 'Ammar chose Sharqiya for his anthropological research because of its hybrid background of Egyptians, northern and southern Arabs, Turks, Moreans, and Berberized Arabs. 'Ammar thus hoped to use it as the perfect test case to demonstrate the ethnological uniqueness of Egypt despite its ethnic heterogeneity (or perhaps even because of it). A total survey of the province in every sense—biological, demographic, and social—*The People of Sharqiya* represented, as 'Ammar's advisor Herbert John (H. J.) Fleure wrote in the work's preface, "a many-sided effort. . . . And this carefully objective synthesis has been built up by a loyal son of Egypt to contribute a basis of accurate knowledge for framing schemes to improve standards of living and of health in Sharqiya and in Egypt as a whole."[71] 'Ammar's study—part racial science and part social survey—was consistent with an interwar trend in British anthropology that was moving increasingly towards coordinated knowledge in imperial settings.[72]

After his undergraduate education, 'Ammar received financial support from the Egyptian government and from Fu'ad I University to continue his studies in England, where he was trained in the measurement techniques of the Manchester School of Anthropology by H. J. Fleure and Elwyn Davies. In conducting his Egyptian fieldwork 'Ammar collected physical anthropometric data on approximately 1,000 men, blood agglutination data, genealogical data, demographic data, and a social survey of about 250 families. In his study of the racial history of the province of Sharqiya, 'Ammar set out to detail "the main elements that have contributed to the people of

Sharqiya with special reference to the Arab influence."[73] Eschewing "dogmatic statements based on mere descriptive evidence and insufficient craniological evidence," 'Ammar rejected the loose use of terms such as "Arab" or "Semite," especially when used to indicate homogeneous racial types.[74] Instead, relying heavily on Arabic sources—notably, the work of Arab historians and genealogists—he concurred with their traditional distinction between the Southern Qahtanite and Northern Adnanite types, finding anthropometric corroboration for this classification.

Because of Sharqiya's northeastern geographical location, 'Ammar viewed the province as being effectively an Arab corridor into Egypt. The objective of 'Ammar's historiographical survey was to ascertain the different historical waves of Arab migrants who had reached the province, and to specify the different contribution of Qahtanites and Adnanites to the local race. Through a highly critical reading of the Arabic and Orientalist historical sources, 'Ammar reconstructed a history of Arab migration and divided the regional population movements into three principal phases: a preparatory stage, four or five centuries before Islam; an active stage of migration from the seventh-century Arab conquest until the end of the thirteenth century; and a final stage of assimilation.[75] In effect, 'Ammar was able to align the new racial sciences with the "prior knowledge" of the Arabic medieval histories, using those histories as a guide for the formulation of his research hypothesis. This strategy, as Partha Chatterjee points out, enabled indigenous scholars "to locate authorities within Western discursive constellations in order to sustain the claims of indigenous knowledges."[76]

The biological or physical component of 'Ammar's research used two types of measures, serological and anthropometric, and the correlation of the two. Serology was, by 1940, an established field of physical anthropology concerned with the scientific determination of race that used blood typing as a criterion "for the discovery of hitherto unknown, and anatomically invisible, relationship between different races."[77] Given the fixity and stability of blood groups, it was hoped that blood would emerge as an "ethno-anthropological fact" in itself. For 'Ammar, blood groups could be used as an additional marker of race and ancestry. Setting out to create a representative sample of the province in order to ascertain the serological constitution of its population, 'Ammar obtained 1,120 samples from inhabitants who could trace their ancestry back at least four generations—an outstanding number compared to previous whole-country studies of blood groups in Egypt.[78]

The results of the serological study confirmed the Arab influence in the racial history of the province, with the people of Sharqiya appearing generally (on serological grounds) to form an intermediate type between the Arab and Egyptian types.[79] 'Ammar's focus on race as blood may appear to modern sensibilities as anachronistic, but it must be borne in mind that serology had begun to emerge as a classificatory tool for the subdivision of the human races after the discovery of blood types at the turn of the century, and the field had gained momentum after WWI.[80] Further, the "colonial ideology of race as blood," had continued to dominate thinking, as, for example, in the British Empire in India well into the nineteenth century.[81] Indeed, it could be argued that 'Ammar reconciled the "prior knowledge" of Arab genealogical reckoning (in particular, Ibn Khaldun's notion of tribal '*asabiyya*—premised, in part, on ideas of tribal groupings bound to each other by blood ties) with the new racial sciences that relied on blood-group classification.

The second component of 'Ammar's study was an anthropometric survey, the object of which was to begin "local anthropometric investigations" within Egypt, in contrast to earlier whole-country studies. Measurements were taken from 1,000 adult male residents of Sharqiya.[82] Finding the greatest range of cephalic indices to fall within the dolicocephalic (long-headed) range, 'Ammar broke the data down by specific districts within the province. This revealed that the people of Sharqiya were not racially homogeneous, and also showed a gradation in cephalic indices as one moved from north to south, but a more significant gradation moving eastwards or westwards. Thus analyzed, neither the anthropometric survey nor the serological study contradicted the historical evidence—namely, that the Arab influence was what lent Sharqiya its "ethnic individuality."[83] Nor could 'Ammar "determine the exact ethnic status of Sharqiya in relation to the so called Arab stock on the one side and the *Egyptian People* on the other," as the available data were insufficient for a comparative study.[84]

'Ammar used all the major methodological tools of positivist anthropological inquiry: representative sampling, data collection (and reduction, analysis, and interpretation), statistical correlations, frequencies and indices, and field surveys. Such tools were geared toward the correction of former anthropological studies whose principal methodological errors were inadequate samples, dogmatic attitudes, vagueness, and the use of ambiguous popular anthropological terms, such as "Semite." 'Ammar's fundamental position on race was that within any given group great complexity, rather than homogeneity, would be found. His research results pointed to the conclusion that Sharqiya was not ethnically homogeneous, but rather represented a range of mixtures of Arab and Egyptian stocks, and that it was the Arab element in Sharqiya that lent the province its ethnic individuality. 'Ammar's emphasis upon the Arab (rather than, say, the pharaonic) element as the sign of ethnic individuality was emblematic of the larger trends within Egyptian nationalism of the 1930s and 1940s, and in particular of the nationalist rejection of pharaonicism and the embracing of Egypt's Arab and Muslim identities. Indeed, *The People of Sharqiya* foreshadowed 'Ammar's later arguments regarding the unity of the Nile Valley region, in which he explicitly linked Egyptian and Sudanese ethnic identities as a people with the region's Arabization and Islamicization. 'Ammar chose to emphasize the commonalities of culture, language, religion and geography shared by the peoples of the Nile Valley. This led to the privileging of Egypt's Arab and Islamic heritage, in keeping with the contemporary tends in nationalist thought, which by the time of 'Ammar's writings was entering a pan-Arabist and pan-Islamist (rather than pharaonic) phase.[85]

Sociological Considerations

Unlike the turn-of-the century fixation with identifying the racial origins of the ancient and modern-day Egyptians while placing them within a universal taxonomy of races, 'Ammar's research involved a pragmatic component as well. One of his aims was to identify the demographic and socio-economic problems of Sharqiya province in order to facilitate policy formulation. It may seem curious for 'Ammar to have combined racial history, demography, and conditions of life in his research agenda, yet this was precisely the type of holistic research project that would characterize the research of the Egyptian intelligentsia during the interwar and post-war periods.[86] Concern for the future of cultural groups was a question important not only to nationalists, but also to interwar European anthropologists concerned with colonial administrative practices.[87] 'Ammar was influenced in part by his advisor Raymond Firth. Firth, a social anthropologist and former student of Bronislaw Malinowski, was a New Zealander interested in the "difficult social and economic problems" of the Maoris.[88] Firth, who served as secretary of the Colonial Social Science Research Council, was an important figure in the training of anthropologists in the British colonial administration. He was particularly interested in contemporary social problems, and he felt that "basic ethnographic field investigation and fundamental studies of social structure were indispensable to provide the anthropological knowledge required for tackling the manifold practical problems involved in the development plans formulated by the colonial governments after the war."[89] For 'Ammar the exigencies of social-scientific research in a nation-state aspiring to complete political independence from the colonial powers were even more pressing.

'Ammar's demographic survey of Sharqiya was published independently as a monograph by the London School of Economics, under the advisement of Firth and the noted British demographer A. M. Carr-Saunders (and it has been recently republished by BERG).[90] This study attempted to track the growth of population, as well as the relation between the number and quality of the people, and one of its primary objects was to spur local demographic studies in different provinces within Egypt, in order to better ascertain the social conditions and standard of living of the community, and eventually formulate population policy. In addition to his demographic survey, 'Ammar conducted a social survey of the province in 1939 that was meant to guide future social reconstruction, and which he condensed into a study of "the conditions of life in rural Sharqiya." "Sentiment," 'Ammar opined, "must be supported by fact if any who still doubt the depth of rural poverty are to be convinced. Thus, the object of the socio-economic survey was to obtain precise first-hand data about the living conditions of its people, to investigate into the causes of the different problems and the effect of such problems on the life of the local community."[91]

In his results, 'Ammar emphasized the poverty of the majority of the people, as revealed in the distribution of capital invested and the indebtedness of the fellahin. 'Ammar spared no criticism of the official attitude toward the peasantry—one that consistently placed blame for poverty on the ignorance of the peasantry rather than on its true causes: "unjust traditional distribution of wealth, the lack of equilibrium between human fertility and land potentialities, the apathetic outlook of the fatalist fallah, the misunderstanding of the real needs of the rural community and the vague idea about social reconstruction in the minds of high officials and authoritative circles."[92] This pragmatic approach would dominate 'Ammar's work over the next few decades, as his research increasingly began to focus on community studies and the twin evils of poverty and unrestrained population growth.

'Ammar's contribution to Egyptian social science was pioneering in several respects: he was one of the first Egyptian nationalist intellectuals to systematically address the issues of race scientifically; he was among the first to employ community and social surveys; and he was one of the first to see demographic inquiry as a critical component of national planning. 'Ammar's combined interests in historical, ethnological, and sociological issues led him to a methodologically eclectic approach in which he drew from innovations in racial science as well as from the canonical historical texts of Arabic medieval history and the sociological tradition of Ibn Khaldun, which addressed human geography, racial admixture, and cultural diffusion—in particular in the relations between settled and nomadic communities.⁹³ 'Ammar's Manchester training was most pronounced in his anthropometric and serological research, in which he relied heavily on the methodologies and findings of prominent figures in racial science: Charles Myers, Charles Seligman, Ernest Chantre, Aleš Hrdlička, and Carleton Coon.

A discussion of anthropological-geographical work on the unity of the Nile Valley can help to contextualize some of 'Ammar's concerns with race within the broader political field of Egyptian discussions of the Anglo-Egyptian Sudan. It is here that we encounter the political and racialist ramifications of arguments on "ethnological uniqueness" in their purest form.

The Unity of the Nile Valley

> Have they not journeyed in this land, and seen what hath been the end of those who flourished before them? More were they than these in number and mightier in strength and greater are the traces of their power remaining in the land: yet their labours availed them nothing.
>
> —*The Holy Qur'an*⁹⁴

In an insightful discussion of the colonial underpinnings of nineteenth-century Egyptian expansionism in the Sudan, Eve Troutt Powell notes the transformations that occurred throughout the century in racial understandings of *bilad al-sudan*. She argues that the writings of the renowned Egyptian writer and educational reformer Rifa'a Rafi' al-Tahtawi on the Sudan represent a "hardening" of Egyptian attitudes towards their southern neighbors, and the beginnings of sharp racial differentiations between the Egyptians and the Sudanese.⁹⁵ By the mid-nineteenth century, she notes, Egyptians began to define their own national and racial identity against that of the "less civilized" Sudanese. Rather than making graded distinctions between *bilad al-'arab* and *bilad al-sudan*, Egyptian colonial ambitions toward the Sudan materialized, serving, in effect, to constitute Egypt as Egypt.⁹⁶ For Powell, the colonial ambitions that made the Sudan into an object of scientific exploration under Mehmed 'Ali's regime, and the Egyptians' own sense of alienation and exile within the space of the Sudan were both lessons learned from their French imperial masters.⁹⁷ Her narrative questions the simple distinctions between "colonizer" and "colonized" by accounting for a colonized peoples' own imperial endeavors.⁹⁸

Interpretations of Egypt's claims to the unity of the Nile Valley are often cast in instrumentalist terms that see claims to unity as a thinly veiled ploy for colonial ambitions in the Sudan or that posit Egypt as mimicking lessons of empire learned from the French and British imperial centers. But claims to the Sudan could be grounded in affective terms as well, and were often emotionally charged issues for nationalists. Powell astutely addresses the intimate nature of links between Egypt and the Sudan in the minds of nationalists and their conceptualization of the unlinking of the Sudan as a form of amputation. Such an intimacy was derived at least in part, she argues, from the long history of black slaves in Egypt and the tradition of Sudanese servitude in Ottoman-Egyptian elite households. Simply put, for many Egyptian nationalists slavery, the Sudan, and the family were intimately connected.[99]

Rather than focus on the affective or instrumentalist motives for Egypt's colonial relationship to the Sudan, however, I concentrate on Egyptian claims to the unity of the Nile Valley, not as a simple ruse for access to water and goods, but as an ideological bid for territorial integrity based on ethnographic and geographic claims. It is essential to see those ideological claims as grounded in the scientific production of knowledge. I therefore focus on the production of ethnographic and geographical knowledge about the Sudan by Egyptian nationalist intellectuals in the twentieth century.

The unity of the Nile Valley and the demand for the sovereignty of Sudan were themes that ran through much Egyptian nationalist literature. Although modern Egyptian involvement in the Sudan dates back to the Mehmed 'Ali era, the British conquest of the Sudan (1896–1898), and the establishment of an Anglo-Egyptian condominium in 1899 after the defeat of the Mahdist forces, all magnified the importance of the Sudan question for the Egyptian nationalist elite.[100] Nationalist demands to establish Egyptian-Sudanese unity were made at the 1919 peace conference, at the 1920 and 1921 British Egyptian negotiations, at the Lausanne conference in 1922 and 1923, and in the first drafts of the Egyptian constitution of 1923, and the first parliament of independent Egypt stated, "the Sudan is an inseparable part of Egypt."[101] Historians of Egyptian nationalism Israel Gershoni and James Jankowski insist on the instrumentalist tenor of the call for Egyptian-Sudanese unity (based on the need for Egyptian control of the Sudan, and especially Nile waters, rather than on belief in a metaphysical or ethno-historical unity), and the preeminence of the call for Egyptian independence. In fact, they claim "the concept to have been in large measure only an extension of the Egypt-centered nationalist orientation of the 1919 revolution as a whole."[102]

Indeed one could argue that the tenor of the debate changed once Egypt had achieved its nominal independence in 1922.[103] By the 1930s a renewed interest had developed in the question of the Sudan. Political views supporting the idea of Nile unity varied in the geographical expanse they deemed necessary to reinstate, ranging from the grandiose 1832 historical borders of the "Egyptian empire" to the slightly more modest borders set by the British commonwealth.[104] For example, throughout the 1930s the political platforms of the Young Egypt party called for Egyptian-Sudanese unity; although the party's leader, Ahmad Husayn, did not visit the Sudan until 1938.[105] In the party's March 1940 platform it demanded a unified infrastructure (social, economic, health) for Egypt and the Sudan, as well as equality in parliamentary representation.[106]

According to Gershoni and Jankowski, the newer Egyptian Arab nationalism, as opposed to the territorial nationalism of the 1920s, emphasized cultural and linguistic aspects of Nile Valley unity, rather than geographical and environmental elements. Thinkers such as Ahmed Ramzi and Sulayman Huzayyin emphasized the unity of the valley on the basis of the spread of Arab and Islamic culture.[107] "Thus an earlier territorial bond between Egypt and the Sudan whose implications were Egyptianist was transformed by Egyptian Arabists into a cultural link with supra-Egyptianist connotations."[108] In a 1947 edited volume, however, all aspects—geographical, environmental, cultural, linguistic, and historical—of the valley were mobilized in support of the nationalist claim to unity. Contrary to Gershoni and Jankowski's contention that many of the themes of nationalist discourse were emotional, irrational, or mythological in content, it can be shown that, in this instance at least, the orientation of certain nationalist ideological writings was in fact scientific.

The volume in question, *The Unity of the Nile Valley: Its Geographical Bases and Its Manifestations in History*, was published under the Presidency of Council of Ministers in 1947, and is exemplary of Egyptian colonial discourse regarding the Sudan.[109] Among its contributors were three history professors from Fu'ad I University, Shafiq Ghurbal Bey, Ahmad Badawi, and Ibrahim Noshi; one geographer, 'Abbas Mustafa 'Ammar; and the director of the Military Museum in Cairo, Lieutenant Colonel Abd al-Rahman Zaki. In the words of Shafiq Ghurbal, who was also dean of the Faculty of Arts at Fu'ad I University, the essays aimed at explaining the "physical, ethnographical, cultural and economic foundations on which the Unity was built and to present the manifestations and forms in which that Unity was expressed through ancient and modern times."[110]

In part a response to British colonial military intervention and the 1899 establishment of the Anglo-Egyptian Condominium in the Sudan, many of the essays in the volume established the historical relationship between Egypt and her southern neighbors in the Sudan as one of paternal benevolence, social uplift, and the "moral and material" improvement of the native population.[111] In this respect, these writings embody a classically colonial attitude towards the Sudan. Thus, for example, authors characterized the regimes of Mehmed 'Ali and Khedive Isma'il not as the Egyptian *conquest* of the Sudan but as attempts to *modernize* the Nile Valley under a unified regime of power—in the north and south alike.[112] Furthermore, it was the independence and Unity of the Valley that, Shafiq Ghurbal argued in characteristically colonial parlance, "saved the Nile Valley from the fate which befell the rest of Africa," partition and forcible tutelage.[113] Egyptian authors cast British policy as a ruse to eradicate Egypt from the Sudan and establish British hegemony over the Sudan in the wake of the devastation wrought by the Mahdist revolt.[114] Egypt, authors paternalistically argued, was best suited for the civilizing mission in the Sudan.

'Abbas Mustafa 'Ammar's contributions to this volume laid the geographical foundations for the unity, pointing to the absence of physical barriers and the slow gradation of change (physical or natural, ethnographic, and cultural) from north to south in the Valley. 'Ammar's conclusions, according to Ghurbal, pointed to the following, "whenever the control of the affairs of the Valley has been in the hands of its people, whenever, that is to say, they have not been forcibly attached to external political entities, some measure of harmony between the physical and the human environment is established and the interests of the inhabitants are then best served. But when superior force imposes on them economic, political and cultural developments dictated by extraneous ends, then moral and material disaster befalls them."[115] 'Ammar's assertion of the unity of the Valley was based on physical, ethnic, cultural, and economic foundations.[116] The subtle gradations of topography, climate, flora, and fauna lent credence to his claim that "one is justified in stating that the present frontiers between Egypt and the Sudan are but artificial boundaries based on no natural or geographical demarcation. In fact, all natural factors favour the unity and fusion of North and South."[117]

Proving the ethnic and cultural bases for the unity of the Nile Valley, however, was a more difficult task, and 'Ammar devoted considerable attention to it in his essays for the *Unity of the Nile Valley* collection. In fact, 'Ammar's anthropological arguments represent, to borrow a phrase from Helen Tilley, the "ambiguities of racial science."[118] 'Ammar and others used the nationalist notion of Egypt's Arab-Islamic heritage to argue for the unity of Egypt and the Sudan. Yet, in proposing such a unity in opposition to British colonial claims on the Sudan, proponents of Nile Valley unity advocated the sub-colonization of the Sudan by Egypt. Egypt, they argued with characteristic paternalism, was endowed with the "capacity of bringing that part of Africa within the orbit of world civilization."[119] Yet at the same time 'Ammar's writings on Anglo-Egyptian Sudan focused on the malleability of racial categories, and even the heuristic limitations of the category of race itself. Racial categories, he argued, often derived their power from political, and specifically colonial, rather than scientific considerations.

> (a) Racial unity does not mean at all either complete uniformity of morphological characteristics or thorough fusion of physical peculiarities. Purity of race is a myth, with no basis in biology or in human history. All that can be expected is a high frequency incidence of similar inherited features, on the one hand, and the absence of such extreme contrasts—that make intermarriage undesirable—on the other.
>
> (b) The racial boundaries indicated on ethnographic maps are hypothetical and general. Racial regions overlap each other and there are transitional zones of mixed elements and heterogeneous population.
>
> (c) The term "race" is absolutely misused by politicians, who are more concerned with cultural than with morphological facts. Nationalists of all countries have always been under the influence of linguistic and historical considerations.
>
> (d) The existence of ethnic minorities—peculiar in their cultural and physical characteristics—within particular nationalities—is a well known fact to students of political geography. Complete ethnic homogeneity might be overlooked for economic and strategic considerations and such ethnic minorities can enjoy cultural autonomy as well as equal opportunities if international law is applied and fair treatment guaranteed by the majority.[120]

This more fluid, relativistic, and historical view of race allowed 'Ammar to contend that views that espoused a Negro and Caucasian Africa were exaggerated for purposes of the general public—and that any theory which attempted to divide the Nile Valley could be easily "exploded." 'Ammar's conception of race was very much influenced by that of his Manchester advisor, H. J. Fleure, who had vigorously critiqued notions of racial purity as political myths, with no basis in scientific fact. Fleure viewed the historical development of races as the product of human intermingling, migration ("drifts of mankind"), and adaptation to local environmental conditions. Avoiding a stance of Boasian environmentalism (or an extreme view of racial impermanence), Fleure espoused an evolutionary Mendelian view of "descent with modification." As such, races were seen not as based in a fixed origin, but as "a present phase toward which there has been a long and continued convergence."[121] Specifically, the "proportionate occurrence of physical characteristics in a people is thus not something derived from an original pure race or fixed from far antiquity into an unchanging and unchangeable frame."[122] According to Fleure, each individual was a composite of features from various races: "we are nearly all mosaics of inheritance from our varied ancestry."[123]

Despite his view of the malleability of race, 'Ammar did nevertheless argue for the predominantly Hamitic character of the ancient Egyptians and Nubians. Thus, he asserted that the early Hamitic influence upon the peoples of the Sudan lay "in the racial formation of its inhabitants."[124] Relying heavily on Cambridge anthropologist Charles Seligman's work on Egypt and "Negro Africa," 'Ammar concurred with his research findings, namely, that there were substantial affinities between northeastern and eastern Africa and Ancient Egypt, which supported "the idea of an underlying Hamitic culture layer." It is indeed a curious historical irony that some thirty years after Seligman first published his research in support of the Hamitic origins of the ancient Egyptians and Nubians, his work would be mobilized against the British control of the Sudan by a nationalist Egyptian geographer and anthropologist.

Seligman was a medical pathologist by training and a member of the original Torres Straits expedition. Along with his wife Brenda Salaman and with official sponsorship, he had collected ethnographic data on physical types, customs, material culture, kinship, and social organization in the Anglo-Egyptian Sudan, during three expeditions between 1909 and 1911.[125] Seligman and W. H. R. Rivers, constituted the core of the Cambridge School of Anthropology, and Seligman was influential in training a generation of fieldworkers and members of the Colonial Administrative Service, including the renowned E. E. Evans-Pritchard, who conducted studies for the Sudan administration.[126] Seligman's original hypothesis was that many of the physical types, customs, and ideas that were found in the Sudan were not of negro, Arab, or Islamic origin, but rather Hamitic.[127]

'Ammar was clear to point out that Arabization of the Sudan had not eliminated the Hamitic influence, although the Arab-Semitic influence had contributed greatly to the ethnic identity of the Nile Valley. The Arabization of the Sudan occurred well before the arrival of Islam, 'Ammar noted, and its distribution was related to environmental factors, and would have continued into the southernmost regions—in contrast to the strict British policy of separation. Arabization itself was viewed by 'Ammar as principally a linguistic and cultural process, as "the Hamites and the Semites are of one racial stock, differing but little in morphological characteristics."[128] Thus did 'Ammar argue that the peoples of the Nile Valley were united in their racial composition (Hamitic) as well as in their linguistic and cultural makeup (Arabized).

'Ammar's focus on unity was problematically premised on Egypt's role as a civilizing force in Africa—itself predicated on a hierarchical notion of a graded humanity in which Egypt constituted the pinnacle of civilization in Africa and southern Sudan the nadir. Yet, at the very same time, 'Ammar denied that Arabs were guilty of racialist thought. He vehemently attacked a 1945 Fabian publication that accused Arabs of "pushing out . . . the original inhabitants" of the Sudan, and of maintaining a strict "color-bar," racial hostility, cruelty, and contempt between Arabs and blacks; 'Ammar countered that the unity of the Sudan would have been achieved had it not been for the imperialistic designs of the British.[129] To back up the cultural unity of the Nile Valley, 'Ammar posited the long historical trajectory of Egyptianization, which he viewed as simultaneously a civilizing agent and a developing force in the valley. As a dominant world civilization and cultural force in the region, Egypt provided influences, ranging from domesticated plants and animals to religious culture (Christian and Islamic), that were spread to the uppermost reaches of the White Nile. 'Ammar repeats, as it were, Seligman's affirmation that "the Hamites were, in fact, the great civilizing force of Black Africa."[130] "Far-reaching Arab influence," 'Ammar noted, "shows that the division of the Sudan into North and South is based upon a deliberate misrepresentation of facts, because the area which had not been affected by Arab influence occupied but an insignificant part of the South. It would indeed be wrong to look upon the Sudan and the Sudanese as being divided into two distinct groups, one Arab and the other non-Arab."[131] Indeed, the need for an "African Negro bloc," Ammar asserted, was only to be found in the minds of imperialists.

According to 'Ammar, the spread of Islam throughout the Nile Valley should be encouraged to follow its natural course, in order to allow for a compact cultural bloc covering every part of the Sudan.

> (a) Cultural homogeneity is essential in peoples of the same nationality for real cooperation and mutual understanding. The overwhelming majority of the Sudanese speak Arabic and follow the teachings of Islam. It is, therefore, in the interest of the remaining minority to fit in the frame of the prevailing culture, especially if it is worth remembering that the culture of the Nilotic tribes is, by no means, worth preserving.
>
> (b) The Southern Communities do not form one cultural unit. On the contrary, they are divided, linguistically and culturally, into a great number of different groups—a fact that makes intellectual homogeneity impossible without some external common medium. . . . The Arabic language is perfectly suitable for being the "lingua franca" of the Nilotes. . . .
>
> (c) Islam has always appealed strongly to primitive peoples. . . .

(d) Lastly it has to be mentioned that the present tendency prevailing amongst European colonizers and exploiters is towards keeping primitive peoples within the framework of their native culture. This policy might be reasonable if there were a culture worth preserving but should it be applied in Southern Sudan, there would be nothing but intellectual rigidity and cultural stagnation. Let us always remember that we are now living in an age of world-wide relations and international interdependence and such a tendency towards maintaining "Ethnographic Museums," would, therefore, be out of harmony with the spirit of the present age.[132]

'Ammar's extreme racialist position—that the southern Sudanese did not have "a culture worth preserving" is clearly delineated, but it is articulated as a critique of European colonial discourse. Thus postulated, the civilizing mission of the southern Sudan could not be left to the British. Rather than foist "a totally foreign culture" on the region, cultural change had to be accomplished through a mediating force with affinities to the indigenous culture—that force, 'Ammar declared, had always been the Egyptians "in cooperation with the Northern Sudanese—who have always been the civilizing force in the whole Nile Valley, and who have the will and the capacity of bringing that part of Africa within the orbit of world civilization."[133] Southern Sudan forms the limit zone, as it were, of 'Ammar's critique of European racial thought—the distance between a culture entombed in ethnographic museums and a culture not worth preserving.

'Ammar ends his discussion of Nile Valley unity with an examination of economic interests, which entailed the interdependence of agricultural, industrial, and commercial interests, and the complete reliance on the Nile's waters. According to 'Ammar, the British organized the Sudan with the aim of making "the Sudanese economy subservient to British industrial needs."[134] "On the other hand," he declared "Egypt has always considered the common interests of the two parts of the Valley as a single entity."[135] A unified economic policy, he noted, would help the two countries to organize production and consumption in a complementary fashion, and gear the Sudanese economy northward.[136]

> The British allege that their mission in the Sudan is a purely humanitarian one, that their aim is to civilize its peoples, afford to them all the elements of progress, and lead them rapidly towards independence. This allegation has similarly been made by every colonizing power whose methods of colonization have now become notorious and have been described as the worst form of exploitation.
>
> The fact is, however, that the British have definite economic and strategic interests in this part of Africa which form the chief motive for Britain's ambition to govern the Sudan, monopolize the authority therein and attempt to dislodge completely the Egyptians from it.

The most important of these interests are as follows:

Firstly.—To exploit the natural resources of the Sudan and its cheap labour and later to take advantage of its potential value as an exclusive market for British goods. . . .

Secondly.—To take advantage of the Sudan's military and strategic situation, along the British Imperial lines of communication in Africa, and to the Far East. . . .

Thirdly.—One of the most potent reasons which impel the British to remain in the Sudan and pursue a particular policy in its Southern part is the fact that they are well aware that the Sudan, as an integral part of an independent unit having its national status, threatens their colonial ambitions in Central and Eastern Africa, where at present strong currents prevail tending towards a national revival which imperialists are attempting to quell by all the means in their power.[137]

Thus ending his tirade against the political and propagandistic efforts of the British to oppose the unification of the Nile Valley into a larger unit ("a desire supported by the great majority of the inhabitants of the Sudan"), 'Ammar called for a British withdrawal and a Sudanese plebiscite.[138]

'Ammar's critique of European discourses of race as applied to both Egypt and the Anglo-Egyptian Sudan was premised on several postulates: that purity of race was not only a myth, but also an ideological tool in the hands of politicians and imperialists; that cultural homogeneity rather than racial or ethnic purity was the foundation for nation-states; that because Egypt and the Sudan shared a common language, religion, history, and culture, their minor racial and ethnic differences were not insurmountable; that, as such, the unity of the Nile Valley was a social fact; and that, therefore, the project of a civilizing mission in the southern parts of the Sudan was best accomplished by the Egyptians, as they shared the same culture and would not cause the "moral and material disaster" that the radically alien culture of the British imperialists would.

'Ammar's critique of racial science, then, was premised on maintaining Egypt in a position of imperial trusteeship over the Sudan. 'Ammar expounded a policy of unification and integration as an alternative to the British "Southern policy," which was the maintenance of a "separate development" program for the South.[139] The rhetoric of safeguarding Egypt's role in the civilizing mission of Africa was couched in the racialized discourse of Arabism that posited the superiority of Arab culture and civilization over that of Africa. 'Ammar's racial blindness is particularly telling because it did not focus on an elusive search for racial origins—namely, the divergence or concurrence of Arab and African racial types—but relied on notions of culture and history to posit racial inferiority and superiority. Ethnological uniqueness or unity functioned within 'Ammar's ethnological account as an exclusionary mechanism. 'Ammar secured the role of social patriarch for Egypt by asserting that whereas the British sought to keep "primitive peoples within the framework of their native culture," Egypt would bear Sudan's future prospects in mind. The nationalist intelligentsia cast itself as executor of the future, avatar of progress, and custodian of the educability of native subjects—aspiring to extend its dominion over Egyptians and Sudanese alike.

. . .

The two trends within Egyptian nationalist discourse—pharaonicism and Arabism—had vexed relationships with the notion of "race" as understood scientifically throughout the first half of the twentieth century. The work of twentieth-century polymath Salama Musa is an exemplar of discourses that popularized race within the nationalist context. Musa's conception of race was specific enough, however, to be transformed into a notion of "national personality." Locating the specificity of Egypt's national personality within its pharaonic heritage, Musa's writings established the continuity of Egyptian identity from the pharaonic era to the present, thereby creating a unified collective national subject. Yet pharaonicism also functioned as an exclusionary discourse, situating Egypt within a heritage highly prized by the West and disembedding it from its African context. In a similar vein, by juxtaposing pharaonicist nationalist discourses with an earlier statist discourse on peasant disregard for antiquities, Elliott Colla has demonstrated "the way in which the nationalist discourse on community was actually based on the subordination of certain groups to others, peasants to urban elements, the South to the North, the countryside to the capital."[140]

Egyptian anthropologist 'Abbas Mustafa 'Ammar, on the other hand, was representative of a later phase of Egyptian nationalism that sought, using anthropological and historical evidence, to demonstrate the ethnological basis of the unity of Egypt and the Nile Valley, focusing on the region's specifically Arab and Islamic heritage. Rather than trying to assimilate Egypt into the Mediterranean world, 'Ammar asserted Egypt's Arab identity. 'Ammar challenged many colonial ethnological claims, such as the racial division of the Nile Valley, even while relying upon the same repertoire of racial science—anthropometry and serology—as his European counterparts. Thus, although colonial and indigenous anthropological methods and epistemological orientations often overlapped, the larger ideological projects within which they were embedded remained fundamentally distinct. As a nationalist, 'Ammar premised his research not on the assumption of the "colonial difference" between the European and the colonized, but on the basis of the uniqueness of the collective national subject. Demonstrating the "ambiguities of racial science," however, 'Ammar remained mired in a racialist discourse that posited hierarchical distinctions between Arab and African and between northern and southern Sudanese.

As Timothy Mitchell has argued, conventional histories of nationalism overlook "the more mundane and uncertain process of producing the nation.... History is written to describe the growing self-awareness or imagination of a collective subject. This imagination takes the form of a gradual revealing of the collective subject to itself.... There is no encounter with otherness, except as part of a world beyond the self."[141] 'Abbas Mustafa 'Ammar very much embodies this pedagogical attempt to create the nation through the imagination of the uniqueness of the collective national subject. What is so interesting about the work of 'Ammar is the way in which he opens up the field of nationalist pedagogy, exposing its indeterminacies and the interstitial production of difference as constitutive to the making of the modern nation. Thus, in arguing for the unity of the Nile Valley, and in arguing for the Arab elements in Sharqiya and in the Sinai, 'Ammar did not argue for racial or ethnic homogeneity. Rather, he argued, quite precisely, for unity in ethnic heterogeneity, or unity in difference. He further elaborated the creation of that unity as a social construction—the product of historically contingent processes such as religious, cultural, and linguistic conversion. Of course, such projects of conversion were inherently underlined by violence and paternalism—the violence of making the other resemble the self.[142] Indeed, 'Ammar agued for the colonial transformation of the Sudan to resemble Egypt, eliminating the southern Sudan as such. It was 'Ammar's colonial contention that Egypt was more capable of civilizing the Sudan than Great Britain, precisely because of its underlying affinity with and resemblance to the region's inhabitants.

'Ammar's focus on the importance of similitude between the cultures of the conqueror and the conquered was reminiscent of his interpretation of Ibn Khaldun's *Muqaddimah*, in which Ibn Khaldun delineated the tendency toward cultural diffusion among cultures of conquest. In other words, both conquerors and conquered tended, through imitation, toward cultural borrowing. So much so that 'Ammar expounded the law of similarity ("that can be attributed to the equality of human 'races' in fundamental innate endowments and to the diffusion of culture and the 'factor of imitation,'" e.g. between conquerors and conquered) as one of Ibn Khaldun's three fundamental social laws.[143] The two other laws were the law of causality (which eliminated chance in the social process) and the law of dissimilarity (based on the existence of different environment types).[144] 'Ammar's discussion of Khaldunian social laws enables us to see more clearly how his work differed from his European counterparts.

In fact, Ibn Khaldun's theories of cultural transmission and diffusion meshed well with several modern theories of race and culture, such as those of H. J. Fleure, that emphasized the importance of cultural diffusion and the migration of peoples to the creation of modern-day "races." In his full-length treatise on Ibn Khaldun, 'Ammar devoted considerable attention to his conception of racial difference, although ultimately disagreeing with Ibn Khaldun's assertion that race was exclusively the product of environmental forces. Nonetheless, 'Ammar emphasized the element of Ibn Khaldun's thought that viewed differences in culture as the product of historical differences in social environments and which was "wholly against the vulgar view that attributes such differences to innate inferiority of racial quality."[145] Indeed, 'Ammar hailed Ibn Khaldun as the initiator of notions of racial equality, as well as the first thinker to take human society as such as his object of study, and to understand history as based on "the existence of certain universal laws which govern all societies."[146]

We would therefore surely be mistaken if we attributed 'Ammar's research solely to the translation of innovations within Western anthropology and geography, for his work drew much from the study of society initiated by the medieval Muslim social philosopher Ibn Khaldun. However, this does raise the difficult question of the extent to which European epistemologies, methodologies, and ideologies were translated in their non-European colonial contexts, and how those translations became authorized as knowledge. 'Ammar's epistemological orientation remained by and large positivist, although he combined the genealogical method of conjectural history (the Arabic medieval histories) with the Khaldunian understanding of natural social laws to formulate his research hypotheses and interpret his research findings. As a result, 'Ammar was methodologically eclectic (or perhaps "creative" is a better term), combining historical, serological, anthropometric, and demographic evidence, as well as the use of the holistic case study, to extrapolate larger arguments regarding social and cultural phenomena. Ideologically, 'Ammar differed most from his European counterparts. Arguing for a nationalist ideology based on ethnological uniqueness, rather than racial homogeneity or purity, 'Ammar went far in destabilizing the heuristic value of the category of race itself. In the process he overturned inherited racial taxonomies, and in fact eventually dispensed entirely with the search for racial origins. Yet, rather than reify the racial division of the Nile Valley,

'Ammar uncritically substituted a notion of the superiority of Arab and Islamic history and civilization as the basis of Nile Valley unity.

'Ammar would eventually abandon his research in anthropology, embarking instead on a career devoted to innovations in social-welfare research and social-policy design, mirroring larger trends within Egyptian social sciences, which became increasingly concerned with the pragmatic implications of the field. Indeed, anthropologists would not make serious inroads into the study of Egyptian society. This may be related in part to the historical dominance of Egyptology, which was often premised on the Orientalist assumption that ancient, rather than modern, Egypt was the object most worthy of study. It is noteworthy that Winifred Blackman's 1927 *The Fellāhīn of Upper Egypt* (recently translated into Arabic), perhaps the first anthropological text to be written on Egypt, was motivated by the study of ancient Egyptian survivals in modern-day Egypt. It may also be related to the colonial genealogy of anthropology, linked as this was to the colonial state apparatus (if not directly in Egypt, then certainly in the Sudan).[147] Perhaps, too, indigenous scholars, much like 'Ammar, viewed the European use of the term "culture" as simply the new term for race, a ploy for "museumizing" indigenous peoples. It would not be until 1974 that Ahmed Abou-Zeid would establish the first and only academic anthropology department in Egypt, at Alexandria University. In keeping with trends in Western anthropology, serious scholarship was relegated to the study of marginal groups, such as Abou-Zeid's own ethnographic studies of various oases and tribal peoples. It is important to note that anthropological networks of knowledge in Egypt were themselves formed at the intersection of anthropology and geography.[148] 'Ammar himself was trained as a geographer, and many anthropological discussions among Egyptian scholars turned on the importance of environment, milieu, and Nilotic character in the formation of a peculiarly Egyptian essence. The distillation of that essence was to be found in the village community.

II   *From Ethnographic Realism to Social Engineering:*
    The Problem of the Peasantry, 1925–1945

3 The Painting of Rural Life

Rural Egypt, recollected Sayyid Qutb, was populated by demons (*'afarit*), saintly wild men (*magazib*), and superstitious villagers seeking to mollify the evil intentions of the spirit world. As the writer and Islamist recalled from the days of his youth, the "filthy" quarters of the traditional *kuttab* school functioned as a counterpoint to the modern government school, the vehicle that would catapult him into the world of the Cairo *effendiyya*.[1] Yet much as the *'afarit* continued to haunt his dreams (although he had purged himself of such superstitious irrational beliefs), so too did the specter of the peasantry—of poverty, disease, and ignorance—pervade his early career and social-scientific writings. Themes such as social reform, moral edification, and national progress cropped up in writings that demonstrated a keen awareness of the rural dimensions of social problems and reforms.[2]

Indeed, throughout the interwar period academic social-scientific discourse in Egypt moved, much like Qutb's own writings, toward the study of society, conceived of now as an object or a series of objects ("the peasantry," "population"). Scholars have argued that the peasantry, specifically, became an object of discourse and political intervention by "both the colonial regime and Egyptian intellectuals."[3] What could be termed, in historical hindsight, "peasant studies" was the domain of Egyptians and European "men on the spot" alike. In Partha Chatterjee's words, "within the same historical career of the modern state both colonial and nationalist politics thought of the peasantry as an object of their strategies, to be acted upon, controlled, and appropriated within their respective structures of state power."[4] In Egypt, as in France, Russia, and Mexico, the question of the peasantry and its modernization entailed considerations related both to labor discipline and to the presumed cultural chasm between the peasantry and the metropolitan elite.[5] The Russian case is especially instructive in this regard, as the efforts of *narodniki* (populists) aimed at the peasantry often mirrored efforts aimed at the assimilation of Russia's ethnic minorities— both populations were targeted (or colonized) as sources of backwardness.[6]

The British occupation highlighted existing tensions between metropolitan elites and rural masses in Egypt. As Samera Esmeir has noted, the British colonial mission often focused on the material improvement of the conditions of the fellahin, and aimed at eliminating their oppression and exploitation at the hands of elites through a series of juridical reforms.[7] In the words of Sir Evelyn Baring, "there can be no doubt that it was the hand of England which first raised him [the Egyptian fellah] from the abject moral and material condition in which he had for centuries wallowed."[8] "Improvements," such as the abolition of corvée, moved in tandem with the scientific management of agriculture and nature—a principal concern of the turn-of-the-century colonial and local elite that gained momentum after the 1898 foundation of the Khedivial Agricultural Society, which supported research into agricultural production.[9] New forms of scientific knowledge, social organization, and administrative expertise addressing rural Egypt emerged throughout the twentieth century.[10] The expansion of the domain of agricultural scientific knowledge production is a crucial component of the story of science in modern Egypt, but here I focus on the human subjects of knowledge—the Egyptian peasantry—tracing discourses that traverse amateur ethnography, literary realism, and positivist human geographical studies.

The emergence of peasant studies within social-scientific inquiry in Egypt during the interwar period and up through World War II must be understood within multiple historical contexts. One setting is the struggle against British colonialism, in which Egyptian anticolonial nationalists attempted to incorporate and mobilize the peasantry as "demographic mass" into the fabric of national life. Such a process of incorporation valorized the peasantry as the "true sons" of Egypt, the repository of national cultural values, but also localized them as a sphere of backwardness to be uplifted and modernized, a process similar to that engaged by the Russian intelligentsia in the late nineteenth century.[11] On another front, the spread of capitalist relations of production into the Egyptian countryside led to the increasing alienation of the Egyptian peasantry from both the urban classes and the agrarian bourgeoisie, which presented an obstacle to the unification of the population in the face of colonial domination. This was a familiar problem faced by anticolonial nationalists all over the world, from French Indochina to Algeria: the contradictory needs for national unification against the colonial power on one hand, and the need for a fundamental restructuring of capitalist class relations on the other.[12] It is also significant that the field of peasant studies emerged simultaneously with waves of peasant rebellions against occupying powers—in Egypt as well as in other colonies such as French Indochina, Mexico, and the Middle East (Syria, Egypt, Iraq, Palestine)—during the interwar period.[13]

At their core, interwar discourses were founded on the fear of the undisciplined rural subject perceived, as Timothy Mitchell has shown, as alternating between the two poles of, on the one hand, passivity and lassitude, and, on the other, irrational outbursts of violence.[14] Such representations served both to rationalize the expertise of social scientists and reformers and to underscore the civility of the urban middle-class *effendiyya*. Thus the discourse on the peasantry was also a discourse of power, elucidating the inextricable links between the elite intelligentsia and the rural population they purported to describe, fictionalize, study, reform, and uplift.

We may view the peasantry as the central contradiction of national identity within Egyptian colonial society—at the same time that they were localized by the nationalist elite as the repository of cultural authenticity, they were also demarcated as a locus of backwardness to be reformed and reconstituted as modern moral subjects of the nation-state. This dialectic of modernist versus romantic thought regarding the peasantry inaugurated a positivist project of formulating a science of the countryside—in which the peasantry became an object of social scientific intervention and engineering—and simultaneously initiated an anthropological and romantic process of recounting and describing the peasantry as cultural artifacts of national identity. The ambivalence of the bourgeois nationalist project was fought on the backs of the peasantry.

Colonial Affronts and Indigenous Discontents: 1906 and 1919

The intersection of anti-colonial nationalism, class struggle, and peasant rebellion in twentieth-century Egypt is best understood against the backdrop of two climactic events: the 1906 Dinshaway "incident" between British officers and Egyptian peasants, and the 1919 nationalist revolt and "peasant rebellion." The attempt to incorporate Egypt into the British empire was a process that began with the bombing of Alexandria and the Battle of Tall al-Kabir in 1882, and the 1883 appointment of Sir Evelyn Baring (later Lord Cromer) as agent and consul-general of Egypt, which he remained until 1907.[15] It was after the British occupation that the peasantry became "an important political factor, regarded as the object of politics by both the colonial regime and Egyptian intellectuals"; this was due in part to the increased contact between Egypt's professional and literary classes (the *effendiyya*) and the peasantry, and in part to the incident at Dinshaway.[16]

On June 13, 1906, several British soldiers went pigeon hunting near Dinshaway, a village in the Delta province of Menufiyya. Pigeon hunting was controversial because it targeted peasant livelihood, and the villagers were provoked when the soldiers then accidentally set fire to a field. After two of the soldiers were beaten (one later died of sunstroke), and the other officers opened fire, fifty-two villagers were arrested and put on trial. In a legal case that became the center of intellectual and political debate, a tribunal that included Mirrit Butrus Ghali and Ahmed Fathi Zaghlul condemned four of the peasants to death by hanging, twelve to prison, and nine to public flogging. On the following day, June 28, the inhabitants of the village were forced out of their homes to witness the executions and floggings.[17] The incident became a rallying cause uniting the nationalist intelligentsia (including Ahmed Shawqi, 'Abd al-'Aziz Jawish, and Mustafa Kamil) and the fellahin who mourned the wrongful deaths of the peasants.[18] Folk songs were composed that lionized the peasants as national martyrs. Less than one month after the incident, a short story titled "Adhra' Dinshaway" ("The Maiden of Dinshaway") was penned to be published in serialized form. Written in a style that could be described as documentary realism, the piece (according to Yahya Haqqi, the first published Egyptian short story to deal with the peasantry) expressed the traumatic events of the summer of 1906 in a narrative that gave truth precedence over fiction, leaving the names of the peasants unchanged.[19] The events at Dinshaway would ultimately lead to Cromer's resignation.

The British establishment of a protectorate in Egypt in December of 1914 and the imposition of martial law came in the midst of other difficulties faced by the Egyptians during World War I, including conscription among the peasantry and economic hardships for the general populace. Seven Egyptian representatives formed a *wafd* (delegation) on November 13, 1918, and three of them—Sa'd Zaghlul, 'Abd al-'Aziz Fahmi, and Ali al-Sha'arawi—met with High Commissioner Sir Francis Reginald Wingate. The wafd's call for complete independence for Egypt, although refused, became a hallmark of the nationalist movement. Later, the Wafd Party became one of the most popularly supported political parties in Egyptian history, and its leader, Sa'd Zaghlul, was enshrined in the Egyptian public imagination as a rural national leader (*fellah ibn fellah*, a peasant son of a peasant—a man of the people). Hagiographical literary depictions of Zaghlul, such as Najib

Mahfuz's *Bayn al-Qasrayn* and Tawfiq al-Hakim's *'Awdat al-Ruh*, illustrate his exalted position in the nationalist imagination.[20] Born to a "prosperous peasant family" in Gharbiyya, and trained initially at al-Azhar and later in law, Zaghlul used his considerable skills as an orator to rally wide public support in the countryside as well as in urban areas.[21] His exile to Malta in March of 1919 led to a series of uprisings, strikes (including a general strike in April of 1919), demonstrations and popular revolts, and widespread social antagonism, first in urban areas and later in the countryside, inaugurating what Jacques Berque has referred to as a dialectic of the people and the Wafd.[22] Nevertheless, the Wafd Party was plagued with internal difficulties ranging from decision-making conflicts among the executive committee to internal divisions based on ethnicity—a Turco-Circassian aristocracy pitted against "pure" Egyptians. With a class base that included the urban middle class, intelligentsia, workers, students, and medium landowners in the rural areas (although party leadership always retained large landowners), the Wafd had a more populist bent than did the more exclusively elitist other parties, such as the Liberal Constitutionalist Party or the People's Party, which comprised mostly large property holders.[23]

By the end of the turbulent year 1919, some 3,000 Egyptians had been killed and 1,400 wounded by the British armed forces.[24] High Commissioner Wingate was replaced by General E. H. H. Allenby, and the Wafd attended the Paris Peace Conference. After two years of stalled negotiations, the British abolished martial law and granted Egypt unilateral nominal independence from British colonial rule in February of 1922. The British continued to maintain control over four points: the security of imperial communications, the defense of Egypt, the protection of foreign interests and minorities, and the Sudan.

It has been argued that the 1919 revolution had two stages: the violent and short period of March 1919 that involved large-scale mobilizations by the peasantry that were suppressed by British military action; and the protracted phase beginning in April 1919 that was less violent and more urban, with the participation of students, workers, lawyers, and other professionals.[25] The mobilization of the peasantry and momentary subversions of the rural order did not in fact materialize into a wide-scale peasant revolution, as the Wafd with its moderate program aimed at political sovereignty, parliamentary democracy, and social justice continued to oscillate throughout its tenure between populism and social conservatism.[26] As many have pointed out, the 1919 revolution, at least from the perspective of the Wafd, did not aim at the radical transformation of the social structure or class relations, but rather at the assertion of territorial nationalism.[27]

Reinhard Schulze's discussion of the 1919 revolution shifts the viewpoint away from the perspective of the elite classes to that of the peasantry. Schulze argues that the Egyptian countryside experienced the spread of agrarian capitalism in the form of colonial regionalization, an uneven process of integration into a hierarchical and centralized system of capitalist production based on the extensive cultivation of two principal cash crops, cotton and sugar cane.[28] This process, what Schulze refers to as the colonization of the countryside, was begun in 1820–21 with the introduction of the long-staple cotton crop, along with the heightened tax and conscription demands placed on villagers under Mehmed 'Ali.[29]

Throughout the nineteenth century the transformation of the Egyptian countryside entailed a shift from basin irrigation to perennial irrigation; a shift in the system of land use from the Ottoman *iltizam* tax farming system to the ownership of land as private property; a shift to the cultivation of cotton as the dominant crop; and population growth.[30] These changes led to the commercialization of agriculture; the establishment of large landed estates (*'izab*, sing. *'izba*); the growth of an agricultural middle class; and the fragmentation of peasant landholdings.[31] In particular, the emergence and spread of large landed estates in the late nineteenth century signaled a new form of power over rural space, movement, and labor.[32]

The social implications of this process of colonization, according to Schulze, were the elimination of autonomous forms of rural social organization, the centralization and urbanization of political power, and the increasing curtailment of the peasantry's ability to mobilize politically in the face of a highly extractive economy.[33] Schulze notes the gradual shift from collective to individual resistance, from millenarianism to brigandage and to individual cases of agrarian crime between 1820 and 1910.[34] Nevertheless, there were documented peasant uprisings, during the 'Urabi revolt (September 1881–September 1882) and shortly after the British occupation; these uprisings generally occurred between March and October—between cotton planting season and harvesting season, as Schulze points out.[35]

The economic and political crises of World War I, experienced in Egypt as the expansion of the colonial-state bureaucracy, the forced conscription of Egyptians, the state appropriation of cotton production, and the forcible provision of supplies for British troops, resulted in a crisis of political control.[36] In the competition for political power that ensued between the *effendiyya* nationalists and the colonial regime, the Wafd Party and the 1919 rebellion were born. Schulze's contribution to the historiography of the revolution, however, overturns the nationalist account of a unified uprising in which peasants and politicians coalesced in support of a nascent nationalism.³⁷ He argues instead that the nationalist call for "independence, freedom, and justice," could not have held the same meaning for peasants. Whereas the *effendiyya* took the colonial state as the target of their efforts, the peasantry took the "wholesale colonization of their economic life" as their object of anger.³⁸ According to Schulze, the upheavals of 1919 are to be read less as the success of the nationalist elite in mobilizing the peasantry, than as the actions of "fellahin, pure and simple, whose goal was to liberate the fellahin from the *'izab* [latifundia] organization and restore their economic position as peasant farm workers or share-croppers."³⁹

Indeed, Schulze claims that with the nominal "political victory" achieved by the nationalists, and the uneasy coalition of *effendiyya* and notables, the contest for power over the colonial state and economy reached a new zenith, leaving the peasant community divided. On one side were landowners, *effendiyya*, and notables, whose interests were represented by the Wafd, and on the other were sharecroppers, agricultural laborers, and small-scale farmers, whose world had now been completely colonized. According to Schulze, this "led to the elimination of autonomous forms of social organization in the countryside and the assertion of central control in the hands of the British, mediated by the monarchy, the notables, and the *afandiyya*."⁴⁰

Whereas Schulze takes the economic colonization of the countryside to be the primary impetus behind the 1919 revolution, Nathan Brown and Ellis Goldberg instead interpret the violence that erupted in March and April as a reaction to British policy during World War I. Both dismiss views that portray 1919 as a social revolution against large landed property, based on the formation of independent republics and the seizure of estates, accounts they claim are somewhat exaggerated. Brown views the revolution as a "popular, broadly based national and political revolution against British rule," and Goldberg sees the "peasant revolt of 1919 [as] centered mainly on preventing goods and men from being transported by the rail system," a direct response to food shortages and labor requisitions.⁴¹

My interest in 1919 is neither to catalog it definitively as an event that embodies an insurgent peasant consciousness (Schulze's account) or as a nationalist peasant consciousness (Brown's account), nor to dismiss it as the spontaneous pre-political (in Hobsbawmian terms) irruption of peasant volatility, nor even to see in it the rational and pragmatic response to the threat of imminent starvation (Goldberg's account).⁴² It is rather to note its troubled presence within the colonial and elite archive as potential Bolshevism and hence as part and parcel of a certain incitement to discourse.⁴³ This incitement to discourse represented both colonial and elite anxieties regarding the disciplinization of the agrarian population and its integration into Egyptian economic, political, and cultural life. Thus, nationalist writings on the peasantry flourished in the attempt to integrate the peasantry as "demographic mass" into the fabric of national life.

Mentalité and Culture: The Painting of Rural Life

The anthropological and romantic process of cataloguing and describing the peasantry as cultural artifacts of national identity spawned a variety of genres, from the literary painting of rural life (Muhammad Haykal's novel *Zaynab*) to journalistic and descriptive accounts of the countryside ('Aisha 'Abd al-Rahman's *The Egyptian Countryside*) to analyses based on social psychology (Henry Habib Ayrout's *The Fellahin*). Within this corpus of writing it was the fixity of the Egyptian peasant—characterized by an unbroken stability, timelessness, and changelessness—that was emphasized. There were two literary traditions for writings on the culture and *mentalité* of the peasantry: the European Orientalist tradition of "manners and customs," often based on participant observation; and an anecdotal, descriptive, and at times autobiographical literary tradition of realism and naturalism in nationalist literature (*adab qawmi*).[44]

Research on the *mentalité* of the peasantry included the representation of their everyday life, manners, and customs, and the collection of folkloric material. This anthropologically inclined approach was often rooted in metaphysical constructs ("culture," "mentalité") and was descriptive and explanatory in method. At its extreme, this position led to an ahistorical romanticism—for example, in the imaginative attempt to capture the cultural essence of the peasantry. Such attempts foregrounded the specificity of place, that is to say, the location of the peasantry in the countryside, and above all their proximity to and intercourse with nature.

Ethnographic Orientalism

European and Orientalist writings on the culture and *mentalité* of the peasantry drew on nineteenth-century European writings on the Middle East (such as Edward Lane's *Manners and Customs of the Modern Egyptians*). As with Orientalism itself, a core set of *idées reçues* came to distinguish ethnographic discourse on the Egyptian peasantry in twentieth-century writings. Such writings also drew on eighteenth- and nineteenth-century notions of national character—theories that were revitalized by turn-of-the-century social psychology (most notably the ideas of Gustave Le Bon).[45] Ethnographic studies on the peasantry began to take shape at the turn of the century. Members of the Royal Geographic Society, in particular, began writing on the peasantry as an ethnographic entity, that is to say, as a racially distinct and culturally unique population in itself. Early examples are the writings of Piot Bey and Abbate Pasha, both active members of the RGS.[46] Several texts, from both the turn-of-the-century and interwar periods, can be seen as emblematic of the core set of *idées reçues* that marked the Orientalist discourse on the peasantry.[47]

In an 1899 article entitled "Causerie ethnographique sur le fellah," Piot Bey, the director of veterinary services on government estates and secretary of the Institut Egyptien, described the Egyptian peasantry ethnographically, proceeding categorically through racial origins and classification; manner of dress and decoration for men and women; marriage and fertility patterns; labor and wages; agricultural instruments; housing; hygiene; food consumption patterns; leisure time; the use of substances such as hashish, alcohol, and tobacco; marriage and death ceremonies; and popular songs.[48] As a psychological or character type, the fellahin, according to Piot Bey, were indolent in nature; a childlike people ill equipped for reason or judgment, the result of moral decadence and a continual retrogression of intellect.[49] Nor was the peasant amenable to instruction. Illiterate, he had only rudimentary knowledge of religious law, and of political events he knew only those that affected irrigation.[50] Ignorance left the peasant susceptible to superstitious beliefs and practices: the use of amulets and the belief in magic, jinns, and spontaneous generation.[51] Centuries of oppression had left the peasant defiant and suspicious, evasive and impudent, susceptible to stealing, tyrannical with his inferiors, arrogant with his equals, submissive with his superiors, obtuse in sensibility, and stoic in comportment.[52]

Piot's discussions of peasant indolence, passivity, fatalism, and superstition echoed numerous Orientalist discussions of the Egyptian mind or character. The Egyptian or Oriental was presumed to be indolent by nature; Islam as a religion was thought to lead to fatalism and passivity; and the lower orders were thought to be inclined toward superstitious practices. Despite his somber depiction of the state of the agricultural population of Egypt, Piot Bey noted that the race was heir to a history that the more content peoples of the world could not even approximate.[53] Thus, although he did not explicitly state the correlation, Piot equated the degeneration of the individual Egyptian fellah (which he described as an analogy to the degeneration of the fellah's faithful companion, the donkey) with that of his civilization. As the once vivacious and intelligent young peasant underwent a "regressive metamorphosis," so too did Egyptian civilization.[54]

In a different vein, the lawyer Yusuf Nahhas argued that the secret behind the passive submission of the fellah was not innate character, but the voluntary servitude engendered by the naturalization of oppression since Mamluk times.[55] This was an argument drawn from the sixteenth-century French text of Étienne de la Boétie (the beloved friend of Michel de Montaigne), *The Discourse of Voluntary Servitude*, which tried to explain the inexplicable servitude of millions of serfs as the product of custom bequeathed by generations of individuals who had never experienced liberty. Nahhas's text, *Al-Fellah*, which was originally published in French in 1901 and translated into Arabic in 1926, was a key text on the peasantry. Although it reiterated certain themes regarding peasant ignorance and passivity, at the time it was unique in its elucidation of the relationship between history, peasant "character," and educability. Nahhas argued, in effect, that although the historical weight of oppression had habituated the peasant to servitude, he was nonetheless still amenable to education. Indeed, the progress of Egypt as a civilized nation depended on the rehabilitation and education of the peasantry. Servile labor was less productive, but also unbefitting the civility of the modern world. Nahhas called for the creation of agricultural credit unions, and for state legislation to protect the interests of the fellah and place limits on his exploitation at the hands of usurious moneylenders. Nahhas's text was an exception among early writings on the peasantry, asserting as it did the preeminence of historical, political, and economic considerations, rather than favoring an ethnographic and folklorized vision of peasant "character."

A little over a decade after the publication of Nahhas's text in Arabic, a less sophisticated but ultimately far more influential text on the peasantry was published; the major themes of Jesuit father Henry Habib Ayrout's study, *The Fellaheen* (originally published as *Moeurs et Coutumes des Fellahs*), appear in all subsequent studies on the Egyptian peasantry.[56] Ayrout, an Egyptian of Syrian Catholic origin, received his doctorate from the University of Lyon, and upon his return to Egypt in 1940 established a benevolent association known as the Association for the Free Schools of Upper Egypt (*Jama'iyyat al-Sa'id*).[57] Ayrout's study, an amalgam of human geography, anthropology, and social psychology, described the peasantry in terms of their manners and customs, psychology, and social relations in the home and community, as well as their relationship with the geography and sociopolitical history of Egypt.

Whereas Nahhas's text was analytical and historical, approaching the peasant as the product of a particular historical moment, Ayrout's was ethnographic and descriptive. Father Ayrout developed his work through ethnographic observation, based "principally on personal observation over a period of years in various provinces of the Nile Valley ... [and] on personal intercourse with people of every rank, and on reflection upon things actually seen and heard."[58] As a whole, Ayrout's study succeeded in describing what might be termed the character or *mentalité* of the peasantry, characterized by changelessness. A 1940 reviewer described the work as a "study in social continuity and resistance to cultural change" that demonstrated that the agrarian population "has been an ethnological and psychological continuum from prehistoric times to the present day."[59]

Within a few years of the French text's 1938 initial release, a revised edition (with a preface by Fu'ad Abaza Pasha) was produced. Not long after that edition's 1943 publication, it was translated and annotated in Arabic by Muhammad Ghallab. Ghallab had written his doctoral thesis, "Les Survivances de l'Égypte Antique dans le Folklore Égyptien Moderne," at the University of Lyon a decade before Ayrout presented his doctoral thesis at the same institution.[60] Two years later, in 1945, the book was translated into English by Hilary Wayment, under the title *The Fellaheen*. Ayrout's study, like Nahhas's was widely read and cited by Egyptian writers concerned with "the problem of the peasantry," including members of the independent study group known as La groupe d'études (*Jam'at al-buhuth*), which included the future leaders of the Workers' Vanguard.[61]

Ayrout's text should be situated within its historical moment—one of cultural revival for the intelligentsia and economic misery for the demographic masses. The period following the 1919 revolution—the 1920s and early 1930s—were characterized by a great cultural efflorescence, with the Egyptian intelligentsia involved in journalism, public oratory, and the development of new national literary genres. Thinkers such as Muhammad Husayn Haykal, Tawfiq al-Hakim, Taha Husayn, Ahmad Shawqi, and 'Abbas Al-Aqqad helped to formulate new genres of prose and poetry.[62] Yet, the interwar years were also years of political upheavals and vicissitudes (among the palace, the Wafd Party, and the British), with the 1924 elections leading to a landslide for the Wafd. The victory was short-lived, however—the assassination of the Egyptian army *sirdar* and governor-general of the Sudan, Lee Stack, led to Sa'd Zaghlul's resignation. This initiated a period of great instability in Egyptian political life, with political parties and ministries shifting power frequently.[63] The years after 1929 were the years of the worldwide economic depression, which gravely affected Egypt's economy, and rural wages and annual per capita income plummeted.[64] The combined effects of a newly instituted tariff reform, inflation, and the increasing problems of rural indebtedness further exacerbated an already difficult time for the urban and rural poor.

Ayrout's study does indeed deal with some of the unrest of the 1930s, and addresses in particular the confrontations between peasants and the state, such as the attempt to foreclose a *'izba* in Kafr al-Zayyat in April of 1936.[65] Yet Ayrout sees such instances as fleeting moments in the life of normally obedient and passive peasants. Among the principal features of the fellah's *mentalité*, according to Ayrout, were changelessness (physical, social, and mental) and stability, due to the "wedlock" of land and people—the fellah's symbiosis with the soil.[66] It was, above all, the proximity of the peasantry to nature that defined their social existence; the fellah was viewed as the substratum of society, "the primal mass," "raw-material," and "subsoil" upon which government and society rested.[67] For Ayrout, the fellah was above all a physical being, determined by nature. "Water, soil and sun are the physical agents which explain and often even determine the physical constitution of the fellah."[68]

As a social being, the fellah was distinguished by his lack of individuality—his status as a member of a group, the village. "The village in Egypt is not a community in the social sense; it is not an organism, but a mass."[69] Ayrout emphasized the idea of the village as a homogeneous hivelike mass—a primitive, formless agglomeration. The Egyptian village, characterized by the same types of people, the same customs, traditions, modes of life, standards of living, and physical structure, repeated itself across the countryside. "Nothing is more like one Egyptian village than another Egyptian village."[70] As a psychological being, the fellah was distinguished by a collective rather than an individual psychology, and equally shaped by his physical environment. He was characterized by absolute dependence (on the soil, on the "social pyramid") leading to utter slavishness. The commonality of "country, race, religion, social status and manner of life . . . entitle us to write in the singular of the fellah's soul."[71] The peasant collective psychology was static rather than dynamic, passive and submissive (because of centuries of oppression); uncreative and lacking personality and initiative, as well as sensibility.[72] Although peasants were capable of repetition, memorization, and reproduction, any form of understanding was beyond their grasp.[73] Above all it was the peasant's torpidity, his passive resignation and "mental languor," "a semi-consciousness which abates suffering" that sustained him.[74] Such torpor erupted into fury in the wake of a wrongdoing, and led him to vengeance.[75] The peasant's mind was "walled in between ignorance and tyranny."[76] As a cultural being with his own peculiar psychology, the fellah was marked by his maintenance of customs and traditions "of the soil," customs of marriage and childbirth, of honor and vengeance, of superstitious practices and peasant mysticism.[77] As a moral being, the peasant, although pious, was ignorant of religious precepts—but his primitive "natural morality" could lead him to a profound faith in the providence of God, resulting, ultimately, in resignation and fatalism.[78]

With Father Ayrout we see the ethnographic and romantic description of the peasantry—emphasizing continuity over change and geography over history—at its extreme. A hallmark of romantic writings on the peasantry was the assumption of a collective unconscious psychology, a *mentalité*, that unified the peasantry. Such an approach inhibited historical investigations into the social, political, and economic conditions of the peasantry, proposing instead a folklorized vision of peasant life. Nor was Ayrout's assessment of the peasantry novel in any way—many of his themes were already evident in the turn-of-the-century writings of Abbate Pasha and Piot Bey. Within this body of writings, the peasantry (both as the demographic mass and as cultural representatives of the population) came to form an important node in the anthropological project of the observation and description of native peoples. The peasantry was often viewed as a unique subpopulation, with its own culture, mores, and values, which was at the same time the atavistic distillation of Egyptian culture from antiquity to the present.

Literary Orientalism

Samah Selim has argued that "a whole mythology, an entirely new and singular, if quixotic, discursive structure grew up around the figure of the peasant over the course of the twentieth century."[79] This mythology, she contends, was linked to two historical processes: the formation of the modern national state in Egypt, and the development of new literary genres (the journalistic essay, the short story, and the novel). Egyptian intellectuals in the interwar period were actively involved in the attempt to formulate a national literature. *Adab qawmi* emerged in the wake of the nationalist upheavals of 1919, and it materialized a nascent discourse of national identity. Above all, it sought to imprint the collective national subject within literary writings. The contradictory nature of nationalist discourse—at once extolling and denigrating the peasantry—is perhaps best exemplified in this development of a national literature during the 1920s and 1930s, and especially in the village novel.[80]

The creation of an Egyptian national literature involved the formation of new literary genres, such as the novel and the essay, and new aesthetic and linguistic sensibilities, such as romanticism.[81] Thinkers such as Ahmad

Dayf, Ibrahim al-Misri, and the vastly influential Muhammad Husayn Haykal began to formulate a complex set of ideas regarding the symbiotic relationship between literary creativity and its geographical and historical context. Environment or milieu was, in turn, thought to be determinative of national character, and notions of Egyptian national character permeated literary writings. Thus, concepts of national personality or character, as well as the "uniqueness of the Nile Valley"—ideas we have already encountered in the writings of Salama Musa and 'Abbas 'Ammar—were crucial components of nationalist and literary discourses alike. Thematically, the areas of focus were pharaonic heritage, the natural environment and landscape of Egypt, and the Egyptian peasantry. Stylistically, this led to realism and naturalism in literary discourse.

Mustafa al-Daba' has noted that literary representations of the peasantry from the turn of the century until the 1952 revolution characterized peasants by a lack of effective agency (until the appearance of 'Abd al-Rahman al-Sharqawi's *al-Ard*), with the fellah appearing as the mere expression of his surrounding environment.[82] Thus, he argues, in Egyptian literary representations the peasantry came to embody the dialectic of man and nature, social mores, social conditions, and human conflict, and to express historical events, or the nature of government itself.[83] Never social actors in their own right, the peasantry were instruments for the representation of events, traditions, morals, and social conditions.

The peasantry was a central focus of nationalist writings, which led to the collective creation of a "myth of the fellahin"—a process analogous to the creation of "peasant icons" among Russian populists (*narodniki*).[84] Valorized as the embodiment of Egypt's heritage, the fellahin were portrayed by authors such as Salama Musa as the quintessence of cultural authenticity. Nationalist writers identified romantically with the peasantry, as the "true sons of Egypt"—the essence or origin of the nation—in part because of the importance of the specificity of place (the "uniqueness of the Nile Valley") within the nationalist imaginary. Realist novels such as Haykal's 1914 *Zaynab* (subtitled "*Manazir wa akhlaq rifiyya*," "Countryside Scenes and Manners"), and even autobiographical works, such as Taha Husayn's 1932 *al-Ayyam* (*The Days*), Tawfiq al-Hakim's 1937 *Yawmiyyat na'ib fi al-aryaf* (*Diaries of a Prosecutor in the Countryside*), or Sayyid Qutb's *Tifl min al-qarya* (*A Village Childhood*), resembled each other in their thick description of the natural beauty of the countryside, and of the manners and customs of rural life. Although idealized, these representations were nevertheless often brutally critical of village life, social mores, educational practices, folk religion, and superstitious practices.[85]

Human Geography: The Study of Rural Habitat

In tandem with ethnographic representations of the peasantry as the archetype of the Egyptian race, a parallel social scientific literature developed that took as its object the relationship between the geographical environment of Egypt and peasant modes of life. This field became known as human geography—those branches of geography concerned with the relation between human activity and geographical phenomena, such as the study of human establishments. In the early 1930s, human geography, which at that time was a predominantly European enterprise, animated much of the work of the Egyptian Royal Geographic Society. At the forefront of such research were the various taxonomical studies commissioned on human establishments, as the positivist project of formulating a science of the countryside emerged in studies of rural housing and village organization.

Throughout the interwar period, the RGS was involved in comprehensive attempts to survey the conditions of life in the countryside, in particular through work on human geography that included studies of rural housing, *'izab*, and village organization.[86] The society's human geographical studies began in the early 1920s and 1930s, most notably with the 1925 International Geographical Conference held in Cairo on the occasion of the fiftieth anniversary of the RGS. The "dual importance of this event, both from the point of view of the intellectual work and the advancement of science" led to the selection of many outstanding committee members.[87] In attendance were delegations from around the world and leading Egyptian officials and intellectuals such as Taha Husayn and Ahmed Lutfi Al-Sayyid. At an April 3 function to celebrate the society's anniversary, King Fu'ad received an honorary membership to the London Royal Geographical Society, Ahmed Hasanayn Bey received a medal from the Philadelphia Geographical Society for his Libyan explorations.[88] The RGS also mounted an exposition, which included a map by the Department of Public Hygiene tracing the routes of epidemics and diseases in Egypt; a miniature reproduction of the Suez canal, Isma'iliyya, and Port Said prepared by the Suez Canal Company; a reproduction of the barrages at Aswan, Isna, and Mazura produced by the Department of Irrigation; several physical relief maps of the Nile Valley prepared by the Survey Department; a collection of insects from the Entomological Society; specimens and drawings illustrating the transformations of cane into sugar by the Société des Sucreries et Raffineries d'Égypte; and a complete series of the different varieties of cotton, prepared by the Cotton Research Board.[89] The exposition itself exemplified the importance of agricultural production to geographical understandings of Egypt.

It was at the 1925 Congress that renowned French geographer Albert

Demangeon, a professor of geography at the Sorbonne, called for nations to cooperate and participate in the study of rural habitat.[90] The result was the International Geographical Union's formation of a Commission on Rural Habitat (which Demangeon presided over), which operated for a decade, until it merged with the organization's Commission on Population.[91] At the same Cairo conference, Demangeon presented what proved to be an influential paper on the effects of agrarian regimes upon modes of habitat in Western Europe.[92] Demangeon's conception of rural habitat was expansive, including the study of the rural house, peasant modes of agglomeration or dispersion, social and economic conditions of rural life, and the evolution of rural economies.[93] In fact, it has been argued that the study of rural habitat itself, which gained momentum during the interwar period, was in large part a result of the enthusiastic efforts of Demangeon.[94]

The next significant geographical congress attended by Egyptians was the one held in Cambridge in July 1928. Its importance lay in its principal theme of rural habitat; Egypt was to be the second nation (the first being Belgium) to commission a large-scale survey and study of rural housing.[95] Two smaller surveys of rural habitat had been undertaken in the 1920s— both in French-occupied North Africa by Augustin Bernard, a Sorbonne professor of geography who later was appointed by Fu'ad I to supervise an RGS publishing project in history and geography.[96] Bernard was a believer in the uplifting effects of the colonial project: "l'Européen aura ainsi rempli vis-à-vis de l'indigène son rôle d'initiateur, de grand frère bienfaisant, ce qui est la veritable objet et la raison d'être de la colonization."[97]

Demangeon himself had an interest in colonial geography, as evidenced by his 1925 text *L'Empire Britannique*, in which he traced the history, political-economic institutions, and overseas expansion of the British Empire. Demangeon's inquiry encompassed the genesis, tools, and results of British overseas colonization, and the final section of the text dealt with the problems and disintegration of empire.[98] Paul Claval has argued that the novelty of Demangeon's work lay in his examination of the effects of colonial contact upon the territorial and social structures and, concomitantly, on the spatial organization of the colonized.[99] Demangeon undertook to

> study the contact between two types of people who are to be associated in a colony: an advanced one, well provided with capital and material equipment and searching for new riches, spatially mobile, open to the notion of adventure, the unknown, and the exotic; the other closed in on itself, faithful to the old ways of life, with limited horizons. . . . Research consists of explaining how the colonizing people acted in order to exploit this domain, to create wealth, to dominate and use the natives, and how the colonized country, according to

its natural setting and the state of civilization of its inhabitants, reacted to the breath of the new spirit.[100]

The interwar interest in rural habitat was a component of the larger colonial concern for the study of the peasantry, invigorated on the one hand by the surge of peasant uprisings in French Indochina, Mexico, and the Middle East (Syria, Egypt, Iraq, Palestine), and on the other hand by the attempt to document, in the manner that Demangeon had suggested, the reaction of the colonized "to the breath of the new spirit."[101]

One of the scholars on the International Geographical Union's commission concerned with rural habitat was Albert Demangeon, who had gone to Egypt in order to survey in person the preparation for the rural questionnaire.[102] An Egyptian, Mustafa Maher Pasha (who we met in Chapter 1), presided over the Egyptian National Commission on Rural Habitat, and in charge of the survey were two young French members of the RGS who had trained at the University of Paris, Jean Lozach and Georges Hug. The objective of the survey was to cover all aspects of geography:

> The shape of houses, the nature of materials used for their building, and chiefly their position and density are at least in the country in sharp relation with the nature of soil, with water, and means of communications, and belong to Human Geography the aim of which is the study of intercourse between Man and Earth. For instance, was not the Egyptian village built on natural or artificial heights (*kom*) in order to protect it from the Nile flood? And as perennial irrigation replaced basin inundation are not these villages spreading all over the country, and settling small groups of peasant houses, which they call ezbehs? It is the human geographer's duty to study the reasons of this evolution, to see the direction and area; at the same time, he acquires a better knowledge of the country he lives in. . . .
>
> The enclosed queries constitute the basis of an inquiry, the aim of which is to study methodically and precisely the geographical economical, political, and ethnical reasons explaining the shape, disposition and chiefly the situation and the dissemination or concentration of the rural houses in Egypt.[103]

The questionnaire, distributed to all the provinces of Egypt, consisted of three sections: the house, the village, and relations between villages (including the '*izba* and relations between '*izab*).[104] Early in 1927, members of the RGS had the opportunity to review the rural-habitat questionnaire prior to its finalization.[105] As data were being collected and tabulated for the rural survey, members of the RGS were kept abreast of all details—translations, expenses, maps, and plans.[106] Questionnaires, in Arabic, French, and English, were distributed to village heads, large property owners, and agricultural engineers. With the assistance of Tharwat Pasha, the questionnaire was successfully distributed to all villages.[107] By February of 1928, close to 4,000 responses had been received. Lozach and Hug were pleased with the high rate of response, and conjectured that the anonymity afforded by the questionnaire made their respondents more willing to answer candidly.[108] The questionnaire responses were translated into French by the RGS secretary, Henri Munier, and Lozach and Hug visited various research sites to verify data and photograph the research sites.[109] The two researchers prepared a preliminary report for the 1928 International Congress at Cambridge (although they did not attend the meeting themselves), covering four provinces in Egypt, two from the Delta (Beheira and Gharbiyya) and two in Upper Egypt (Beni Suef and Fayum).[110] The final report was published in 1930 by Lozach and Hug, under the auspices of the RGS, as *L'habitat rurale en Égypte*.[111]

Lozach and Hug were influenced in part by the writings of Jean Brunhes, whose magnum opus, *La géographie humaine*, was a systematic elucidation of the objects and methods of human geography, and "an attempt at a positive classification."[112] In 1912 Jean Brunhes defined human geography as the study of the relation between human activity and geographical phenomena—with man himself understood as a geographical agent. Broadly understood as an ensemble of interconnected phenomena, the field included studies of the soil, climate, plant and animal life, travel, and human establishments.[113] For Brunhes, human geography should ally itself with the positivist scientific method entailing, above all, observation. Human geography was animated by the geographic spirit, which (although occasionally guided by the historical spirit) privileged space and place. That is to say, the geographical conditions of human activity—and its localization in space—was to be the primary object of study, rather than the origins and historical transformations of phenomena.[114] Despite this view, Brunhes maintained that the "house is not only a geographical fact, but also an historical fact."[115]

Brunhes's discussion of the "house in Egypt," which appeared almost two decades before Lozach and Hug's work, surveyed the geographical literature on Egypt. Brunhes pointed to the degree to which the ordinary Egyptian peasant house had gone unnoticed. Nonetheless, Brunhes recapitulated certain Orientalist conceptions, especially that of the unchanging stability of peasant life. Indeed, he went so far as to quote a description from Edward Lane's classic Orientalist text, *An Account of the Manners and Customs of the Modern Egyptians*, as evidence of the constancy of the peasant house.[116] His own observations of Egypt, however, were discriminating enough to distinguish between the north and the south. As Brunhes noted, the peasants, especially those of the delta, used unbaked bricks made of mud kneaded with water and left to dry in the sun, to build their houses, with or without a roof. Sometimes roofs were built with vaults, as in Upper Egypt, or with a little cupola (Delta). Brunhes ranked the crude houses of the delta as the simplest forms; followed by the craftsmanship of the Upper Egyptians—with their ability to bake bricks in a kiln and build vaults, and south of Aswan, to build houses with stone (cubical and with a single door in the front)—and finally, the more developed and almost artistic houses of the Fayum. "Everything is more trim, better finished, and we might almost say more artistic at Fayum. The house is of the same type as that of Egypt [sic]; but just as its approaches and annexes show more care, so the arrangements and details of its walls of pressed earth show a more developed taste and even art."[117]

Although sharing the north–south distinction (Upper and Lower Egypt), the work of Lozach and Hug had much stronger affinities with that of Albert Demangeon, who wrote the preface to their book. According to Demangeon, the distinctive feature of their text was their reconciliation of the facts of rural habitat with the facts of rural economy. In fact, in contrast to Orientalist representations of peasant life as remaining static for centuries, Demangeon himself had written a piece on Egypt that historicized rural life between 1875 and 1925.[118] Noting population increase and the penetration of European civilization (and the subsequent shift to commercial agriculture) as the two most influential forces affecting rural life, Demangeon traced the evolution of Egyptian agriculture—the shift from basin to perennial irrigation, the adoption of commercial fertilizers, transformations in cultivation techniques, the development of monoculture, the dramatic increase in private property ownership, and in particular, the shift from densely populated and concentrated villages (due to the constraints of corvée labor and collective taxes) to more dispersed forms of habitation, of which the self-contained farms or *'izab* were emblematic.[119]

Demangeon, as well as his students Lozach and Hug, were Vidalians. Vidalian geography was characterized mainly by a socially (rather than biologically) oriented conception of human geography. Following the lead of the prodigiously influential Paul Vidal de la Blanche, this important French school of geography took a less deterministic approach to human geography in which historical, social, and material conditions of existence, or milieu, rather than physical geography, played a fundamental and determining role. According to Paul Rabinow, milieux were "composite products of historical, geographical, ecological and demographic elements," and therefore socially constituted.[120] This allowed for the possibility of social amelioration, insofar as "living beings could be improved by ameliorating milieux."[121] Vidal also introduced the concept of *genres de vie* (modes of life) as a principal focus of human geography and emphasized rural and regional locales as units of geographical analysis.[122]

Divided into two books—Lower Egypt was covered by Lozach and Upper Egypt by Hug—*L'habitat rural en Égypte* was a comprehensive synthesis of the massive body of questionnaire data from the 1928 survey. Lozach's method was primarily descriptive, with romantic undertones; Hug's work was far more functionalist, at times historical (predominantly using economic forces as his explanatory criteria) and typological or classificatory. Strongly influenced by Demangeon, Hug adopted his mentor's hallmark method—the combination of typological and functionalist modes of analysis—as well as his economic determinism.[123]

Jean Lozach, a professor at the Royal School of Law in Cairo, took the transformations of the nineteenth century noted by Demangeon (and their effect upon peasant housing) as his principal research issue. Concerned chiefly with the disintegration of tradition—as embodied in collective work and life—and the urbanization of peasant tastes, needs, and desires, Lozach asserted that, in provinces located closer to Cairo, peasants had developed an urban *mentalité*. This in turn influenced housing, such that in those areas in proximity to city centers one found the juxtaposition of modern and traditional housing forms, and the emergence of a hybrid form. Perhaps, he argued, the primary feature of traditional peasant housing was the tendency toward dense agglomerations. In the twentieth century, and in areas north of Cairo, the tendency toward dispersion had become more pronounced. In these areas, smaller hamlets—groups of houses on the periphery of larger villages established by the state, by landed proprietors, or by peasants themselves—had begun to make an appearance. This disintegration of the densely knit village form led, according to Lozach, to the transformation of the spirit of the fellah, which he identified as a weakening of the collective spirit and of the attachment to specific geographic locales. In addition, the formation of modern *'izab* by large landowners included the creation of modern geometrical plans with uniform subdivisions. Indeed it was this excessive modernism that led Lozach to assert in a romantic tenor that, "in terms of actual evolution, Lower Egypt will reach a point in common with many of the rest of the European countries. It will then lose its originality and its picturesque and charming qualities. But, beauty and progress are rarely in accord."[124] Despite his lamentations, Lozach nonetheless found the solution for the creation of modern, hygienic peasant housing to lie with the formation of *'izab* by comfortable landowners.

Georges Hug, a graduate of history and geography at the Sorbonne, and a lecturer at the Faculty of Letters at the Egyptian University, had been trained by Demangeon and Emmanuel de Martonne, another Vidalian.[125] Focusing on Middle Egypt (Giza, Beni-Suef, Minya), Upper Egypt (Asyut, Girga, Qina, Aswan), and the Fayoum, Hug transformed the reams of questionnaire data into a systematic exposition of the modes of dwelling, habitation (*peuplement*), and agglomeration present in the Egyptian countryside. For Hug, the house and the various forms of agglomeration provided a translation of the social and economic conditions of individual peasants as well as of the countryside itself—the two factors he privileged above the brute facts of physical geography and climate. Continuously interrogating the relationships among architectural form, physical geography, conditions of agricultural production (systems of cultivation, irrigation, and land tenure), economic conditions of existence, and political regimes of power, Hug tried to explain such architectural facts as the existence of vaults only south of Isna and the expansion in the use of baked (red) brick in Middle Egypt.

Using historical evidence—in large part French travel accounts from after the Napoleonic invasion—Hug explicated architectural facts in a structural-functionalist fashion. Thus, for instance, the *herméticité* of the village house—its enclosure—was explained as both a cultural artifact (an exaggerated sense of propriety and the Oriental prejudice of male-female separation) and a historical artifact (an organ of defense against brigandage, nomadic invasions, revenge crimes, political instability, and the corruption of power in the pre-Napoleonic era).[126]

The most critical aspect of Egypt's rural habitat that Hug had to explain was the transformation of the countryside from dense and agglomerated villages to more dispersed forms of habitation.[127] The historically older pattern of concentrated villages—rooted in a combination of physical or geographic factors (for example, the need for collective surveillance efforts during Nile flooding), and political-agrarian regimes (and concomitant labor and taxation requirements, especially from the sixteenth to the eighteenth centuries) had, according to Hug, steadily given way under the reign of Mehmed 'Ali's *paix publique* to rural dispersion. Hug identified three principal causal factors: an agricultural revolution (the shift from basin to perennial irrigation); the advent of private property; and the establishment of agrarian capitalism. With the commercialization of agriculture—the advent of new systems of labor organization such as the *'izba*, new cultivation and irrigation techniques, and new crops such as cotton and sugar cane—an ensemble of forces worked to transform older village forms into a more dispersed format, in particular the semi-dense groupings of hamlets ('*izab* and *nag'a*) located in pastoral regions or alluvial regions bordering the desert. The creation of agricultural colonies, however, required central zones from which to market goods and services. This in turn created a centrifugal movement—and a new mode of habitat had evolved since the reign of Khedive Isma'il, as the older zones of cultivation gave birth to a new intermediate zone of habitat that united the original opposition between concentrated older villages and the dispersion of hamlets into boroughs. In fact, as argued by Hug, the Napoleonic expedition was a watershed in the transformation of the Egyptian countryside. In this classically Orientalist interpretation of Egyptian history, the Napoleonic invasion ushered in a significant series of events: the eventual downfall of the Mamluks and the rise of the Ottoman viceroy Mehmed 'Ali Pasha. This led to the subsequent modernization of Egyptian agriculture, industry, education, and society. As did Demangeon, Hug identified the progressive evolution of Egyptian agriculture with its increased Europeanization.

How did the taxonomical observation and classification by type of this French Vidalian geographic tradition affect Egyptian geography? According to Donald Reid, Francophone geography was unable to make serious inroads into Egyptian academic life, in part because of the early demise of French geographer Marcel Clerget's career, the 1926 replacement of Georges Foucart by British geologist W. F. Hume as president of the RGS, and the training of Egyptian geographers Mustafa 'Amir and Muhammad 'Awad by British geographer P. M. Roxby.[128] But perhaps Reid somewhat overstates his case. Even students trained in the tradition of British academic geography, such as 'Abbas Mustafa 'Ammar, referred to Lozach and Hug's canonical text, not to mention the countless references to their work as authoritative by other academics.[129] The influence of the French Vidalian school may be seen more generally in the trend toward social amelioration projects premised on the idea of social reform through the transformation of milieux, such as those of the Royal Agricultural Society and the Egyptian Association for Social Studies. Indeed, the French geographical tradition was supplanted in the field of peasant studies by an indigenous group of researchers who supplemented taxonomy and classification with in-depth field experiments, case studies, and community surveys geared not only at the observation and understanding of rural life, but also at the formulation of concrete social-engineering projects aimed at the moral and material uplift of the rural population.

. . .

In contrast with the descriptive studies discussed above, many of the Egyptian nationalist intelligentsia of the 1930s and 1940s viewed the peasantry as the ultimate object of social reform. Peasants were to be refashioned as national subjects and citizens. Many of the very same features that writers such as Ayrout denigrated were valorized by nationalist thinkers as part of the very fabric of Egyptian national life. And although much of the nationalist literature on the peasantry also denigrated "irrational" peasant customs such as superstitious practices, the reform of those practices was incorporated into a concrete framework of social engineering that entailed the education (*ta'lim*), cultivation (*tarbiya*), discipline (*tahdhib*) and social uplift (*tarqiya*) of the peasantry. As the social uplift of the peasantry was yoked to the nationalist project of social reform, reformers attempted to argue that understanding the *mentalité* of the peasant was important for creating viable reform projects. To reform the peasantry required an understanding of that "primal mass" that was to constitute the raw material of reform. To create model villages, then, one first had to create a model peasant, *al-fellah al-namudhaji*.[130]

4 Rural Reconstruction
The "Road to a New Sanitary Life"

I have just come back from a trip in the country and what unmistakable signs of revolution I saw: what indications of resentment and what unrest! I wish some of the Ministers, magnates, or feudal lords were with me to hear with their own ears how their names were mentioned. I wish they were with me when I went through the vast feudal estates of the Minister of the Interior and those of his relatives.

—*Ahmad Husayn*[1]

We could argue that it is always the specter of an open rebellion by the peasantry which haunts the consciousness of the dominant classes in agrarian societies and shapes and modifies their forms of exercise of domination.

—*Partha Chatterjee,* The Nation and Its Fragments

In 1932 two men from the village of Badari in Asyut Province in Upper Egypt, Ahmad Ja'idi and Hasan Abu 'Ashur, were charged with the murder of a rural superintendent (*ma'mur*). The convicted men made impassioned accusations of torture, which included multiple humiliations, privations, and brutalities that ranged from being bound, beaten, and dragged, to sodomy. As a legal case the incident highlighted the repression and torture of the peasantry at the hands of provincial notables, but the murder under scrutiny also underscored the peasant propensity toward "revenge" and the resulting potential vulnerability of members of the state apparatus and *kibbar al-mullak*, or the landed elite.[2] Indeed, there was sufficient cause for alarm that at the outbreak of World War II in 1939 the state ordered the removal of firearms from peasant households and even sequestered a group of known bandits in Jabal Tur.[3]

The incident at Badari illustrates the larger social context of the emergence of the "peasant question" as a discourse of social welfare and the reproduction of power relations. The reform of the Egyptian village and its inhabitants formed a principal locus of concern within the discourse of social reform.⁴ Beginning in the middle of the 1930s, a core group of Egyptian nationalist researchers and social reformers began to formulate social-scientific agendas that took the peasantry as their principal object of study and reform. In fact, the entire question of the educability, rather than stagnation (*jumud*), of the peasantry emerged at this time, as the call for a rural renaissance (*al-nahda al-qurawiyya, al-nahda al-rifiyya*) reached its apex in the mid- and late 1930s. Egyptian intellectuals often invoked graphic images of rural decay and criminality to demonstrate the urgency of social reform. Representations of uncivilized peasants served to rationalize both the expertise of social scientists and reformers and to underscore the civility of the urban *effendiyya* (Egypt's emergent middle class). It also enabled a series of positivist interventions geared at the creation of a *nahda rifiyya* (rural renaissance). Such reformist projects were meant to lead to the creation of new forms of social and spatial organization guiding the peasantry to "reformed" norms of behavior, modes of life, and social and cultural practices appropriate to the progress and civility of the modern world.

Indeed, the question of culture has been central to the construction of the "peasant problem" in multiple historical contexts. Most notably, in the Latin American context the question of the peasantry and its role in national culture and in the development of an economically efficient and productive modern nation-state has drawn considerable scholarly attention. Florencia Mallon has explored the significance of peasant struggles in nation-building projects in Mexico and Peru, and Mary Kay Vaughn has explored the cultural politics of the Mexican revolution by focusing on rural schools.⁵ Guillermo Palacios has noted, in the context of pre-Cárdenas Mexico, how the construction of *campesinidad* (peasant-ness) and attempts to construct the "new rural man" were bound up with differing interpretations of the role of culture in the state's projects of modernity by its emissaries—rural schoolteachers who were portrayed as the protagonists of a national drama.⁶ In keeping with revisionist interpretations of the Mexican revolution, Christopher Boyer has contended that in 1920s Michoacán "issues of land reform and cultural reconstruction came to constitute the key axes of negotiation between the state and peasant communities in the 1920s and 1930s."⁷ Kim Clark has argued that racial ideologies informed land policies in 1930s Ecuador, illustrating that debates on national development were textured by cultural conceptions of Indians as non-progressive and traditional.⁸

In Egypt, the social uplift of the peasantry was understood to involve a complex of social and cultural values that needed to be inculcated and cultivated; these included education (*al-tarbiya wa al-ta'lim*), civility and refinement (*tamadun*), culture (*'umran*), progress (*raqa*), and proper comportment (*adab*), and were thought to lead to the elimination of vice, depravity, wretchedness, and general decline. The village, writers claimed, was a microcosm of Egypt, so without its arousal, the nation would not be able to progress.⁹ "There is no doubt," claimed Mahumd Shakir Ahmad, "that the sight of the fellah's village and housing would greatly pain intellectuals. . . . .The village is, after all, a microcosm of our country. . . . They must think thoughtfully about its improvement. . . . for it to be on the road to a new sanitary life."¹⁰ Thus posed, the renaissance of the modern nation (*nahdat al-umma al-haditha*) was contingent upon the revival of the Egyptian village. One of the key elements in this transformation was the modification and revival of the built environment, or in the words of renowned writer and politician Muhammad Husayn Haykal, the creation of a *nahda 'umraniyya* (renaissance of the built environment).¹¹ In this body of writing the social uplift of the peasantry was yoked to the nationalist project of social reform. This corpus of knowledge directly informed various nationalist projects in which the peasantry became an object of social-scientific intervention and engineering.

A plethora of recent works have dealt with the question of prerevolutionary rural Egypt. Samah Selim focuses on the interconnection between the development of new literary genres, such as the novel, and the centrality of the figure of the Egyptian peasant; Amy Johnson focuses on rural reconstruction in pre- and postrevolutionary Egypt as a precursor to rural development; Mercedes Volait looks at the significance of the built environment to both rural and urban reform projects; and Sylvie Chiffoleau argues that rural reform signaled the medicalization of village life.¹² Rather than isolate the question of rural reform, however, I seek to situate the emergence of the "peasant question" within a set of broader social and political processes that took place throughout the second third of the twentieth century.¹³ The "peasant question," I argue, emerged in tandem with the "problem of population."¹⁴ Both questions were embedded within a discourse of social welfare and reform that may be related to an impending crisis in the social reproduction of labor power in the 1930s. The principal signs of this crisis were the increased impoverishment of the Egyptian fellah and the dramatic increase in rural crime in the 1930s and 1940s.¹⁵ As such, social reformers increasingly came to rely on discourses of positivist criminology, social hygiene and welfare, architectural modernism, and neo-Malthusianism to explain and remedy rural poverty and anomie.

The Undisciplined Rural Subject

Much of the rural reconstruction work that was undertaken in the 1930s and 1940s was a response to the need for greater control over the laboring agricultural population. The 1930s and 1940s were characterized by sustained rural violence, and the post-Depression era was, economically and politically, a difficult one for agricultural labor. As the need for more systematic mechanisms of control over the rural population arose, various rural reform projects were formulated that aimed at the holistic improvement of village life. As argued in the previous chapter, peasant studies emerged in Egypt in the interwar period because of the convergence of the struggle against British colonialism, the spread of capitalist relations of production in the countryside, and the wave of peasant rebellions against colonial powers. The peasantry, I argue, became ever more central to the social-scientific research agenda of 1930s and 1940s Egypt, as concerns grew about the frequently antagonistic relationship between peasants and landowners, which crystallized in the figure of the undisciplined rural subject. Discourses of social hygiene and positivist criminology emerged throughout this period as part of a discourse of social welfare meant to "regulate" peasant modes of life.

The undisciplined rural subject was seen by many to be the product of a specifically peasant character that entailed a propensity to violence and various forms of social anomie. Yet the increase in crimes both by and against property owners, and rural violence more generally, may be related to a crisis in the social reproduction of labor power, which had become acute by the 1930s. The years after 1929 were the years of the worldwide economic depression, and during this time agricultural wages fell an estimated forty percent.[16] The thirties were characterized by "violence and unrest," with increased activity of peasants, workers, and trade unions, student agitation and demonstrations."[17] This is, in part, related to what Abdel-Malek has called "a moat of injustices" that had left the rural population (the hardest hit by inflation) increasingly devastated in the wake of the Great Depression, especially by the final years of World War II.[18] Indices of rural economic depression during the WWII era are numerous and varied: a drop in national average income, a rise in prices, the fact that earnings of the average agricultural laborer did not even meet subsistence needs, a concomitant dramatic rise in agricultural rents, and an increase in sharecropping.[19] Thus, for example "[w]hereas in the United States in 1945 an average acre of farm land was worth the equivalent of less than ten days of the average farm worker's wages, in Egypt an equivalent farm land area claimed a price equal to about 20 years of the average worker's wages."[20]

Politically, the 1930s were volatile years. Between 1930 and 1933 the Sidqi regime was characterized by state violence, election fraud, and the general abrogation of constitutional rights. Isma'il Pasha Sidqi, often described as authoritarian, reactionary, and anti-constitutionalist (with an "iron-fist" policy), held close ties to the business community and consistently privileged their interests as well as those of the agrarian landowners over the working poor.[21] In 1936, with the Italians in Ethiopia and Cyrenaica, and following the death of King Fu'ad and the installation of his son Faruq, an Anglo-Egyptian treaty was signed by the nationalist and newly-elected Wafdist government (with Nahhas as prime minister once again); this established Egypt's legal independence but allowed for the continued military presence of British troops in the Suez, and Britain's right to defend Egypt in case of attack. Shortly thereafter the capitulations were finally abolished, at the 1937 Montreaux Convention.[22] During much of the period from 1936 to 1945, the Wafd was in power, although not without dissension and division.[23]

The convergence of independence from the British and the drive to build an indigenous capitalism in the post-1936 period led, as Robert Tignor has argued, to a "concern for the social costs of capitalist growth" on the part of Egyptian elite.[24] The reformist tenor of this period was evident in the platforms of the various political parties (the Wafd, the Sa'dist party, and the Kutla bloc), as well as in the general cultural climate. It is crucial to note that individuals of widely varying political orientations engaged in the politics of social welfare generally, and rural reform in particular—for example, Wafdists ('Abd al-Wahid al-Wakil), non-partisans (Dr. Ahmed Husayn), Liberal Constitutionalists (Hafiz Afifi Pasha), Royalists (Ali Mahir), and members of the National Renaissance Society (Mirrit Butrus Ghali), of Young Egypt (Ahmed Husayn), of the Muslim Brotherhood (Hasan al-Banna), and even of the royal family (Prince Umar Tusun). This illustrates the pervasiveness of social reform as a language of political and social debate, and its dominance as a discourse of power and social reproduction.

The situation in the countryside throughout the 1930s and 1940s was characterized by grave economic hardship and increased outbreaks of violence by peasants against landowners, *'ayan* (notables), and members of the state apparatus enforcing land foreclosures, debt acquisitions, and settlements.[25] Many writers complained that the increase in absenteeism among landowners had exacerbated class antagonisms and created an unsupervised rural environment.[26] An entire series of measures both before and after the British occupation (and beginning roughly in the second half of the nineteenth century) point to the increasing encroachment of the state into the countryside, and the exercise of control over agricultural land and labor.

Ranging from the establishment and spread of agricultural estates that "fixed" the peasantry to the land, to new forms of policing, criminal investigation, law enforcement, and adjudication of disputes, these changes enmeshed the peasantry into increasingly centralized systems of governance.[27] As Sayyid Ashmawi has argued, however, increased state repression and violence against peasants by landowners and the state did not end autonomous political action on the part of the peasantry; there remained multiple avenues for the expression of political dissatisfaction on the part of peasants.[28]

Rural violence, however, should not be understood to refer solely to violence by peasants. Large landowners, first and foremost, engaged in the politics of violence, or what Timothy Mitchell, following Michael Taussig, has referred to as a culture and economy of fear.[29] The general climate of fear in the countryside, so as to subjugate an erstwhile unruly peasant population, was achieved with coercion, threats, and actual violence (including torture and murder), as incidents of violent rural crime gained notoriety in the public press.[30] Even legal routes for the political organization of the peasantry were foreclosed by the elite. Law 85 of 1942 prohibited the formation of agricultural labor unions, on the premise that strikes by agricultural laborers would damage national welfare.[31] By the late 1940s and early 1950s, the situation between landowners and peasants bordered on incendiary. In the summer of 1951 several peasants attempted to express their discontent at the grossly exploitative practices of the Badrawi landowning family in the village of Bahut, only to be attacked by hundreds of police and later accused of spreading communism.[32]

According to Nathan Brown, there were two principal forms of resistance on the part of Egyptian peasants from 1882 to 1952: atomistic and communal. Brown characterizes atomistic action as "acts by individuals or small groups involving little coordination. . . . Atomistic activity consisted of attempts by individuals or small groups to strike out at local manifestations (and perceived injustices) of the prevailing order."[33] Atomistic acts, which included attacks on the persons or properties of figures of power, (*'umdas*, local notables, merchants, foreigners, landlords, village officials, external officials, agents of landowners, and so forth) were often violent crimes, such as murder, as well as so-called agrarian crimes (crop destruction, etc.).[34] Such acts were important for several reasons, argues Brown: because of their targets, because of the "conspiracy of silence" surrounding them, and because of their "newsworthiness," since they were seen as a direct threat to landowners.[35]

Communal acts, on the other hand, involved "instances in which peasants, acting in large numbers, take matters into their own hands to try to enforce their will. Such actions can truly be regarded as communal when they involve entire villages, estates, or significant sectors of them."[36] Such acts were generally unplanned and in response to specific threats to the community (a court order for the confiscation of land, raising of rents, arrest of a community member, decision to cut off water).[37] With the exception of the 'Urabi revolt and the 1919 revolution, communal action often centered around disputes over irrigation water, expropriation of land, and payment of rents.[38] Brown notes the structural basis of communal action—that is, the propensity of permanent peasant workers on commercial estates to act communally, whereas seasonal workers and commercial and subsistence smallholders were less likely to act communally.[39] The *'izab*, or commercial estates, were more prone to violence because of the system of obligations that existed between peasants and landowners, and disputes arising from them.

Rural reformers were acutely aware of these dispersed yet consistent acts of individual and collective violence committed by and against property owners and their agents. Without excessively romanticizing peasant resistance, we may simply note the dialectical relationship between the forms of peasant resistance and the modes of domination that came to enclose the countryside. Discourses of peasant "character," positivist criminology, and social hygiene were meant to address the dramatic increase in rural crime in the 1930s and 1940s and the impoverishment of the Egyptian fellah. In order to "regulate" peasant modes of life, various rural reform projects were formulated that aimed at the holistic improvement of village life. The "social uplift" of the peasantry thus served to keep at bay the crisis of the social reproduction of labor power and to deflect attention away from the radical restructuring of class relations, by emphasizing piecemeal and palliative reforms for the laboring classes.

Criminality and Peasant "Character"

A discourse of peasant "character" had since the beginning of the century linked the peasantry to pernicious habits such as drug addiction and theft, as, for example, in Muhammad 'Umar's turn-of-the-century *The Present State of the Egyptians or the Secret of their Retrogression (Hadir al-misriyyin aw sirr ta'khuruhim)*. The 1930s and 1940s, however, mark the beginnings of a discourse that centralized the production of statistical and substantive knowledge about peasant crime. For example, the Central Narcotics Intelligence Bureau began to collect data on the use of addictive substances as hashish, opium, and black tea, linking their use to criminality and other social ills. The collection of statistics on rural crime, and violent crime in particular, helped cultivate a discourse on peasant character that emphasized the fellah's lack of moral sense.

Criminological studies emerged in the late 1930s as Egyptian social scientists began to compile studies, statistical and descriptive, on the rate, prevalence, and types of crimes being committed. Two key texts published during World War II were Muhammad al-Qolali's *Essai sur les causes de la criminalité en Egypte* and Muhammad al-Babli's exhaustive study *Al-ijram fi Misr (Crime in Egypt)*.[40] Muhammad al-Babli's study was the canonical work on criminology at the time, extensively reviewing the methodological approaches to the study of crime and focusing in particular on the use of statistical data, as well as analyzing the various theories regarding the predisposing factors to criminality. When he wrote the book, al-Babli was the director of the School of Police, and had originally been trained and employed as a lawyer.[41] Al-Babli and al-Qolali were good friends and cooperated extensively in their research.

Criminology was part of a larger social and political process that occurred in tandem with the construction of the modern Egyptian state. As Nathan Brown has noted, this process included the redefinition of criminality, in part to address the increased mobility of the rural population as the need for migrant labor increased in the interwar period. In effect, Brown argues, the concept of crime was transformed from a local village concern to an issue of national importance. Thus, the monitoring, reporting, and adjudication of rural crime was centralized as a national and civic duty. The idea of justice was to be transformed from a familial or communal obligation to something dispensed at the level of the state. Brown sees this new state-sanctioned conception of criminality as divergent from preexisting notions of crime and justice, and it led to many conflicts of interest.[42] Indeed, as al-Babli noted, after 1919 attacks on members of the police and the state apparatus increased at a conspicuous rate.[43]

One of the hallmarks of criminological studies in Egypt was its sociological classification of criminality as either urban or rural. Studies of criminality reified notions of a unique peasant *mentalité* by dividing crime into urban and rural types. Each of these distinct types was considered to have a vastly different etiology and morphology from the other. On the whole, writers argued, urban crime was materially motivated, whereas the hallmark of rural crime was its violent and affective nature—crimes of revenge and passion. Social reformers such as al-Babli argued that peasant ignorance was a predisposing factor in rural crime.[44] The peasant's naturally patient and submissive character, it was often argued, was labile and could become vengeful at any moment, particularly because of his attachment to rural manners and customs (*adat wa taqalid*) such as *tha'r* or vendetta.[45] It was noted that crimes of passion (and not cupidity) were more common in Egypt than in the West. This tendency was more pronounced in the countryside, where "revenge" crimes (murder, assault, arson, destruction, poisoning of crops or livestock) were far more common than crimes whose aim was material gain.[46] In a 1940 article addressing the specific nature of rural crime, Muhammad al-Qolali, characterized urban crimes (which accounted for the majority of convictions in Cairo, Alexandria, and Suez) as materially motivated, and as relegated to a particular class of individual, namely the urban criminal. Rural crime, on the other hand, was characterized by cruelty (*al-qaswa*).[47]

What, then, were the motives behind rural crime? "Revenge is the blood wound in the social life of the countryside."[48] Most rural crime, even against property, was believed to be motivated by revenge or by the preservation of self or honor. Thus, the most discussed aspect of rural crime by far was the custom of *tha'r*, or vendetta, understood as retribution for a breach of familial or personal honor. *Tha'r* was considered especially pernicious because it widened individual feuds to a family level. Factionalism was another aspect of rural life that was seen as exacerbating criminality because it allowed individual disputes to escalate to the level of families or moieties.[49] Writers emphasized the triviality of the motives behind rural crime. Peasant crimes, they noted, were often caused by petty disputes, arguments, or minor thefts, usually revolving around land, water, crops, or livestock.[50]

Peasant habits, too, were implicated in rural crime. In particular, the culture of the coffee houses, with its attendant social evils, was thought to play a major role in the moral decadence of the peasantry. The peasantry was thought to have a strong propensity toward addiction to narcotics such as hashish, opium, and black tea.[51] In the coffee houses, peasants stayed out late "killing time," gambled, and were exposed to various narcotics and professional criminal elements. Nevertheless, addiction to substances such as alcohol, hashish, opium, morphine, heroin, and cocaine was thought to be limited to certain small pockets in the rural community. The far more prevalent and destructive rural addiction was black tea—potent, unregulated, often adulterated and consumed by children and adults alike in vast quantities.[52] "Black tea" was used to refer to the product obtained from boiling a quantity of tea leaves and water in a kettle: "during the next twenty-four hours the kettle is never cleaned out but more tea leaves and more water are added with the result that all the so-called tea leaves are boiled six or seven times over producing a black, bitter liquid to which large quantities of sugar must be added."[53] The concern over boiled tea, as well as its commercial adulteration, was serious enough that by 1938 the Ministry of Public Health commissioned a scientific study on tea as bought, prepared, and consumed by the fellahin; the study concluded that although the amounts of caffeine and tannin were proportional to the amount of tea used and not dependent on the length of boiling, the sheer quantity of caffeine consumed by the Egyptian peasant on a daily basis was sufficient to be deleterious to his health, given his physical environment and influences (the presence of endemic diseases, the lack of nutrition, and excessive labor).[54]

Tea itself came to be viewed by social reformers as a narcotic substance because its effects mimicked those of any other addictive substance: nervous and physical stimulation (not dissimilar to cocaine's effect, and resulting, in cases of excessive and continuous use, in trembling of hands, insomnia, and heart failure); psychological and physical dependence; decreased productivity; and even a propensity to criminal activity.[55] Authorities viewed tea consumption as a lowerclass phenomenon, and marveled at the proportion of income spent on tea by the average peasant household—income that could have been spent on foodstuffs. According to an estimate, the efficiency of the worker was reduced by 25 percent, "based on the time lost and the fact that the tea-drinker is not as able a workman as the non-drinker."[56]

Both al-Babli and al-Qolali continuously resorted to discussions of *mentalité* to explicate rural crime. Social and economic factors play a surprisingly negligible role in their analysis. This was despite the statistical correlation that al-Babli noted between crimes committed and agricultural seasons (crime rates increased during harvesting and storage season), or as Tawfiq al-Hakim phrased it in *Yawmiyyat na'ib fi al-aryaf*, every crop had its crime.[57] Nor did reformers view peasants' unwillingness to cooperate with authorities in prosecuting criminals as a political act. According to al-Qolali, there was more than a fifty-percent chance for criminals to evade the law.[58] Above all, social researchers found the use of brigands or bandits (*al-ashqiya'*) most disturbing, but did not link it to social or economic struggles.[59] Rather than view peasants' refusal to cooperate with the authorities as a deliberate strategy, in keeping with older conceptions of crime and justice, reformers viewed this instead as a problem of ignorance. Similarly, crimes against the persons and properties of landowners or their agents (especially, the so-called agrarian crimes—arson and destruction or poisoning of crops or livestock) were viewed not as crimes that masked class violence or social struggle, but rather as the remnants of an archaic tradition of revenge or vendetta crimes. In fact, al-Babli went so far as to dismiss the potential effects of revolutionary Soviet communist propaganda, saying that Egyptians by nature were not amenable to it.[60]

The closest al-Babli came to social and political analysis was in his discussions of the improvements in methods of communication and transport in the aftermath of World War I, and of the intense politicization of the countryside inaugurated by the 1919 revolution. Such transformations, he argued, had made the fellah more aware of "civilized" life, as well as of his own relative simplicity.[61] Thus, urban migration was thought to have contributed to rural crime in two principal ways. First, easier and cheaper systems of transport from the countryside to the city meant more peasant mobility, and a desire for frequent movement—dislocating peasants from their worldviews and setting in motion social anomie. Second, urban migration was foremost a privilege of the medium and large landowners, who as absentee landlords became unable to monitor the criminal activities of "their" peasants.[62]

What was the solution to peasant criminality? The primary causes of peasant's irrational behavior were ignorance and a lack of *sens moral*, so it followed that through moral and social education (*tathqif*, *tarbiya*) peasants could develop their reflective and rational capacities, as well as their sense of social responsibility.[63] It was hoped that newly formed institutional frameworks such as the Ministry of Social Affairs' Fellah Department would take the initiative in the education of the peasantry, eliminating such social customs as the coffee house and poetic and folk traditions that glorified heroic acts of vengeance. Once peasant ignorance and illiteracy were remedied through a proper upbringing (*tarbiya*), the problem of rural crime could be addressed, and the peasantry would return to their natural contented state.[64]

Model Villages, Model Peasants

Positivist criminology was a central component of discourses on the "peasant question," but by far the most discussed aspects of rural reform in the 1930s and 1940s were the discourses of social welfare and architectural modernism embedded in rural reconstruction. Raising the mental, moral, and material standards of the peasantry through the combat of pernicious superstitions, manners, and customs, the development of village housing, sanitation, and hygiene, and the formation of cooperative societies were all interventions that rural reformers began to discuss and implement in the 1930s. These efforts crystallized in the development of the "model village" as a reproducible prototype across the Egyptian Delta.

The history of model villages began in 1847 under Mehmed 'Ali, when he assigned a French technical commission, which included renowned physician Antoine-Barthélemy Clot Bey, to develop three types of village housing, which were then constructed in the Nile Delta villages of Kafr al-Zayyat, Negileh, and Ghezay.[65] Taking two years to complete, the villages were built in a rectilinear fashion with wide, tree-lined streets, and were provided with a school, a hospital, and public bathrooms.[66] As a twentieth-century commentator later noted, the villages were endowed with a uniformity and order "rare for the Delta," only to eventually return to "their primitive state" (as was the case with Ghezay).[67]

A second, and more pertinent, development in the history of model villages in the nineteenth century was the emergence and spread of large landed estates (*'izab*) in the 1860s and 1870s, which signaled a new form of power over rural space, movement, and labor.[68] The *'izab* were, in effect, self-contained private villages. The term *'izba* originally referred to the temporary straw huts built by agricultural laborers for shelter, but eventually came to refer to a form of "capitalist agricultural colony," in the words of Georges Hug.[69] These colonies contained their own housing complexes for workers, which were eventually planned and supervised, thus reordering the space of the estate itself. According to Timothy Mitchell, this process of ordering and modifying rural space was coeval with the emergence of the private ownership of land, and was part of the attempt to directly control the agricultural process, and in particular the movement of agricultural laborers.[70] Crucially, it also entailed the transformation of the physical landscape of Egypt, including not only the development of the *'izba* system, but also the building of canals and dams, and the shift to perennial irrigation, illustrating the preeminence of geography to the reengineering of the social and physical world of peasants.

Thus, the transformations of the nineteenth century were embodied in the new forms of social control exercised in the countryside over land, labor, housing, and agricultural produce.[71] It is these transformations that mark the emergence of the *'izba* system, and, more specifically, of the attempt to "fix" peasants and Bedouins to the land, thereby establishing a closer and more pervasive social control over the rural population. As such, the emergence of the rural estate may be seen as part of a more efficient set of practices and arrangements that worked to concentrate and contain the peasantry, curbing the excessive mobility of the rural population. In short, the history of the *'izab* was inextricably linked to the creation of a disciplined rural labor population. Such a process of discipline, entailing fixity, concentration, and containment, was a necessary precursor to the creation of a rural labor market, and historically preceded discourses that focused on social hygiene and positivist criminology.

As noted, the *'izab* were more prone to outbursts of peasant violence than were other rural areas. Indeed, following the 1919 revolution, the image of the peasant figures prominently within the colonial and elite archive as potential Bolshevism. The post-Depression era was a difficult one for agricultural laborers. It is not accidental, then, that many rural reconstruction projects were often conceived of as modifications to the *'izba* complex.[72] Various rural reconstruction projects took place in Egypt in the 1930s and 1940s under both governmental and private auspices. Governmental institutions such as the Ministry of Agriculture, the Department of Rural Affairs, and later the Fellah Department, began programs such as the Ministry of Public Health's "program for the reorganization of villages and the improvement of peasant housing." Non-governmental interventions included those of the Royal Agricultural Society, the Egyptian Association for Social Studies, and the Jesuit Fathers. Such projects were prototypes for the more systematized rural reconstruction work undertaken by the Ministry of Social Affairs in the 1940s and 1950s, such as the Fellah Department's large-scale project known as "rural social centers," as well as the "combined units" of the Nasser era.

The model-village programs of the 1930s and 1940s were characterized by several innovations. Whereas earlier attempts to transform Egyptian village life had focused on the transformation of the built environment and the spatial reorganization of village life, rural reconstruction in the 1930s to the 1960s aimed at creating model peasants by reconstructing bodies and minds, constructing a "new Egyptian" as much as reordering the built environment.[73] Model villages are an example of what James Scott refers to as "miniaturization: the creation of a more easily controlled micro-order in model cities, model villages, and model farms."[74] Once replicated in Egypt's 4,000 villages, these miniatures led to the legibility and simplicity so characteristic of modern statecraft and its visualization of the public sphere.[75]

The Royal Agricultural Society: Bahtim Village

The Royal Agricultural Society (hereafter RAS) was among the first non-state institutions to initiate model village programs. Founded in 1898 under Sultan Husayn Kamil I, who served as the Society's president from 1898–1914, the society was concerned with the general improvement of agricultural methods and "the lot of the fellah," and its work encompassed both the practical and scientific aspects of agriculture. The society's goals included improving agricultural methods, organizing agricultural credit, encouraging the creation and management of agricultural syndicates, and augmenting the income of the fellah.[76] The RAS also organized agricultural expositions; for example, it undertook the creation of an agricultural museum in 1920, which was modified into a cotton museum and opened to the public in 1926. In 1939, plans were proposed for the "Fu'ad I Agricultural Museum," which surveyed developments in agricultural production (cotton, seeds, machinery) and agricultural housing, from the reign of Mehmed 'Ali onward.[77] As with the Royal Geographic Society, museum culture was an integral component of the representation and display of Egypt's civilizational progress within a teleological framework.

The RAS had been active in encouraging the development of model farms and housing on *'izab* by private landowners, sponsoring general competitions, and distributing prizes and medals. The model *'izab*, in keeping with the original model villages and estates of the nineteenth century, were rectangular, with gridlike blocks of housing, similar to those of the royal family in Inshas, Idfina and Kafr al-Shaykh.[78] Since 1924 the RAS had awarded prizes for the overall best-kept farms or *'izab*. Several prominent landowners and members of the royal family were recipients of prizes, demonstrating that noblesse oblige still had its place in the twentieth century.[79] Beginning in 1939, to encourage those who could not reconstruct their entire *'izba* or village to emulate the model rural housing of the *'izab*, prizes were awarded to villagers and landowners for modifications or improvements in the following categories: construction and architecture, hygiene, and social institutions.[80]

Three model farm villages were constructed by the RAS in 1934, 1936, and 1941 at Bahtim Village, located in the Delta province of Qalyubiyya. The project at Bahtim was very much the creation of Fu'ad Abaza Pasha, the dynamic director-general of the RAS and a member of a large landowning family from Sharqiyya. Like other reformers of his time, Abaza conceptualized rural reform as a total social plan that would encompass the improvement of peasant housing, health reform, educational reform, and the raising of the social and economic standard of living of the peasantry.[81] Another problem to be tackled was low agricultural productivity, which was attributed to the lack of agricultural guidance.[82] Bahtim was seen as an experimental field for technical, agricultural research, and as a practical demonstration of the link between increased agricultural productivity and the revival of the agricultural laborer and the improvement of the countryside.[83]

The first farm village was inaugurated in November of 1934. It spanned more than three *feddans* and included thirty houses for laborers, three for overseers, and one for a farm manager, in addition to public buildings (a mosque, a school, an assembly hall, and public baths).[84] Father Ayrout described the village as follows:

> The dwellings run from North to South in five rows, and each row is divided into two groups by a street, widening into a square in the middle. Between each pair of rows there is a street six yards wide, so that sunlight can penetrate into every dwelling.
>
> The houses are of red brick, with concrete ceilings, and the floors are raised a foot above street level. The roof is about thirteen feet from the ground. Twenty of the houses are two-roomed, with a yard inside and a shed for cattle. . . .
>
> Six baking ovens have been built outside the housing area, so that the smoke may not trouble the inhabitants. They are used by all families in turn. There are also six shower baths, four for men and two for women, together with laundry facilities.
>
> The village hall will hold seventy people; it is used for feasts, marriages and funerals. The mosque covers 600 square feet. The school, which follows the syllabus for compulsory elementary education, is open to boys and girls. Shops have been opened so that people may buy what they want on the spot, and there is a great enclosure with six depots for storing the various crops, fodder for the animals and agricultural implements.[85]

The spatial nature of the plan was geometric, rectilinear, and grid-like, demonstrating the principles of simplification and legibility in the transformation of rural space. In addition, the creation of a village hall was part of the attempt to create a centralized space for village sociability.

The total cost of the experiment was prohibitive, and therefore could not serve as a model for private persons (large landowners) to emulate.[86] It was decided that a cheaper model village be built on a one-*feddan* plot 600 meters from the original site. In searching for something more economical, the RAS decided on replacing baked (red) brick with raw or unburnt (mud) brick, an idea that was confirmed for Abaza when he saw similar housing in California and Arizona on a trip to the United States in the summer of 1939.[87] The 1934 estate thus became known as the "red '*izba*," and the 1936 one as the "green '*izba*."

Planning for the second farm was begun early in 1936, and work commenced in October of that same year. The architect commissioned for the village was Mustafa Bey Fahmi, a graduate of the École des Ponts et Chaussées in Paris who is considered Egypt's first modern architect.[88] Indeed, it is significant that two of the architects who worked on Bahtim, Mustafa Bey Fahmi and Hassan Fathy, were major figures in the development and modification of architectural modernism in Egypt throughout the twentieth century.[89] Fu'ad Abaza described the new village in terms nearly identical to those of Father Ayrout, emphasizing the geometrical layout of the village, which was meant to ensure "a maximum amount of sun penetrating the houses."[90] The cost of the individual houses had been reduced to five times the original price. As Abaza noted, "these houses, providing sufficient accommodation for the needs of the Fallah and his family, sanitary arrangements and other amenities, are calculated to ameliorate the conditions under which he has lived in the past and generally to improve his health and well being."[91]

A key ideological component of rural social reform throughout this period was the firm belief, in the words of Father Ayrout, "that matter determines form."[92] As such, Bahtim was meant to be more than the provision of low-cost housing for peasants; rather, the transformation of peasant space was meant to ensure the overall well-being of the peasantry. The development of model homes was a direct response to the arresting visual image—repeated continuously in the first half of the twentieth century—of the fellahin living side by side with animals in "aggregations of dirty, badly ventilated mud houses, intersected by narrow lanes encumbered with dirt and dung."[93]

> [The RAS] feels that it has proved that definite steps can be taken by even the smallest landowners to do their part to rescue the great majority of the nation from that apathy and rot which is undermining the health and strength of the agricultural worker, and to place him in a position in which he can hold his head high and take his place in the life of the nation with pride, realizing that he is an essential factor in the country's progress.[94]

At a reception given in December of 1941 at the Main Hall of Bahtim's new social center, Abaza spoke on the social and economic aspects of rural reconstruction.[95] The Bahtim project had made possible the provision of social services (such as social and agricultural guidance; educational, health, and religious services; and maternal and child health care) precisely because it provided a series of public spaces (in the form of a centralized social center) for such guided communal activities to take place.[96]

The final model estate in Bahtim, 'izbat Abu Rajab, was built in 1941 by internationally celebrated Egyptian architect Hassan Fathy.[97] At the time Fathy was a young graduate of l'Ecole Supérieure des Beaux-Arts, and had recently exhibited his mud-brick designs at the 1937 Mansuriyya Exhibition. One of those designs was to become the prototype for 'izbat Abu Rajab.[98] The work of Hassan Fathy illustrates the tension between the ideas of social reform as a positive scientific project (leading to the creation of reproducible modular types) and as a culturally specific moral project of social uplift. Fathy's ideas and corpus were a fusion of romantic ideas and positivist social-engineering projects, in particular the creation of a "science of human settlements" (later known as "ekistics"), illustrating how such dichotomies as positivism and romanticism continuously broke down in practice. Fathy, who was to become renowned for his use and valorization of indigenous building materials (such as mud brick) and designs (such as the use of vaults), is a more complex figure than he has been represented. He was neither a champion of the rural poor nor a ruthless social reformer. Rather, his work presented a viable critique of architectural modernism and an idealization of the vernacular, but it was ultimately an elitist vision of how the subaltern masses should live.

Committed to the application of scientific method to environmentally sound designs, Fathy was also enamored with the beauty of vernacular architecture. According to biographer James Steele, six general principles lay at the foundation of Fathy's work: "belief in the primacy of human values in architecture; the importance of a universal rather than a limited approach; the use of appropriate technology; the need for socially oriented, co-operative construction techniques; the essential role of tradition; and the re-establishment of national cultural pride through the act of building."[99]

Fathy, who already early in his career was developing his ideas regarding the superiority of vernacular architecture and indigenous building materials, was the ideal choice for the project at Bahtim, especially given the fact that the RAS had already turned to unbaked brick to meet the requirements of low-cost and hygienic housing for peasants. The years 1940 and 1941 were prolific ones for Fathy, as during that time he designed a number of villas and traveled around the delta with his "itinerant band of masons" testing out his building methods in several rural farms and villages.[100] The Bahtim farm was built as a self-contained complex,

> consist[ing] of housing, a stable for cattle, granaries, and a pigeon-cote, all organized within a boundary wall with one main gate. To provide a large open area for the cattle and to zone this area away from the living quarters, elements are once again strategically manipulated to provide specialized usage of open space. The granaries, which are of necessity very high for adequate natural ventilation as well as maximum storage capacity, become the dominant forms of composition. . . . Both the housing and the stables were designed with flat roofs to be framed with wood in the conventional way, which presented no technical problem, but the vaults and domes of the granaries were another matter.[101]

In his memoirs, *Architecture for the Poor*, Fathy recounts his early experiences with the use of mud brick, especially for building domes and vaults in Bahtim. To create model low-cost housing for the peasantry, Fathy put his faith in the most abundant indigenous building material: mud. According to Fathy, the fact that peasant homes were "cramped, dark, dirty and inconvenient" was not the fault of the mud brick, and "nothing that could not be put right by a good design and a broom."[102] He often bitterly struggled to convince proponents of red brick that, furthermore, building material itself did not dictate progress and advancement.[103]

Fathy's reliance upon this low-cost building material would eventually lead to conflicts with one of Egypt's most powerful contractors, Osman Ahmed Osman, who lobbied against Fathy in order to promote the use of steel and concrete, which would have maximized his construction profits.[104] For the project at Bahtim, which was undertaken during the war when building materials were scarce, Fathy intended to use mud bricks for both the walls and the roofing. The search for a technique to use mud for roofing vaults and domes would lead Fathy on a quest that would ultimately help define his career as an architect.

> Normally, to roof a room with a vault, the mason will get a carpenter to make a strong wooden centering which has to be removed when the vault is made; this is a complete wooden vault, running the full length of the room, held up by wooden props, and on which the courses of the masonry vault will rest while being laid.
>
> But besides being elaborate and requiring special skill to insure [sic] that the voussoirs are pointing toward the center of the curve, this method of construction is beyond the means of peasants. It is the kind of thing used in building a bridge.
>
> Then I remembered that the ancients had built vaults without such centering, and I thought I would try to do the same. About this time I was asked to do some designs for the Royal Society of Agriculture, and I incorporated my new ideas in these houses. I explained my wishes to the masons, and they attempted to put up my vaults without using centering. The vaults promptly fell down.[105]

Repeated trials brought no success, and a dejected Fathy turned to his elder brother, who at that time was under commission to work on the Aswan dam. His brother noted that Nubians were roofing their houses and mosques by building vaults that stood up during construction without the use of wooden supports. "Perhaps the answer to all of my problems, the technique that would at last let me use the mud brick for every part of the house, was awaiting me in Nubia."[106] Returning to Bahtim with Nubian masons, Fathy was finally able to complete the project, exemplifiying the importance of indigenous practical knowledge, or what Scott refers to as *mētis*, in the man-made adaptation to the natural environment.[107] Fathy was indeed in the vanguard of architectural theory and practice in his attempt to combine architectural innovation and scientific principles, with vernacular architecture—itself a countercurrent within twentieth-century movements of architectural modernism.

To one contemporary observer much impressed by Fathy's work at Bahtim, this experiment represented the attempt to formulate a pragmatic, economic, and rational adaptation of the vernacular—one that accentuated the Egyptian or Nilotic character of the rural built environment.[108] Indeed, the notion of vernacular peasant architecture as scientifically valid was developed by Fathy in both *Architecture for the Poor* and *Natural Energy and Vernacular Architecture: Principles and Examples with Reference to Hot Arid Climates*.[109] Fathy, although a proponent of social planning and scientific method, remained distinct from the architectural modernism of the International Movement in several ways. First, Fathy aimed for the unity of man and nature, in what he called the "God-made environment." Hence, he valorized the vernacular as the embodiment of the unity of man with his environment. Second, Fathy privileged proper functioning over form "in the human not the mechanistic sense."[110] Third, rather than being interested in a continuous attempt to express the contemporary and the modern, Fathy was fascinated with origins—in particular the historical continuity of the building techniques and methods of the ancient Egyptians. Fourth, Fathy rejected the repetitive uniformity of the modern movement, aiming instead for housing that was varied and individualized in character.

Fathy was eventually afforded the opportunity in 1945 to realize his dream "to build a village where the fellaheen would follow the way of life that I would like them to."[111] His success at Bahtim led to his selection by the Egyptian Department of Antiquities to head a project to relocate the village of Gourna, originally located on the site of the Tomb of the Nobles near Luxor in Upper Egypt. Some seven thousand Gournis were to be relocated, clearing squatters from the site of the necropolis. Fathy considered the village to be a model project in the sense of being an embodiment of "standards markedly higher than those prevailing before" and a "prototype to be repeated."[112] The story of Gourna, its architectural innovations and visions, and its ultimate failure has been told elsewhere and continues to be the subject of debate as the Egyptian government continues to attempt to demolish the village of New Gourna.[113] In brief, the Gourna project was never completed. Fathy, caught between the government that commissioned him and the peasants he was meant to relocate, faced continuous obstacles: Machiavellian machinations and bureaucratic intrigues at the Department of Antiquities; difficulties obtaining basic supplies; unwilling Gournis who were loathe to leave their original village (and the profitable antiquities trade there); the outbreak of a cholera epidemic in 1947; and a flooding of the new village.[114] Eventually the project was abandoned, and allegations circulated that the project at Gourna had been too costly, that mud brick was an inappropriate building material, and that Gournis had not wanted to relocate to the new village.[115] Even today adaptations of Fathy's designs are visible: residents have sealed up the wind catches, covered courtyards, and rebuilt collapsed domes with reinforced concrete.[116] Fathy continued to work in Egypt, however, designing villas under private commission and participating (along with several other influential architects, notably Sayyid Karim) in a government-commissioned committee for village planning in the early 1950s.[117] In 1956 the architect left Egypt for Athens, joining the firm of Constantinos Doxiades, where he was assigned to work on a housing project in Iraq.[118]

The Egyptian Association for Social Studies

The Egyptian Association for Social Studies (EASS), founded in 1936, was involved in social research, the training of social specialists, and experimental social studies such as village reconstruction projects and the reform of juvenile delinquents.[119] In October of 1937 the association also founded the Cairo School of Social Work (CSSW), whose mission was the modern scientific training of specialists to study social problems, and the uplift of various populations through the provision of social services.[120] The school's curriculum was created bearing in mind Egypt's most important social issues, such as health and rural issues, workers' problems, juvenile delinquency, and village reconstruction. The three-year program included two years covering twelve subjects, with the third year devoted to practical training and conducting social studies.[121] The CSSW was active in both governmental and non-governmental associations involved in social work activities, and it provided assistance in the form of information, lectures, and written reports.[122]

With thirty teachers and an initial student population of 50, the school had grown to around 150 students in the early 1940s (30 of whom were female).[123] The topics of instruction included general psychology; personal health and first aid; mental health; public health; sociology and economics; rural issues; means of social service; the organization of social service agencies in Egypt; workers' problems and social anomie; juvenile delinquents and handicapped children; and social statistics. Students received practical training in affiliation with various social agencies in Egypt. For example, students would take individual cases that had been transferred to the school from the Ministry of Social Affairs, in keeping with the school's policy that each student specialize in a particular facet of social service. Students in their third year wrote theses on social issues, taking on topics as varied as "Vagabondage in Egypt," "Social Research in an Egyptian Village," and "Play as a Means of Uplifting the Social Life of the Poor."[124] At the completion of their course of study, students took a social-service diploma examination supervised by the Ministry of Education. Successful graduates of the school were employed in various fields of Egyptian social services, both private and governmental, such as the Labor Department, Fellah Department, Social Relief Fund, and other divisions of the Ministry of Social Affairs.[125]

One of the strongest components of social service was the study of rural issues. CSSW volunteers undertook numerous studies in the Ministry of Social Affairs' rural social centers. In order to better prepare their graduates for the administration of these centers, the school solicited various of its graduates who were in the Ministry of Agriculture to create a program that encompassed those aspects of social service peculiar to the countryside.[126] The pinnacle rural programs of the EASS were the experimental village projects undertaken in the Delta between 1939 and 1941. The projects were based on principles of scientific and practical experimentation and were meant "to discover through careful observation, study and experimentation, the best possible technique for raising the standard of living in the Egyptian village. An attempt is being made to conduct this experiment on social policy along scientific lines based on the principles of hygiene, economics, sociology, social psychology and philanthropy."[127]

According to Dr. Ahmed Husayn, an agricultural economist and one of Egypt's leading experts on rural reform, the foundational principles of reform projects were that rural reform must take economic, social, cultural, and health factors simultaneously into consideration; reform efforts must be simple and uncomplicated for villagers and not costly; and peasants themselves must be fully convinced of the value of the reform efforts.[128] Two villages in the Delta region were initially chosen for the experiments: Al-Manayil, located in Qalyubiyya Province, and Shatanuf, located in Menufiyya Province. Energies were concentrated on Al-Manayil, with its 1,700 inhabitants, malaria epidemic, and lack of most basic necessities; Shatanuf, a larger village with approximately 5,000 inhabitants, was already endowed with social and economic amenities. Reconstruction work began in both villages in October of 1939.[129]

The original plan for the research on the villages was actually formulated by Wendell Cleland, a professor at the American University in Cairo and among the first to comment extensively upon Egypt's population problem. As a first step, detailed studies of all aspects (social, economic, educational, hygienic) of village life were compiled, social surveys were conducted of all families in the village, and complete medical examinations were made of all villagers.[130] In each village the project then establisehd a social center supervised by a social worker (a graduate of the CSSW); a maternal and child welfare center supervised by visiting nurses (graduates of Qasr al-'Ayni hospital), who were assisted by local midwives (trained for six months); and a health unit for endemic diseases founded by the Ministry of Public Health.[131] Services included reconciliation committees to arbitrate village disputes, and religious-reform committees to organize sermons and supervise religious festivities.[132]

The eradication of illiteracy and the generalization of primary education were critical components of these new efforts to reform the rural population.[133] Critics complained that only a small percentage of children who should be receiving compulsory education were actually enrolled in rural schools.[134] The educational curriculum itself was thought to be at fault, given its excessively abstract and theoretical content, far removed from the quotidian requirements of a peasant's livelihood. Proposals for educational reform suggested a two-pronged curriculum consisting of the basic requirements of knowledge—Arabic, arithmetic, Qur'an (or religious training), and general knowledge—on one hand, and on the other, a practical and vocational component that included training in agricultural and artisanal techniques, household handicrafts, and, for females, a working knowledge of the requirements of sanitation, health, hygiene, and household management.[135]

A successful example of this type of reform was the experimental rural school established by the EASS in the village of Al-Manayil. The villagers in Al-Manayil had drawn up a petition to the Ministry of Education requesting that a school be established in their village. The request was approved, and the villagers themselves drained and filled the pond at the site where the school was built. Education was structured with a core syllabus, along with outdoor workshops providing the vocational training thought necessary to creating a "good and happy citizen, useful and capable of serving his country."[136] Activities "suitable for country-dwellers" were chosen: "The boys worked in the fields and workshops, planting crops, vegetables, etc., starting a garden or dairy farming, breeding animals, bees, making furniture . . . and weaving cotton and rugs. The girls took silk culture . . . fruits and vegetable preserving, sewing and poultry."[137] Students also used a four-acre "model experimental field" where they were educated in natural history and agricultural practices. As a prototype, the Al-Manayil experiment proved influential in the reorganization of rural education that was undertaken by the Ministry of Education in 1942.[138]

A meeting hall was also established in Manayil, as well as a series of novel interventions: workshops for youths, cooperative societies, a women's campaign, and a village cleanliness campaign.[139] Lectures, meetings, radio broadcasts, and other forms of propaganda were disseminated primarily through the meeting hall, with one day a week devoted specifically to women. On occasion a "health propaganda car" visited the village, dispensing health information to villagers through a loudspeaker.[140] Social workers called "health visitors" were responsible for a range of activities including immunizations, follow-up medical care, home visits, hygiene instruction, and cleanliness inspections. They were meant to become members of the village community.[141] Mohamed Shalaby described how the ethic of cleanliness became internalized among the villagers:

> After leveling the streets of the village and cleaning them, it was hoped that they were kept clean and that cleanliness would enter the houses. The nurse and the writer devoted part of their time daily to talking with the people and encouraging housewives to clean the streets and their homes. A group of boy and girl pupils was formed to keep watch over the cleanliness of the houses. They received badges to distinguish them and for their encouragement. . . . Later the elder leaders in the village became interested in the question of cleanliness and decided to conduct a contest over a period of time to judge the cleanest house. The contest was announced, the houses were inspected, and the owner of the cleanest house was rewarded by having his house whitewashed free of charge. . . . After a period of time most of the people of the village got the habit and cleanliness of houses and streets was automatically practiced.[142]

Perhaps the most distinctive aspect of these reform projects was the presence of trained medical and social specialists. The peasant *mentalité* of passivity and lassitude, reformers argued, required the dynamism of trained individuals.[143] Social workers were viewed as indispensable components of successful social reform, and many reformers also suggested the recruitment of patriotic youths for village amelioration.[144] The constant presence of health inspectors and visitors, social workers and monitors, and other trained personnel ensured the level of guidance and supervision thought necessary for educating peasants and inculcating them with the spirit of reform so that they would come to desire it for themselves. The support workers were also thought to offset the damaging influence of the village elders who, reformers argued, often reinforced harmful social customs and traditions.[145]

It must be noted that these ideas regarding rural reform were unique neither to the EASS nor to Dr. Ahmed Husayn.[146] Indeed, they were pervasive throughout the 1930s and 1940s. For example, many writers put forth the idea of guidance (*irshad, tawjih*) as a critical component for the reeducation of the peasantry. The edification of the peasantry, it was argued, required a battery of practices—guidance (*irshad*), advice (*nasiha*), religious sermonizing (*al-waʿz al-dini*) and the corollary processes of cultivating and disciplining minds and selves (*tahdhib al-ʿuqul wa al-nufus*).¹⁴⁷ The responsibility of providing the peasantry with moral education and guidance, reformers argued, fell on the religious and provincial leaders of the countryside. It was precisely the peasant's imitative faculties that were believed to have led him astray from the proper religious way of life and toward indulgence in un-Islamic practices such as alcohol and drug consumption. Yet, paradoxically, it was this very same propensity to imitate that held out the possibility for reformed norms of behavior and social practices—provided village elders and authorities could serve as role-models for wayward peasants.¹⁴⁸ Social guidance and the moral uplift of the peasantry were consistently represented as a nationalist and religious duty (*wajib watani wa dini*) that was to lead to the much-needed rural renaissance (*nahda rifiyya*).

In an important sense, then, to "civilize peasants" was both a moral and a material project. The focus on the peasant *mentalité* of ignorance, superstition, and fatalism was in many ways a repetition of the colonial perception of the "backwardness" of the Egyptian fellahin. The lack of modern educative practices—*ʿilm* (scientific knowledge) and *thaqafa* (cultural knowledge or literacy)—among the peasantry, writers noted, had led to the persistence of older social customs and traditions. Reformers observed how peasants drew from an eclectic blend of ancient Egyptian beliefs, Arab medicine, and distorted Islamic and Coptic religious beliefs, such as the beliefs in magic, envy, and the evil eye; the use of talismans and amulets to ward off evil; the use of folk remedies such as cauterization derived from Arab medicine, or *zar* (a ceremony performed for spirit possession); the cult of saints; and a strongly fatalistic attitude of reliance upon the providence of God.¹⁴⁹ Peasants' irrational and pernicious manners, customs, and superstitions would have to be remedied before any effective social reconstruction of the countryside could take place.¹⁵⁰ Rural mothers in particular were singled out as being the most susceptible to superstitious practices, and the most inclined to consulting mystics and charlatans rather than doctors—thus harming their children's health and well-being.¹⁵¹

Reformers also suggested that the relevant ministries, such as the Ministry of Education, the Ministry of Social Affairs, and the Ministry of Health, participate in the moral uplift of the peasantry by providing financial and technical support for propaganda and guidance projects. Through the use of films, radio, and lectures (even mobile units were suggested), a vast number of villages and peasants could be provided with health, religious, agricultural, and social propaganda which could combine entertainment and education.[152]

Governmental Interventions

During the 1930s reformers began to call for greater governmental involvement in rural reconstruction. "With the establishment of the Ministry of Public Health," claimed Mahmud Shakir Ahmad, "and the study of all affairs related to village improvement and reform," along with a doubled budget, "the projects to be undertaken will enable the fellah to take his place in the nation, as a vibrant element worthy of care, uplift and thought." [153] Ahmad discussed several projects that the Ministry of Public Health was developing at the time as an organized strategy for dealing with health, economic, educational, and social factors as interconnected issues: improving the availability of clean drinking water, the draining of *birkas* and marshes (contaminated yet often used for a water supply), the provision of sewage systems in the villages, the construction of public bathrooms, and the organization of the villages and improvement of the housing of the fellah (*birnamij tanzim al-qura wa tahsin masakin al-fellah*).[154]

Perhaps the most instructive aspect of this reform proposal was the project for reorganizing the villages, which was characterized by a high degree of detail and instruction. The detailed nature of these plans related to the construction of a new internal space, one that would be ordered according to the scientific and sanitary principles of health and hygiene. In congruity with much of the reconstruction work that had come before, the Ministry of Public Health ascertained that the new housing projects required separate areas for baking and for animals, and an open courtyard—measures intended to ensure hygiene, ventilation, and sunlight.[155] Areas around the village were to be bought and used for building new houses. All houses from then on were to be built according to the models approved by the Ministry of Health. Rebuilding of entire villages was only to be attempted when a village was destroyed by fire or flooding, or after severe epidemics. Depending on the size and importance of the village, there would be a mosque with hygienic washing installation and latrines, an elementary school, a village hall, police and fire stations, a market hall, a slaughterhouse, and sheds for storing straw. Village councils were expected to supervise the implementation and maintenance of these projects.[156]

The wide-ranging plans of the Ministry of Public Health were never fully implemented, as government involvement in rural reconstruction often took place under conditions of disaster or forced relocation (such as in Mit al-Nasara or Gourna). The ministry did, however, become involved in the construction of rural health units, adding a rural health section to the Ministry in 1939, but implementation was slow.[157] By and large, however, rural services were undertaken by the Fellah Department (a subdivision of the Ministry of Social Affairs)—itself a point of contention and interministerial rivalry.[158]

Nevertheless, the health and hygiene of the fellah remained at the forefront of ministerial concerns, and, once again, addressing the *mentalité* of the peasant was considered a sine qua non of any reform efforts; writers argued that model villages were futile if the tenacious problem of peasant ignorance remained.[159] As one Ministry of Public Health official explained rural affairs,

> the root of all this is poverty and ignorance. How many diseases would be prevented if the fellah separated himself and his children from his cow? If he knew how to let air and sun into his room? If he covered his feces with dirt? If he cleaned from his home the piles of filth and removed it far from the village? If he did not drink dirty water? All these and more would drive nails into the fellah's coffin, if it were not for the sun and the grace of God.[160]

Perhaps the most important component of the peasant's re-education was health and hygiene instruction. According to 'Abd al-Wahid al-Wakil, a prominent Wafdist and member of the EASS who had been appointed Minister of Health in 1942, the fellah, because of his ignorance, would be incapable of using in a sanitary fashion the model homes and villages built for him.[161] The principles of rural hygiene, he argued, were understood only in theory; their applicability to the Egyptian village would require careful study and experimentation. In this way, everything from the most suitable latrine to the best architectural plan for peasant homes could be determined experimentally.[162] The dissemination of hygienic practices among villagers, reformers argued, required some form of monitoring, either by nurses or social workers or by groups of villagers themselves.

A crowning moment for governmental intervention in rural affairs came on May 5, 1941, when the project for the rural social centers was inaugurated by the Fellah Department of the recently formed Ministry of Social Affairs.[163] The project's existence was due in part to the success of the EASS's experimental village projects, and to the initiative of the director of the Fellah Department, Ahmed Husayn, whose lobbying efforts led to the formation of the rural social centers project on an experimental basis. The Fellah Department was

> concerned with the study of problems connected with the life of the Fellah, in an effort to improve his lot, and to raise the standard of living of the Egyptian village.... The fellah department ... has as its goal, the awakening of the rural population, and educating them as to their need for reform, *so that they will harken to the call willingly, and participate morally and materially* having once been convinced of the need for reform.[164]

A scheme for the reconstitution of Egyptian villages and the reeducation of the Egyptian peasant through a decentralized collection of rural welfare centers was begun in 1942 with six centers, which were increased to eleven in 1943. Each center was initially established to serve 10,000 villagers.[165] In 1946 the Supreme Council for Rural Welfare recommended an increase of 30–40 centers per annum. By 1950 there were 136 centers, serving 1.5 million of the rural population.[166]

The first *Annual Report on the Rural Welfare Centers* issued by the Ministry of Social Affairs positioned the fellahin as the repository for the welfare of the nation, and hence in need of uplifting for the construction of a modern Egypt.[167] The centers were supplemented by rural reconstruction societies composed of villagers themselves, under the supervision of the department, who were "forming committees to distribute supplies and look after the cleanliness of the village, and to encourage popular co-operation, to educate the illiterate and to settle disputes."[168] Most villages, through an elected administrative council, formed five committees: health, educational, charitable, conciliatory, and economic and agricultural.[169] The centers' main concerns lay with the general amelioration of the conditions of agricultural workers, including landlord–tenant relations, extension of small landholdings, improvement of agricultural production, introduction of agricultural handicrafts, reduction of taxes, nutrition of the fellah, popular education and literacy training, and social conciliation.[170]

In a format common to this period, the centers provided health services aimed at eliminating unhealthy habits, generalizing cleanliness, sanitation and hygiene, and teaching women proper child care, household cleanliness and order. Each center had three main employees:

> The *Social Worker*: ... His duties are to raise the fellah's standard of living economically, socially, physically, mentally and morally.... He tries to cure bad and unhealthy habits, supervises the cleanliness of the village, its roads, and its population. He is to attain these aims through the help and cooperation of the people themselves.... [A] *Medical Doctor*: His duties are to study the conditions of the village, give a physical examination to each inhabitant and to

> draw up a complete survey. He instructs the villagers in hygiene and prophylactic measures. . . . With the help of the social worker he must fight against superstitious and unhealthy habits. . . . [A] *Health Visitor*: . . . She takes care of the pregnant women and the babies of the village. She strives to raise the village women's standard of living by teaching them cleanliness, order, housekeeping, and some useful cottage industries such as needle work, dress making and the like which enable them to use their leisure time profitably. She also trains promising young village women to be nurses. She visits the village school to teach the girls and boys how to be clean in a very practical way by cutting the boys' hair, cleaning, combing and brushing the girls' hair, and trimming the boys; and girls' nails, and collects the sick pupils for treatment. She regularly visits each house in the village and teaches and demonstrates household cleanliness and order.[171]

The passage illustrates quite vividly the detailed nature of instruction felt necessary for the uplifting of villagers. The description of tasks embodies the conjuncture of the discourses of health and hygiene and the welfare of the nation—that is, the attempt to transform rural life by creating model peasants.

. . .

Rural reconstruction projects attempted the complete reconstitution of the Egyptian village. The emphasis was upon reconstructing bodies and minds: building and cleaning villages, homes, and children, and thus constructing a "new Egyptian." The concern with the welfare, and specifically the health and hygiene, of women and the peasantry was part of the nationalist and reformist project of generating a productive and vital population. The larger social and political context for this discourse of social welfare and social hygiene lay, as I have argued, in the increased rural violence (both by and against property owners) of the 1930s and 1940s and in the depressed economic state of the countryside and rural laborers, all of which had led to a crisis in the social reproduction of labor power.

This crisis crystallized in the figure of the undisciplined rural subject and the fear of potential Bolshevism, and led to the attempt to contain radical social change through piecemeal social reform and amelioration of the conditions of the laboring classes. A totalizing model of social welfare, meant to encompass economic, social, and political factors, was developed alongside an interventionist policy of social planning and engineering. New discourses—notably, positivist criminology, social hygiene and welfare, architectural modernism and neo-Malthusianism—were formulated throughout this period.

This ideological discourse of social welfare was inextricably linked to the creation of new public and social spaces (the village hall, the rural social center, the maternal and child welfare clinic), new social practices (biomedical health care, such as large-scale vaccinations, "guided" village arbitration, religious reform), and new "public" individuals (the village doctor, the social worker, the health visitor). Such reformist projects were meant to lead to the creation of new forms of social and spatial organization, guiding the peasantry to "reformed" norms of behavior, modes of life, and social and cultural practices appropriate to the progress and civility of the modern world.

The body politic (already viewed as depleted by the vices of poverty, ignorance, and disease) and the peasant (enervated by schistosomiasis, ancylostoma, and numbed by narcotics) became the protagonists of a nationalist tragedy. By 1942, as Erwin Rommel's troops were beyond the border at al-Alamein, the tragedy intensified when Egypt was invaded by a deadly malaria epidemic.[172] From March of 1942, when the first case of the disease was reported in Upper Egypt, until February of 1945, when the *Anopheles gambiae* mosquito (which carried the parasite) was finally eradicated, the malaria epidemic was the centerpiece of nationalist and reformist debate.

Rural reconstruction, public health, and village sanitation, formerly the purview of ancillary state apparatuses, social reformers, and intellectuals, entered the realm of politics, both domestic and international. The epidemic claimed the lives of an estimated 100,000 individuals, mostly Upper Egyptian agricultural laborers. It generated a complex web of politics between the Wafd, minority parties, the Palace, and the British; a mobilization of elites (through the Mabarrat Muhammad 'Ali and the Red Crescent Society); philanthropic efforts on the part of political parties and groups ranging from the Communists to Young Egypt to the Muslim Brothers; and British and American rivalries that led ultimately to the involvement of the Rockefeller Foundation with Egyptian public health.[173] Timothy Mitchell has argued that the malaria epidemic was translated by political elites into a more radical program of social and political reforms. The malaria epidemic did indeed accelerate the call for more activist social change among Egypt's political elite, but the social and political processes it intensified had already been under way in the 1930s.[174]

The two protagonists in Asyut with whom our chapter began, Ahmed Ja'idi and Hasan Abu 'Ashur, were ultimately convicted of premeditated murder, receiving sentences of capital punishment and life imprisonment with hard labor. Their case illustrates the efficacy of a culture of fear, if not in imposing obedience, then in securing dominance. It is no wonder, then, that after a 1935 visit to the Royal Agricultural Society's model village of Bahtim, characterized as it was by social welfare services, amicable social relations and the absence of poverty and disease, journalist A'isha Abdel-Rahman declared it the "heaven of the countryside."[175] By the middle of the 1930s, social reformers had found that the softening of relations of domination in the countryside through the provision of social welfare was a more humane and effective means of social regulation.

III   *The Problem of Population, 1925–1945*

5 Barren Land and Fecund Bodies
The Emergence of Population Discourse in Interwar Egypt

The rapid growth in numbers.
In 100 years from now Egyptians would number 49,600,000.
In 300 years from now they would total 500,000,000.
In 425 years Egyptians would equal the present population of the earth at 2,000,000,000.
In 968 years Egyptians would occupy not only the whole earth but several other planets as well at 973,300,000,000.
— Wendell Cleland, "The Necessity of Restricting Population Growth in Egypt"[1]

Between 1936 and 1939, the Egyptian Medical Association held a series of forums on birth control and the population problem; the first full-length book on Egypt's population problem was published; the first life tables for Egypt were calculated; a group of university professors organized under the rubric of "The Happy Family Society" to discuss the need for planned families; the first religious edict (*fatwa*) on birth control in the twentieth century was issued by the mufti of Egypt, Shaykh Abd al-Majid Salim; and the Ministry of Social Affairs was created, with part of its mandate being to study the population problem.[2]

The constitution of population both as an object of knowledge requiring observation and management through "numbers, statistics, material phenomena," and as a social problem to be remedied for the progress of the human race, took shape in Egypt during the interwar period.[3] However, the parameters within which the problem of population were discussed during this time were far broader than the discussions of the later twentieth century, entailing fields of knowledge as varied as medicine, geography, and sociology, in part due to the embryonic nature of specialized fields of expertise such as demography, vital statistics, and eugenics. Population politics at this time was marked by this convergence of overlapping fields of knowledge that took the calculus of life and death, of the fecundity of lands and bodies, into consideration, and that concerned itself with the scientific reform of society.

David Horn has detailed a similar process in Italy in the 1920s and 1930s, focusing on the formation of reproduction and welfare as objects of social-scientific knowledge and new social technologies "intended to confront the 'problem' of declining fertility." Ann Anagnost has explored the notion of China as a nation that is "excessively populous" analyzing how the meaning of the one-child policy in China expanded from a "remedy for under-development" to a "a sign of the modern itself." She notes that since the one-child policy was issued in 1978, population has been posed not just as a problem, but also as a principal causal factor in China's failure to progress. Both authors treat population as a discursive construction. That is to say, they do not engage with the question of whether China is really overpopulated or Italy really underpopulated. Instead, they treat demographic programs and their cultural meanings as solutions to a culturally constructed problem rather than as effects of objective crises, or "mere propaganda." My intentions are similar.[4]

The interwar period is, indeed, unique in the history of population politics in Egypt. The Mehmed 'Ali period up until the British invasion was characterized by an expansionist conception of population and embedded within the imperial framework of the Ottoman Empire. Population concerns were driven by a conception of population as strength in numbers (to provide for military and fiscal exigencies) and the expansion of imperial wealth.[5] Some scholars have also argued that the governmentalization of population—or the harnessing of population, the management of its growth and characteristics, to colonial concerns of state—occurred during the colonial period after 1882.[6]

I emphasize, however, the precise moment at which population concerns became harnessed to Egyptian national and nationalist concerns, and embedded within the wider framework of the study of social phenomena. This shift corresponds, as Timothy Mitchell has argued, to "the collapse of the colonial organization of power, knowledge and exchange, and the rise of the national state as producer of statistical knowledge and custodian of the economic."[7] I seek to uncover the new modes of governance, expertise, and social knowledge that defined a distinctive era of population politics in interwar Egypt.

Debating Population

Throughout the interwar period, population was viewed primarily in terms of the problem of the quantity (*'adad, kam*) versus the quality (*naw'*, *kayf*) of the nation's inhabitants, and configured as a component of social welfare.⁸ Population debates thus revolved around two points, both related to the problem of population as a problem of social intervention and engineering. The first issue was the debate over the neo-Malthusian reduction of the birth rate. This concern generated a flurry of empirical, statistical studies on historical demography, and debates as to whether Egypt was in fact overpopulated. The second issue was the improvement of the characteristics of the population either through the encouragement and enhancement of "types" or the elimination of "defectives" by social welfare and eugenics. "Quality" encompassed the social uplift of the mother-child unit (often through maternal welfare programs) and of the peasantry (through rural reconstruction projects)—it thus dovetailed with the concerns of rural reformers. What is unique about this time period, however, is the confluence of these two issues. Writers dealt with population as a "total social fact," that is to say, arguments regarding historical demography could not be separated from issues of social welfare.⁹ The quantity of the population could not be divorced from its quality.

Prior to the middle of the 1930s, population concerns were varied. Colonial administrators such as James Ireland Craig worried about overpopulation or population maldistribution as early as 1917; members of the indigenous intelligentsia, such as Mustafa 'Amir, noted vast increases in population. By and large, however, there was neither sustained debate nor consensus on the state of Egypt's population. For example, in the late 1920s some writers on family law held that Egypt suffered from underpopulation, thereby providing a legitimization for polygamy.¹⁰

After the mid-1930s a veritable onslaught of publications, conferences, and debates on population appeared in both the mainstream press (newspapers and journals such as *Al-Ahram*, *Al-Hilal*, and *Al-Muqtataf*), in specialized professional meetings and journals (such as that of the Egyptian Medical Association), in the women's press (*al-Nahda al-Nisa'iyya* and *al-Mar'a al-Misriyya*), and within the religious establishment (*dar al-ifta*). Major establishment figures, including members of parliament and landowners such as the reformist Mirrit Butrus Ghali and the somewhat feudal Hafiz Afifi Pasha, in keeping with their class interests, argued that the causes of Egypt's poverty were overpopulation and poor public health and housing, rather than the unequal distribution of property.¹¹

In fact, it can be argued that the clichéd discussions of the vicious cycle of "poverty, disease, and ignorance" centered on the problem of population, which was to be resolved through the regulation of women and regulation of the peasantry. By "regulation of women," I mean the process of fixing women in healthy, modernized, and regulated reproduction.[12] The regulation of women is apparent in the multitude of maternal- and child-welfare programs that emerged in both rural and urban areas of Egypt in the twentieth century. By "regulation of the peasantry," I mean the process of reforming rural and peasant life in order to lead the peasantry to modes of life and social practices appropriate to the progress and civility of the modern world. These included such measures as rural reconstruction projects and model village programs.

Inserted into the larger social and political context of Egypt's new-found independence from the British, and the dislocations that had taken place in the aftermath of World War I—the nascent industrialization of the interwar period, the emergence of a large urban working class and an organized labor movement, the heightened importance of the land question, the increased scale of agricultural unemployment, and the increase in crime, prostitution, narcotics, and other social maladies—the question of social reform had reached a heightened pitch by the middle of the 1930s. To resolve what came to be called the social question (*al-mas'ala al-ijtima'iyya*), middle-class reformers turned to the management of population and the regulation of women and the peasantry. It is not accidental that the two populations most systematically targeted for improvement were those responsible for the reproduction of labor power and the extraction of wealth from the land.

In many respects, the focus on population represented a naturalized explanation of the problem of rural poverty. Indeed, it was the acute nature of the social and economic state of Egypt's agricultural laborers in the post-Depression period and the impending crisis of the social reproduction of labor power that rendered the problem of population salient in the first place. Yet it would not be until the mid-1940s that the relationship between population, poverty, and land reform would be articulated in a coherent fashion. The agrarian question did not emerge full-blown until the final years of World War II, at which point the economic state of the rural proletariat had deteriorated to the point that the question of land reform and a more frontal assault on social reform was all but necessary to avoid the dangers of revolutionary ferment. This was further underscored by the increased politicization of the countryside and urban centers in the late 1930s and 1940s. From the middle of the 1940s on, the agrarian question entered into and dominated public debate, although no substantive actions were taken to ameliorate the economic situation of the peasantry until the advent of the revolutionary regime.[13]

Population politics under Nasser continued to be framed within the larger issue of national and familial welfare, although population growth was problematized to a far greater extent than during the preceding period. Nasserist political discourse characterized population programs as part of social welfare—the primary object of state concern. The government-sponsored programs of family planning under Nasser mobilized ideologies of nationalism and national progress, which emphasized family planning as an integral component of the welfare of the state and its people, a culmination of the discourse on welfare of the 1930s.[14]

I focus, however, on the interwar period as the years in which the most vigorous and sustained debates on population took place, and in which antinatalist and pronatalist views were promulgated. I analyze 1930s and 1940s debates on population, in order to draw out the relationship between population debates and state-building projects. The problem of population was viewed by its theorists as principally a problem of land and labor, to be resolved through the improvement of the dispositions of one or the other—for example, through the increase of cultivatable land or the improvement of the quality of the population. In its totality, however, the problem of population was seen as a component of social welfare, and moved in tandem with the identification of women and the peasantry as objects of moral and material improvement. This led to wide-scale attempts at their social uplift through various efforts, such as rural and village reconstruction projects, maternal-child welfare centers, and the various activities of the Ministry of Social Affairs.

The various international developments in demography, eugenics, and population studies provided a key backdrop for the emergence of population debates in 1930s Egypt. The convergence of international interest in the question of population in the 1920s and 1930s may be related to several factors: the disintegration of empire, the negative association of eugenics with fascism, European fears of depopulation, and the development and refinement of new forms of geopolitical representation, such as the use of aggregate and comparative statistical measures and the development of historical demography.[15] The interwar period witnessed the proliferation of international birth control movements and conferences, in which birth rates, rather than racial hygiene or eugenic merit, were the main focus of attention. The 1927 World Population Conference held in Geneva under the organization of Margaret Sanger may be taken to mark the beginnings of the construction of population as an international problem and as an object of scientific prediction and management. In the words of one participant, "production can only be rationalized if one undertakes to rationalize reproduction just as intensively and intelligently."[16] The conference proceedings, which were widely read by the Egyptian intelligentsia, were very influential in the formation of Egyptian debates on population, and in particular regarding the question of the demographic optimum for population.[17]

In contrast to the European colonial concern with depopulation and military expansionism, population debates in the postcolonial national context were deeply enmeshed in the bourgeois project of nation building. Throughout the interwar period Egyptian elites mobilized nationalist arguments in debates on population. In 1936, as the Egyptian elite was aspiring to independence from the British, social planners were eager to assert their own control over the realm of population—a new object of "governance" in the post-independence period. Population was to be rationalized as an object of knowledge and managed in the interest of the people. These concerns were especially salient given the imperialist ambitions of fascist nations such as Italy and Germany, which made it apparent that population was a critical component of modern warfare and politics. With Italy on Egypt's borders, in Cyrenaica and Ethiopia, such concerns were part of the recognition of the importance of numbers—or demographic weight—in the modern era.

"Numbers, Statistics, Material Phenomena"

Unquestionably, the development of population as an object of study owes its genesis to that quintessential sign of modernity—the national census. The first countrywide enumeration of the Egyptian population, known as the census of 1848, was made at the behest of Mehmed 'Ali. The census was driven largely by fiscal and military concerns (taxation and conscription), as well as the knowledge that "the causes of the progress and civilization of other nations is the precise enumeration of their people and the orderly administration of their interests."[18] As Kenneth Cuno and Michael Reimer have argued, the 1848 Egyptian census was very much a part of the overall Ottoman effort "to enumerate the empire's population rather than a separate undertaking."[19] It is precisely this "Ottomanness" of the census that distinguishes it from later censuses, which were embedded within colonial or nationalist contexts.

The next census of Egypt took place in 1882, just months before the battle of Tall al-Kabir. In that year, the population was enumerated on a single day, by Western definitions, a modern census count. It was the 1897 census, however, that was viewed, by British colonial officials and modernizing Egyptian technocrats, as Egypt's first reliable attempt at the statistical enumeration of the population. Successive censuses were taken decennially (1907, 1917, 1927, and so on). By 1917 there was an entire apparatus in place for census taking, ranging from a general statistical office, modern counting and tabulating Hollinger machines, active census propaganda (*nashr al-daʿwa*), and house numbering. Nevertheless, census taking in Egypt was, in the words of James Ireland Craig,

> characterized by a complete absence of continuity in its preparation and method. Owing to the absence until 1905 of a general statistical office, or a proper registrar, familiar with the problems of population, a census office had on each occasion been constituted *de novo*. On the termination of the work the office was wound up, the staff dispersed and the documents mostly destroyed, so that those in charge of the next census were altogether deprived of the benefit of the verbal or written tradition of previous experience.[20]

Craig was a central figure in the development of the Egyptian census and the use of statistical data in Egypt.[21] At various points in his career he served as director of the Computation Office of the Egyptian Survey Department, controller of the Statistical Office and Census Office, controller general of the Census, controller of the Supplies Control Board, and financial secretary of the Ministry of Finance. As Craig was wont to point out, the timing of censuses in Egypt proved to be a frequent and awkward problem.

The 1882 census, for example, was taken at a most inopportune moment: the ʿUrabi military revolt had taken place the year before, in January the British and French governments presented their joint note to the Khedive, in July Alexandria was bombed, and in September the Battle of Tall al-Kabir was fought.[22] According to the director-general of the 1907 census, "there has probably not been a single year in the last thirty years when conditions more unfavourable for census taking prevailed than in 1882."[23] The 1897 census took place while a saint's festival (*mulid*) was being held in the town of Zaqaziq, which led to a surge in the population of that province, and a corresponding decrease in the count for that same province in the following census (the Egyptian census was based on the *de facto* population—all those present in a district at a given moment—rather than *de jure*). The 1917 census was taken during World War I, when the British demand for labor had caused a temporary emigration of Egyptian laborers, in addition to the fact "that not a few people had objected to the taking of the census."[24] In addition, because of the Muslim use of the lunar calendar and the imperative of avoiding census taking during the month of Ramadan, the date of enumeration shifted from census to census. Not to mention the "vagueness and ambiguity" of terms used in the census schedules, a problem generally endemic to the operation of a census.[25]

Timothy Mitchell, drawing on Georg Simmel, has discussed the process of creating a world of "unrelenting calculability," illustrating how the relationship between calculability—whether in the cadastral survey or the modern census—and concomitant new forms of social expertise, led to the creation of an effect of distance between the expert and the object calculated. This separation created its own forms of instability and crisis that ultimately "destabilized the process of making a world of calculation," as the difficulties discussed above demonstrate.[26] Yet despite this seemingly slipshod and chaotic collection of census data, the modern census, with its principles of collection, classification, and enumeration, has remained one of the principal modalities for the regulation and transformation of national subjects and citizens in the modern era. As Talal Asad states,

> The point is that the practice of assembling and classifying figures periodically on births, diseases, crimes, occupations, natural resources and so on was, from a governmental standpoint, not merely a mode of understanding and representing populations, but an instrument for regulating and transforming them. This applies also, and even more strongly, to the "modernizing" nation-states that have succeeded European colonies.[27]

J. I. Craig understood this principle well, and was keen to point to the modern census as the most effective monitor of changes in national population and resources. The value of statistics as a science that deals with the "collection and arrangement of facts and figures bearing on the condition—material, social and moral—of a people" lay, according to Craig, in its practical use.[28]

In his discussion of the 1917 census of Egypt, Craig noted that one of the main roles of the census lay in determining whether "the agricultural resources are keeping pace with the needs of the population."[29] By 1926, in underscoring the census's primary political and economic importance, he devoted considerable attention to the question of population as one of the most important issues "moulding human action at the present moment."[30] For Craig, the census could serve as an important gauge of population—of the relation between population and cultivatable land and questions concerning the quality of the population (age distribution, average mortality, size of families, class and social position, education level, polygamous practices, etc.).[31] By 1926 Craig was claiming that Egypt was already feeling "the pressure of population on the means of subsistence."[32]

Craig's concern with the modern census marks a transition from a view of Egypt's population as an agglomeration of disparate peoples, or "as no more than a polyglot mix of different religious, racial and ethnic groups," to a view of population as a homogeneous entity whose quantitative characteristics could be measured and acted upon.[33] Henceforth, the production of statistical data in Egypt would gain momentum, and increased attention would be paid to the numerical relationship between population and resources.[34]

As Roger Owen has argued, Craig initiated a statistical regime in which "data was provided which was abstract, quantifiable and transferable."[35]

Yet the transformation of the notion of population into a discrete and quantifiable entity did not occur immediately. In 1928 Mustafa 'Amir, a professor of geography at the Egyptian University, was sent as one of the Egyptian delegates to the International Geographical Congress held at Cambridge.[36] In his paper "Some Problems of the Population of Egypt," he discussed the issue of population as principally a problem of specific populations.[37] The populations in question were Nubians, Upper Egyptian migrant laborers, and "the foreign elements." The 1902 construction of the Aswan dam and the addition to it in 1910 had resulted in flooding as well as in a northward movement of the Nubian population in search of work in urban centers.

> To control the movements of the Nubians on the one hand, and of the Upper Egyptians (*Saidis*) on the other, and to protect the big urban centres of the North from the unruly elements of both these groups, and especially from those who have no fixed abode and no particular employment, are some of the problems that have to be carefully and speedily dealt with, for the sake of public security. More serious still, and more detrimental to the social and economic structure of Egypt, is the slow but steady trickling in of poor foreign elements from the other side of the Mediterranean.[38]

Less than a decade later, Egypt's population would be thought of not as an agglomeration of disparate populations—Upper Egyptian peasants, Bedouin, Nubians, foreigners—but as a homogeneous mass whose quantitative and qualitative characteristics could be observed, analyzed, in effect taken as an object of study, as a total social fact.[39] As such, population became subject to laws and regularities, which needed to be studied in order to effect the proper transformation of the social and natural world, to align the fecundity of bodies with that of the soil.

Barren Land and Fecund Bodies

The first comprehensive treatment of population in Egypt was Wendell Cleland's 1936 *The Population Problem in Egypt*.[40] Cleland, an American who had lived in Cairo since 1917, was a member of the faculty of the American University in Cairo, where he taught Psychology, and was "deeply engaged with Protestant activism directed at the Copts."[41] His involvement, as a member of the Egyptian Association for Social Studies, with prominent ministry officials working on issues such as irrigation, public health, sanitation, and hygiene impressed upon him Egypt's most serious social issues, and it is emblematic of the connections between the issues of population and social welfare. Cleland's work was to become a point of entry for subsequent writings; virtually all studies of Egypt's population take Cleland as a reference point, and his text's enduring impact on Egyptian population debates should not be underestimated. Henceforth, the neo-Malthusian approach (in which artificial mechanisms such as birth control are proposed to curb population growth so as to regulate the relationship between population and resources) achieved an unparalleled level of dominance in population studies.[42] As late as the middle of the 1960s, Cleland's groundbreaking book was still considered a hallmark of sociological writings on Egypt.[43]

The Population Problem in Egypt was divided into two sections, "one quantitative and the other qualitative;" the first surveyed the numerical trends in Egypt's population, and the second examined the standard of living.[44] He noted the importance of a study of standards of living, given that "a study of the known resources of modern Egypt leads one to conclude that they are quite inadequate to support so great a population on any higher standard of living than present, and, furthermore, if the quality of people is of any importance, then somehow a limitation of numbers must be brought about."[45] Cleland's methodology was straightforward. It entailed the simple juxtaposition of estimated general trends in population (based on birth and death rates) versus the "capacity of the land," which he calculated by applying "to the whole of the habitable country the density ratio of the most populous section outside of the large cities."[46] Thus, he concluded (in a classically Malthusian formulation) that based on a comparison between the growth of population and that of cultivatable lands, "the people appear to multiply more rapidly than the acreage."[47]

Cleland argued that the density of population and scarcity of arable land, the exceedingly low standard of living and the high rate of unemployment among agricultural laborers, were all indicative of overpopulation, and that the solution was an interventionist population policy advocating the use of birth control.[48] He wrote,

> It is obvious, therefore, that the growth in the agricultural products has not kept pace with the growth in population. As agriculture is the chief occupation . . . and the products of the land the chief source of wealth, it is inevitable under present conditions that this constant running ahead of the density beyond the productivity of the soil must result in a steady decline of the already low standard of living.[49]

It was this "constant running ahead" of the fertility of man (and, hence, density of population) over that of the soil that led to the deplorably low standard of living and low quality of the population.[50]

Cleland's formulation differed from a strictly Malthusian one in which population, subject to the laws of nature, was checked by misery. For Malthus, misery included starvation, disease, and death, and it was the principal limit on the growth of the poor population; thus the natural tendency for the laboring classes to increase would be checked by their inability to receive the subsistence necessary for their preservation and reproduction.[51] For Cleland, the laboring poor and the peasantry reproduced "unchecked," as "half-living listless people," undernourished and debilitated by enervating diseases such, as bilharzia and ancylostomiasis, that "deplete[d] the vitality of the laboring classes" and reduced the efficiency of peasant labor.[52] This was a common concern among officials in the Ministry of Public Health, among them 'Abd al-Wahid al-Wakil. Al-Wakil, a member of a prominent landowning family with strong Wafdist ties, was a medical doctor, health inspector of Cairo, and member of the EASS, and had been active in formulating sanitary requirements for Egyptian villages in a manner consonant with what was then understood as the peasant *mentalité* ('*aqliyya*).[53] Al-Wakil became minister of health in 1942.[54]

The concerns about the labor efficiency and productivity of the population, particularly the peasantry, were echoed at the 1937 Conference on Birth Control sponsored by the Egyptian Medical Association.[55] Several speakers most notably Muhammad 'Awad Muhammad, one of Egypt's first professional geographers and a member of the EASS, and Mustafa Fahmi, a professor of social science and an official in the Ministry of Education—argued that high birth rates led to lower standards of living and lowered the productive power of the nation.[56] With Egypt's low average life expectancies, "most [citizens] die without benefiting the nation with their productive efforts. The important thing is to improve their health and life, thereby increasing production."[57] Infant and child mortality, which in 1937 was estimated to account for 65 percent of deaths in Egypt, was also considered a serious cause of productivity loss.[58]

Such arguments had become increasingly common in the second half of the 1930s, foreshadowing the future dominance of a neo-Malthusian perspective in Egyptian social science and population debates. The year following the publication of Cleland's book, Hamid El-Sayed Azmi, a statistician at the Ministry of Finance, delivered a lecture at the American University in Cairo in which he characterized "rapid and continuous population growth" and population "mal-distribution" as among Egypt's most serious problems, going so far as to suggest the need to develop a population policy.[59] Several notable Egyptian public figures and social reformers, such as Mirrit Butrus Ghali and 'Aisha 'Abd al-Rahman, began writing about the problem of Egypt as primarily a problem of rapid population growth in relation to the dearth of agricultural land.[60]

Mirrit Butrus Ghali was a major intellectual figure in interwar Egypt. A member of a prominent large-landowning Coptic family, in 1944 he founded, along with several other intellectuals, the Jama'at al-nahda al-qawmiyya, which called for the social reform of Egyptian society.[61] Ghali was a member of the Chamber of Deputies in the 1940s, and served as minister of municipal and rural affairs in the Najib al-Hilali cabinet, which was toppled by the 1952 revolution.[62] Ghali's well-known 1938 text *Siyasat al-ghad* targeted population growth that was too rapid in proportion to agricultural growth as Egypt's first and foremost economic and social problem. In this text Ghali explicitly rejected European socialist theories that low standards of living were caused by the unequal distribution of national wealth. He argued that distribution played an insignificant role in the economic and social ills of Egypt, and that, instead, "the economic difficulty of Egypt is simple enough; it is the result of overpopulation and of the poverty of economic resources."[63]

But even writers who identified with the European socialist tradition, such as Salama Musa, argued in favor of neo-Malthusian principles. In a 1930 text Musa discussed the population problem in Darwinian and Malthusian terms, noting that the more evolved the species, nation, or class, the less fertile its population.[64] Furthermore, lower birth rates were in the interest of the working classes, because a smaller laboring population would mean higher wages, Musa argued, noting the resistance to the call for birth control among conservative newspapers and parties. High birth rates, Musa claimed, simply led to high death rates and the general immiseration of the laboring classes.

Thus, the issue of population was discussed in terms of a material relationship between the number and quality of the nation's inhabitants and its national wealth and resources. This often metonymized in the image of a family that could not sustain itself because it continued to grow although its income was fixed. As Cleland put it, "if capital and income are insufficient for a large national family, and the national family exists in misery, then the next generation should learn its lesson and limit the size of the family, so as to elevate its standards and remove its miseries. Surely a people can be as proud of the quality of its people as its quantity."[65] Cleland, Ghali, Azmi, Musa, and others posited a fundamental antagonism between population growth rates (quantity) and standards of living (quality), and therefore the productive power of Egypt.[66]

The Uplifting of Women and Peasants

What solutions existed for such a dire national situation in which population was purportedly outstripping resources? Cleland had proposed a plan for reducing births, which included raising the standards of living and hygiene (which would result in decreased fertility—that is, a rise in culture would be followed by a decline in the birth rate[67]); promoting birth control clinics; and eugenic measures to stop the propagation of future dependent classes—that is, legislation "to restrict propagation of the unfit, limit free social services and raise the age of marriage."[68]

To control the peasantry's "natural" libidinal tendencies, Cleland argued, required social intervention, in the form of birth control as well as moral education and psychological training—a position referred to as neo-Malthusian.[69] Although the task would be difficult, "in view of the national ambition for size, the ignorance of the people, the strength of custom and the religious fanaticism. . . . People today are afflicted by the megalomania of ultra nationalism, which seems to demand larger and larger populations."[70] Many Egyptians at the Conference on Birth Control agreed. Muhammad 'Awad Muhammad compared Egypt to China and India, noting favorably the Indian government's efforts to promote artificial birth control.[71] Kamal al-Din Fahmi, a sanitary engineer and member of the EASS, presented a detailed and triumphalist history of the various birth control movements in Europe and Japan, in order to illustrate the acceptance that birth control had gained over time and place, despite the resistances encountered.[72]

It was, however, the attempts to improve the standard of living that proved the most advocated population policy in the 1930s and 1940s. The concept of standard of living was understood to mean all the components related to the health and hygienic standards, that contributed to the wellbeing and strength of the population and thus optimized its ability to produce and provide for the needs of the nation. Regardless of their position on birth control, those who wrote on the population problem in the 1930s and 1940s were able to agree on one issue: the obligation of the state to provide social services for women and the peasantry in order to improve the health and hygiene (i.e., standards of living) of the population. This included various state-sponsored efforts for the social uplift of women (through maternal and child welfare programs) and the peasantry.

The regulation of women was most directly exhibited in maternal-child welfare programs. Beginning in the mid-1920s, philanthropic organizations and government clinics worked on informing maternal practices and improving child welfare in order to reduce infant mortality. By 1936, Wendell Cleland could describe child welfare as an arena that had made great gains in Egypt:

> There is a commendable industry among the officials of these centers in attacking the mountain of ignorance and superstition under which the vast majority of Egyptian mothers are buried. Instruction is given by lectures, moving pictures, demonstrations and printed matter at the centers and in the homes and schools, government physicians, midwives, and health visitors all participating. Much excellent work is being done in the child welfare centers in removing the superstitious confidence of mothers.[73]

The regulation of the mother-child unit formed one locus of the interwar concern with the welfare and productivity of the population; the other was prominently occupied by the fellah. According to Azmi, Ghali, Cleland, and others, the most fundamental component of any government population policy would be raising the standard of living of the fellahin. In keeping with the work of the EASS, Wendell Cleland's ultimate vision was one of structured, hygienic communities of peasants living in a manner in keeping with the progress and civility of the modern world.

> In the following plan I see an average family of from three to five children with intelligent, literate parents, living healthy lives in solid, clean houses, very simply furnished, which will belong to well-ordered, sanitary communities, all members having equal opportunities for plenty of clean water, electric light and power, a well balanced diet with enough protective foods, simple but adequate clothes, steady and sufficient work to bring an income of not less than L.E. 100 per year or its equivalent.[74]

The image of an average family living "in solid, clean houses . . . which belong to well-ordered, sanitary communities" was a powerful one, which many of Cleland's ministerial colleagues had been attempting to implement throughout the 1930s and 1940s. Wendell Cleland was himself involved in the operationalization of such ideas in governmental programs and policies in Egypt, such as the experimental village projects undertaken in the Delta between 1939 and 1941 by the Egyptian Association for Social Studies (discussed in Chapter 4).

It must be emphasized that projects such as those of the child-welfare centers and the EASS were an essential component of interwar population discourse in Egypt. Thus the concerns of population theorists, which encompassed the social uplift of women (through maternal welfare programs) and the peasantry (through rural reconstruction projects), often dovetailed with the concerns of rural reformers.

"L'Éloquence des Chiffres"[75]

Writing in 1942, Elie Nassif, a Professor at the Royal Faculty of Law in Cairo, composed a book-length article directly criticizing Wendell Cleland's proposition that Egypt was suffering from a population problem and that the solution was to embark on a birth control program.[76] Nassif was one of many writers in Egypt at this time who opposed the call for birth control. Both historical and sociological in his approach, he persistently claimed that population doctrines, as well as population itself, had to be historicized. Nassif's view of population corresponded most closely to that of Italian statistician Corrado Gini. Gini saw Malthusian theories of the geometric increase of population as being premised on one fundamentally flawed assumption—that "the reproductive powers of populations remain constant throughout their generations."[77] Gini had formulated a theory known as the theory of the cyclical rise and fall of population, whose underlying postulate was that rates of increase differed among different populations according to race and class, on the basis of evolutionary biological difference. According to Gini, populations, like societies, individuals, and other organisms, had life cycles of birth, evolution, and death. The implications were decidedly anti-neo-Malthusian, as intervals at diverse points in history could represent transitory phases of over- or underpopulation.

Elie Nassif's work was meant as a theoretical intervention into the existing literature on population and demography. This approach was unique among Egyptian writings on population at the time. In his extensive theoretical overview of the criteria of demography, the core of Nassif's critique rests on the impoverished, reductive, abstract, and ahistorical nature of the Anglo-Saxon idea of the demographic optimum.[78] In the 1920s and 1930s, many Anglo-American demographic arguments on the problem of population turned on the elusive concept of an optimum. "Demographic optimum" referred to the ideal numerical relationship between the natural resources of a country and the size of its population; this was usually calculated as the population at which per-capita real income could be maximized.

Nassif argued that in defining the demographic optimum as the population corresponding to the highest real individual income, the "Anglo-Saxon doctrinaires" excluded the possibility of diverse demographic optima corresponding to the progressive evolution of the social and economic structure of a society and its complexity.[79] Following Gini, he maintained that in certain instances an elevated population density corresponded to economic (or other) advantages. National psychology was key. Whereas some races (such as Anglo-Saxons and Scandinavians) did not require demographic pressure to stimulate a spirit of initiative, others (such as Italians and Egyptians) needed it as a stimulant to progress; for yet others (such as the Indians and the Chinese), demographic pressure might have no effect.[80]

Nassif therefore tried to develop a methodology that would account for the historical and cultural determinants of population, that is, its specificity to Egypt. He relied on a concept of social evolution in which he could allow for the natural evolution of societal structures, so as to account for Egypt's imputed overpopulation as a necessary stimulant to its social, political, and economic development. Further, he argued that political and moral considerations were key to discussions of population. In particular, he claimed, the difference between the rates of growth of the higher and lower classes had given birth to an ascending demographic movement, in which the fertility and vitality of the lower classes were continuously outstripping those of the upper classes. The ramifications of neo-Malthusian practices in the Occident were only just beginning to be felt:

> Need I mention the effects of this [birth control] policy on Western countries? Birth control had the effect . . . of reducing the births amongst the intellectual class who should have been encouraged to multiply; so the best of social classes was the first sacrifice of this policy. . . . [S]ociologists and economists in the West are now concerned with . . . the continuous decline in overall birth rates. . . . Is it not necessary, then, to review Professor Cleland's arguments before following through with his suggestions? . . . We need to measure changes in population and standard of living before we assume any relationship between the two.[81]

Indeed, a crucial component of nationalist thought in the 1930s was the concern for the formation of a *classe dirigente* that would lead Egypt toward becoming an indigenous modernizing nation-state. The solidification of such a nationalist elite required the maintenance of an appropriate balance among the social orders. Social reformers remained concerned that any attempt at inaugurating neo-Malthusian practices would lead to the cannibalization of the productive and innovative middle classes by the lower orders. Issues of class remained at the heart of population debates. Criticizing both the eugenics and birth-control movements as having led to declining birth rates, Nassif suggested that efforts turn instead to the development of the domestic economy—perfecting national industry and augmenting capital, in order to reestablish an equilibrium between human agents and natural factors of production. Indeed, the "existence of an economic elite could remedy demographic pressure while its absence could aggravate it."[82]

Many opponents of birth control at the 1937 Conference on Birth Control agreed. Muhammad Hasan and Hasan al-Banna (leader of the Muslim Brothers) argued that it would be the educated middle classes that would heed the call to birth control, with harmful national consequences.[83] According to Hasan,

> the class which uses birth control is the middle class—the enlightened and intelligent class of the nation—the class which produces *'ulama*, inventors and innovators in every art and science, the class from which extraordinary men are produced in all nations (such as, in the case of Egypt, Sa'd Zaghlul, Mustafa al-Nahhas, Tal'at Harb, Shaykh Muhammad 'Abduh, etc.). . . . It is not proper that this class, which transmits its unique characteristics of intelligence and talent to its offspring through heredity, should consider limiting its progeny.[84]

Similarly, 'Abd al-Majid Nafi'a, a member of the Chamber of Deputies and lawyer noted for his fervent economic nationalism, argued that the call for birth control was a "national crime and not a social necessity."[85] Arguing that birth control was antinationalist, and indeed a form of national suicide (as the historical example of France illustrated), Nafi'a urged the reconsideration of Malthus's population doctrine. He called instead for a return to the belief in the strength of population numbers as the vital force (*quwa hayawiyya*) of the nation. Population discourse thus entered what Roger Owen has termed "the ideology of economic nationalism," which entailed the assertion of Egyptian national identity in the consolidation of independent economic interests in industry, agriculture, and finance.[86]

How, then, was the relationship between Egypt's population and and its natural resources to be judged? Nassif summarized his findings:

> All these reflections lead me to determine the demographic optimum based on two essential elements (positive, concrete and measurable): on the one hand, *standards of living*, as objectively prescribed by specialists as necessary and useful for the normal activity of an individual, given geographical conditions; and on the other hand, *resources*. Insofar as resources can support the requirements of *standards of living*, one should not invoke the necessity of birth control.[87]

To determine the demographic policy Egypt should follow, he argued, one had to assess the country's population growth in relation to the standard of living of its inhabitants, relying on a concept of a "welfare optimum." The concept of a welfare optimum was developed by E. F. Penrose (an American population theorist who had written on Japan), and involved a consensus among qualified individuals on the requirements for optimum welfare (e.g., biochemists determining the optimal food requirements for physiological welfare, medical scientists determining public hygiene needs, architects determining housing needs, and so forth).[88] "In the case that national resources suffice to cover actual and future needs, one should not hesitate to allow the population to follow its natural course."[89]

Nassif's lengthy and sophisticated theoretical prolegomenon was followed by a far more detailed analysis and evaluation of Egypt's standard of living in comparison to its resources. In evaluating *les niveaux de vie*, Nassif relied on various scientifically established criteria.[90] "In demonstrating that agriculture has amply covered the needs of an eminently prolific population and that it will continue to do so in the coming decade, one can perhaps prove that the deterioration of the standards of rural life will not be a definite consequence of demographic growth in Egypt."[91] Nassif contested the notion that standards of living need necessarily be inversely related to increases in population size. For Nassif, people were resources of national wealth. If resources and standards of living were commensurate, there would be no need to reduce birth rates or arrest population growth.

Nassif analyzed what he deemed the three component factors of standards of living: the nutrition of the fellah, health and labor productivity, and housing. Taking each factor, he tried to show how it might be improved irrespective of population size—thereby contesting Cleland's arguments. Nassif claimed that malnutrition had been inadequately studied; that innovations in irrigation techniques and affordable medical treatment had been shown to reduce the incidence of schistosomiasis and ancylostoma; and that the successful creation of several model villages had led to improvements in hygiene and sanitation.

Disagreeing with Cleland's superficial assessment of population only in terms of already-cultivated agricultural land, Nassif saw no reason to assume that an increase in population would be problematic if the increase in the rate of agricultural production continued, and innovations in irrigation, draining, and cropping techniques were incorporated—without any consideration for industrialization or external immigration.[92] The only population "problem" Nassif would admit to was one of inequities in the spatial distribution of the nation's inhabitants. Foreshadowing what would effectively become, within a decade, a crucial part of Egypt's future population policy, Nassif suggested internal colonization (*une veritable politique de colonization intérieure*) to achieve an optimal distribution of population.[93] At the same time that the barren lands in the northern Delta were being reclaimed, he suggested, massive transplantations of people—a grandiose plan for interior colonization—could be coordinated. Nassif felt he had proven that the standard of living of the fellah was not as low as Cleland would have had us believe, that it had been ameliorating slowly but surely over the preceding decade, and that it would continue to improve, participating in the gradual and natural evolution of the nation toward a better social future.[94]

Naturalism in the Sciences of Man

Nassif and Cleland represent two poles of an important debate—one that was to dominate the Egyptian political scene for the remainder of the century. Wendell Cleland exemplified the triumph of neo-Malthusian thought in population debates, the perspective that later became hegemonic. Elie Nassif, on the other hand, represented an evolutionary perspective that held that population should not become an object of conscious political strategy, but was best left to natural laws. More subtly, however, Nassif argued for the privileging of social, cultural, and historical specificity in determining the optimum population of a nation, corresponding to the evolution and complexity of its social and economic structure. For both scholars, the formation of a nationalist elite that would lead the economy and polity of Egypt—and the demographic mass toward their own well-being—was essential.

The considerable discrepancy between the two perspectives outlined above, however, should not blind us to the limits of the interwar discourse on population. Both views remained imprisoned in naturalism—itself the legacy of Malthusian thought (indeed, Karl Polanyi has linked Malthus to the emergence of naturalism in the sciences of man[95]). In this respect, it is important to note the influence of Malthus on Darwinian theories of natural selection, and on Herbert Spencer's discussion of the necessary antagonism between individuation and genesis.[96]

The evolutionary perspective of Nassif and the neo-Malthusianism of Cleland were in effect linked through the naturalism of the Malthusian tradition. In particular, they were related in their attribution of overpopulation and poverty to natural laws, evolutionary or otherwise. Perhaps there is no greater evidence of this than their egregious omission of the effect of the distribution of wealth upon the problem of poverty. Yet it was the critical social and economic state of Egypt's agricultural laborers and the impending crisis of the reproduction of labor power (as manifested in starvation, disease, and misery) that rendered the problem of population salient in the first place.

The question of Egypt's putative overpopulation had surfaced at this time as a potential obstacle to economic development, particularly if biological reproduction was outstripping agricultural and industrial production. The promotion of a population plan was tied to the proper management of the relationship between the population (the problem of labor) and the natural resources of the nation (the problem of land). With a decline in the total value of agricultural wages, rents, and production, and a radical drop in the nominal value of the cotton crop, the post-independence period was characterized by an attempt at economic recovery and the reformulation of

Egypt's major social problems along the lines of social welfare and etatism.[97] In many respects, the focus on population was a naturalized explanation of the problem of rural poverty.

The perception of the population problem was thus a translation of the dire state of Egypt's agrarian population. This was further underscored by the increased politicization of the countryside and of urban centers in the late 1930s and the 1940s, as evidenced in peasant jacqueries, an increase in rural crimes committed against property holders, a movement toward unionization and more militant labor organization, and the increase in student protests and demonstrations.[98] Rather than attribute poverty or over-population to existing social, economic, and political conditions, however, the authors in question relied upon the "inexorable laws" of nature as explanatory devices. The flood of writings on population between 1936 and 1942 thus represented several interrelated concerns: fears regarding the ability of the working classes to reproduce themselves in a viable fashion (one that could keep up with the demands of labor discipline and agroindustrial production); the need to coordinate the organization of production with that of biological and social reproduction; and the shift of the problematic away from the redistribution of land and toward the reduction of population numbers or the improvement of standards of livings.

Those who were engaged in debates on population in 1930s Egypt viewed the problem of poverty, as (1) a problem of excessive fertility, (2) a dearth of natural resources, (3) the inefficient exploitation of natural resources (land or labor), or (4) the improper distribution of resources among the population. The first two (fecund bodies and barren lands) were explanations that naturalized poverty as the result of "inexorable natural laws," and hence, suggested neo-Malthusian solutions for the reduction of the birth-rate. The second two were social and political explanations, which placed the question of the moral and material welfare of the population within a political framework of social reform. In all cases, however, the problem of population was inextricably linked to the state as the arbiter of social welfare, which was, first and foremost, and interventionist project—whether accomplished through a population policy, a program for land reclamation or social welfare, or the moral education of the demographic masses.

6 Body Politics
Gender, Reproduction, and Modernity

> There is a belief that we must not interfere with such a natural process as child bearing. In the present state of our knowledge we do interfere in every stage of child bearing and birth either to allay pain or to bring an end to prolonged suffering or to avoid evil results and complications. . . . We have been actuated by factors of progress and development to wipe out merciless epidemics and to lengthen the life span of the human being through better modes of living, sanitation and hygiene. These factors played no unimportant role in the adjustment and limitation of the human race in this world. Now it is time to control the production of the human race in this world in accordance with our needs and our comprehension of human welfare and prosperity. It might be well at the outset to dismiss the erroneous intermingling of abortion with our subject of tonight—namely contraception. Abortion is in reality manslaughter, but birth control is an act of philanthropy—at present an intelligent and constructive production of the human race. The future is awaiting for it as part of Eugenics.
>
> —A. M. Anous, *"The Dangers of Frequent Child-Bearing and Necessity of Birth-Control"*

In the speech quoted above, A. M. Anous, a medical doctor, was addressing an array of prominent medical practitioners, social scientists, and ministry officials, from fields including medicine, education, religion, sociology, geography, and political economy. All were in attendance at the April 1937 conference Birth Control in Egypt, sponsored by the Egyptian Medical Association. The conference proceedings were published as a collection of articles in a special issue of the *Journal of the Egyptian Medical Association (Al-Majalla al-Tibiyya al-Misriyya)*, thus ensuring a wider readership within the medical and paramedical professions. Among the numerous participants in attendance were Najib Mahfuz Bey, perhaps the most renowned of Egyptian doctors; Muhammad 'Awad Muhammad, one of the first professional Egyptian geographers; Hasan al-Banna, the leader of the Muslim Brothers; and numerous medical doctors, health inspectors, and university professors.[1]

Taking the conference as its centerpiece, this chapter explores the central role of reproduction in the formation of a national modernity in interwar Egypt, using an empirically grounded case study of the discourse of population quality in demographic debates. Whereas the previous chapter explored the construction of population as a statistical and material phenomenon—an object of knowledge requiring observation and management—here I focus on social-scientific discourses surrounding the optimization of the species body and its "biological processes: propagation, births and mortality, the level of health, life expectancy and longevity."[2] Such attempts at the "intelligent and constructive production of the human race" necessarily relied on a statistical and empirical notion of population as a quantifiable essence (as explored in Chapter 5), but they operated predominantly through the instrumentalization of the family.

In this process, the family was transformed from a metaphor to an instrument of governance. Beginning at the turn of the century and throughout the interwar period, the family became a new site of regulatory controls, including maternal and child welfare, birth control, and eugenics, in the Middle East as elsewhere. Late Ottoman thinkers, whether Islamist, Westernist, or Turkish nationalist, sought to reconstruct the family as a social and cultural institution.[3] Beginning in the Hamidian era, and particularly from the late 1880s, Turkish writers began to focus on the relationship between proper childrearing, social reform, and the health of society. Child-health treatises and childrearing manuals drawing on the French sociological and psychological traditions flourished, and pediatrics itself emerged as a specialization.[4] Throughout the interwar period, European welfare states too, whether fascist or liberal, were characterized by social interventionism targeted at families, a phenomenon that Mark Mazower has referred to as the "state as paterfamilias."[5]

In colonial Egypt since the turn-of-the-century reforms of Muhammad 'Abduh, Talal Asad has argued, "the family" became no less than a juridical unit of shari'a law.[6] Lisa Pollard finds that familialism, or "the equation between a particular kind of political order and the shape and form of the family," was fundamental to the iconography of revolutionary nationalist discourse in Egypt during the British occupation.[7] Marilyn Booth has explored female biographies as a matrix through which the construction of female and national identity emerged in late-nineteenth- to mid-twentieth-century Egypt.[8] Hanan Kholoussy has discussed the so-called "marriage crisis" in pre-1919 Egypt as a central vehicle through which ideas regarding masculinity and femininity (or the creation of husbands and wives) and national identity were formulated.[9] The vast increase in discursive practices surrounding the role of women and the family since the turn of the century highlights the fact that, far from being a sacrosanct domain of private life, the family as a site of public discourse hinges on the interconnection between the private and the public sphere.[10]

Rather than follow the traditional focus on the domain of public politics as the quintessential site of nationalism, I address reproduction and reproductive politics as a key locus of nationalist ideology. Population discourse in twentieth-century Egypt normalized monogamous sexuality within the parameters of modern family life—bourgeois companionate marriage, small family size, and middle-class hygiene—while organizing reproduction within a framework of social reform.[11] This entailed the dual process of fixing women in healthy, modernized, and regulated reproduction and childrearing, and of relegating to men the management of birth control, either in their domestic capacity as heads of household, or in their political capacity as social reformers. The modernization of reproduction was a crucial component of the nationalist ideology of social planning and scientific progress.[12] The historical conjuncture of national independence from the British and the increasing attempts to relegate reproduction to the domain of politics led, effectively, to the effacement of women from the political discourse surrounding reproduction.

As practitioners in their various fields, social reformers outlined the problem of population as a problem of social intervention and engineering. Regardless of their stance on birth control, almost all of the participants in the 1937 Birth Control in Egypt conference concluded that Egypt must work to improve the quality of its inhabitants, to produce "healthy sons of the nation." The identification of women and the peasantry as objects of concern moved in tandem with the problematization of population, and the problem of population and the regulation of women and the peasantry crystallized in the drive to modernize the family unit. To create the modern family (indeed modern citizens) required the creation of new dispositions (self-governance, self-improvement), new habits of cleanliness and hygiene, and the cultivation of new sensibilities appropriate to the order of the modern world.[13]

Civilized Reproduction

One of the most basic and most contentious issues to arise at the 1937 Cairo conference was the appropriate terminology for the organization of reproduction. Discussion centered on the use of the term "birth control"—in Arabic, *tahdid al-nasl*. *Tahdid*, the contested term, refers to a process of limitation, restriction, or curbing; *nasl* as a noun refers to progeny or offspring, and comes from the root "n-s-l" meaning to beget, procreate, or sire. The alternative proposed was *tanzim al-nasl*, indicating a process of organization, adjustment, or regulation—that is, the organization of reproduction rather than its prevention.[14] The closest English correlate would be "birth planning."

Although the conference was called *Tahdid al-nasl* (birth control) several speakers urged the Egyptian Medical Association to change the title to *Tanzim al-nasl*.[15] According to Mustafa Fahmi, birth planning was preferable to birth control, because the latter denoted prevention and thus contradicted the call for the care of offspring (*al-'inaya bil nasl*). Other terms, especially eugenics (*tahsin al-nasl*), "which signals care for what exists and control over what does not," were also suggested.[16] For Kamal Fahmi, a sanitary engineer, "control" denoted the prevention of offspring or the limitation of childbearing, whereas the goals of "planning" were "to organize child bearing such that it accords with the parents' health and their economic abilities, so that every child may be raised in the best possible environment. Birth planning is thus in the best interests of the child, parents, family, and nation."[17] Once birth planning was posed in terms of child, familial, and national welfare, critiques of it could be cast as misguided and misinformed.

The resistance to the idea of preventing (rather than planning) births lay in its association with more problematic measures, such as abortion, infanticide, and sterilization, and thus the permanent prevention of a living being or potentiality (indeed, of God's grace) and a lack of faith in God's ability to provide for the future. Planning, on the other hand, entailed a concern for and preservation of procreation—one of the key aspects of *shari'a* doctrine, as well as a sign of civility itself.[18] As one speaker at the birth control conference noted, "if even savages have accomplished this task [organizing the production of offspring] albeit by reprehensible and evil means . . . then we should take up this matter in a civilized fashion based on science and study."[19] Yet the concept of birth planning or organization stood in a somewhat contradictory relation to the progress and civility of the modern world. For some scholars, the control of reproduction was itself a transhistorical and cross-cultural phenomenon, in existence among both primitive and civilized peoples. For others, it was the mark of modern progress and civility itself. Still others claimed that along with civility, fertility would come to regulate itself.

In his discussion, the geographer Muhammad 'Awad Muhammad relied heavily on A. M. Carr-Saunders's account of the history of birth regulation, citing abortion, infanticide, celibacy, and homosexuality as methods used in the past to reduce offspring. "Why," he asked, "has this desire to establish an economy of offspring appeared all over the earth at all times?"[20] The answer lay in the relationship between population and resources, which led nations to be underpopulated, overpopulated, or stable at an optimum population. Controlling their own numbers, then, was simply the mechanism by which nations had tried to optimize their population throughout history. The gap between the barbaric or backward peoples and the civilized was exemplified in the means used to reduce their numbers, "reprehensible and evil," on the one hand and "scientific and medical" on the other.[21] For Mustafa Fahmi, the measure of civilizational progress was man's success in discovering and harnessing the civilizational laws that dictated societies. In a Comtean fashion, Fahmi declared the age of metaphysics over, and called for the practical and positive study of social problems. It was by following and applying the laws of society to the life of the group (without trying to change or correct the course of civilization) that society could be directed toward progress, civility, scientific advances, and the general good. "In calling for birth control in Egypt, the sociologist is not trying to change human nature or stand in its course, rather he is trying to direct it in the best possible way, by heeding its organization, formation and future course, and in relying on numbers, statistics, material phenomena and practical experimentation."[22]

Even opponents of birth control were able to use the concept of civilizational progress to their advantage. Medical doctor Filib Shidyaq discussed the two activities that concerned living entities: the care of the self (*al-muhafza 'ala al-nafs*) and the care of progeny (*al-muhafza 'ala al-nasl*). The care of progeny entailed the coordination of natural resources and the tendency to procreate. According to Shidyaq, those tendencies remained unchecked in the early or primitive stages of history. As man became civilized, however, he developed demands beyond nutritional sustenance (namely, mental and spiritual sustenance), which consequently led to a lessening of numbers. In nations where people geared themselves toward the satisfaction of simple or basic needs, their numbers remained high so long as they remained at a primitive level of culture. Thus, the more advanced a culture, and the greater the equality of women, the more fertility regulated itself (*al-nasl yuhadid nafsu bi nafsu*).[23] Others made similar arguments, noting that among the effects of civilization were an increase in the length of education and a corresponding increase in the age of marriage.[24] The Spencerian notion that an increase of civilization (*hadara wa madaniyya*) led to a decrease in fertility was taken throughout interwar Egypt (as it was in much of Europe) as an axiom of demography.

Eugenics: *Tahsin al-nasl*

The primary conceptualization of the population problem in Egypt at this time was in terms of quality versus quantity.[25] Quality encompassed the general characteristics of the population (age, sex, number of individuals per family, growth rate), their standard of living (which included the level of health, hygiene, and sanitation), and the prevalence of hereditary illnesses, such as feeble-mindedness, insanity, sexual diseases, or physical disabilities. Referred to as *tahsin al-nasl*, or the improvement of offspring, eugenics was not discussed in the Egyptian context as a racial (*jinsiyya*) issue, but predominantly as the removal, through sterilization, birth control, or confinement, of mental and physical "defectives" from the body politic (*jism al-jama'a*).[26]

In its larger sense, however, *tahsin al-nasl* emphasized positive eugenics (encouraging the propagation of the fit), and encompassed sanitation, public hygiene, child and maternal welfare, and puericulture (the cultivation of children—*tarbiya*). Population politics during this period was embedded within the larger issue of the health, hygiene, and vitality of the population. The depletion of the social body by the presence of "idle and ill-fed bodies" had to be addressed and remedied through the uplift of the lower classes. Thus, the creation of sound families, the improvement of the characteristics of the population through the encouragement and enhancement of "types," and the uplift of the laboring poor and peasantry through social welfare projects were all crucial to these discussions.[27]

Tahsin al-nasl was further understood to relate to the improvement of what we would now refer to as the demographic characteristics of the population—age and sex distribution—in order to augment or improve the productive segment of the population. This could be adjusted through improvements in medicine, hygiene, and sanitation, thereby reducing the infant mortality rate or prolonging the longevity of life. Finally, it could subsume attempts to alter the differential fertility of the social classes and their relative distribution throughout the population. At this juncture, then, the quality (and not quantity) of the population was arguably the principle contradiction, for birth planning at this time was not consistently linked to or advocated as a means for reducing population growth.

Eugenics (which was sometimes also referred to as *al-yujiniyya*) was divided into positive and negative eugenics. The former entailed the propagation of the fit—those who could most contribute to the well-being of the nation—whereas the latter called for the prevention of mentally or physically "inferior" individuals from reproducing.[28] For instance, at the 1937 conference there were those who advocated birth control not as a means to reduce population growth, but as a form of negative eugenics. For Kamal Fahmi, Ali Bey Fu'ad, and Mustafa Fahmi, both birth control and sterilization were negative forms of eugenics, and although less desirable than positive eugenics, were nonetheless deemed necessary.[29] They therefore recommended not only that doctors encourage the sick or infirm (those with illnesses such as heart disease, cirrhosis of the liver, or diabetes) to use birth control, but that sterilization or confinement be used when necessary for those with sexual diseases and for the insane and feeble-minded.[30] Repeatedly, they emphasized the importance of quality (*naw'*) not quantity (*'adad*). "It is to the nation's benefit to have children of healthy build and sound mind rather than a plentiful but disabled and weak minded progeny. . . . Better to live as a progressive nation of small numbers than a populated backward nation."[31]

Abd al-Hakim al-Rifa'i, a professor of political economy at the Faculty of Law in Cairo and an avowed proponent of birth control for the purposes of reducing Egypt's population, believed that sterilization should be a crucial component of the state's population policy.[32] Discussing the issue at great length at the conference, al-Rifa'i overviewed the history of sterilization, its 1907 legalization in the United States, its application in other major nations in the late 1920s and early 1930s, and its target population, namely those with untreatable physical or mental diseases such as hereditary madness, schizophrenia, periodic or recurring madness (*al-junun al-dawri*), epilepsy, Huntington's chorea, hereditary blindness or deafness, any dangerous hereditary deformity, and any severe addiction such as alcoholism.[33] "Sterilization is a necessary step for the creation of a sound generation . . . it should only be performed in exceptional cases in which the disease has been proven untreatable."[34] Arguing that the rights of the individual must be sacrificed to prevent general societal harm, al-Rifa'i contended that just as the state intervened in combating epidemics and establishing quarantines, so too must it ensure the general good (*maslaha*) of future generations.[35]

Indeed, social-cost arguments had become increasingly common at this time, and reformers would even go so far as to calculate the exact financial losses suffered by the state from unproductive "human waste" (infant mortality). For al-Rifa'i, once the amount that would be spent on treating incurable diseases was calculated and the state's duty in providing housing and work for fit elements (*al-'anasir al-salima*) was considered, then sterilization was clearly "the duty of society." Further, the "duty of every state is to work towards the *constitution* of the people's welfare, that is, the development of their physical and mental characteristics."[36] Thus, sterilization, he argued, was the best way for Egypt to prevent the procreation of those afflicted with mental or physical illnesses; it was an unavoidable, necessary evil—one that would protect society from the danger of too many weak offspring (with limited productive power) and that would lead, eventually, to the elimination of hereditary diseases.[37]

Mustafa Fahmi, the only participant to discuss natural selection at the conference, noted the factors affecting the characteristics of the population:

> the population of any environment will not be able to maintain its characteristics entirely over time. It will be affected by three factors: firstly, natural selection [al-intikhab al-tabi'i], that is, the increase of one over another stratum [tabaqat] of the population due to its ability to adapt; secondly, elimination, that is, a weakening of one particular stratum of the population due to its inability to overcome the natural factors of its environment and its exposure to disease and extinction; thirdly, is the mixing [ikhtilat] of different races [ajnas], that is, the marrying of individuals from one society of members of another race. This encourages the appearance of another segment with its own unique characteristics, which differ from the original characteristics of the population.[38]

Fahmi argued that elimination, in particular, had played an important role in the Egyptian environment. Many of those who would not have been cared for by society were exposed to environmental or hereditary factors that they would not survive. In the long run, it was better "to remove defectives from the body politic [jism al-jama'a] without providing social services, as we do not want these corrupt elements procreating, or their offspring increasing over generations, nor do we wish to have their diseases and deficiencies among the group."[39] Surely, thought Fahmi, opponents of birth control would not disagree with prohibiting the negative elements from reproducing their hereditary illnesses.[40] Further, he argued, according to the most recent (1927) census results, there were 140,978 such negative elements, and if these persons were not sterilized, their offspring would reduce the strength of the next generation.[41]

For Filib Shidyaq, birth planning was of the utmost necessity in Egypt, not for the reduction of births, but for the improvement of offspring, in keeping with contemporary civilization and progress.[42] Given his view that fertility adjusted itself along with civility, Shidyaq's focus was on increasing the standards of health and hygiene of the mass of peasants—the elimination of enervating diseases, instruction in rural sanitation, and the improvement of the mental standards of the peasantry. Those whose progeny would be unhealthy should be sterilized, and those who were of sound mind and body should be asked to multiply,

> so that they may become, if they wish, as many as 50 million. Because the Nile's water . . . is sufficient for them. Look at the English Isle, it is, as you know, a

country impoverished in food resources and yet its millions are not dying—these resources are brought to it and its population increases daily in culture and comfort. Why? Because its population is educated, healthy and active. Because the British are strong. Why must we remain in darkness for generations to come? Why must we measure and control the number of our population by the number of heads that sprout in our fields?[43]

Others had similarly critiqued the birth control movement for reducing the numbers of the sound and the unsound alike, thereby ignoring quality. They argued instead for birth selection. Birth selection would reduce the numbers of those not fit for survival, through negative eugenics (thereby reducing numbers generally), but it would also propagate and cultivate the fit.[44]

These eugenicist concerns regarding the removal of mental and physical "defectives" were not simply the social-Darwinist musings of a select group. In a series of articles in the popular journals *Al-Hilal* and *Al-Muqtataf* in the 1930s, authors emphasized eugenic considerations (the health and strength of the population; and the presence of weak, feeble-minded and criminal elements) for any population program.[45] For example, 'Abd al-Wahid al-Wakil, future minister of health, noted that prior to thinking of birth control, Egypt should strive to be free of diseases, hereditary and otherwise. He therefore suggested medical examinations for couples before marriage to ensure the health of the couple and the absence of diseases, especially sexually transmitted ones.[46]

Similarly, an article published in the *Journal of the Ministry of Social Affairs* in April of 1941 proposed the reconsideration of a law in Egypt that called for the medical testing and certification of individuals before marriage by government physicians to ensure the sexual and reproductive health of the couple.[47] The law, drawn up by medical doctor 'Abd al-Rahman 'Awad, had been originally proposed to the senate in March of 1928, and was being resubmitted in a modified form in 1941 by the Ministry of Health.[48] The *Journal of the Ministry of Social Affairs* article was replete with estimates of mental and physical illnesses in Egypt, as well as examples of other national experiences (e.g., Germany) with sterilization and marriage licensing. Surely, it argued, the benefit of such a law, which would protect the future generations of the nation, outweighed its drawbacks (medical licensing was considered too expensive and too difficult to implement, in particular in rural areas). This failed attempt to medicalize marriage was one component of state efforts to assert control over the reproductive process. As healthy childbearing became a "national duty," nationalist discourse increasingly took up the women's question, encouraging the mothers of the future to "reproduce less in order to reproduce better."[49]

Mothers of the Nation

Ultimately, it was positive rather than negative eugenics, and maternal and child welfare in particular, that was the most successfully pursued policy in Egypt.[50] Population questions merged with the nationalist preoccupation with the women's question, which was closely entangled with the improvement of the quality of the population. Both secular nationalist and Islamist texts on proper mothering and child rearing identified women as both a "locus of backwardness" and a sphere of transformation essential to the nationalist project. The intellectual genealogy of the concept of *tarbiya*—or the proper upbringing, education, and cultivation of children—and its relationship to European colonial and indigenous nationalist discourse at the turn of the century has been discussed elsewhere.[51] Briefly, Egyptian discussions of motherhood entailed the constitution of a private sphere of bourgeois domesticity, with motherhood recast as a rational, scientific, and hygienic vocation aimed at the cultivation of new types of children. Motherhood figured centrally in turn-of-the-century modernizing discourse, and was essential to the nationalist project. The focus on proper rational and scientific mothering was thus situated within both the colonial discourse on motherhood and the nationalist discourse on modernity.[52]

Partha Chatterjee has argued that Bengali Hindu anticolonial nationalist discourse situated the woman's question within an inner domain of spirituality, localized in the home and embodied by the feminine. This enabled nationalist discourse to construct a cultural essence distinctive from the West.[53] Thus, he finds, "the relative unimportance of the women's question in the last decades of the nineteenth century is to be explained not by the fact that it had been censored out of the reform agenda or overtaken by more pressing and emotive issues of political struggle. The reason lies in nationalism's success in situating the 'women's question' within an inner domain of sovereignty, far removed from the arena of the political contest of the state."[54] In contrast to Chatterjee's assertion, the women's question in Egypt clearly linked both the moral and the material domains. Although Egyptian nationalist discourse sought to uphold women as a source of cultural integrity, it also identified them as an arena for the social, political, and cultural progress of the nation. That is to say, the advancement of the nation in the "material" fields of law, administration, economy, and statecraft (what Chatterjee refers to as the "outer domain") was positioned in such a way that progress for the nation could not be achieved independently of progress in the domain of women, and more specifically mothers.

The contours of Egypt's maternal and child welfare programs illustrate the extent to which Egyptian turn-of-the-century discourses on proper child rearing were "operationalized" beginning in the mid-1920s. Maternal and child welfare was a cornerstone of the modernization of reproduction, itself a crucial component of the nationalist and reformist ideology of social planning and scientific progress. Although maternal and child health care was geared toward the reconstruction of the modern family and the optimization of its health and welfare, programs targeted women—rural and working-class in particular.

The adoption of modernist reforms by the Egyptian elite entailed the emergence of a prescriptive and didactic discourse directed toward working-class and peasant mothers. The problem of child bearing and rearing was localized and attributed to the "ignorance" of lower-class mothers, who were faulted for their inability to teach children disciplined habits. Maternal ignorance was often blamed for faulty hygiene and the neglect of children, and this justified programs such as physical education, feeding schoolchildren, and providing food, clean milk, and hygiene and cookery classes for girls and mothers. In Egypt, as in Europe, education and pedagogy for working-class mothers sought to address maternal ignorance of nutrition, diet, and sanitation through lectures, pamphlets, manuals, female health visitors, women's sanitary associations, and infant consultations.[55] These associations helped set a middle-class standard of hygiene. Schools were often crucial in the attempt to transform working class life by instilling an ideology of domesticity and the habits of discipline. These forms of pedagogy helped disseminate a middle-class ideal of motherhood and domesticity as a national duty.[56]

The institutionalization of such ideas and their dissemination across class lines did not begin to crystallize until the middle of the 1920s, mainly through philanthropic organizations and government clinics aimed at informing maternal practices and improving child welfare. Egyptian mothers were portrayed as ignorant of the principles of cleanliness and hygiene, which children's dispensaries and maternal and child health clinics sought to address through the instruction of mothers "in the methods of cleanliness and the proper feeding and bringing up of their children."[57] An interest in the scientific organization of the protection of childhood began to develop, and Egyptian delegates were sent to attend international conferences on the subject.[58] Public governmental organizations, as well as private philanthropic initiatives such as the Lady Cromer Memorial dispensaries, the Society for the Protection of Children, Mabarrat Muhammad Aly (Ouevre Muhammad Aly, Dispensaire pour les femmes et les enfants- Centre de Puericulture et de Pediatrique Preventive), Mme. Huda Sha'arawi dispensaries, the Egyptian Feminist Union, the Egyptian Child Welfare Association, and the Jama'iyyat ummuhat al-mustaqbal (Société des mères futures), were responsible for the diffusion of health propaganda to mothers and children all over Egypt.[59] Midwives and health visitors conducted home visits in which they instructed mothers how to feed, clothe, and bathe their children.

By 1925 state efforts at protecting childhood included antenatal care, focusing on provincial hospitals and emphasizing the supervision of pregnancy and early treatment of syphilis (venereal clinics were also being established in all state hospitals); natal care, including efforts to raise the standards of midwives, with eight schools available for midwives in lower and upper Egypt; and postnatal care, which included welfare centers and children's dispensaries.[60] Such centers emphasized prevention, providing individual and collective talks on elementary hygiene and mothercraft. In 1925 there were twenty-two of these child welfare dispensaries and centers, thirteen of which were run by the state or local municipalities. In 1924, 90,000 babies received attention, with the total number of visits amounting to nearly half a million. Health visiting had also begun, but would require a better supply of suitably trained staff before service could be generalized and improved.[61] At the 1925 Congress on Child Welfare, the Egyptian delegation noted that

> a prolific cause of high infant mortality in Egypt, as elsewhere, is the ignorance of the populace in all matters appertaining to the hygiene of infants and proper mothercraft. The Egyptian government is fully aware of the importance of Education, not only general, but also specialised instruction so that a campaign may be conducted to diminish the infantile mortality rate in the Country, and already steps are being taken to achieve the object. The teaching of hygiene, both general and personal, is being introduced into the primary as well as the secondary schools for girls and boys. Infantile hygiene in particular is being taught in the training colleges for girls.[62]

In 1927 a special unit called the Child Welfare Section was created within the Department of Public Health; this division was responsible for permanent and traveling child welfare centers, children's dispensaries, and schools for midwives.[63] The objectives of the Child Welfare Section were

1. Attention to the treatment of hereditary diseases and the treatment of the off-spring;
2. Attention to motherhood, and education of mothers as to the means of care and prevention, together with encouraging them to fully perform their duties as mothers;
3. Attention to children welfare and to their good health with a view to reducing their mortality.[64]

In 1929 there were twenty-one such government child-welfare centers, and public health doctors attended fewer than 2 percent of births that year. By 1933, however, thirty centers were operating, and doctors attended 5.2 percent of total births.[65]

Government involvement was only one component of efforts aiming at the social uplift of mothers. Indeed, the first and most dramatic inroads into the regulation of lower-class urban and rural women's home environments had been made by the women's philanthropic movement. Egypt's philanthropic movement began around the turn of the century, initially operating dispensaries for poor women and children, such as the Mabarrat Muhammad 'Ali societies. The services of these associations later expanded to include vocational and literacy training as well as detailed instruction in health and hygiene, and eventually child care.[66] The Egyptian Feminist Union (EFU), which was central to the women's feminist and philanthropic movement in Egypt, was from its inception fairly active in pedagogy for the working classes.[67]

The predominantly upper-class members of the EFU were engaged in class-consolidating activities that were both nationalist and feminist. As with their European counterparts of the nineteenth and early twentieth centuries, their activities often centered on the instruction of working-class women in proper domestic and child-rearing practices, which attempted to efface and recast class differences by formulating a middle-class ideal of domesticity and motherhood.[68] The EFU's activities included the establishment of dispensaries for poor mothers and children "to take care of women and children and teach mothers the elementary knowledge of hygiene and child care"; the creation of a center for instruction in domestic arts (sewing, weaving, embroidery) and handicrafts; and the formation of a professional and domestic school which feminist Saiza Nabarawi announced would create "a conscious [female] working class, which at the moment does not exist, and which Egypt greatly needs in the task of social reconstruction underway.... Above all our goal is to form women members of the working class conscious of responsibility for their own existence."[69] Among the committees formulated by the EFU were the following:

> *Committee for Child Care*: Its duty was to take care of children from the sanitary and health aspects, as well as from the literary aspect. The members of this committee had to read all that was written at the time about child care, both the mental and the physical.... They visited poor mothers and showed them the proper care of children. They gave them food, clothing, and, if necessary, sanitary equipment for them and for their children.... *Committee for Health Affairs of Women and Children*: This committee has under its care sixty children whom it gives over-all attention regarding food, clothing, cleanliness and

health. . . . The committee takes special care of the cleanliness of the children and mothers. It gives them soap twice a week and instructs the mothers in the proper way of child care. It encourages those who take good care of the cleanliness of their children by giving them a prize in cash.[70]

The EFU was not the only privately organized association involved in maternal-child health care. The Société Internationale pour la Protection de l'Enfance (S.I.P.E.), was established in 1927 at the instigation of several doctors, including Ahmed Bey Sa'id and one Dr. Dolbey of Qasr al-'Ayni Hospital, who thought it necessary to have a free dispensary for the care of poor children, regardless of their religion or nationality.[71] Young doctors began offering their services free of charge at this dispensary. Under François Cassingena's presidency the society opened an office in downtown Cairo on Qasr al-Nil, where it flourished between 1927 and 1937. Among the society's activities were the organization of a comprehensive conference on childhood in 1928; an antituberculosis campaign in the early 1930s; and the provision of clothing, medicine, and medical care to poor children. The volume of patients was high; in 1928, for example, 33,311 medical cases were treated, and the number went up to 48,056 in 1929.[72]

The Red Crescent Society (Fédération Royale des Associations Internationales d'Assistance Publique en Egypte, founded on 13 May 1907 to provide public assistance in cases of sickness or injury due to accidents, public calamities, and epidemics) also provided hygienic advice to mothers.[73] Additionally, independent private organizations located in specific districts often included a component of maternal-child health, such as that of the Heliopolis Social Service Association.[74] Begun in Heliopolis as a movement for social reform and public service, this association was originally formed to support the establishment of the Heliopolis Hospital for the free medical care of the poor classes and a center for maternal and child care. This experience, however, illustrated "that medical care alone is insufficient and that the poorer classes are in need of social care to reduce ignorance, sorrow etc., to uplift them and to guide them towards means for achieving an appropriate life which would raise them to a human level."[75]

The Heliopolis association provided services such as medical treatment and nutrition for the poor and for pregnant and nursing women and children; referrals to social and health agencies, especially for children and women; help for the poor with furnishing; and social research. Among its specific social-reform projects was the creation of a social dispensary for the common classes (*mabarrat ijtima'iyya lil tabaqat al-sha'abiyya*):

> From our experience we decided that the best method for the uplift of the popular classes is that social reform occur in their midst. As such the associa-

tion decided to establish a *mabarrat* in the popular area of Heliopolis. This *Mabarrat* includes baths for the poor, washers for washing their clothes, a nursery for children, and care of deprived childhood and motherhood, a small cafeteria providing nutritional food, the *mabarrat* also contacts the families, and schoolchildren to follow up and hopes to make the *mabarrat* the social center for providing services to the poor from all health, moral and social aspects.[76]

A common component of many social-uplift programs were cleanliness campaigns in which participants would compete with each other to have the cleanest homes. The Heliopolis association chose forty poor families to enter a competition in cleanliness "in order to encourage their children towards cleanliness and health especially with respect to childrearing." The Minister of Health himself awarded prizes to the winning families and presented a donation to the association. "We should mention that the competition had the effect of creating a competitive spirit among the poor families in the popular districts of Heliopolis, and these classes began to appreciate the importance of cleanliness and to follow the principles of health and hygiene which were taught them by the social specialists working at the association."[77]

These forms of regulation of the daily lives of families, particularly mothers and children, show the detailed level of intervention by private organizations and agents of the state in the lives of the urban and rural poor. The creation of the modern family required new dispositions and new habits of cleanliness and hygiene. Further, instructing women and peasants in proper hygiene—"civilizing" them—ensured the well-being and strength of the laboring population and thus optimized its ability to produce and provide for the needs of the nation.

The Arithmetic of Welfare

Such long-standing concerns with maternal and child health entered into the 1937 debates on birth control: many thinkers, rather than emphasize negative eugenics, preferred to underscore the effects of birth control as raising the family's moral and material level, and by implication the nation, by building "able-bodied and sound-minded progeny.[78] The call for healthy sons of the nation was part of the imperative (in the words of Ann Anagnost) to reproduce less in order to reproduce better. Writers emphasized that birth planning was not meant to ease the life of parents, but rather was related to a fundamental concern for procreation itself, a concern for those children who would bear the future of the nation.

Many assumed that even the most ardent opponents of birth control would not call for the unrestricted growth of offspring of any kind. As geographer and anthropologist 'Abbas 'Ammar noted, unrestricted and unplanned births along with narrow economic resources would lead to a large population, but one that would encumber the nation. "What use is a large population which debases the nation—weak of body, devoid of strength, distressed in mind, ill bred, and of poor moral constitution? . . . We want progeny that benefits society and uplifts it and . . . we hope birth planning becomes a national policy for Egyptians. . . . We want progeny that benefits society, raises its level, and to avoid the multitude that saps our efforts and returns nothing to our lives but negative harmful effects."[79]

In rebutting arguments that birth control would lead to depopulation, authors argued that, even in instances where this was true (such as France) it had resulted in a higher standard of living and culture, and had virtually eliminated unemployment.[80] Furthermore, they argued, a high birth rate could lead to a halting of population growth, because of lower standards of living. In fact, statistics from other countries showed that increased births covaried with increased deaths, leading to the same net population growth.[81] Thus, although it was agreed that the prevalence of contraception led to the lowering of the growth rate, reformers asked what kind of growth was implicit in countries with high birth rates, poor health, poverty, and poor childrearing. Thus, Muhammad 'Awad Muhammad concluded that a decrease in population could be compensated for with improved health, higher standards of living, and greater longevity. Individuals, he argued, could contribute more to society if they lived longer and more productive lives.[82] Often the demographic characteristics of a population—age distribution (and its effect on national productive power); sex (and its effect on fertility); average family size (and its effect on the strength of offspring); and growth rate (and its effect on standard of living)—were analyzed in an attempt to refine measurements of population growth. For example, in contrast with the European nations, Egypt appeared to have a preponderance of youths and adolescents in comparison to the productive (20–65) segment of the population.[83]

This unrelenting emphasis on labor productivity was a crucial component of many post-independence reform efforts that advocated economic nationalism. Economic nationalism sought to place Egypt on the path to a successful and indigenous modernization, through an ideology of economic self-reliance. This form of nationalism, which gained popularity in the 1920s, entailed the consolidation of independent economic interests in industry, agriculture, and finance. As an ideology it may be said to have been inaugurated with the 1918 *Rapport de la Commission du Commerce et de l'Industrie*. The *Rapport* underscored the importance of industrialization and of the predominance of local interests and capital in diminishing foreign control over the economy.[84] The trend toward the indigenization of the economy took shape during the interwar period, and in particular under the influence of Tal'at Harb and the Bank Misr industries. At the time that nominal independence from the British had been attained, the Egyptian elite was preoccupied with the efficiency and maximization of agricultural and industrial productivity.

Thus at the 1937 birth control conference, Egypt's high infant mortality rate was considered among its gravest problems. Infant mortality was estimated in 1937 to account for 65 percent of deaths in Egypt, and was considered a serious loss in productivity.[85] As Mustafa Fahmi pointed out in a graphic arithmetic of life and death, each year the nation and government lost a multitude of children.

> If we calculate the money lost per year with an average longevity of 6 months, at a rate of [expenses of] 20 piastres/month and 100 piastres for childbearing, that is a total of 56,000 £/year. What does the government lose on children who die before 10? Assume the average age at death is 7 years; assume the family spends £7 per child/per year and the government £8 per year on schools, and 30 piastres on clinics, hospitals, etc. These are minimum estimates and amount to £2 million spent yearly by state on children who go to their graves by the age of 10.[86]

Citing Alfred Ploetz's research in the U.S. on the correlation between multiple childbirths and high infant mortality, 'Ammar noted that children of large families were more likely to suffer weakened health due to malnutrition, poor housing, and early child labor. Interestingly, moral arguments were used as well, as large families were thought to deprive children of proper household child rearing, and of sufficient maternal affection. The combination of neglect, lack of discipline, and poverty was thought to lead to moral depravity.[87] With the appearance of the nation as a "breeding ground for humans" the family could not conceivably undertake proper childrearing.[88] The image of the dissolute Egyptian nation as merely a "breeding ground for humans" was a powerful one. As we have seen, social reformers posited birth control in a complex relationship to modernity, civility, and progress. The modern family—marked by small family size, proper childrearing, and middle class hygiene, and the general concern for thoughtful procreation—was viewed as a sign of modernity itself.

Demographic Weight

The modernity of the Egyptian family was, of course, something to be judged comparatively. As such, the international context of the birth planning movement was a consistent framework of discussion for Egyptian reformers. The international birth control movement's use of comparative statistics was the method of measurement by which nations were judged to be over- or underpopulated. India, China, Japan, and the European welfare states came to symbolize key poles of debates on population, and Egypt was often compared to countries such as India or China. Population concerns were especially salient given the imperialist ambitions of fascist nations such as Italy and Germany, which made it apparent that population was a critical component of modern warfare and politics. The pronatalist policies of fascist and liberal-democratic nations provided an alternative conceptualization of and path to population policy. In addition, the history of the birth control movement itself, including the various international congresses on world population, provided a larger context for debates on population. The interwar period, with its vast array of specialists involved in studies of population and the widely discrepant and often irreconcilable differences of opinion on issues such as class fertility or the declining European birth rate, provided a rich and varied series of questions for discussion.

Muhammad 'Awad Muhammad noted that Egypt, like China and India, faced the potential of unchecked population growth which would continue to increase beyond the availability of natural resources, resulting in a decline in standards of living and health.[89] Citing discussions by Indian speakers at the 1931 population conference in Rome, he praised the Indian government's resolution regarding poverty, population growth, standard of living, and health as an example that could be followed by Egypt: "There is currently in India a movement (I hope it will be blessed) for regulating the numbers of the population along scientific lines."[90] He noted that India's 1931 census stated the following:

> A definite movement towards artificial birth-control appears to be taking place and is perhaps less hampered by misplaced prudery than in some countries, which claim to be more civilized; thus not only is birth-control publicly, advocated by a number of medical writers, but Madras can boast a neo-Malthusian League with two maharajas, three High-Court Judges and 4 or 5 men very prominent in public life as its sponsors.[91]

Others were less sanguine, and the pronatalist policies of the fascist nations were consistently raised as an objection to any attempt to inaugurate a population policy in Egypt. Arguments centered on the military requirements of the nation-state and the nature of its defense needs, and all agreed that a careful study of the situation was necessary before embarking on a limitation of numbers.[92] Hilmi Bey sarcastically noted "a curious coincidence of circumstance": At the same time that the Egyptian Medical Association was holding a conference on birth control, a telegraph was published in the *Al-Ahram* newspaper on 17 April 1937, regarding the "Italian project encouraging people to marry and procreate,"[93] which included government bonds for married couples with children, and tax exemptions for fathers.[94]

In 1937, then, as the Italian Fascist Council was passing laws regarding preferences for heads of households over bachelors in the public sector and as Germany was providing tax exemptions for parents, reformers in Egypt wondered if their country was waging war on parenthood. Was it logical or nationalist to reduce births at the same time that militant neighbors were increasing theirs? Lawyer 'Abd al-Majid Nafi'a, linking pronatalism and nationalism inextricably, urged mothers to produce soldiers for the nation, and to leave behind misguided notions of the liberation of women (*tahrir al-mar'a*).[95]

The provision of social welfare was another key point of comparison between Egypt and other nations. In the West, it was argued, tax exemptions for parents, free education, and family rights were safeguarded. For those who argued from a Muslim perspective, the Islamic tradition contained within itself the principles of social welfare and social justice, which, ironically, were being upheld in the Western nations. Thus, for Muslim Brother Issa 'Abduh, it was peculiar to see the European nations providing familial welfare benefits while in Egypt—where Islam should have ensured the equitable distribution of wealth—poor families were struggling to subsist.[96] Obligatory Muslim practices such as tithing ensured the alleviation of "the burdens of poor families. . . . The unfortunate and needy have a claim over the more affluent; they are not simply to be sterilized or prevented from marrying."[97] Rather than promote social justice, the state had turned to birth control as a solution to its social problems.[98]

Policies such as the protection of parenthood (through tax exemptions and other financial incentives), the criminalization of abortion, and anti–birth-control legislation were increasingly commonplace in interwar Europe.[99] According to 'Abduh, Egypt had separated itself from the civilized nations by denying the rights of fathers. 'Abduh's discussion of European welfare practices was intended as a critique of Egypt's contemporary economic situation (particularly the hardships endured in the immediate aftermath of the post-Depression period) and the lack of an effective social policy to remedy the conditions of the working poor. Most interestingly,

'Abduh used Islamist rhetoric to mobilize the language of paternal privilege and responsibility (rather than maternal ignorance) to highlight the state's obligation to safeguard the family.[100]

Class Politics

As Ian Hacking has astutely noted, "the 'population problem' denotes both the population explosion of other peoples and too low a birth rate of one's own people. During the nineteenth century in France one's own people were French, the others German and British. In Prussia . . . the others were Jewish. Today the others are the Third World. In late-Victorian England, the others were the labouring classes."[101] The question of whose births to control often condensed a complex set of meanings, usually of relationships of domination. Numerous historical studies of population control movements in a variety of contexts have shown how the lower classes, "inferior" races, and ethnic minorities have often been most vigorously targeted by birth control programs.[102] In the Egyptian context, the lynchpin was class. Middle-class and elite social reformers had numerous concerns regarding birth control and class politics. With respect to class differences in fertility, on the whole, it was agreed that the lower classes (the urban poor and the peasantry) were more fertile than the middle or upper classes. Why this was so and what should be done about it, however, were subjects of heated debate. What factors affected the differential fertility of classes? Was fertility simply inversely related to civility and therefore class? Should certain classes be encouraged to propagate more than others? If a general birth-control program were to be launched, would there be unintended class consequences?

Perhaps the most eloquent participant at the 1937 Birth Control in Egypt conference to address the issue of class explicitly was 'Abbas Mustafa 'Ammar, who in 1953, as Chairman of the National Commission for Population Problems, would write the seminal memorandum "The Population Situation in Egypt."[103] At the conference 'Ammar presented his case for birth control as a philanthropic issue, explicitly targeting the rural and urban lower classes as the primary beneficiaries of a birth-control program.[104] Describing in Dickensian-like detail the life of the poor, overburdened as they were with children, he argued that workers and peasants were the most fertile class, that this resulted in their narrowed resources, and that overpopulation was the cause of Egypt's poverty. According to 'Ammar, there were three reasons behind this state of affairs: first, the poorer elements were less cognizant of the burdens of married life and less concerned with the condition of their children; second, many of these people married early because they viewed marriage in sexual terms only; and finally, many of the poor were completely ignorant of the methods of birth control, and so viewed children as disasters (*masa'ib*) that could not be helped, inescapable manifestations of God's will.[105]

In contrast, speakers such as Ali Fu'ad, Hasan al-Banna, and Muhammad Hasan argued that it was precisely the peasantry who would be unwilling to take up birth control. These authors argued that the peasantry was intentionally prolific, relying on their children to work in the fields. As Ali Fu'ad put it, children in the countryside were a laboring wealth (*tharwa 'amila*) and a patriarchal treasure.[106] For Islamist Hasan al-Banna, too, children represented a source of capital and wealth, and it was the peasantry who were thus most in need of offspring.[107] As Muhammad Hasan noted, the peasant with many children could work more land and amass more wealth—the more children he had, the prouder he was.[108]

'Ammar, himself from the Delta province of Menufiyya, attacked the opponents of birth control by accusing them of being insulated from the demographic masses.

> Perhaps there are some from the opposition who cannot imagine the level of misery that the majority of our citizens live in. And perhaps there are some who are so far removed from that environment, by their wealth and comfort, that they cannot comprehend the level to which millions of the sons of the nation have sunk. . . . You must immerse yourself among these classes to see how they live, crammed into narrow rooms, without sun or air, ill nourished. . . . Yes, you must live with the peasantry and interact with the workers in order to imagine the disruption society will face from excessive childbearing in these classes.[109]

It was through an identification with and immersion in the lives of workers and peasants that 'Ammar validated his interpretation of the state of the lower orders.

There was also the objection that birth control would affect the leading classes rather than the lower orders. Reformers felt that the birth rates of the enlightened classes had to be increased, thereby upholding the distribution of society, ensuring the maintenance of social standards, and increasing the likelihood of cultural renaissance.[110] Indeed, in answering those who were critical of the idea of birth control, the differential fertility of the various social classes was used explicitly to support pronatalist arguments. It was feared that the middle classes—postulated by Muhammad Hasan, Hasan al-Banna and 'Abd al-Majid Nafi'a to be the creative, intellectual, and productive sector of the nation—would be the ones to implement birth control. As the Islamist al-Banna said, it would be the educated classes who would accept the call to birth control, with harmful consequences for the nation. How could Egypt, he asked, "increase the progeny that will serve the nation" and obtain a multitude of sons?[111]

To these types of class-specific pronatalist arguments 'Ammar responded that there was no option but to maintain the "demographic metabolism" existent between the classes, which entailed continued birth planning among the more advantaged classes and the dissemination of birth-control propaganda among the poor, placing a limit on their shocking excess.[112] "Thus," he said, "we ask those who oppose the idea of birth planning: is it in the nation's interest for the less developed classes to exceed the other classes?"[113] Class was a controversial and divisive issue of debate. Reformers questioned the potential outcome of a sustained birth-control movement—particularly if middle-class families, the cornerstone of national life, succumbed to such antinatalist tendencies. Perhaps equally contentious was the issue of religion. In particular, disagreements arose as to whether or not birth planning was permissible according to Islamic dictates.

Religious Discourse

Included in the 1937 conference proceedings was the first *fatwa* (religious edict) in the twentieth century regarding birth control or planning. The text of the *fatwa*, issued in January 1937 by Shaykh Abd al-Majid Selim from Dar al-Ifta, responded to a question regarding the permissibility of child spacing as a safeguard against the inability of the inquirer to raise and care for his children (*tarbiyat al-awlad wa al-'inaya bihim*), or the possibility that he might suffer from ill-health or a nervous breakdown, or that his wife's health might deteriorate because of repeated pregnancies. The *fatwa* sanctions the prevention of pregnancy in the circumstances cited in the inquiry, with the following qualifications:

> The basic position in the school is that it is not the right of the man to ejaculate outside the vagina except with the permission of his wife and that it is not for the woman to shut off the opening of her uterus except with the permission of her husband. But it may be allowed (according to later *Hanafite* jurists) for the man to ejaculate outside the vagina without permission of the wife if he is afraid that the child born may act evilly because of the corruption of the age (*fasad al-zaman*). . . . By analogy, later jurists have said that the woman may obstruct her *os uteri* without permission of her husband if she has a justifiable reason. Briefly, then, the husband or wife may with the consent of each other use contraceptive measures to prevent male semen from reaching the woman's uterus. Further, according to later jurists, either the husband or wife may use

contraceptives . . . without the consent of the other party if he or she has excuses already cited or similar ones.

One more point needs to be discussed, namely, is it permissible to prevent pregnancy by abortion after impregnation occurs, but before life has breathed into the fetus? *Hanafite* jurists have differed on this issue. Although abortion has not been sanctioned as a rule, it has now been accepted that an exception may be made and abortion be permitted before the child is gifted with a soul, if the present pregnancy endangers the life of the previous child (e.g. stopping the mother's flow of milk so that the child will starve, or refuse to suckle from a wet nurse or if the father is unable to afford a wet nurse). Once a child is gifted with a soul abortion is strictly forbidden.[114]

Birth spacing or planning has a long history of debate in the Islamic tradition. The earliest and most comprehensive statement on permissibility of coitus interruptus (*al-'azl*) in Islamic jurisprudence is the medieval text of the *Shafa'i* scholar Imam Abu Hamid Muhammad al-Ghazali.[115] Al-Ghazali deemed coitus interruptus permissible when done for the following reasons: to avoid fathering children who would become slaves, to preserve the wife's beauty in order to ensure marital bliss, and to avoid economic hardships and "embarrassment" (*haraj*).[116] It was within the Islamic discursive tradition, then, that a modern jurist such as Majid argued, usually extrapolating by analogy (*qiyas*) from the justification of *al-'azl* to modern methods of birth control.

Majid's *fatwa* was argued on the grounds of moral and material improvement, that is, the fear that the newborn child might act evilly (because of general societal religious decline) or be improperly cared for (because of economic, health or social stresses faced by parents). In this sense, it was historically continuous with older edicts, which emphasized the fear of the child's moral corruption as the predominant motive for birth control. However, throughout the twentieth century and within the context of the modernizing nation-state, the emphasis would increasingly come to be placed on rational planning—planning for a family and for the future in accordance with one's social and economic abilities, and planning for the nation-state in accordance with its resources. It is in this sense, then, that Majid's *fatwa* may be considered modern.[117]

Shaykh Majid's *fatwa* was not, however, taken as axiomatic, and several participants at the conference—most notably the supreme guide of the Society of Muslim Brothers (*al-Ikhwan al-Muslimun*), Hasan al-Banna—took it upon themselves to discuss and qualify in detail the religious aspects of birth control or planning. Al-Banna had founded the Muslim Brothers, later to become a political party on par with the Wafd, in 1928, originally as an alternative association aimed at encouraging an Islamic revival and introducing Islam into all aspects of everyday life and society.[118] In 1932 the society relocated to Cairo, where it gained a following that included lower- and middle-class Egyptians (civil servants, urban workers, students, lawyers), estimated at hundreds of thousands by World War II. Committed to the ideals of social justice, anti-imperialism, pan-Islamism, and a free Palestine, al-Banna founded a daily newspaper, *Al-Ikhwan al-Muslimun*, to express the principles of the society.[119] For al-Banna, Islam was a total system that encompassed all human affairs, practical and spiritual.[120] First and foremost, Islam required the maintenance of rightly guided religious and ethical practice through an adherence to the precepts of the *Qur'an*, *Shari'a*, and *Sunna*, which set general and foundational principles for the life of the individual and of the community. Such adherence, however, could not be assumed—rather, it required an active entity to ensure it and to "convince those weak and recalcitrant selves who do not accept evidence and proof," and "if the people cloak proof and stray, then war is preferable to the world of safety."[121]

According to al-Banna, therein lay the Islamic justification for *jihad*, or holy war, in which a noble army attained victory through truth, and without oppression, material exploitation, or self-interested colonization. Thus, he argued, Islam ordered a continuous state of preparedness and strength for *jihad* as a religious duty. For al-Banna, the logical corollary was that "Islam commands a multitude of offspring, it incites it and calls for it, and does not ask for control or lessening."[122] Of course, there were instances in which necessity and the specificity of individual and familial circumstances could allow that which was forbidden (*yubih al-mahzurat*).[123] For al-Banna, those instances were indeed exceptional and did not alter what he considered the fundamental interdiction against birth control. Issa 'Abduh (the other Muslim Brother in attendance at the 1937 conference) concurred with al-Banna. *Jihad*, he argued, was obligatory, and thus necessitated a glorious military presence and plentiful army. 'Abduh argued that the contemporary example of the Ethiopian war ("the current destruction of Africa by Rome") was an instance of military superiority premised on the destruction and annihilation of weaker races, and thus was the antithesis of the Islamic ideal of *jihad*, conversion, and assimilation with conquered peoples.[124]

One of the key points of contention between Islamists and others was whether or not birth control practiced out of the fear of poverty was permissible, or was simply evidence of a lack of faith in God's beneficence. In the most extreme cases, speakers at the conference equated birth control with infanticide, as did 'Abduh: "do not murder your children, fearing want, we will provide for them and whosoever has murdered them has erred greatly."¹²⁵ To prevent a living being from coming into existence through the use of contraception, by this account, was a crime equivalent to murder, no different than infanticide, and to commit the act out of fear of poverty or want was to doubt God's grace and wide beneficence.¹²⁶ For Issa 'Abduh, interference in childbearing was permissible in the case of "harm," whether that harm be a threat to the mother's health or a threat to society posed by unsound offspring. 'Abduh specifically excluded the fear of material need, assuming parents and potential offspring were of sound mind and body.¹²⁷ Instead, he posited the encouragement of child bearing as the highest ideal for the Muslim family, arguing that Egyptian family life had become mired in luxury and required a return to simplicity.¹²⁸ 'Abduh blamed the un-Islamic state, which, forgetting the importance of the family to the nation's prosperity, had neglected the fate of the family, leaving the head of the household to bear the social and economic burdens of the postwar period.¹²⁹ Social welfare projects formed the cornerstone of the Muslim Brothers' response to the economic difficulties of the interwar and postwar periods, and were the foundation of their critique of the secular state.¹³⁰

Al-Banna, too, urged conference participants to think more critically regarding the causes of Egypt's social and economic problems. He asked,

> have we ascertained with certainty that the cause of our social predicament is too many births? Is there any other social cure? Is it possible that birth control will not solve the problem at hand . . . but that we will simply have fewer offspring? That is to say, will birth control lead to stronger progeny (or just fewer)?¹³¹

As advocates of a pan-Islamist supranational vision, both al-Banna and 'Abduh argued that Islam did not follow the political divisions of nations in the Muslim world. As a religion, nation, and race (*al-Islam din wa watan wa jinsiyya*), Islam recognized no borders or limits. As such, population excess in one part of the *umma (Islamic community)* could fill a dearth in another.¹³² Al-Banna's position was what Gershoni and Jankowski have referred to as Supra-Egyptian in orientation. That is to say, al-Banna, like many other Islamists, rejected the exclusive emphasis on territorial Egyptian nationalism, arguing instead for a broader pan-Islamic geographical conception, with profound implications for conceptions of population.¹³³

Normalizing Gender, Normalizing Sexuality

Religious leaders were not the only ones to draw on moral arguments in making a case for birth control. Medical doctors, even though they focused on the medical benefits of birth control, also resorted to moral argumentation. At times the medical dangers of excess childbearing were foregrounded, especially by those inside the medical profession, as one of the principle reasons for the use of birth control. According to A. M. Anous, the "dangers of frequent childbearing" included "reproductive insanity," criminal abortion, liver trouble, weakening of uterine musculature, difficult labors, misdirection of uterine axes, and accidental hemorrhage. These diseases made it clear that "the only salvation for us lies in birth control and that what we might lose even in instituting birth control will be more than amply compensated for by having healthier and more useful mothers, and healthier, more vigorous and better trained children."[134] Indeed, criminal abortion was considered one of the more serious effects of the lack of widespread knowledge of birth control, as was the use of folk methods to prevent conception.[135] Abortions could be legally performed only in cases of medical danger to the mother's health, and only in the first trimester. The use of folk methods was assumed to be widespread, and although statistics on the prevalence of abortions were largely unknown, there was thought to be a large segment of the poorer classes who would resort to criminal abortion out of desperation and poverty. Scientific birth planning was viewed, then, a means to eradicate criminal abortions associated with the dangerous under classes.[136]

The devaluation of both illicit sexuality (sexual activity outside of marriage) and celibacy was evident in discussions of prolonged bachelorhood.[137] For Fu'ad, Anous, 'Ammar, and Muhammad, the prevalence of a large number of bachelors in society was considered a cause of social anomie. They argued that birth spacing therefore maintained marital bliss, and would aid in the prevention of social perversions such as prostitution, illicit sexual relations (*zina*), homosexuality, and abstention.[138] Those who encouraged birth control for these reasons felt early marriage to be "morally and materially uplifting," as it would help prevent illicit social relations, effectively normalizing middle-class sexuality.[139] "Of the other ways of shirking the responsibilities of bigger families and too many children—including such morbid conditions as abstention from marriage or its postponement, sexual perversions, prostitution, and criminal abortion—contraception is by far the most safe and reasonable method, especially if practiced properly and under competent guidance."[140]

One dissenting voice, however, noted that the use of birth control was itself a form of sexual perversion and an "unnatural" act. Hilmi Bey noted the various symptoms and diseases that resulted from unnatural acts during sexual intercourse. Such symptoms included dyspnea (asthma), sciata, and impotence in males, headaches, constipation, and nervous diseases. In his discussion of abnormal intercourse, Hilmi discussed coitus interruptus in detail. For Hilmi, any state of incomplete ejaculation or orgasm (in men and women) eventually resulted in pathology (premature ejaculation and impotence in men, and nervous and psychological diseases in anorgasmic women).[141]

Normalizing sexuality within the parameters of bourgeois companionate marriage, along with organizing reproduction within a framework of social reform, has often effaced women's centrality to reproduction, as Rayna Rapp and Faye Ginsburg have argued.[142] It was no different in Egypt, where women remained objects of population discourse, effectively excluded from the public discourse on birth control, until the middle of the century. Women's erasure from the discourse of birth control, however, did not go entirely unnoticed throughout the 1937 conference. One speaker, whose address was aptly titled, "A Word for Women on Birth Planning," pointed out that men dominated the entire conference, and that she would present "a woman's voice on a woman's issue." Zahya Marzuq, a member of the Egyptian Association for Social Studies, reprimanded the audience for their neglect of women's role in childbearing.[143] Like many feminists of the time, Marzuq based many of her arguments on maternalist assumptions that relegated reproduction, as well as child rearing, to the domain of women. Marzuq argued that in order for women to attend properly to child care they had to avoid the perils of early marriage and excessive childbearing. Further, she warned against the creation of unwanted children, which would lead to juvenile criminality, vagrancy, and unsociability. Asserting that children should be three to four years apart, she cited psychological studies that indicated the negative effects of large families on children's psyches.[144]

'Abbas 'Ammar, the only other conference participant to address gender, argued along maternalist lines, but addressed the liberation of women (*tahrir al-mar'a*) directly. Indeed, he faulted the Egyptian women's movement for not incorporating birth planning in their agenda. He argued that birth planning would leave women free to fulfill their duties in the home, as well as to undertake the necessary reform of Egyptian society—a burden that he felt would increasingly come to fall on women (the secret of the progress of the civilized nations).[145] How, 'Ammar asked, could women liberate themselves if childbearing took up all their time? Birth planning would enable women to coordinate their household and societal duties. For 'Ammar, the choice was to be made by women—"the dividing line between her freedom and her enslavement" lay outside the home, in the reformist politics of the day.[146]

As we have already seen, productive involvement in social reform (often in maternalist and child welfare programs) was among the first spheres outside of domestic activity that upper-class Egyptian women became involved in. However, rather than emphasize the opportunities that birth planning would afford women and society, most discussions of population in the 1930s and 1940s posed birth control as a question of social reform (quality), or alternately, political economy (quantity), thereby relegating it once again to the male domain of governance and reformist politics. Above all, it was the social reform and uplift of the countryside and urban poor, in order to contain social anomie, that received the most attention.

The Question of Reform

Although no formal population policy would be promulgated in Egypt until 1953, some proposals for a population policy that would address the question of social reform were put forth in the interwar period. Abd al-Hakim al-Rifa'i, for example, encouraged the establishment of scientific associations that would study population scientifically, before prescribing particular policies. This would include the study of demographic patterns and the determination of an optimum population. Birth planning, according to al-Rifa'i, could be accomplished without legislation, through the formation of private associations that would encourage a later age of marriage or birth prevention for the poor. "I want to underscore the importance of the population issue in Egypt, and suggest the establishment of a national commission for the scientific study of population, composed of doctors, economists, lawyers and other interested parties."[147] According to al-Rifa'i,

> By population policy is meant the sum total of steps taken by the state to encourage the procreation of sound elements [al-'anasir al-tayibba] and prevent the procreation of harmful elements [al-'anasir al-darra], and provide for the comfort of the people. By following this policy, the state is working toward the benefit of society [maslahat al-mujtama'] over that of the individual. . . . Egypt, in its current state, is in need of a general strategy of population, due to the great increase in numbers and the decline in standard of living. This is evident to anyone who observes life in the countryside, where the basic necessities of life are lacking, materially (e.g., homes, clothing, etc.) and morally (e.g., general culture, education . . .). There is no doubt that the proliferation of ignorance and illiteracy prevents the peasant from using modern scientific methods in agriculture, and as such he cultivates the land using arcane methods. Further, the peasants' health has declined due to smoking, black tea, and exposure to germs and diseases such as schistosomiasis and hookworm. We feel the government population policy disseminated through education and generalized hospitals should be directed toward: birth planning, the increase of agricultural and industrial production, and raising the people's standard of living and providing a comfortable life to them.[148]

Al-Rifaʿi's statement indicates, quite precisely, the convergence of concerns regarding rural reform and the population question. The deplorably low standard of livings of the peasantry was intimately bound to their overpopulation. His remarkably prescient proposals for the establishment of a statist population plan and commission would not become a reality until the early 1950s, when a scientific commission for the study of population was established in Egypt.

But what if the concern for numbers was simply a deflection from the social issues at hand? According to Ahmad Khayri Saʿid, this was precisely what the debate between pronatalists and anti-natalists had caused—a digression from the practical question of social reform. Surely, he argued "we should prevent the mentally deranged, mentally ill, and those with weak nerves, from procreating. But how can we enforce this in our country? We have large numbers of victims of pellagra, hookworm, schistosomiasis, and large numbers of the mentally and physically weak. Shall we sterilize half or one-third of the fellahin . . . ?"[149] The solution, he opined, was radical social reform, or the creation of a new Egypt, which required no less than men like Mustafa Kemal, Mussolini, or Hitler.[150]

> The revolution against social conditions and class differences has begun. People leave the countryside migrating to the city looking for work. And as numbers have increased beyond available jobs, migrants join the ranks of thugs, smugglers, and evil-doers. The unemployed educated urban youths, too, revolt in small ways—by demonstrating, taking hostages in schools, and work. This is the true Egypt. Pronatalists have gotten what they want, and antinatalists have ammunition for their argument. As I said, neither the increase nor the decrease of numbers is a solution for the problems at hand. What matter if a country increases or decreases in number but maintains the status quo? These are the symptoms of the illness and its diagnosis- but what is the treatment? Thinkers have differed. Reform should not be patching or mending. Old clothes no matter how much mended, or old buildings no matter how much repaired, will eventually fall apart.[151]

"The revolution against social conditions and class differences" had indeed begun, not as a radical "frontal assault" against the social structure, but in the regulation of the demographic metabolism between the social classes and the promotion of ameliorative social reform projects for the laboring classes.

. . .

The modernization of reproduction in interwar Egypt was a cornerstone of social-scientific research, as harnessed to the nationalist project of regenerating Egyptian society through the reform of women and the peasantry.

Debates over the benefits and disadvantages of birth control condensed complex issues of class, gender, and religion, as well as the nature of modernity within the Egyptian polity. As such, population discourse was fundamental in the constitution of notions of the modern family and the creation of new habits of modernity: cleanliness, hygiene, and thrift; and habits of home: monogamous sexuality, bourgeois companionate marriage, and small family size. Further, the statist projects of "civilizing" women and peasants was a crucial component of ensuring the well-being and strength of the laboring population and hence optimizing its ability to produce and provide for the needs of the nation. Many social reformers (both pronatalist and antinatalist) exhibited concern for the fate of the Egyptian family, particularly in the arduous post-Depression years, and demanded interventionist social policies from the Egyptian state in order to safeguard the interests and welfare of the family. Thus, a more radical frontal assault "against social conditions and class differences" was deferred, and replaced by regulation of the demographic metabolism between social classes and the promotion of social-reform projects—be they rural reconstruction or population management—for the "lower orders."

IV *The Revolutionary Moment*

7 Etatism

Theorizing Egypt's 1952 Revolution

> My basic thesis is that it is not possible to pose these questions (and therefore to answer them) *except from the point of view of reproduction.*
> —Louis Althusser, Lenin and Philosophy

It is not difficult to imagine the scene in Tahrir Province (the definitive land reclamation project inaugurated under Gamal Abdel Nasser) upon the arrival of a high profile visitor—such as the Yugoslavian ambassador, who visited in January 1957, or the representatives of the newly formed National Assembly, in September 1957.[1] Former peasants appeared now as citizens, the men dressed in gingham shirts and overalls, the women in white shirts, black skirts, and printed headscarves, looking quite picturesque for the cameras. Early-morning visitors would no doubt witness the call to attention, the daily salutes and nationalist songs sung in unison. Visitors would also surely note, as did scholar Doreen Warriner during her 1956 visit, that settlers had been subjected to "complete human reconditioning. . . . Every aspect of their lives was disciplined and standardised."[2] They might also have remarked upon the rows of new houses, each identical to the other, "consisting of two rooms, a hall, a kitchen, and a bathroom . . . a front terrace and a backyard," all "carefully planned and built according to health conditions."[3] The village itself, with its wide, straight roads and a main square situated in the center (with buildings for village administration, a cooperative center, school, nursery, and clubs for migrants and employees), would have appeared quite unlike any other "typical" Egyptian village in the Delta.[4] An especially astute observer might also have noticed the peculiar absence of any children running around the village—all were safely ensconced in day-care centers.

The totalizing model of social welfare embodied in the Tahrir Province project is evident in the multitude of social welfare projects that marked women and the peasantry as objects of moral and material improvement, and which occurred in tandem with the emergence of the problem of the population, since the 1930s. These attempts at the reconstitution of the Egyptian mother-child unit and the peasantry focused upon individuated detail—the emphasis was on reconstructing bodies and minds: building and cleaning villages, homes, and children, and thus constructing a "new Egyptian."

During the interwar period, and up until the end of World War II, two sets of debates dominated social-scientific discourse in Egypt: the problem of the peasantry and the problem of population. These concerns remained central to the post–World War II era, up through and including the Nasser period. Although Egypt achieved nominal independence from the British in 1922, and furthered the terms of its independence in 1936 with the signing of the Anglo-Egyptian Treaty, its postcoloniality is considered to have begun with the 1952 revolution, led by Gamal Abdel Nasser and organized around state socialism. Yet rather than interpret Egypt's 1952 revolution as marking a fundamental disjuncture with the previous sociopolitical order, I suggest that Egyptian history from the 1930s to the 1960s is best viewed as part of a single historical bloc.[5]

I propose an alternative framework for understanding the organization of the postcolonial Egyptian state and society, which I call a "social-welfare mode of regulation" underpinned by an economic system of etatism.[6] A social-welfare mode of regulation is premised upon the state apparatus as arbiter not only of economic development, but also of social welfare. Some of the salient features of this mode of regulation are the rejection of the maximization of economic utility as the sole telos of social life; a view of "the people" (the demographic masses) as resources of national wealth (the motor of its development, as it were) and as the primary object of governance; the attempt to contain radical social change through piecemeal social reform and amelioration of the conditions of the working poor; the development of an interventionist policy of social planning and engineering; and a totalizing model of social welfare, meant to encompass economic, social, and political factors at the same time.

Social welfare, of course, should not be understood solely as an idealist, benevolent process whereby the state or social scientists shepherd citizens in their own welfare. Rather, it refers quite specifically to the social and political process of reproducing particular social relations (often based on violence and coercion), such as those between the city and the countryside, at least partly to ensure the successful reproduction of labor power and to minimize class antagonisms.

As Karl Polanyi has shown, the continuous expansion of the market economy may be seen in terms of a double movement of the principle of liberalism—laissez-faire and free trade on the one hand, and the principles of interventionism and protectionism on the other hand.[7] The latter provides a check on the market force in the form of protective legislation, and is meant to safeguard against the market's own self-destructive tendencies (to annihilate land and labor). That is to say, the tendency is to simultaneously commodify and find institutions that place limitations on the processes of commodification and exploitation, in order to avoid exploiting land and labor to the point of destruction, or to the point after which it can no longer reproduce itself.[8]

Social-welfare regulation in Egypt can be best understood by examining the ancillary components of the state apparatus—namely those members of the state apparatus who in various capacities, mostly educational and technocratic, were politically responsible for addressing the key issues of Egypt's transition from a colonial to a nationalist postcolonial social and political modernity.[9] Tracing the new modes of governance, expertise, and social knowledge that defined a particular era of nationalist politics, I eschew an interpretation of Nasserism that focuses on populism, or charismatic claims of national sovereignty and identity.[10] Instead, I underscore how Nasserism built upon the historical processes and structures that preceded it, and also the extent to which Nasserism was based on an assemblage of institutional apparatuses, technocratic practices, and modes of knowledge production, rather than simply on emotive appeals.

Etatism

As Egyptian economist Mourad Magdi Wahba has argued, the development of etatism in Egypt (understood as the interaction of economic developments, ideology, and government policy) can be said to have begun in 1916 with the convening of the Commission pour le Commerce et l'Industrie, which represented the first "conscious attempt by a capitalist group to promote industrialization and to enlist the help of the state in the process."[11] Wahba notes the speed with which the transition was made in Egypt between a free-market economy with strong links to foreign capital to a quasi-industrial economy with state hegemony over the productive process.[12] Contesting the predominant historiography, he contends that there was indeed a strong capitalist class in Egypt before 1952, "strong enough to promote the growth of etatism."[13] Wahba locates the formation of the etatist system between 1916 and 1957, and its implementation between 1958 and 1961. What, then, were the principle economic features of etatism?

According to Wahba, the series of economic crises relating to cotton prices that plagued Egypt between 1902 and 1914, and especially the crisis of 1921, conveyed to Egyptian businessmen and policy makers the precarious nature of an economy dependent on monoculture, and the disruption of trade during World War I provided a boost to local manufacturing and commerce, making the necessity of economic diversification clear to all.[14] By the time of the publication of the commerce commission's report in 1918 (the *Rapport de la Commission du Commerce et de l'Industrie*) many key elements of etatism had crystallized, namely: the assertion of industrialization as the path to progress, the need for state assistance in that goal, and economic nationalism (or the conflict between foreign and local capital). Wahba provides two examples of etatism for this period: the establishment of a *régie* (administration)for the Société des Sucreries et des Raffineries d'Egypte, which granted the sugar monopoly in Egypt the advantage of prohibitory tariffs on sugar imports, as well as government controls on sugar-cane acreage and farm-gate prices; and the well-known Piastre Plan (*Mashru' al-qirsh*), which was intended to foster the growth of a local fez industry.[15]

One facet of etatism, the privileging and indigenization of industry, took shape in the late 1930s and 1940s. Spurred on by the effects of World War II on the Egyptian economy (the disruption of international trade, increased industrialization to meet import substitution, increased demand), industry was strengthened and Egyptianized during this period, and the state played an increasing role in the economy (for example, it became involved in military factories, as a result of the failure of the 1948 war in Palestine).[16] Important markers of etatism, according to Wahba, were the development of the first five-year plan in 1946 to organize production and infrastructure; the 1947 creation of an Industrial Bank; the passing of laws for the Egyptianization of corporations; and the injection of state capital to form the Crédit Agricole et Foncier d'Egypte (thereby moving in the direction of state organization of agriculture).[17]

It is interesting to note that at precisely the same time that a concern for industry was beginning to engage the interests of the agrarian and industrial bourgeoisie, there emerged the question of population. Indeed, writers often linked the question of overpopulation to the development of industry. In the late 1930s, both Hamid El-Sayed Azmi and A. E. Crouchley argued that industrial development would absorb Egypt's excess agricultural population into the labor force.[18] Yet, despite the ideological fixation on the question of the peasantry and rural social reform, interwar writings on the peasantry and on population were marked by the eclipse of questions of income or land distribution, evidenced in the focus on the geographical or natural foundations of poverty (too little land, too many people).

How are we to explain this egregious omission in the literature on the peasantry and on population—had no one noticed the gross maldistribution of Egypt's landownership? As has been pointed out by Gabriel Baer, the question of the distribution of private property "engaged Egyptian public opinion only to a slight degree before the 1940s. Apart from the proposal advanced by the insignificant Communist Party in the early 1920s, no demand was made to limit the size of great estates or to confiscate them, and there was no public discussion of the question."[19] For instance the land problem was ignored by all political party platforms in the 1930s. According to Baer, this could be related to the hegemony of the landowning classes—and in particular their strong political and parliamentary presence after 1936. In the 1940s, however, the agrarian question was beginning to occupy center stage in political discussions, and a series of books touching on the issue were published.[20] What caused this shift? Baer finds a variety of factors, including the Anglo-Egyptian Treaty of 1936 and the 1937 ban on the Capitulations, which led to a political shift toward domestic affairs; the social and economic dislocations caused by war; the malaria epidemic in Upper Egypt; and the circulation among the intelligentsia of ideas surrounding social justice.[21]

In fact, the construction of "the problem of population" effectively served to displace any discussion of an agrarian crisis in Egyptian political-economy writings at this time. The onslaught of writings on population between 1936 and 1942 was itself a response to the acute nature of the social and economic state of Egypt's agricultural laborers in the post-independence period. It was this crisis in the social reproduction of labor power—the inability of the agricultural classes to reproduce themselves in a viable fashion, along with the need to coordinate the organization of production with that of biological and social reproduction—that led to a growing concern for the reduction of population and the improvement of standards of living.

The problem of population was made salient by the attempt to politically contain the historically determined problems of the 1930s and 1940s—gross mal-distribution of agricultural land; rises in agricultural rents; increased rural crime; and a drop in the average income of the rural laborer, despite an increase in national income. This was accomplished through a naturalization of poverty, a focus on overpopulation as a cause of poverty rather than a symptom of existing conditions of capitalism (the radical alienation of the peasantry from the means of production); and the problematic was thus directed away from the question of redistribution of wealth. The agrarian question did not emerge full-blown until the final years of World War II, at which point the economic state of the rural proletariat had sunk to such depths of poverty that the questions of land reform and more radical social reform were all but necessary to avoid the dangers of revolutionary ferment. From 1942 to 1945 (and beyond), the agrarian question dominated public debate, although no substantive actions were taken to ameliorate the economic situation of the peasantry until the advent of the revolutionary regime.

In the mid-1940s, analyses of the countryside began to deal with the historical and political-economic dimensions of the agrarian question, as issues of landownership and class became central, and attempts were made to forge a unified front between workers and peasants.[22] Two landmark texts were published at this time that represented divergent ideological agendas: Mirrit Butrus Ghali's reformist *Al-islah al-zira'i* (*Agrarian Reform*), and the Marxist analysis of Ahmed Sadiq Sa'd, *Mushkilat al-fellah* (*The Problem of the Peasantry*). Thus, by 1945 the agrarian question was at the top of political agendas, with the first plan for agrarian reform being proposed in the senate by Muhammad Khattab Bey in 1944 (a plan that writer and head of the Liberal Constitutionalist Party Muhammad Husayn Haykal, and general secretary of the Wafd Muhammad Sabri Abu 'Alam agreed to bury), and a flood of texts being published on the need for agrarian reform.[23] The attempt to contain radical social change in the countryside led to the elision of the question of the distribution of wealth and landed property from the political agenda of interwar Egypt. By the end of World War II, however, the question of distribution emerged to dominate public discourse—setting the stage for the 1952 revolutionary land reforms.

Passive Revolution

It now remains to explicate the mode of historical transformation embodied in Egypt's 1952 revolution. Partha Chatterjee's discussion of the national postcolonial state hinges on a conception of passive revolution as "the general framework of capitalist transition in societies in which bourgeois hegemony has not been accomplished in the classical way."[24] Following Chatterjee's analytic framework, it may be argued that Egypt's 1952 revolution, rather than inaugurate either a national bourgeois revolution or the radical socialist transformation it espoused, effected what amounts to piecemeal, molecular, legal and reformist revisions of the previous political-economic order, without radically dismantling class relations and power structures. This relates primarily to the postcolonial problematic of establishing national independence on the one hand, and eradicating social inequalities, engendered or exacerbated by colonial domination and capitalism on the other. As Nasser put it, it was the problem of simultaneously enacting the political revolution, *al-thawra al-siyasiyya*, or national sovereignty and self-determination, and the social revolution, *al-thawra al-ijtima'iyya*—a dilemma faced by many anticolonial nationalists and widely discussed at the Second Congress of the Communist International.[25]

In consolidating an anticolonial nationalist regime, the postcolonial state in Egypt created an alliance between the ruling class and segments of the older dominant classes; constraining both in effecting either a radical national socialist project or a bourgeois hegemony. This is so for several reasons. In the first place, the institutional structures and logic of rational authority (administrative, bureaucratic, managerial state apparatus, and the logic of planning) were in many ways continuous with those set up in the period of colonial rule. In addition, no full-scale assault was launched on the previously dominant classes, despite state ownership of the means of production; rather, their former power was limited, and attempts were made to bring them into "a position of subsidiary allies within a reformed state structure."[26] Furthermore, no radical restructuring of class relations took place; rather, class antagonisms were contained by several mechanisms, most notably moderate land reform and various concessions and palliatives to labor. Politically, the regime sought to contain the possibility of any broad-based revolutionary movement, hence the attempts at cooptation and the violence perpetrated against its two main ideological contenders, the Muslim Brothers and the Marxist-Communist Left, as well as the abolition of political parties and organizations. Finally, what the post-1952 regime effectively created was as an etatist welfare regime, characterized by a social-welfare mode of regulation, continuous with the earlier period of the 1930s and 1940s. The postcolonial state's concern for welfare thus illustrates a continuity with the post-independence period, rather than the fundamental disjuncture usually presumed to have occurred with the 1952 revolution.

What the postcolonial state achieves, according to Chatterjee, is a "synthetic hegemony. . . . The reification of the nation in the body of the state becomes the means for constructing this hegemonic structure, and the extent of control over the new state apparatus becomes a precondition for further capitalist development."[27] As I will argue, the political-ideological legitimacy of the postcolonial state lay in its role as the purveyor of national welfare, articulated in the name of the interests of the demographic mass of the population, that is, as the representative of the national-popular. As

Abdel-Malek framed it quite early on, the fundamental problematic of post-1952 Egypt was the reconquest of political power and economic power, and, more importantly, the reconquest national identity.[28]

Capital and Class

As several analysts chronicle it, the Nasser regime concentrated its efforts upon dismantling the old landed aristocracy through agrarian reform and co-opting the old industrial bourgeoisie to further its own aims of large-scale national industrialization.[29] The new class that emerged and characterized the state public sector, however, was a "state bourgeoisie," made up of the new class of technocrats together with older elements of the industrial, financial, and commercial bourgeoisie who insinuated themselves into the public sector. Both classes obstructed the nationalist government's plan for guided industrial and economic development, furthering their own interests instead. As Malak Zaalouk states, "while the genesis of a public sector was being created and the old bourgeoisie was being threatened and dismantled as a 'class' towards the end of the period, some of its members had managed to survive and help give rise to a new class within the state ruling class, i.e. a 'state bourgeoisie.'"[30] The strength of Zaalouk's analysis lay in her illustration of the various ways in which the old bourgeoisie (agrarian, industrial, and commercial) continued to play a crucial role up through the Nasser period, indeed until *infitah*. The Free Officers, she argues, inadvertently facilitated the old bourgeoisie's continued hegemony, allowing them to retain their former economic dominance and political influence. What is crucial to recognize in all of this is the extent to which the economic policy of the state inadvertently intersected with the interests of the older capitalist bourgeoisie.

As in Nehruvian India and Kemalist Turkey, the importance of state planning in Nasserist Egypt centered around the key issues of national independence and socioeconomic progress, with large-scale industrialization and centralized national planning at the forefront of the agenda.[31] The trajectory of state planning marked out the regime's initial path of a collaborative effort with the capitalist bourgeoisie and an active search for domestic private and foreign investment in order to subsidize large-scale industrialization projects. This was followed by increased state control over the ownership of the means of production, nationalization of foreign companies, the formation of a National Planning Committee, and the formulation of the first industrial plan. Between 1961 and 1967, the creation of a state sector was marked by massive nationalization policies and centralized state control for directed economic development; state-led initiatives in industry, banking, finance, and commerce; the extension of government control over the private sector; and the more rapid growth of a state technocratic class—all embodied in the first five-year plan (1960–65) and the various National Planning Commissions.

The regime's policy towards labor activism and trade unionism was characterized by a two-pronged policy of co-optation of labor and union leaders (their incorporation into the state apparatus) and extensive revisions of labor legislation (for example, legislating job security and improved material benefits).[32] Such strategies mollified workers by improving their standards of living, and were perceived as part of the regime's efforts at social justice. Autonomous labor action and the political independence of the trade unions were curtailed by a legislative ban on all strikes, laws on the arbitration and conciliation of labor disputes, and a new trade-union law. These patterns of political containment, corporatism, government conciliation and arbitration, political heteronomy, and outright violent repression should be thought of neither as endemic to Egyptian political culture nor as unique to the Nasser period.[33] Rather, they were both continuous with, and the effect of, earlier patterns under colonial tutelage that had sought to diffuse forms of political and labor activism.

Land reform, in many respects the locus of the regime's self-definition, was promulgated under several laws that established land ceilings. Although successful in dismantling the large estates, these laws were less effective in redistributing land to the smaller landowners. Simply put, what land reform succeeded in was redistributing land to the rural middle class, leaving the predominance of landholdings in the arena of 50 to 100 *feddans*; it thereby eroded the landed aristocracy and the mercantile rural elite, and transformed rich and middle peasants into a new rural elite engaged in capitalist intensive agriculture. For small proprietors, and especially for the poor and near landless peasants, the reforms were less propitious. Although their relative number and percentage ownership of cultivated land did increase, serious inequities remained, and poor peasants continued to rely on wage labor, as proletarianization among migrant farm workers continued. The ability of the agrarian bourgeoisie and even the old landed aristocracy to continue to insinuate itself and consolidate its holdings through subversions of the intent of land redistribution should not be underestimated. Land inequity continued to be a substantive problem. Agricultural cooperatives, both productive and consumptive, served to further palliate rural labor, and were continuous with the cooperative policies of the 1930s and 1940s that had aimed at ameliorating the standards of living of the peasantry, as well as providing holistic social welfare. Thus, the land reform policy ushered in a new system of agrarian stratification while at the same time containing class conflict by minimizing glaring inequities and providing concessions to the small landholders, and by freeing peasants from complete social, economic, and political dependence on large landlords.

Rational State Planning, Ideology, and Modern Power

> Adequate socialist planning is the only path that would ensure the complete use of our natural resources—material, natural and human—in a practical, scientific and humane manner that would enable us to achieve the welfare of the entire people and make a comfortable life available to them.
>
> —*Egypt's National Charter*

Interpretations of Nasserism have centered on the state apparatus. Discussions have tended to focus on the authoritarian-bureaucratic state structure, characterized by a highly state-centralized process of socioeconomic development, a corporatist, prebendal, or patrimonial state bourgeoisie, a single-party system bolstered by a repressive state apparatus, and a populist nationalist ideology. This political formation, interpreters argue, proved incapable of radically restructuring the Egyptian state, society, and economy, as signified by the failure to build an industrialized, capitalist or socialist, liberal democratic nation-state.[34] Such accounts, however, define Egyptian postcoloniality by a series of lacks or absences, and leave untheorized the discursive field mapped out by the contested ideological terrain of post-1952 Egypt.[35] Crucially, they do not adequately answer the following question: How did the Nasser regime attempt to secure and maintain hegemony, or organize and educate consent?[36] Rather than focus on the state-apparatus, following Chatterjee, I shift the terms of the debate to the formation of a postcolonial national popular. As Chatterjee notes, the postcolonial state becomes the embodiment of a rational consciousness—as executor of the nation's resources—distinct from the colonial state in its concern for the development of the nation, rather than the exploitation of its resources.[37] The Nasser regime was marked by a new focus on comprehensive national planning based on principles of objective scientific research and a concern for national welfare.

However, Chatterjee's assertion that the distinctive and positive content of the postcolonial state is to be found in a developmentalist ideology seems unfounded. In the case of Egypt, planning did come to embody the rational consciousness of the state under Nasser, but that rationality was contingent upon a conception of social welfare as the telos of government. This mode of regulation was continuous with the social-welfare projects of the 1930s and 1940s. State power, then, lay in the rationality of planning and the rationalization of political power, embodied in Egypt in the new technocratic-managerial class, and state legitimacy lay with the state's project of social welfare. It is in this capacity, as the provider of proper welfare rather than as proponent of the process of socioeconomic development, that the Egyptian postcolonial state marked its distinctive content.

The Nasser-period projects were distinguished from the earlier period by the scientific nature of socialist planning.[38] The aim and object of planning were conceived as an organic whole, understood as government and people, geared towards economic and social progress. Planning was never simply about the construction and implementation of schemes. Rather, within the nexus of the socialist project, planning also constituted the collectivity ("the people") in the construction of the social-welfare project. Egypt's precolonial backwardness was to be expunged through rigorously planned schemes that would utilize the nation's resources in the general interests of all citizens, but within the rubric of an aggregate concept of welfare.

The Nasser period is distinguished from later periods in the continuation of the idiom of social welfare. Social-welfare schemes emphasized the ability to create a productive, rationally and scientifically managed state that could adequately provide for its population and the goals of a postcolonial and post-exploitative industrialized modernity. The fact that these projects were framed within a model of social welfare does not diminish the fact that the modernist focus on national and individual production and efficiency was firmly in place. The importance of increased productivity during this phase related to the proper scientific management of the resources of the state and their distribution throughout the population in a manner consonant with the state's goal as provider of proper welfare, and not economic "development." There were two principal domains of statecraft in which the revolutionary regime attempted to assert its hegemony in an etatist welfare mode: land reclamation and resettlement, and population planning.

People and Land under Reclamation

> Building factories is easy, building canals is easy, building dams is easy—but building men, that is the harshest difficulty.
>
> —*Gamal Abdel Nasser,* Takwin wa tanmiyat al-mujtama'at al-jadida fi al-aradi al-mustasliha

Land reclamation projects were launched under Nasser to address the slow rate of expansion of cultivated land area relative to rapid population growth. Government efforts focused both on reducing population growth through the nascent family-planning programs and on expanding horizontally to reclaim land. Land reclamation and resettlement was primarily the purview of governmental agencies such as the Permanent Organization for Land Reclamation, established in 1954 and consolidated in 1966, along with several other agencies, into the Egyptian Authority for the Utilization and Development of Reclaimed Land (EAUDRL).[39] Numerous actors, institutional formations, and political blocs (in particular, the burgeoning technocratic elite of the Army Corps) competed to engineer the development and maintenance of land reclamation projects such as Tahrir Province. Newly formed state agencies, such as the Organization for Land Reclamation, as well as reinvigorated ministries such as the Ministry of Agriculture and the Ministry of Social Affairs, were actively involved in the development of social-welfare policies aligned with the new political orientation of the Nasserist regime. These agencies fostered the development of a technocratic elite (the hallmark of the Nasser era), and the cultivation of new forms of expertise, in fields ranging from agricultural engineering to social work.

Although the main objectives of land reclamation were to provide farmland for landless peasants and increase agroindustrial output, there was a strong emphasis on social objectives as well. Reclamation schemes under Nasser have often been viewed as the creation of a "new rural social order" that would entail a shift to "a new peasant, owning his land and a house in the modern village, a healthy and educated citizen."[40] The attempt to construct a new peasant, healthy and educated, was far from a novel attempt, however, as we have seen with the earlier rural reconstruction projects of the 1930s and 1940s. The Nasser period differentiated itself, however, by its attempt "to free the peasantry from the bonds of exploitation" and its efforts at the inculcation of communitarian socialist values and ethics as an essential component of the statist project. These goals were most often accomplished through "organizations such as cooperatives, community councils, and women's organizations . . . viewed as the main vehicles for social change, the development of positive social attitudes, the creation and organization of new institutions and services, and the growth of community self-help spirit."[41] These formats were almost without exception drawn from earlier models.

The Tahrir Province project was presented by the revolutionary regime as its quintessential enterprise—"one of the major pioneering programs for the invasion of the desert."[42] The project aimed at increasing national production through the expansion of cultivatable land, and, more importantly, also attempted to create a "model rural community based on Socialist principles" and "give self-confidence to individuals by demonstrating their capacity to undertake large projects, especially that this project is totally undertaken and supervised by Arab technicians without any foreign assistance."[43] The project, located west of the Delta and south of Alexandria, began shortly after the revolution in 1952, under the supervision of Magdi Hasanayn, himself a free officer.[44] Hasanayn became head of the Tahrir Province Organization, administering the province for several years along a controversial socialist-utopian model. In the words of Hasanayn, the object of the project was to "accustom our people to the desert, to make the young intellectuals practically active in reclamation, and to give more work."[45] Hasanayn also intended to demonstrate that the Arab world could compete with the much-vaunted Israeli "colonization of the desert."[46]

The process of settlement was by no means indiscriminate. A policy of migration began with the completion of the second village in the province (Omar Shahin), after which the migration committee moved to Menufiyya Governorate (the most crowded governorate in the republic) to choose the first group of citizens who would occupy the new community. Settlers (*al-'anasir al-bashariyya*) had to fulfill numerous requirements to qualify for migration:

> In order to qualify for reclaimed land, the settler must possess Egyptian citizenship; have been engaged in agricultural work for at least two years; own five *feddans* or less, with preference given to landless farmers; be in good health and free from any contagious diseases such as tuberculosis, leprosy, bilharzia, and encylostoma; have a clear police record, with preference given for obviously good conduct; be between the ages of 21 and 50 years; have not more than five members in his family; and be literate ... He must agree to move with his family to the new settlement and cultivate the land by himself with the help of family members; to join the community development council which helps promote the social standards of the community; and to become a permanent resident of the community.[47]

Families were then selected from Menufiyya and Dakhaliyya governorates for medical, psychological, and occupational testing. Settlers were expected to be mentally fit and emotionally stable, which would enable them to learn and benefit from the new system (*al-nizam al-jadid*) in the new community, and would facilitate their becoming sound, cooperative, and productive citizens. They were also required to have a certain standard of skill/artisanry (*mihara*) in manual labor, to have some knowledge of reading and writing, and to have an ability to acclimate.[48]

Writing on the selection of settlers in Tahrir, Doreen Warriner recounts the words of Major Gamal Zaki, director of the Social Affairs Department:

> Settlers, he said, are selected scientifically on social, medical, and psychological tests. ... Of 1,100 applicants so far, all had the right social qualifications, but

only 382 families were accepted medically, because while most of the men were healthy enough, the women and children fell far short of the standard. Only 180 families survived the psychological test.... Of these, 132 are now undergoing the six months' training, which includes a three-month probation period. "*We consider both people and land to be under reclamation.*" When trained in the central village, they will be moved out to other villages as nuclei for the future settlements.[49]

The first transfer of families occurred on October 23, 1955, when 131 families were moved to Tahrir Province, followed by 30 families on February 1, 1957.[50]

> Remember this day well
> Remember every day that dawns on the nation
> Remember every time a new migration occurs in this great battle
> It is 23 October 1955.[51]

The image of building men of metal in the middle of the desert infused the literature on Tahrir province and mobilized an armature of metaphors of factories, steel, and a vanguard of soldiers (*masana' al-salb al-bashari*). Yet the specifically rural nature of the endeavor was always underscored, hence the organic metaphor of "a new human plant" (*nabat bashari*) grown in the desert as a retort to "those who accuse the Egyptian fellah of backwardness and stagnation (*ta'akhur wa jumud*)."[52] The specificity of Tahrir lay precisely in this hybridization of metallic and organic metaphors—in the creation of peasants made of metal.

Upon their arrival, the new citizens were trained in the village of Omar Shahin, after which they would be relocated to their new villages. Social specialists (including social workers and public-health workers) organized a comprehensive six-month training program for settlers (*al-tadrib 'ala al-hayat fi al-muwatin al-jadid*), to facilitate their mental and practical acclimation to their new environment. Social training took place on individual, family, and group/community levels, and was intended to introduce and acclimatize settlers to the principles of the revolution and of the new community and its way of life—through both practical and intellectual means, such as lectures, radio programs, cultural programs, and various publications.[53]

Prior to the settlers' move to their new homes, the following were to be accomplished by the migration agency: an explanation of the principles of the revolution, and what productive and political projects it had undertaken; a description of the foundations of the Tahrir Province project; a study of social acclimation, and measurement of the direction of social change that settlers were faced with in their encounter with a new life and community in Tahrir Province; training of settlers in the practicalities of cooperative life—the organizing principle in the new village; and the dissemination of health awareness.[54]

The vanguard settlers in Omar Shahin village would begin their day with communal athletic exercises, the disciplinization of the body occurring in unison. This would be followed by public lectures on topics such as the "Socialism of Islam." The aim was nothing less than "purity of spirit," "soundness of body," and "care for the general interest and mutual cooperation."[55] "For the first time in Egypt, in all of the East, we see a peasant son of the nation who argues with you about religion, talks to you about music, discusses economic issues, and invites you to a new life whose basis is . . . Islamic socialism, he is truly happy because he lives in Tahrir Province."[56]

Training and instruction were to be fairly extensive, and included primary and vocational education, child care, household care, and hygiene. In the words of an observer, "Everything is disciplined, standardized, new."[57] Settlers had a daily schedule and wore uniform clothing, and all children left their mothers' care at the age of two to be placed in nurseries. The province had a social service center that aimed at providing inhabitants with the necessary training for "raising the standard of their production capacity," and social workers supervised virtually all aspects of social life—including athletics and the use of leisure time.[58] Life and labor in the province were characterized by the ubiquitous presence of experts. Indeed, there were experts for every crop and for every field of agricultural, industrial, and social expertise—all available on site.[59]

Settlers received this "total care" to help them acclimate to their new environment and to foster self-help and governance. All aspects of life in the province, such as the daily salutes and singing, were attempts to foster group unity and a sense of shared principles and goals. Even the uniform clothing served a purpose—that of effacing differences and creating a sense of equality.[60] Above all, the new society was to foster the principle of equality. Indeed, in the recollection of Ahmed El-Hammami, an engineer who worked on the project under Hasanayn, the idea that women were equal partners in labor was among the most marked features of life in Tahrir.[61] According to Hekmat Abu-Zayd, a prominent social scientist who worked extensively on the project and conducted a 1957 survey there on social acclimation, settlers were meant to come to view the state differently. The hope was that they would not see it as the repressive apparatus of domination (*ruh al-saytara*) familiar to them from the army, police, and courts, but rather would see the state in the faces of vocational trainers, social workers, and agricultural engineers, all sharing the same goal of collective cooperation.[62]

Magdi Hasanayn's supervision of the Tahrir Province project was short-lived and beset by administrative difficulties and political rivalries. In November of 1957, following a heated debate in the inaugural session of the National Assembly, Hasanayn, a proponent of a socialist model loosely based on Soviet models and the communal ownership of land, was ousted and replaced by Sayed Marei, a bourgeois conservative who chaired the Higher Committee on Agrarian Reform (which was responsible for land redistribution) who favored a far less radical smallholder model.[63] The early days of Tahrir Province proved no more than an experimental attempt to create a new rural community based on socialist principles. Although Hasanayn was later vilified in the press (accused of being a communist with bourgeois tastes), many of the Tahrir settlers poignantly recalled the days of Hasanayn as among the best in their lives, an attempt to correct the historical record.[64]

Despite its short life, the Tahrir project was an important conceptual model of land reclamation and social welfare under the revolutionary regime. What is most striking about Tahrir Province, and most distinctive about this particular phase of postcoloniality, is the accent placed on scientific socialist planning and the extremely structured environment that was created for its inhabitants—much of it centered on welfare, health and hygiene, communitarianism, and cooperation. First and foremost, reclamation projects aimed at the creation of new model communities of citizens, entailing "the addition of productive units to society"; the transformation of wastelands into productive resources; the creation of a "happy family made of workers and peasants"; and the inculcation of individuals with communitarian and socialist ethics.[65] In short, they aimed at "building men," through "unity, discipline, and labor," as much as building new societies. The key to these new communities was the supervision of their composition and the direction of their development by the state. Such features as the selection of settlers with the knowledge of the state (*bi ma'rifat al-dawla*), and the organization of relationships among citizens within the framework of social and economic institutions, in order to fulfill the goals of the state for a model community, were indeed innovations in state power.[66]

During the period from the 1930s to the 1960s, rural space was problematized and privileged.[67] Within a socialist welfare framework that sought to increase the health and productivity of the population through land reclamation and resettlement schemes, plans were both comprehensive in scope and individuated in detail. What differentiated the discourse on space and population under Nasser from later periods was precisely the continuation of this idiom of social welfare.

Planning the National Family

Eight years after World War II and only one year after the 1952 revolution, Egypt's political climate was characterized by an etatist ideology of rational planning, scientific research, and social welfare. Although under Nasser population growth was problematized to a far greater extent than in the previous period, population politics continued to be framed within the larger issue of national and familial welfare. Socialist political discourse characterized population programs as part of social welfare (and not development)—the primary object of state concern. The government-sponsored programs of family planning under Nasser mobilized ideologies of nationalism and national progress, which emphasized family planning as an integral component of the welfare of the state and its people, a culmination of the 1930s discourse on welfare.

In 1953 the minister of social affairs, 'Abbas Mustafa 'Ammar (our erstwhile anthropologist) submitted a memorandum to the Permanent Council for Public Services highlighting the gravity of Egypt's population problem and its implications for the health, education, and welfare of the people.[68] The memorandum inaugurated an official state discourse on population and family planning, and urged the formation of a "National Commission for Population Problems," to be established within the structure of the Permanent Council for Public Services. The memorandum stated:

> Whereas the policy of the present era is to face facts objectively and courageously, and whereas the method of government in dealing with all problems is to go deeply into the roots rather than to treat the symptoms, it is essential for the responsible authorities to take a definite attitude towards the population problem and to play a positive role in alleviating all evil consequences. . . . In our opinion, any reforming and welfare policy which disregards population growth is but a short-sighted policy.[69]

The new commission's charge was to study population trends in Egypt, to examine the impact of population growth on economic development, to assess methods for influencing population trends "in such a manner that may advance the welfare of the individual, family and society," and to make recommendations for a population policy that would agree with Egypt's national objectives and would enhance Egypt's international status.[70]

The commission's first meeting, in January of 1954, included twelve members, among them the ministers of social affairs, public health, and agriculture, and economists, demographers, statisticians, and physicians. The tasks of the commission were distributed among demographic, economic, and medical subcommittees, all of which placed heavy emphasis on social planning and scientific research. Interestingly, the medical sub-committee was "to help spread sex-education at different levels through audio-visual aids; to inaugurate family planning clinics for the purpose of experimentation with various contraceptives to determine the actual degree of acceptability and effectiveness"—among the first programs of this kind in the Middle East.[71]

As early as 1954, when Lieutenant Colonel Husayn al-Shafa'i, a minister of social services, was asked during a press conference his opinion on birth control policies and replied:

> Not only do I approve of birth control, but I also believe that it has become a social necessity. Over-production in population, as well as in other fields, becomes waste. Human waste, which has resulted from unlimited reproduction, has created complex social problems. . . . If we continue to reproduce with the maximum biological impetus, without regard to the capacity of society to provide for the basic needs of its members, we shall have more weaklings, vagrants and beggars.[72]

Al-Shafa'i conceptualized population as another component aspect of production, arguing for the incommensurabilty between material production and biological reproduction. Similarly, in a speech given at Al-Azhar the same year, on the second anniversary of the revolution, President Nasser declared:

> Our greatest calamity, a legacy of the past, was continuing to live on limited resources which did not increase. It was similar to a family whose children were continuously increasing, on a constant income that never grew. Past governments neglected productive programs, particularly industrial ones, both through sheer ignorance and on purpose.[73]

Nasser's comparison of the state to a family that could not feed itself highlights the paternal, etatist role of the state, and underscored population growth as a process related to a set of fixed resources. It followed from this, then, that government efforts would concentrate upon either a lowering of birth rates or territorial expansion in the form of land reclamation.

The scientific nature of planning was integral to this phase, and family planning, along with all other social programs, was to be undertaken scientifically. The significance of the family (and its instrumentalization) to national planning is inscribed in Egypt's 1962 National Charter and reiterated in the literature of the day:

> The family is the first cell of society, and the socialist family is the path to the socialist society that will enable it to reach its goals and ambitions. It is within the sphere of the family that socialist values may be inculcated, and from it

may spring a generation with such [socialist] principles.... And every effort expended on the preservation and insurance of the well-being of the family is at the same time a necessary effort in the building of a socialist society.[74]

Here, the emphasis is on the family as the unit of instrumentality; it is the family that must first inculcate the values of socialism in the citizens of the state, and planning becomes the means for ensuring the good (socialist) society. The National Charter further demonstrated both the importance of "modern scientific planning" and the state's push to increase production, with population growth increasingly articulated as a threat.

Population increase constitutes the most dangerous obstacle that faces the Egyptian people in their drive towards raising the standard of production in their country in an effective and efficient way. Attempts at family planning deserve the most sincere efforts supported by modern scientific methods.[75]

The declaration was heralded as a breakthrough in the scope of state intervention in family planning; henceforth, limits on the provision of contraceptives would be lifted, mass media efforts would be mobilized, and research efforts aimed at enhancing the public promotion of family planning would be inaugurated.[76]

In 1964 a ministerial committee composed of demographers, sociologists, educators, psychologists, journalists, and theologians was organized to plan and evaluate the dissemination of family-planning information.[77] Social scientists began research on family structure, family-size ideals, and reproductive behavior patterns; demographers analyzed census data and vital registration; and biomedical experts investigated contraceptive acceptability. Together with this work, a vast expansion of training in these specialized fields also helped to lay the groundwork for the formulation of a population control strategy.[78]

In public speeches, President Nasser began to more explicitly invoke population control as essential for the nation's progress:

The prime minister Zakariah Mohieddin presides over the Birth Control Council.... Listen to his plans in the field of social development.... We will be unable to provide a decent standard of living to a family that produced many children. There is no need to produce many children at the expense of the mother's health.... We know that God provides. God of course said that although he is dependable, we should work. The prophet appealed to our rational thinking and told us to stop being fatalistic.... If you do not, you are lost and the plan will be equally lost.[79]

Nasser also became more direct in his appeals for the practice of family planning and "assumed the role of educator, supporting his speeches with

Qur'anic and prophetic citations and emphasizing the importance of maintaining the nation's health."[80]

In 1965 Nasser established the Supreme Council of Family Planning (SCFP), which had as its mandate to establish a total plan for family planning in the country; to study, encourage, and coordinate all population affairs, including medical, statistical, social, economic, and all other scientific studies pertaining to family planning; and to develop cooperative links between the various organizations participating in the program's organization.[81] The council was to expand family-planning clinics and services to all parts of the country in order to reduce population growth. The formation of the SCFP marked the crucial move from the researching of population issues to the implementation of family-planning and population-control programs.

Yet family planning was not the purview of secularist state discourse alone. Religious discourse on family planning during this period also posited the problem of population in terms of the coordination between biological and material production. In 1950 Islamist Khalid Muhammad Khalid, an Azhar graduate, discussed the importance of "planning both the materials and human production of society if a balance between them is to be achieved." He stated,

> There is no hope of improving the standard of living so long as birth-rates are increasing. . . . The problem is complicated by the fact that our society does not realize that it is facing a crisis which may threaten its welfare and progress. . . . This crisis is due to our misconception of religion. Islam permits birth control in the interest of society and for the welfare of the individual . . . [82]

Religious discourse during the Nasser era shifted in focus towards planning. Within the historical context of socialist planning and the modernization of reproduction, the issue of family planning (and indeed even the term) related to the entire issue of planning: planning for a family, planning for the future in accordance with one's socioeconomic capacities and needs, and planning for the nation-state, in accordance with its resources.

Two *fatawi* (religious edicts) issued during this period exemplify the extent to which the issue of family planning was embedded within the social-welfare discourse of the time. A *fatwa* issued by Shaykh Mahmud Shaltut in 1959 dismissed the possibility of a birth-control policy that would be obligatory for everyone, regardless of the condition of their health or finances. Rather, he stated that birth control may be allowed only under certain circumstances, for

> women who bear children too quickly in succession, or suffer from contagious diseases, and for the minority whose nerves are weakened and cannot face up

to their manifold responsibilities and do not find assistance from their government or the wealthy members of their society that would enable them to shoulder their responsibilities. In such cases, where birth control is individual and specific, it is a remedy designed to avoid well-known evils and through which strong and righteous progeny may come into being.[83]

Shaykh Hassan Ma'mun issued a *fatwa* along similar lines in 1964 that was published in *Akhbar al-Yawm*. Ma'mun began by elaborating upon the original intent of the Islamic call for procreation and multiplication, which had been both legitimate and suitable at the time because "its early followers were few and weak in the midst of a vast majority of aggressive and oppressive people, by reason of their wealth and social standing." He went on:

> But now we find that conditions have changed. We find that the density of population in the world threatens seriously to reduce the living standards of mankind to the extent that many men of thought have been prompted to seek family planning in every country, so that the resources may not fall short of ensuring a decent living for its people and to provide public services for them. Islam . . . has never been opposed to what is good to man. . . . I see no objection from the *Shari'ah* point of view of the consideration of family planning . . . if there is a need for it, and consideration is occasioned by the people's own choice and conviction, without constraint or compulsion . . .[84]

These *fatawi* are similar in their emphasis on the household unit as the level at which the issue of family planning was to be decided. Indeed, in relying upon the Islamic tradition for argumentation, all the *fatawi* on this subject emphasize maternal and familial health and welfare, as well as issues of morality and virtue. What differentiated these *fatawi* from earlier edicts was the shift in emphasis from familial health to the welfare of the nation-state. Here the discussion has already moved to the level of the world's ability to sustain a population that can enjoy a reasonable standard of living. Family planning, thus postulated, became a concern tied to the viability of the welfare of the nation and its citizens.

. . .

Nasserism built upon the previous historical edifice of the 1930s and 1940s through the continuation of an older social-welfare mode of regulation, evident in the management of population, rural space, and the national economy. Through directed efforts such as child-welfare centers, rural and village reconstruction projects, land reclamation projects, cooperative societies, and the various activities of the Ministry of Social Affairs, totalizing social projects were formulated that marked the health, wealth and welfare of the population, and by extension the nation, as their object. It is this "armory of holistic social engineering," to use Vaclav Havel's phrasing, that characterized the postcolonial state in Egypt.[85] It was by means of an interventionist state and socialist planning geared towards social welfare, and not through socioeconomic development, that the Nasser period marked its distinctive content.[86] Within this etatist welfare regime, the demographic masses (the "people") were valorized as generating the dynamism behind the expansion and consolidation of the nation-building project.

Nationalist social science in Egypt constituted itself as the purveyor of the well-being of the population through the apparatus of knowledge production. Often enough, this was accomplished through the scientific constitution of "society" as an object or a series of objects of study—be it an anthropological unit of study ("the modern Egyptians")—an occupational unit of study ("peasants")—a regional unit of study ("Sharqiya")—or the population conceived of as a demographic whole ("Egyptians").

Conclusion

It has by now become a platitude to argue the danger of exaggerating the coherence and efficacy of dominant discourses and technologies of power. Yet, within the Egyptian postcolonial context the continued and marked persistence in quotidian life of discourses of identity (*al-shukhsiyya al-misriyya*, "Egyptian character"); of discourses of governance (neo-Malthusianism, social-hygiene, social-uplift); and above all of notions of backwardness, illustrates the resilience and hegemony of dominant nationalist categories of thought often inherited from colonial rule. The preceding narrative demonstrated the hegemonic power of colonial and nationalist discourses of progress and improvement that targeted subaltern populations. Two theoretical and methodological issues are raised by these contentions. First, insofar as the object of colonial and nationalist political governance was the subaltern masses, the question of the appropriate level of historical analysis is raised. Should historians focus their attention on the historical "recovery" of the subjectivity and agency of those masses, or on the illumination of the pressure that subalternity exerted upon dominant discourses, be they colonial or nationalist? Second, the question arises as to whether this approach suggests that the versions of modernity, and power, produced in colonial contexts were identical to the models of the colonizers.

Scholars have long demonstrated the heuristic value implicit in the concept of subalternity. Drawing upon the work of Antonio Gramsci, the Subaltern Studies collective has argued for the centrality of relations of domination and subordination in the history of colonialism. This relational and mediating view of power has enabled historians to narrate subaltern history along the axes of class, caste, gender, race, and region. Initially, the collective took as its task the restoration of the subaltern as the (autonomous) agent of a history denied it by elite historiography.¹ Discussions of subalterns (especially of peasants and women), in South Asian scholarship and elsewhere, have tended to view both categories as composed of self-constituted historical agents who stand in a relation of opposition to the state (colonial or postcolonial), a dominant bourgeoisie, a capitalist economy, or patriarchal structures. This may be seen as part of a larger movement in anthropological and historical writing bent on recovering the subject as an autonomous agent.² Ironically, as Talal Asad has noted, at the same time that these works attempted to subvert metanarratives of capitalism or colonialism (perceived to have subordinated subaltern histories and to reproduce colonial or capitalist structures), they also revealed a certain affinity with liberal-humanist notions of agency and subjectivity—specifically, the idea that historical agents imbued with consciousness "make their own history."³ Responding to such criticisms, the collective shifted its focus toward the emergence of subalternity as a discursive effect, reconceptualizing the subaltern as radically heterogeneous to, though not autonomous from, dominant discourses.⁴ This relocation of subalternity in relation to dominant discourses has led scholars to locate the pressures that the "intractable presence of subalternity" exerted upon dominant discourses—whether colonial, metropolitan, or nationalist.⁵

I have similarly tried to highlight the centrality of the recalcitrant presence of subalternity to the intellectual history of twentieth-century Egypt. Thus, I argue that the development of peasant studies was a direct result of the fear of potential bolshevism spawned by the peasant insurgencies of the 1919 revolution, and of the dramatic increase in rural crime throughout the 1930s and 1940s. So, too, did population studies emerge out of anxieties concerning the regulation of women and mothers. The development of "population" as an object of knowledge and social control, therefore, entailed the modernization of reproduction through the cultivation of small family size, mothercraft, and eugenics. Subalterns were as central to the formulation of social scientific agendas as they were the objects of political intervention and governance.

An understanding of the social reproduction of power relations—the regulation of the relationship between the nationalist elite and subaltern masses—as part and parcel of the history of ideas debunks the myth that ideas, epistemological orientations, and structures of knowledge are removed from the social and political realities of "people on the ground." Structures of knowledge are, of course, integral to the creation and reproduction of social, economic, and political orders and hierarchies. Against the conventional belief that ideas are immaterial or disembodied, I have tracked some of the material effects that were produced by particular social groups (social scientists and reformers) who upheld certain social-engineering practices such as rural reconstruction and family planning, that had social consequences.[6] Indeed, as the postcolonial nation-state became further absorbed by the "logic of planning," the organization, appropriation, and domination of knowledge became ever more important.

The putative identity of colonial and nationalist discourses has been amply refuted by the voluminous literature on colonialism. Scholars have shown that the formulation of a postcolonial national modernity under the constraints of colonialism and capitalism did not entail a mere process of imitation, nor did it lead lead to total homogeneity.[7] As Talal Asad astutely observes, "when a project is translated from one site to another, from one agent to another, versions of power are produced. As with translations of a text, one does not simply get a reproduction of identity."[8] Clearly, the emergent regime of governance under postcolonial nationalism was one in which earlier precolonial modes of order, authority, and domination were hybridized with colonial modes of domination.

In fact, reversing Ranajit Guha's formulation of the colonial state as "dominance without hegemony," we could say that it was precisely the intersection between colonial and modern forms of power—their mobile and improvisational nature—that enabled the transformative power of colonial formations (their hegemony) as well as their irreducible heterogeneity in non-European contexts.[9] Thus, for example the notion of "progress" itself, that archetypal sign of the modern (and the yardstick brandished over categories of persons thought to be backward—peasants, women, and tribes) was generated out of a complex convergence of meanings, both precolonial and colonial. It should come as no surprise that categories of thought such as "progress" and "society" were forged out of older, preexisting notions—an existing cultural lexicon.

Hence, our promising young geographer 'Abbas Mustafa 'Ammar asked in 1941: "To what extent would it be possible to fit the idea of a society moving in a cycle as visualized by Ibn Khaldun into the general scheme of a progressing humanity?"[10] The medieval Muslim social philosopher Ibn Khaldun had conceptualized the movement of history as one in which states rose and fell cyclically, declining after lapsing into luxury and extravagance. 'Ammar wished to ascertain whether Ibn Khaldun believed in progress. This explicit juxtaposition of secular, unilinear, progressive time (an endless linear progression into the future) and cyclical time constitutes a rare moment in which the multiple temporalities of the postcolonial reformer are acknowledged.[11] On the one hand, 'Ammar was the inheritor of classical notions of time as cyclical and nonlinear, but he was also the bearer of a scientific tradition of positivism that embodied unilinear progressive time. It is precisely this creative synthesis of the prior knowledge of Ibn Khaldun and the new sciences of positivism that I refer to as the process of *translation* within the postcolonial moment.[12] To quote 'Ammar:

> The views of Ibn Khaldun recall of the classical conception of history as an endless series of cycles and consequently raise the question of whether after all our Muslim writer believed in progress? . . .
>
> But whereas the classical writers had always looked back to the "lost golden age," regarded the present as a period of degeneration and conceived improvement or progress only in terms of regeneration, Ibn Khaldun did not commit himself to such doctrines. He did not state whether the following cycle would start from the same starting point as the previous cycle or would benefit from past experience and therefore take a further step along the path of progress.[13]

Thus conceived by 'Ammar, Ibn Khaldun represented the possibility of a synthetic notion of time as both cyclical and linear. Endless progression, once coupled with cyclical time, would lead one into an ascending spiral, thereby coalescing multiple and heretofore discrete temporalities.

Perhaps the challenge of our postcoloniality entails this simple acknowledgement of the multiple and discrete temporalities of modernity, eschewing the hegemonic colonial and nationalist vision of history as a simple, layered sedimentation that propels one forth into the future. Perhaps we must also eschew the critiques of unilinear temporality within the European post-Enlightenment tradition. The Nietzschean and Freudian tropes of remembering and forgetting (the "plastic power" of mnemotechnics), or loss and nostalgia (the time of repetition, the time of the symptom) continue to configure particular kinds of temporality as unilinear and teleological. Thus, in their relegation of nonlinear temporality to the time of pathology (the pathology of modernity, of modern man, of the herd animal), the fin-de-siècle critiques unmask the notion of worldly progress and history as a movement and acceleration oriented toward an open-ended future as being a mere ruse.[14] Human development, Nietzsche teaches us, is halting, hesitating—it takes long and moves back and in circles, because the herd instinct is always what is inherited best.

What if we abandon both the calendrical unilineal time of the future and the "pathological" nonlinear time of the "herd" and of the "symptom"?[15] To experience time as cyclical, contrapuntal, filiative, or expansive is, perhaps, to acknowledge other modes of being that we, as a condition of our postcoloniality, inhabit inconstantly.

Notes

In citing works in the notes, short titles have generally been used. Full citations are provided only for archival sources and primary-source periodicals published in Egypt. For a list of archives and periodicals consulted see the Bibliography.

Introduction

1. Husayn's thesis, "Étude Analytique et critique de la Philosophie Sociale d'Ibn Khaldun," was translated into Arabic as *Falsafat Ibn Khaldun al-ijtimaʿiyya: tahlil wa naqd*. On Husayn's education see Mahmoudi, *Tāhā Husain's Education*. I am grateful to Donald Reid for helping me clarify aspects of Husayn's education.

2. T. Hussein, *The Days*, 363.

3. Lévy-Bruhl had written extensively on primitive mentalities. Fahmi was accused of denigrating Islam in his 1913 thesis, which argued that the advent of Islam had caused the status of women to deteriorate. Fahmi's thesis had caused such "commotion and outrage" that four years later Husayn was required to present his thesis not only to his Sorbonne committee, but also to an Egyptian professor for approval. See Reid, *Cairo University*, 64–67; T. Hussein, *The Days*, 364–65.

4. T. Husayn, *Falsafat Ibn Khaldun*, 58–65.

5. Stephen Dale discusses Ibn Khaldun as the first *Annaliste* historian, formed by the same Aristotelian rationalist tradition that influenced Durkheim and his progenitor Montesquieu. See Dale, "Ibn Khaldun." In this sense Husayn was identifying points of intersection or commensurability between the rationalist tradition of Islamic philosophy and that of the Western social sciences.

6. See the analytic organization of Porter and Ross, *The Cambridge History of Science*.

7. See, for example, Barshay, *The Social Sciences in Modern Japan*; Trillo, "Stereophonic Scientific Modernisms."

8. See Prakash, *Another Reason*.

9. Asad, ed., *Anthropology and the Colonial Encounter*; Driver, *Geography Militant*; T. Mitchell, *Rule of Experts*; Khanna, *Dark Continents*.

10. Lévy-Bruhl as quoted in Conklin, *A Mission to Civilize*, 197; on Durkheim and Lévy-Bruhl's relation to ethnology in France, see Sherman, "'Peoples Ethnographic.'"

11. For histories of European and Anglo-American social science see Horne, *A Social Laboratory for Modern France*; Poovey, *Making a Social Body*; Poovey, *A History of the Modern Fact*; Porter and Ross, eds., *The Cambridge History of Science*; Steinmetz, *Regulating the Social*; D. Ross, *The Origins of American Social Science*.

12. Chatterjee, *The Nation and Its Fragments*; Chatterjee, ed., *Texts of Power*; Cohn, *Colonialism and Its Forms of Knowledge*; Cooper and Stoler, eds., *Tensions of Empire*; Dirks, *Castes of Mind*; Goswami, *Producing India*; T. Mitchell, *Colonising Egypt*; T. Mitchell, *Rule of Experts*; T. Mitchell, ed., *Questions of Modernity*; Pels and Salemink, eds., *Colonial Subjects*; Prakash, *Another Reason*; Rabinow, *French Modern*.

13. Barshay, *The Social Sciences in Modern Japan*; Barshay, "The Social Sciences in Japan"; Chatterjee, "A Modern Science of Politics for the Colonized."

14. I thank one of the anonymous reviewers of Stanford University Press for drawing my attention to this critical issue.

15. Deringil, *The Well-Protected Domains*; Makdisi, "Ottoman Orientalism"; Rogaski, *Hygienic Modernity*.

16. On the Napoleonic invasion of Egypt from 1798 to1801, see Al-Jabarti, *Napoleon in Egypt*; Godlewska, "Napoleon's Geographers"; Godlewska, "Map, Text and Image."

17. Egypt became a province of the Ottoman Empire in 1517. On Mehmed 'Ali, see Fahmy, *All the Pasha's Men*; on transformations in Egypt's military and educational apparatus under the Ottoman ruling family, see T. Mitchell, *Colonising Egypt*, 34–40, 63–94.

18. Asad, *Formations of the Secular*, chap. 6; Esmeir, "The Work of Law in the Age of Empire"; T. Mitchell, *Colonising Egypt*. Egypt achieved nominal independence from the British in 1922 and furthered the terms of its independence in 1936 with the signing of the Anglo-Egyptian Treaty and the abolition of the capitulations (grants of extraterritoriality allowed to European residents); but its postcolonial period is considered to have begun with the 1952 revolution, led by Gamal Abdel Nasser and organized around state socialism.

19. I borrow the idea of Napoleon's long shadow from Joshua Schreier, "Napoleon's Long Shadow."

20. See Powell, *A Different Shade of Colonialism*; Jeppie, "Constructing a Colony on the Nile."

21. See Chatterjee, ed., *Texts of Power*; Chakrabarty, *Provincializing Europe*; Césaire, *Discourse on Colonialism*; Senghor, *The Collected Poetry*. The Négritude movement similarly grappled with the tensions between the universal and the particular and its relation to European modernity; see Cooper, *Colonialism in Question*, 34, 55.

22. See Chakrabarty, *Provincializing Europe* for a discussion of the critique of

Enlightenment taxonomies and universal (secular) histories and hierarchies within the Indian context.

23. Recently, the idea of "post-Enlightenment rationality" has come under fire for reifying European social thought and presenting a unified picture of what was, in reality, a fragmented social and intellectual landscape; see, for example, Cooper, *Colonialism in Question*. Although European ideas after the Enlightenment were, clearly, heterogeneous, certain ideas were arguably central to *Encyclopedist* European thought: namely, that knowledge entails the history of the rational progress of scientific inquiry; that there is a unity of truth and reason embodied in a single and unitary conception of rationality; and that progress encompasses not only rational scientific inquiry, but moral progress as well. See MacIntyre, *After Virtue*; MacIntyre, *Three Rival Versions of Moral Enquiry*.

24. On the concept of a disinterested and impartial ideal rationality, based on universal and ahistorical principles—independent of social, cultural and historical particularities (or what Hans-Georg Gadamer has referred to as the "Enlightenment doctrine of prejudice")—see Gadamer, *Truth and Method*, 270–85.

25. Cromer, *Modern Egypt*, 1:328. On Cromer, see Owen, *Lord Cromer*.

26. On the significance of the narrative emplotment of colonialism for imagining postcolonial futures, see D. Scott, *Refashioning Futures* and *Conscripts of Modernity*.

27. Chatterjee, *The Nation and Its Fragments*, 16–22.

28. Nicholas Dirks's discussion of the state in post-1857 India as an ethnographic state is entirely relevant insofar as it accounts for the unremitting taxonomical drive of the colonial state, but it fails to capture the extent to which the colonial state was also geared toward the maximization of the economic resources of a bounded geographical entity (which Dirks relegates to the pre-1857 period in the form of a revenue state). Such an attitude allowed the colonial state apparatus to posit the cultural and racial essence of the colonized as the distinct form of colonial difference (that which could not be surmounted in order to develop, progress, attain historical becoming, nationhood, etc.), while at the very same time economically exploiting those racial differences. See Dirks, *Castes of Mind*; cf. Goswami, *Producing India*, and Ghosh, "A Market for Aboriginality."

29. For other versions of this argument see Asad, *Genealogies of Religion*; Asad, "Conscripts of Western Civilization"; Cohn and Dirks, "Beyond the Fringe"; and D. Scott "Colonial Governmentality."

30. See Chakrabarty's useful discussion of the violence attendant on national modernity's idealistic and reformatory impulses, in *Provincializing Europe*, chap. 1; see also T. Mitchell, *Rule of Experts*, especially chap. 6.

31. Partha Chatterjee, "The Disciplines in Colonial Bengal," 16, 19.

32. As Manu Goswami points out in *Producing India* (p. 25), "colonial and nationalist forms, although distinguishable, were not separable."

33. See Zayed, "Seventy Years of Sociology in Egypt"; Zayed, "Al-nazariyya al-ijtima'iyya al-mu'asira wal-waqi' al-'arabi"; Wafi, *Al-falsafa al-ijtima'iyya li Ibn Khaldun wa Auguste Comte*.

34. Dipesh Chakrabarty, *Provincializing Europe*, 5–6.

35. Sociology was established in the Egyptian University's Faculty of Arts. "This department has since embraced the principles and methods of the French school as initiated by August Comte and firmly established by Emile Durkheim" (Hasan al-Saʻati, "Tatawur al-madrasa al-fikriyya li ʻilm al-ijtimaʻ fi Misr," *Al-Majallat al-Ijtimaʻiyyah al-Qawmiyya / The National Review of Social Sciences,* National Centre for Sociological and Criminological Research January 1964, 21–34; quote is from English abstract, "Development of the School of Sociological thought in Egypt since 1952," 143.

36. For new directions in European historical writing that are beginning to track the post-Enlightenment emergence of "society" or "the social body" as analytic and epistemological categories for conceptualizing human interaction, rather than as reified objective structures or entities, see Cabrera, "The Crisis of the Social and Post-social History." I am grateful to Alvaro Santana for drawing my attention to this article. For a discussion of the emergence and reification of "society" as an object in early Meiji Japan, see Howland, "Society Reified."

37. Stetkevych, *The Modern Arabic Literary Language*, 25; cf. Asad, *Formations of the Secular*, 198, 229, and T. Mitchell, *Colonising Egypt*, 119–20. See also Marilyn Booth's critique of this line of reasoning in her review "Talal Asad, *Formations of the Secular.*"

38. Prakash, *Another Reason*. See also Rabinow, *French Modern*; Wright, *The Politics of Design in French Colonial Urbanism*.

39. Prakash, *Another Reason*, 3–14.

40. Rabinow, *French Modern*, 289.

41. T. Mitchell, "The Stage of Modernity."

42. Asad, *Formations of the Secular*, 13.

43. As Keith Watenpaugh has demonstrated, being modern in the Middle East was neither a simple process of emulating Western metropolitan practices nor the ineluctable outcome of the logic of capitalism and colonialism. Rather, it was a complex and contingent historical process; see Watenpaugh's discussion of eastern Mediterranean modernity in *Being Modern in the Middle East*.

44. See Ussama Makdisi's "Ottoman Orientalism" for a discussion of the new forms of temporality attendant on Ottoman ideas of modernity.

45. Partha Chatterjee outlines a similar intellectual agenda in his "The Disciplines in Colonial Bengal."

46. Asad, *Genealogies of Religion*, 13. See also Spivak, *Outside in the Teaching Machine*; Prakash, *Another Reason*; Chakrabarty, *Provincializing Europe*.

47. Chakrabarty, *Provincializing Europe*, 17.

48. The following two paragraphs are based on my reading of Stetkevych, *The Modern Arabic Literary Language*.

49. On *nahdawi* linguistic innovation, see Samah Selim's illuminating study, *The Novel and the Rural Imaginary in Egypt*.

50. Stetkevych conceptualizes semantic extension as "made possible by a general openness of meaning, and is not to be seen as a simple shift from concrete

to abstract (mostly) or from abstract to concrete (less frequently), but rather as an increasingly conceptualized concentration of meaning in a word, without any qualifications beyond the concept. The way towards this essential meaning ... leads through the metaphor" (*The Modern Arabic Literary Language*, 72). This is crucial given that "the bulk of the modern Arabic verbal lexicon consists not of formal derivations of totally new words, but of semantically extended preexisting ones," (ibid., 38). On *majmaʿ*, see ibid., 20–21.

51. Ibid., 45.
52. Rabinbach, *The Human Motor*, 10.
53. See Steinmetz, ed., *The Politics of Method in the Human Sciences*.
54. On the Saint Simonians in Egypt, see Abdel-Malek, *Idéologie et Renaissance Nationale*, 189–98.
55. Kremer-Marietti, "Comte, Isidore-Auguste-Marie-Francois-Xavier." References to *positivism*, or *social positivism*, throughout my present text refer predominantly to Comtean positivism. French philosopher Auguste Comte (1798–1857) formulated a philosophical system that linked a new epistemological orientation, that of "positive philosophy," to a new social and political arrangement of society. The principal features of Comte's positivism are that science is the highest form of knowledge; that metaphysical claims are pseudo-scientific; and that there is one scientific method common to all of the sciences. This last contention is known as "naturalism," and includes the idea that the social realm is part of the natural world and therefore must be studied by standard scientific methods—laws govern the social world, and social science must identify those laws. A key feature of Comtean positivism (in contrast to later positivism) was the rejection of methodological individualism in favor of holism, which claimed that macro-sociological processes were essential to explanation. Further, for Comte, society should be run by an elite able to discern the social laws and work toward ameliorating society; thus, social problems should be addressed scientifically. See Kincaid, "Positivism in the Social Sciences," and Kremer-Marietti, "Comte, Isidore-Auguste-Marie-Francois-Xavier."
56. Kremer-Marietti, "Comte, Isidore-Auguste-Marie-Francois-Xavier."
57. I use *romanticism* to refer to a general philosophical movement as well as a movement in art and aesthetic theory. In brief, key romantic ideas are "the fundamental doctrine that all reality is ultimately spiritual, derivative from a living spirit and so knowable by the human spirit;" a metaphysical account of nature and man; and an epistemological doctrine that is essentially a creative urge to self-expression. Thus, romanticism is characterized by a metaphysic "that interprets the universe in terms of the concepts of evolution, process, life and consciousness;" and an epistemology that is "exclusively emotional and intuitive, stressing the necessity of fullness of experience and depth of feeling if reality is to be understood. Reason, being artificial and analytical, is inadequate to the task of comprehending the absolute; knowing is living, and the philosopher must approach nature through inspiration, longing and sympathy." "Romanticism," *Dictionary of Philosophy*, 272. In aesthetics, romanticism is marked by "an intense interest in nature, and an attempt to seize natural phenomena in a direct, immediate and naïve manner," an assertion of the

"primacy of feeling, imagination, and sentiment, as opposed to reason," and "a rejection of formal restraints" (ibid., 273).

58. On romanticism in the Egyptian pastoral novel, see Selim, *The Novel and the Rural Imaginary*.

59. This is best embodied in the designs of internationally celebrated Egyptian architect Hassan Fathy. Romantic aspects were never completely purged from his social engineering projects, and the need to create a "science of human settlements" (later known as "ekistics") was shot with tensions. On Fathy see Chapter 4.

60. Abdel-Malek, ed., *Contemporary Arabic Political Thought*, al-'Alim, *Al-fikr al-'arabi bayn al-khususiyya wa al-kawniyya*; al-'Alim, *Al-ibda' wa al-dalala*; Laroui, *The Crisis of the Arab Intellectual*. For a historical unpacking of the epistemological grounding and formation of modern Arab subjectivity and identity, see Sheehi's erudite study, *Foundations of Modern Arab Identity*. For a discussion of narratives of crisis in the Anglophone intellectual history of the Middle East see Gershoni, "The Theory of Crisis and the Crisis in a Theory."

61. Abdel-Malek, ed. *Contemporary Arab Political Thought*, 16. For the decolonizing self, identity is often represented as a wound, or as a double-bind, in the aftermath of colonization. Metaphors of possession, of bondage and servitude abound:

> The overlay of my oral culture wearing dangerously thin.... Writing of the most anodyne of childhood memories leads back to a body bereft of voice. To attempt an autobiography in French words alone is to show more than its skin under the slow scalpel of a live autopsy. Its flesh peels off and with it, seemingly, the speaking of childhood which can no longer be written is torn to shreds. Wounds are reopened, veins weep, the blood of the self flows and that of others, a blood which has never dried.

Assia Djebar, *Fantasia: An Algerian Cavalcade*, quoted in Spivak, "Acting Bits / Identity Talk," 147.

62. Abdel-Malek, *Contemporary Arab Political Thought*, 10.

63. Al-'Alim, *Al-fikr al-'arabi*, 30. Thinkers such as Laroui and to a lesser extent Abdel-Malak reintroduce, ironically perhaps, the same criteria of modernity: unilinear progressive temporality, historicity, and, subsequently, the subjectivity of the self-constituted autonomous subject, of Enlightenment thought, and of colonial ideology and its civilizing mission. That is to say, precisely the ideology that their projects sought to critique. It is almost as though colonialism were a specter eternally destined to revisit as *jinns*.

64. Chatterjee, *Nation and its Fragments*, 6.

65. As the distinction between a bourgeois private sphere inhabited by patriarchal families and a public sphere inhabited by homogeneous citizens was not available to Indian nationalism (because citizenship was denied to colonized Indians); the emergent middle-class nationalism in India utilized the strategy of another distinction—the spiritual/inner (where nationalism forged its hegemony) and the material/outer (where the ground was surrendered to the colonists). Chatterjee, *The Nation and Its Fragments*, 147.

66. His discussion, as Goswami notes, also "tends to reify an indigenous domain as a repository of a pure difference" (*Producing India*, 24).

67. Chatterjee, *Nationalist Thought and the Colonial World*, 30; Chatterjee, *Nation and Its Fragments*.

68. Chatterjee, *Nationalist Thought and the Colonial World*; Chatterjee, *Nation and Its Fragments*.

69. The idea that modernity is antithetical to tradition has been widely criticized as nothing more than Enlightenment prejudice—see Gadamer, *Truth and Method*; MacIntyre, *After Virtue*; MacIntyre, *Three Rival Versions of Moral Enquiry*. In setting up universal rationality against particular or local prejudice, Enlightenment thinkers discredited the notion of tradition. One of the consequences of Enlightenment thought, then, was the subjection of tradition and authority to reason, that is, the formulation of a distinction between faith in authority or tradition (reduced to mere blind obedience) and using one's reason freely. It is this conception of tradition as antithetical to the free use of reason and rationality that MacIntyre combats, both by rehabilitating the notion of the rationality of tradition and by highlighting the Enlightenment conception of morality as the "superstition of modernity." A trenchant critique of such oppositions as they relate to the Islamic discursive tradition can be found in Asad's "The Idea of an Anthropology of Islam" and *Genealogies of Religion*; see also Haj, "Reconfiguring Tradition."

70. Al-'Alim, *Al-fikr al-'arabi*.

71. See Sayyid Qutb, *Khasa'is al-tasawwur al-islami wa muqawimatuhu*. Between 1949 and 1951 Qutb published his *Ma'rakat al-islam wa al-ra'smaliyya* and *Al-'adalat al-ijtima'iyya fi al-islam* in which he argued that Islam was the antithesis of the universal negative of capitalism. Qutb's position represents the radical reformist posture within the Islamic tradition. See Roussillon, "Trajectoires Reformistes, Sayyid Qutb et Sayyid 'Uways: figures modernes de l'intellectuel en Egypte."

72. Indeed, the organization of the Muslim Brothers was, from its inception, involved in modernist projects of social reform; see R. Mitchell, *The Society of Muslim Brothers*. I am grateful to Talal Asad for bringing this point to my attention.

73. Gramsci, *Selections from the Prison Notebooks of Antonio Gramsci*, 52.

74. According to Chatterjee ("The Disciplines in Colonial Bengal," 24), "in the dispersal of the disciplines in the colonies, differences could appear at all four levels: in the formation of objects, in the modalities of enunciation, in concept-formation, and in the thematic choices." These are, of course, the rules of formation of disciplinary knowledge laid out by Foucault in *The Archaeology of Knowledge*.

75. The following discussion of the founding and early years of the Egyptian University relies heavily on Reid's comprehensive account in *Cairo University and the Making of Modern Egypt*.

76. Heyworth-Dunne, *An Introduction to the History of Education in Modern Egypt*; T. Mitchell, *Colonising Egypt*.

77. Between 1917 and 1936, 1,794 students were sent abroad, and between 1935 and 1939, 444 went abroad (Reid, *Cairo University*, 99).

78. Beinin and Lockman, *Workers on the Nile*, 10. For an anatomy of Egypt's social classes based on access to the means of production, see Abdel-Malek, *Egypt: Military Society*, 57–61.

79. Deeb, *Party Politics in Egypt*, 12.

80. As Keith Watenpaugh has noted, this group—despite its profound significance in shaping Middle Eastern modernity—has not been the object of systematic study. He argues that it is crucial to understand their "middle classness" not solely as an economic category, but rather as a complex of intellectual habits, social practices, and cultural comportment, which, taken together, constituted being modern. Watenpaugh, *Being Modern in the Middle East*, 17–26.

81. Najib, *A'lam Misr fi al-qarn al-'ishrin*, 289; Reid, *Cairo University*, 561.

82. Gramsci, *Prison Notebooks*, 52.

83. In Chapter 7, I argue that these concerns remained central to the post–World War II era, up through and including the Nasser period. Egyptian politics during the period from the 1930s to the 1960s is thus viewed as part of one historical block, thereby contesting the interpretation of Egypt's 1952 revolution as marking a fundamental disjuncture from the previous sociopolitical order. Rather, I propose an alternative framework for understanding the organization of the postcolonial Egyptian state and society: a social-welfare mode of regulation underpinned by an economic system of etatism.

84. Surprisingly few recent studies deal with race and class in the Egyptian colonial context, and the interwar period is understudied in Middle East history generally. Notable exceptions are Powell, *A Different Shade of Colonialism*; Chalcraft, *The Striking Cabbies of Cairo and Other Stories*; Thompson, *Colonial Citizens*; Watenpaugh, *Being Modern in the Middle East*.

Chapter 1. The Ethnographic Moment

1. Gaillardot Bey to Khedive Isma'il, 25 March, 1869, Alexandria, Dar al-Watha'iq al-Qawmiyya (hereafter DWQ), Al-Archif al-Urubi: 'Ahd Isma'il, al-jama'iyyat al-'ilmiyya, box 50/6 (25/3/1869–25/5/1875) (I am grateful to Patricia Singleton for pointing out the relevance of this archive to my work). Gaillardot Bey directed the Qasr al-'Ayni School of Medicine from 1879 to 1882.

2. "Projet d'organisation d'un service d'exploration scientifique de l'Egypte présenté à son altesse le Khedive par le Dr. Gaillardot," DWQ, Al-Archif al-Urubi: 'Ahd Isma'il, al-jama'iyyat al-'ilmiyya, box 50/6.

3. T. Mitchell, *Colonising Egypt*, 1–33. For a very different approach to culture and imperialism, see Maya Jasanoff's *The Edge of Empire*, in which she narrates the history of the British Empire from 1750 to 1850 through the lens of individual collectors.

4. See Kinney and Çelik, "Ethnography and Exhibitionism at the Expositions Universelles"; Çelik, *Displaying the Orient*; Said, *Culture and Imperialism*, chap. 2, sec. 4 ("The Empire at Work: Verdi's *Aïda*").

5. Trillo, *Mexico's Presence at World's Fairs*, 3. For a similar discussion of the

Mexican geographical society's efforts at imagining Mexico as a coherent geographical, cartographic, and temporal entity, see Craib, "A National Metaphysics."

6. Trillo, *Mexico's Presence at World's Fairs*, 3.

7. Çelik, *Displaying the Orient*, 11.

8. Barnett, "Impure and Worldly Geography," 239. For similar approaches to the study of geography, see Driver, *Geography Militant*; McEwan, "Cutting Power Lines Within the Palace?"; Kearns, "The Imperial Subject"; Gregory, "Between the Book and the Lamp"; Godlewska and Smith, eds., *Geography and Empire*.

9. Barnett, "Impure and Worldly Geography," 248–49.

10. Exceptions are Trillo, *Mexico's Presence at World's Fairs*; Pels and Salemink, eds., *Colonial Subjects*; Reid, "The Egyptian Geographical Society"; and Reid's excellent account, *Whose Pharaohs?*

11. See, for example, Clifford, *The Predicament of Culture*; Clifford and Marcus, eds., *Writing Culture*.

12. On the formation of British social anthropology see the work of George W. Stocking Jr., including *Race, Culture and Evolution*; *Victorian Anthropology*; *The Ethnographer's Magic and Other Essays in the History of Anthropology*; and *After Tylor*. See also Henrika Kuklick's excellent and comprehensive study, *The Savage Within*. On European classicism see Martin Bernal's *Black Athena*, and the debates surrounding his book.

13. For readability, I refer throughout to the society as the Royal Geographical Society, although it had several names over its history: *La Société Khédiviale de Géographie d'Égypte*; *La Société Sultanieh de Géographie d'Égypte*; *La Société Royale de Géographie d'Égypte*.

14. Société Khediviale de Géographie, *Notice* (Cairo: Secretariat de la Societété Khediviale de Géographie, 1883), in DWQ, *Abdin, al-jama'iyyat al-'ilmiyya, al-jama'iyya al-gughrafiyya, 1895–1949*, box. 198.

15. H. Awad, *La Société Royale de Géographie d'Égypte*, 8.

16. Schweinfurth (1836–1925) was a German explorer and botanist who traveled throughout central Africa. A pivotal figure in Egyptian natural history, he became the first president of the Royal Geographic Society, presiding from its inception in May of 1875 until the end of 1879. On his travels in central Africa, see Schweinfurth, *The Heart of Africa*.

17. Perhaps no one was better received by the RGS than the illustrious explorer Henry Morton Stanley (1841–1904), who came to symbolize both the pioneering and scientific spirits of nineteenth-century colonial civilization. After arriving in Cairo in January 1890, Stanley was received by virtually every important personage in Cairo, including the khedive himself, who hosted a gala dinner in Stanley's honor at 'Abdin Palace. Stanley was also the guest of honor at a banquet sponsored by the Egyptian government. It was there that Stanley recounted his adventures in Africa in attempting to rescue Emin Pasha (née Edward Schnitzler) from Mahdist forces. Months later, in April of 1890, Stanley, who had already been named an honorary member of the RGS upon his return from the Congo in February 1878, was given an honorary diploma to celebrate his last voyages in Africa and the publication of his

In Darkest Africa or the Quest, Rescue, and Retreat of Emin Governor of Equatoria. See "Stanley au Caire," *BSGE* 3, no. 5 (1890): 329–56. Stanley's adventures are recorded in *In Darkest Africa*.

18. Burton (1821–90), who traveled throughout Arabia and Africa, edited the *Arabian Nights* and wrote the notorious *Personal Narrative of a Pilgrimage to al-Madinah and Meccah*. Burton, too, was an honorary member of the RGS. See Dr. Abbate Pasha's obituary notice, "Sir Richard Francis Burton," *BSGE* 3, no. 7 (1891): 481–87.

19. De Lesseps (1805–94) was a Saint Simonian and the architect of the Suez Canal.

20. A French Egyptologist and archaeologist, Mariette (1821–81) founded Egypt's Antiquities Service, supervised many excavations in the Nile Valley, established the Egyptian Museum in Bulaq, designed the Egyptian pavilion at the 1867 Exposition Universelle in Paris, wrote sketches for operatic treatment from which Verdi composed *Aïda*, and helped set up the French Archaeological Institute. On Mariette, see Reid, *Whose Pharaohs?*

21. Victorian polymath Francis Galton (1822–1911) spoke at the RGS on the development of fingerprinting and its relevance to Egypt and criminal justice, having observed Colonel Harvey Pasha's (the Commandant of Police) Identification Office. Galton was much impressed with what he saw, and emphasized the utility of fingerprinting for the British Empire. For vivid descriptions see Francis Galton, "Souvenirs d'Égypte," *BSKGE* 5, no. 7 (1900): 375–80; Galton "Identification Offices in India and Egypt."

22. Foucart and Cattaui, *La Société Sultanieh de Géographie du Caire*, viii–ix.

23. "Memorandum, Ministère de la Guerre, État-Major-Général, Caire le 15 Novembre 1876," DWQ, Al-Archif al-Urubi: 'Ahd Isma'il, Al-Gughrafiyya, box 22/7 (12/9/1876– 15/11/1876). The September 1876 Congress is now remembered more as a colonial ruse than as a scientific gathering, in which Leopold established the International African Association, cementing his hold on what was to become the Belgian Congo. See Hochschild, *King Leopold's Ghost*; Fabian, *Out of Our Minds*.

24. Reid, "The Egyptian Geographical Society."

25. Société Khediviale de Géographie, *Notice*. See also "Statuts de la Société Sultanieh de Géographie" (Cairo: Imprimerie de l'Institut Français d'Archéologie Orientale, 1917), DWQ, Abdin, al-jama'iyyat al'ilmiyya, al-jama'iyya al-gughrafiyya, 1895–1949, box 198.

26. According to Donald Reid, the society's membership in 1881 consisted of twenty-eight high government officials, twenty-four lower government officials, twenty-three liberal professionals, nineteen merchants and industrialists, sixteen professors, fifteen military officers, six cabinet ministers/ex-ministers, six diplomats/consultants, three explorers, one clergyman, and one prince—a pattern not unlike most Western geographical societies. In 1881, 82 percent of the members were Westerners (but by 1928 that number had fallen to 44 percent). See Reid, "The Egyptian Geographical Society," 544, 552.

27. H. Awad, *La Société Royale de Géographie d'Égypte*, 8–9; Foucart and Cattaui, *La Société Sultanieh de Géographie du Caire*, ix.

28. H. Awad, *La Société Royale de Géographie d'Égypte*, 10–11. See also Wheeler, *Report upon the Third International Geographical Congress and Exhibition at Venice, Italy, 1881*, 62–75. Among the Egyptian contributions were a 1559 map of the world (H. Ahmad), cartographic Arabic works and instruments; cadastral surveys of the Khedive's dominions; meteorological and geological tables and charts; the ethnographic collections made by Schweinfurth during the expeditions in Dar Fur, Niam-Niam, and Monbouttou, as well as his maps of the Nile Valley and Arabian desert; and drawings and sketches of plants and African and Asiatic race types.

29. Dr. Abbate Pasha, "Le Congrès International des Sciences Geographique de Paris," *BSGE* 3, no.5 (1890), 272. This, nevertheless, did not prevent Abbate from complaining to Riaz Pacha (the Minister of Interior) that the financial situation of the society was indeed dire. See his correspondence of 6 December 1890 in DWQ, Majlis al-Wuzara: Sharikat wa Jama'iyyat, box 3/alif, 9/1880–2/6/1924.

30. Ibrahim, "The Egyptian Empire, 1805–1885," 198–216.

31. Sharkey, *Living with Colonialism*; Powell, *A Different Shade of Colonialism*; Daly, *Empire on the Nile*; Daly, *Imperial Sudan*.

32. H. Awad, *La Société Royale de Géographie d'Égypte*, 11, Foucart and Cattaui, *La Société Sultanieh de Géographie du Caire*, xviii–xxi.

33. Frédéric Bonola Bey, "Le Musée de géographie et d'ethnographie de la société," *BSGE* 5, no. 5 (1899): 296–324.

34. Ibid., 298–99.

35. Ibid., 299–300.

36. According to Reid, the Society's history may be divided as follows: the African phase (1875–85); the Italian phase (1885–1915); the golden age of royal patronage (1915–35); the phase of Egyptianization and professionalization (1935–55) and the phase of postrevolutionary professionalism (1955 to the present) (Reid, "The Egyptian Geographical Society," 541). As Reid points out, Italians were the second largest foreign community in Egypt after the Greeks, and they had founded the Egyptian postal system and were the most numerous foreigners teaching at the Egyptian University (ibid., 550).

37. Bonola Bey, "Le Musée de géographie et d'ethnographie de la société," 302.

38. Ibid., 302.

39. Ibid., 304–7.

40. Ibid., 308–13, 320–21.

41. Ibid., 316–20.

42. Ibid., 313–16.

43. Mustafa Amer, "Some Unpublished Egyptian Maps of Harrar," *BSRGE* 19, no.3 (1937): 289.

44. Godlewska, "Napoleon's Geographers," 40, 50–52. For a fascinating comparison of the 1798 French expedition to Egypt with Napoleon III's Scientific Commission of Mexico, see Edison, "Conquest Unrequited."

45. Çelik, *Displaying the Orient*, chap. 4.

46. Pels, "The Rise and Fall of the Indian Aborigines"; see also Prakash, *Another Reason*.

47. Chatterjee, *Nation and its Fragments*, 20.

48. Said, *Orientalism*, 86.

49. T. Mitchell, *Colonising Egypt*, 140.

50. Pels, "The Rise and Fall of the Indian Aborigines"; Dirks, *Castes of Mind*; Godlewska, "Napoleon's Geographers"; Godlewska, "Map, Text and Image."

51. T. Mitchell, *Colonising Egypt*, 166.

52. Dirks, *Castes of Mind*, 193.

53. All biographical information on Abbate presented here is from Rhodes, "S.E. LE Dr. Onofrio Abbate Pasha." On Abbate's involvement with the Free Popular University, see Gorman, "Anarchists in Education."

54. Abbate's other publications were *De l'Afrique centrale, ou Voyage de S. A. Mohammed Saïd Pacha dans ses provinces du Soudan* (Paris: H. Plon, 1858) and *Le Soudan sous le règne du Khédive Ismail: Notes d'une decade historique, 1868–1878* (Cairo: [n.p.], 1905).

55. The Cambridge Torres Straits expedition, organized by British ethnographer Alfred Cort Haddon in April 1898, included an extensive series of psychological and physiological tests, as well as the collection of general ethnographic, medical, linguistic, and physical anthropological data. It was described by later anthropologists as "'the beginning of a new phase' in the history of British social anthropology" (Stocking, *After Tylor*, 111). The Torres Straits are located between New Guinea and Australia. See Haddon, *Reports of the Cambridge Anthropological Expedition to Torres Straits*; Stocking, *After Tylor*, 98–115.

56. On cosmopolitanism in Egypt and in the Middle East generally, see Meijer, *Cosmopolitanism, Identity and Authenticity*; on cosmopolitanism in Alexandria, see Ilbert and Yannakakis, eds., *Alexandria 1860–1960*.

57. See Kuklick, *The Savage Within*; Dirks, *Castes of Mind*.

58. Reid, *Whose Pharaohs?*

59. Heyworth-Dunne, *An Introduction to the History of Education in Modern Egypt*.

60. Onofrio Abbate, "Le Positivisme dans les recherches géographiques actuelles," *BSGE* 3, no. 12 (1893): 822–29.

61. Robic, "Geography."

62. Hannaford, *Race*, 187–90.

63. Ibid., 197–202, 213–24; Eze, *Race and the Enlightenment*, 29–33; Balibar, "Fichte and the Internal Border," 61–87.

64. Hannaford, *Race*, 255–70. Lamarck argued for the effects of environmental influences on the modification, growth, and atrophy of the human organs over successive generations. Cuvier, in contrast, argued for the "fixity of type" and unity of the species.

65. Hannaford, *Race*, 214.

66. Stoler, *Race and the Education of Desire*; Stoler, *Carnal Knowledge and Imperial Power*; Balibar and Wallerstein, *Race, Nation, Class*.

67. See, for example, Stocking, *Victorian Anthropology*; Nye, *Crime, Madness, and Politics in Modern France*; Goldstein, *Console and Classify*; Rabinbach, *The Human Motor*.

68. Pick, *The Faces of Degeneration*, 4.

69. Rabinbach, *The Human Motor*, 3–4.

70. Abbate, "Prééminence des facultés mecaniques dans la race Egyptienne," in *Aegyptiaca*, 147–56 (speech originally delivered at the Institut Égyptien, 6 November 1891).

71. Ibid., 146. This discussion is reminiscent of the Indian colonial labor market for aborigines; see Ghosh, "A Market for Aboriginality," and Pels, "The Rise and Fall of the Indian Aborigines."

72. Abbate, "Prééminence des facultés mecaniques dans la race Egyptienne," 146–48.

73. Ibid., 149.

74. Ibid., 150–54.

75. On features such as imitation as being Semitic traits, see Richard Wagner's 1850 article "Judaism in Music."

76. Abbate, "Prééminence des facultés mecaniques dans la race Egyptienne," 153.

77. Abbate, "L'equilibre statique chez la femme Égyptienne," in *Aegyptiaca*, 107–13 (speech originally delivered at the Institut Égyptien, 7 April 1893).

78. Ibid., 107–8.

79. Ibid., 110–11.

80. Ibid., 112–13.

81. Abbate, "La Fixitè de la Race dans la Femme Égyptienne," in *Aegyptiaca*, 339–47.

82. Ibid., 340.

83. Ibid., 342–43. In fact, much of Abbate's work was threaded together by a concern for physiological and organic structural difference, such as the prevalence of a condition known as "asymetria vasorum" among Arabs and Egyptians. On this condition see, Abbate, "Asymétrie cardiaque dans le race indigéne," in *Aegyptiaca*, 257–61 (speech originally delivered at the Institut Égyptien, 27 January 1882).

84. Abbate, "La Fixitè de la Race dans la Femme Égyptienne," 344–45.

85. Ibid., 346.

86. In "Notes on Hasish," Abbate observed the Oriental use of the drug as an aphrodisiac, despite its diametrically opposed actual effects. See his experimental results in Abbate, "Notes sur le haschich," in *Aegyptiaca*, 165–70. On snake charmers, see Abbate, "Les Psylles d'Egypte. Charmeurs des serpents—Nouvelles recherches," in *Aegyptiaca*, 504–18.

87. Abbate, "Sorcellerie Egyptienne: Le Fataa El Mandel en Egypte. Phénomènes de suggestion hallucinatoire," in *Aegyptiaca*, 35–49.

88. Lane, *An Account of the Manners and Customs of the Modern Egyptians*, 263–75. Lane's text was written in Egypt between 1833 to 1835 and based on notes taken in a former visit, from 1825 to 1828.

89. Ibid., 275.

90. Abbate, "Sorcellerie Egyptienne," 37–40.

91. Ibid., 40–41.

92. Ibid., 42–45. A psycho-physiological framework, Abbate argued, could be used to comprehend different levels of consciousness, such as was found amongst the yogis and fakirs in India; and in the practice of *zikr*, among dervishes in Egypt and the Middle East.

93. Ibid., 45–49. Similarly, he notes, Newton could summon the image of the sun before his eyes in the dark; Goethe could voluntarily evoke the image of a flower and, Shelley was the victim of hallucinations of his imagination that became forces independent of his own will.

94. Abbate, "Le Positivisme dans les recherches géographiques actuelles," 827–28.

95. See Abbate, "L'eunuchisme: Notes physiologiques, pour aider a son abolition complete," in *Aegyptiaca*, 633–53 (speech originally delivered at the *Premier Congrès Egyptien de Medicine au Caire*, December 1902); Abbate, "Memorandum and Letter to the Grand Vizir," in *Aegyptiaca*, 654–58.

96. See, for example, Asad, "Reflections on Cruelty and Torture," in *Formations of the Secular*; Mani, "Contentious Traditions"; Dirks, "The Policing of Tradition" in *Castes of Mind*.

97. Abbate, "Bonaparte et l'Institut d'Égypte," in *Aegyptiaca*, 417–32.

98. See Mustafa Amer, "An Egyptian Explorer in Arabia in the Nineteenth Century," *BSRGE* 18, no. 1 (1932): 29–45; Amer, "Some Unpublished Egyptian Maps of Harrar." On the conquest of Harrar, see Douin, *Histoire du Règne du Khédive Ismail*, 602–27.

99. *Société Royale de Géographie d'Égypte*, pamphlet, n.d., in DWQ, Abdin, al-jama'iyyat al-'ilmiyya, al-jama'iyya al-gughrafiyya, 1895–1949, box 198; Ahmed Hassanein Bey, "À Travers le Désert Libyique," *BSRGE* 13, nos. 3–4 (1925): 181–83.

100. *Procès-Verbaux des séances du Conseil d'administration de la Société Royale de Géographie d'Égypte*, 5 April 1928, in DWQ, Abdin, al-jama'iyyat al-'ilmiyya, al-jama'iyya al-gughrafiyya, 1895–1949, box 198.

101. "Hasanayn, Muhammad Ahmad," in Goldschmidt, *Biographical Dictionary of Modern Egypt*, 73–74.

102. Ibid., 73. The RGS included less sensational figures as well. Mahmud Pasha al-Falaki, one-time court astronomer, minister of public instruction from 1884 to 1885, and vice president of the RGS and the Institut d'Egypt, produced the first topographical map of Egypt. A graduate of Mehmed 'Ali's Ecole Polytechnique (where he eventually taught mathematics and astronomy), al-Falaki was sent on a student mission to Paris, where he remained for nine years. Al-Falaki was the Egyptian representative at the 1881 International Congress of Geography in Venice ("Al-Falaki, Mahmud Ahmad Hamdi," in Goldschmidt, *Biographical Dictionary of Modern Egypt*, 53).

103. Reid, "The Egyptian Geographical Society," 558. Fu'ad was not the only

member of the royal family to engage such "adventures"; see Prince Youssef Kamal, "Notes de voyage au Soudan Egyptien," *BSSGE* 9, no. 3–4 (1920): 199–202.

104. Hafez Afifi, "Mon voyage de Benghazi à Garaboub en compagnie du Grand Senoussi," *BSSGE* 8, no. 4 (1917): 289–300.

105. Reid, "The Egyptian Geographical Society," 556.

106. "Projet de Note: Sa Majesté Fouad I Roi d'Égypte," in DWQ, *Abdin, al-jama'iyyat, jama'iyyat' ilmiyya, 1909–1952,* box 200.

107. Société Royale de Géographie d'Égypte, *Record,* updated to the end of May 1928, indicating the activities of the King and the Kingdom of Egypt in DWQ, *Abdin, al-jama'iyyat al-'ilmiyya, al-jama'iyya al-gughrafiyya, 1916–1950.* Archive Box. No. 201.

108. Reid, "The Egyptian Geographical Society," 555. On Augustin Bernard and his surveys of rural habitat in Colonial Algeria and Tunisia, see Chapter 3.

109. Foucart and Cattaui, *La Société Sultanieh de Géographie du Caire,* xvi; G. A. Wainwright, "Ethnology in Egypt," *BSRGE* 16, no. 4 (1929): 257–62. King Leopold II of Belgium designed the Tervuren Museum (named after Leopold's royal estate, and also known as the Musée du Congo) in 1897–98 to promote scientific, commercial, and public interest in the Congo Free State. The museum was greatly expanded between 1904 and 1909, renamed the Museum of the Belgian Congo, and reopened in 1910. After the Congo gained independence, the museum was renamed the Royal Museum for Central Africa. On the history of the museum's buildings, see http://www.africamuseum.be/sitemap/research/about/histobuildings.

110. Sultanieh Geographical Society, *Programme of Work* (in English), Cairo: Printing Office of the French Institute of Oriental Archaeology, 1918, in DWQ, *Abdin, al-jama'iyyat al-'ilmiyya, al-jama'iyya al-gughrafiyya, 1895–1949,* box 198.

111. Ibid., 1–2.

112. Ibid., 1.

113. Ibid., 3–6.

114. Ibid., 4.

115. Ibid., 13–15. An anthropometric study of the inhabitants of Siwa, Baharia, Farafra, Dakhla, and Kharga oases was later published by Mohamed Mitwalli, "The Population of the Egyptian Oases."

116. Barnett, "Impure and Worldly Geography," 242.

117. See Reid, "The Egyptian Geographical Society," 551–55.

118. "Union Geographique International: Comité Nationale d'Egypte," 24 April 1929, in DWQ, *Abdin, al-jama'iyyat al-'ilmiyya, al-jama'iyya al-gughrafiyya, 1895–1949,* box 198; "Congrès de 1925, Comité d'Organisation, Proces-Verbaux," in DWQ, *Abdin, al-jama'iyyat al-'ilmiyya, al-jama'iyya al-gughrafiyya, 1916–1950,* box 201, folder 8; Mustafa Pacha Maher, "L'Oasis de Siouah," *BSRGE* 9, nos. 1–2 (1919): 47–104.

119. Maher, "L'Oasis de Siouah," 103.

120. Ibid., 100.

121. Ibid., 104.

122. Wainwright, "Ethnology in Egypt," 258.

123. Ibid., 259, 261.

124. "Procès-Verbaux des seances du Conseil d'administration de Société Royale de Géographie d'Égypte," 5 April 1928, in DWQ, Abdin, al-jama'iyyat al-'ilmiyya, al-jama'iyya al-gughrafiyya, 1895–1949, box 198. Bovier-Lapierre had previously been a professor at the Faculty of Medicine in Beirut.

125. Ibid. Bovier-Lapierre also wrote on prehistoric Egypt—see Bovier-Lapierre, "L'Égypte Préhistorique."

126. R. P. P. Bovier-Lapierre, "Rapport sur le Musée d'Ethnographie Égyptienne," *BSRGE* 18, nos. 3–4 (1934): 283–92.

127. Charles Bachatly, *Rapport, 1927–1934*, in DWQ, Abdin, al-jama'iyyat al'-ilmiyya, al-jama'iyya al-gughrafiyya, 1916–1950. box 201.

128. Charles Bachatly, "Notes sur quelques amulettes Égyptiennes," *BSRGE* 17, no. 1 (1929): 49–60; Bachatly, "Notes sur quelques amulettes égyptiennes, 2e serie" *BSRGE* 17, no. 3 (1931): 183–88; Bachatly, "Le bosquet sacre de Guizeh," *BSRGE* 18, no. 1 (1932): 97–101. See also Ch. Bachatly and H. Rached, "Un cas d'envoutement en Égypte," *BSRGE* 17 no. 3 (1931): 177–81.

129. For Petrie's view, see Petrie, *Amulets*.

130. Abbas Bayoumi, "Survivances Egyptiennes," *BSRGE* 19, no. 3 (1937): 279–87.

131. On the denial of epistemological value, see Barnett, "Impure and Worldly Geography," 245.

132. On the relationship between ancient Egypt and Africa, see George Foucart, "L'ethnologie Africaine et ses récents problèmes," *BSSGE* 8, no. 3 (1917): 195–288; G. A. Wainwright, "Ancient Survivals in Modern Africa," *BSSGE* 9 nos. 1–2 (1919): 105–30. On the study of survivals, see Hodgen, *The Doctrine of Survivals*.

133. See Maspero, *Du genre épistolaire chez les égyptiens de l'époque pharaonique*; Maspero, *Le contes populaires de l'Égypte ancienne*; Maspero, *Causeries d'Egypte*. Maspero was secretary of the Academy of Inscriptions, director-general of the Service of Antiquities in Egypt, and a member of the Institute of France and of the Egyptian University Board.

134. Artin, *Contes populaires inedits de la Vallée du Nil*; Legrain, *Louqsor sans les pharaons*.

135. Reid, *Whose Pharaohs*, 185.

136. Foucart directed the *Institut Français d'Archaéologie Orientale* and succeeded Gaston Maspero on the Egyptian University's Board of Directors in 1914.

137. Foucart, *Introductory Questions on African Ethnology*, xii.

138. In constructing his questionnaire Foucart tried to avoid some of the pitfalls of earlier surveys, such as the difficulty of separating ethnography from biological anthropology evident in works such as the 1883 *Questionnaire de Sociologie et d'Ethnographie* of the Anthropological Society, and the narrow scope of other surveys, such as J. G. Frazer's 1907 *Questions on the Customs, Beliefs, and Languages of Savages*. It was Joseph Halkin's 1905 "Questionnaire ethnographique et soiologique" that Foucart found the most impressive model, and which he reworked for his own survey. The same model had been used in the *Monographies*

Ethnographiques (1907–14) of the National Sociological Institute of Brussels. Foucart, *Introductory Questions on African Ethnology*, xvi–xviii.

139. Blackman, *The Fellaheen of Upper Egypt*. Of course, the precursor to this work and others like it is Edward Lane's renowned study *An Account of the Manners and Customs of the Modern Egyptians* (1836).

140. Blackman, *The Fellaheen of Upper Egypt*, 9–12.

141. Ibid., 214–17.

142. See also Blackman, "Ancient Egyptian Custom Illustrated by a Modern Survival."

143. On R. R. Marett, see Stocking, *After Tylor*, 163–72.

144. R. R. Marett, foreword to Blackman, *The Fellaheen of Upper Egypt*, 5–7.

145. Ibid., 6.

146. Preface to Blackman, *The Fellaheen of Upper Egypt*, 10.

147. Stocking, *After Tylor*, 167.

148. Stocking, *After Tylor*, 167.

149. Ghallab became a professor of philosophy in the Faculty of Theology at al-Azhar University, and was prodigiously prolific, publishing dozens of books on Greek, Eastern, Christian, and Islamic philosophy.

150. Herzfeld, *Ours Once More*.

151. Gershoni and Jankowski, *Egypt, Islam, and the Arabs*, 164.

152. Ibid., 167. The article cited is Muhammad Husayn Haykal, "Misr al-haditha wa Misr al-qadima," *al-Siyasa al-Usbu'iyya*, 1926.

153. Ghallab, "Introduction," in *Les Survivances de l'Égypte Antique*.

154. Ghallab identifies himself as being from the village of Bani-Khalid in the province of Mellawi.

155. Ghallab pointed out some of the following as common themes (*idées reçues*) in both ancient and modern popular literature: the idea that Egyptians inhabit a privileged land; Egyptians' belief in the superiority of their race; an extreme intimacy and simplicity with family coupled with a savoir-faire with outsiders; an extreme admiration for eloquence; a belief in the supreme power of the word (speech); a joyful being; an ardent sensualism; an amorous psychology; and the importance of the feminine personality. An example of a specific theme is that of the adulterous Egyptian female. Ghallab, *Les survivances de l'Égypte antique*, 55–122.

156. Ibid., 177–206.

157. Ibid., 189.

158. Ibid., 207–83.

159. Ibid., 217–18.

160. Ibid., 236.

161. On the idea of the "Unity of the Nile Valley" in Egyptian nationalist discourse, see Chapter 2.

162. Gershoni and Jankowski, *Egypt, Islam and the Arabs*, 107. The article cited is "Al-adab al-misri wa mizatuhu 'an al-adab al-samiyya," published in *al-Siyasa al-Usbu'iyya* in 1929.

163. Ibid., 116.

164. Fabian, *Time and the Other*; Koselleck, *Futures Past*.

165. Later writings by Egyptians on folklore include Selim Hasan, "Survivals of Ancient Egyptian Customs in Modern Egypt," *Bulletin of the Society of the Friends of Coptic Art* II (1936): 47–71; A. Hasanayn, *Qasasuna al-sha'bi*; A. Amin, *Qamus al-adat wa al-taqalid wa al-ta'bir al-misriyya*; Kamal, *Athar hadarat al-fara'inah fi hayatuna al-haliyah*. Many of these authors drew from Edward Lane's *An Account of the Manners and Customs of the Modern Egyptians*, which was translated into Arabic in 1950. Ahmed Rushdi Salih, a Marxist and noted folklorist, represented a critical juncture in historical writings on folklore and the peasantry. He served as editor in chief of *Al-fajr al-jadid*, director of the Center for Popular Arts in the Ministry of Culture and editor of its magazine, *Folklore*. Two of his classic texts, *Al-adab al-sha'abi* and *Al-funun al-sha'abiyya*, present analyses of folklore based on historical and aesthetic criteria. An interesting discussion of the importance of folklore studies in hegemonic cultural formations is Peter Gran's discussion of the "Italian Road" model of hegemony in his *Beyond Eurocentrism*.

Chapter 2. Anthropology's Indigenous Interlocutors

1. Musa, *Misr asl al-hadara*.
2. Egger, *A Fabian in Egypt*, 127–28, 159 n. 18. Musa claimed to have appropriated the term *thaqafa* from Ibn Khaldun, who he claimed used it in the sense used in modern European literature. According to Egger, *al-thaqafa* was an important term in *Al-Jarida* circles in the pre-war period, and Musa may have been inspired by them. See also Salama Musa, "Al-Thaqafa wa al-hadara," *Al-Hilal* 36 (December 1927): 171–74.
3. Husayn, *Mustaqbal al-thaqafa fi Misr*.
4. T. Mitchell, *Rule of Experts*, 183.
5. Powell, *A Different Shade of Colonialism*, 17.
6. Glassman, "Slower than a Massacre."
7. Ibid., 725.
8. Ibid., 732–33.
9. On Latin America, see Stepan, *"The Hour of Eugenics"*; Trillo, *Mexico's Presence at World's Fairs*, chap.6.
10. *Al-Muqtataf*, founded in 1876 by Ya'qub Sarruf and Faris Nimr, and *Al-Hilal*, founded in 1892 by Jurji Zaydan and one of the most widely circulated Middle East periodicals at the time, were both Lebanese-Egyptian literary-scientific-cultural journals, decidedly secular in tone, that advocated Westernizing reforms.
11. Elshakry, "Darwin's Legacy in the Arab East," chap. 2.
12. "Al-Anthropolojiyya aw 'ilm al-insan," *Al-Muqtataf* 16 (1892): 91–96.
13. "Masa'il wa ajwibatiha," *Al-Muqtataf* 21 (1897): 306–7.
14. "Al-'ilm fi al-'amm al-madi: Al-anthropolojiyya ay 'ilm al-insan" *Al-Muqtataf* 40 (February 1912): 124–25. *Al-Hilal* covered the London conference as well, in "Akhbar 'ilmiyya: Mu'tammir al-anasir," *Al-Hilal* 19 (April 1911): 443–44.

15. "Al-'ilm fi al-'amm al-madi: Al-anthropolojiyya," *Al-Muqtataf* 42 (January 1913): 6; "Al-'ilm fi al-'amm al-madi: Al-anthropolojiyya aw ilm al-insan," *Al-Muqtataf* 44 (January 1914): 29. *Al-Hilal*'s column "Scientific News" also reported on paleontology, see "Akhbar 'ilmiyya: Al-insan fi al-athar al-jiyulujiyya," *Al-Hilal* 12 (December 1903): 190; "Akhbar 'ilmiyya: Athar al-insan," *Al-Hilal* 19 (February 1911): 318.

16. "Alwan al-bashar," *Al-Hilal* 6 (April 1898): 621–23; "Akhbar 'ilmiyya: Al-ru's al-mustatila wa al-ru's al-mufaltaha," *Al-Hilal* 7 (January 1899): 244–45.

17. "Asnaf al-bashar," *Al-Hilal* 9 (October 1900): 50–53.

18. The exact phrase used to refer to monogenesis was *inna sukkan hathihi al-ard mutasalsalun min abb wahidin*. Sometimes this doctrine was referred to as *wihdat al-insan al-awwal*.

19. Jurji Zaydan, "Asl al-insan: Hal wahid aw ghayr wahid," *Al-Hilal* 20 (June 1912): 538–43; "Al-Sulalat al-bashariyya wa ikhtilafuha," *Al-Hilal* 37 (August 1929): 1211–13.

20. "Al-anthropolojiyya wa al-bahth al-jina'i: al-haykal al-athmi," *Al-Muqtataf* 93 (November 1938): 417–20.

21. Jurji Zaydan, *Tabaqat al-umam aw al-sala'il al-bashariyya: Huwa kitab 'ilmi, taba'i, ijtima'i* (Cairo: Matba'at al-Hilal, 1912).

22. Ibid., "Introduction."

23. See Wehr, *A Dictionary of Modern Written Arabic*. In a contemporary dictionary of social-scientific terms, *'unsur* is the term given for "race," and *'unsuriyya* for "racism"; see Madkur, *Ma'jam al-'ulum al-ijtima'iyya*.

24. Musa, *Misr asl al-hadara*, 12. This idea was most probably based on Sergi's *The Mediterranean Race*.

25. Musa, *Misr asl al-hadara*, 14–17. Compare Musa's discussion in *Nazariyyat al-tatawwur wa asl al-insan*, 194–200.

26. Musa, *Misr asl al-hadara*, 7.

27. Gershoni and Jankowski, *Egypt, Islam, and the Arabs*, 164, and see especially chap. 8. For Gershoni and Jankowski, pharaonicism is a component of what they term "Egyptian territorial nationalism," a movement of the first third of the twentieth century (especially the 1920s), in which intellectuals developed four collective images: a territorial image of the Nile Valley as the unique determinant of Egyptian personality; a historical image linking all Egyptians (past and future) within a collective historical experience; a pharaonic image linking the ancient and modern Egyptians; and a cultural image positing a distinct Egyptian national culture (ibid., 131). They oppose "territorial nationalism" to the supranationalist tendencies of the 1930s and 1940s (Egyptian Easternism and Islamism). On Greece, see Herzfeld, *Ours Once More*.

28. Gershoni and Jankowski, *Egypt, Islam, and the Arabs*, 168.

29. Ibid., 165–68.

30. Ibid., 167. This is exactly the intellectual agenda that Muhammad Ghallab set out in his *Les survivances de l'Égypte antique* (see Chapter 1).

31. Gershoni and Jankowski, *Egypt, Islam, and the Arabs*, 183–85. For an

insightful discussion of pharaonicism as a literary movement and its intersection with statist discourses on antiquities, see Colla, "The Stuff of Egypt."

32. Ahmed Shawqi, "Tutankhamun wa hadarat 'asru," *Al-Muqtataf* 68 (January 1926): 5–8. On Shawqi's poetry in praise of ancient Egypt, see Gershoni and Jankowski, *Egypt, Islam, and the Arabs*, 184–5, 187. Other articles on Tutankhamun included "Al-Malak Tutankhamun wa kunuzu," *Al-Muqtataf* 62 (January 1923): 1–8; "Iftitah nawus Tutankhamun," *Al-Hilal* 32 (April 1924): 681–83; "Timthal bad'ia lil malak al-shab Tutankhamun" and "A'imat al-malak Tutankhamun," *Al-Hilal* 35 (March 1927): 518–19; "Athar Tutankhamun," *Al-Hilal* 36 (March 1928): 537–39; "Athar Tutankhamun," *Al-Hilal* 37 (August 1929): 1180–81; "Safinat Tutankhamun" and "Iktishafat jadida fi qabr Tutankhamun," *Al-Hilal* 38 (November 1929): 24–27.

33. Egger, *A Fabian in Egypt*, 70.

34. Reid, *Whose Pharaohs?* 172–212.

35. Gershoni and Jankowski, *Egypt, Islam, and the Arabs*, 165–68. On Marcus Simaika, see Reid, *Whose Pharaohs?* chap. 7.

36. Egger, *A Fabian in Egypt*, 70. Musa had a most prolific career. In the 1910s he wrote for the journal *Al-Muqtataf*, in 1910 Dar al-Hilal published his *Muqadimmat al-Suberman*, and in 1914 he began the journal *Al-Mustaqbal* with Shibli Shumayyil. He began writing for *Al-Hilal* in 1917, and would continue to do so throughout the 1920s; while between 1923 and 1929 he worked as an editor for *Al-Hilal* and *Al-Balagh*. He ran his own journal and publishing house, *Al-Majalla al-Jadida* from 1929 to 1942, and even did a brief stint in 1939 editing the journal of the Ministry of Social Affairs (*Majallat al-Shu'un al-Ijtima'iyya*). See Musa's autobiographical *The Education of Salama Musa*, 123–33.

37. The character is 'Adli Karim, in *Sukariyya* (see Egger, *A Fabian in Egypt*, 236 n.14).

38. Musa, *The Education of Salama Musa*, 50. Musa continues, on the same page, "We had totally ignored this history, because the English had felt that it had better be left unstudied by the descendants of the Ancient Egyptians in the twentieth century as it might incite in them an undue sense of pride and glory, and even foster a demand for independence. Ever since that time I have taken a strong interest in the ancient history and culture of our country and my book *Egypt, the source of civilization*, is a fruit of that interest."

39. Ibid., 139.

40. Egger, *A Fabian in Egypt*, 225.

41. Ibid., 39.

42. On the nationalist ideology of Easternism and Musa's antipathy towards it, see Egger, *A Fabian in Egypt*, 121–32.

43. On these figures see Gershoni and Jankowski, *Egypt, Islam, and the Arabs*, chap. 8. Musa considered 'Abd al-Qadir Hamza, a journalist and social commentator who was trained as a lawyer, an important personal influence. Hamza worked as an editor for the weekly *Al-Balagh al-Usbu'i*, writing articles on ancient Egypt as the source of Greek and Roman civilization, and recounting, in what was a common

journalistic trope of the 1920s, a trip to Upper Egypt during which he became enamored with Thebes. On Hamza, see Gershoni and Jankowski, *Egypt, Islam, and the Arabs*, 88–92, 172–74, 181, 188. On Musa's opinion of Hamza, see *The Education of Salama Musa*, 125, 130, 132, 137, 166.

44. Egger, *A Fabian in Egypt*, 129.

45. "I was much enlightened by the far-flung researches made by Elliot Smith and his colleagues, who sought to explain the traces that were left by the beliefs of the ancient Egyptians" (Musa, *The Education of Salama Musa*, 178). Musa was equally enamored with the encyclopaedic text by James Frazer, *The Golden Bough*, although it directly contradicted many of Elliot Smith's main theses.

46. See Grafton Elliot Smith, *The Ancient Egyptians and the Origin of Civilization* and *The Diffusion of Culture*.

47. W. J. Perry, "Anthropologist and Ethnologist," in Warren R. Dawson, ed., *Sir Grafton Elliot Smith: A Biographical Record by His Colleagues* (London: Jonathan Cape, 1938), 208.

48. Smith, *The Ancient Egyptians and Their Influence upon the Civilization of Europe*, 16.

49. Smith, *The Ancient Egyptians and the Origin of Civilization*, xii.

50. "Wida' al-Duktur Alyut Smyth," *Al-Muqtataf* 35 (July 1909): 717.

51. *Al-Muqtataf* published several pieces by or on Smith between 1912–32. These included Smith, "Nushu' al-insan," *Al-Muqtataf* 41 (November 1912): 417–24, a lecture given by Smith as chair of the anthropological section of the British Association for the Advancement of Science; "Usul al-hidara wa manshu'iha al-awwal. Elephants and Ethnologists: Kitab jadid lil Duktur Alyut Smyth,"*Al-Muqtataf* 76 (January 1930): 102–4, a review of Smith's *Elephants and Ethnologists*; Smith, "Ayna mahd al-insan: Afriqya aw Asya," *Al-Muqtataf* 77 (October 1930): 305–10, a translation of a Smith article from *Scienctia*; and Smith "Tutankhamun: Misr wa usul al-hidara," a chapter from Smith's *The Ancient Egyptians and the Origins of Civilization*. Salama Musa published a series of articles in the late 1920s and early 1930s on Smith's notion that Egypt was the origin of civilization: "Misr asl hadarat al-alam," *Al-Hilal* 35 (December 1926): 183–86; "Muluk al-alam," *Al-Hilal* 37 (November 1928): 39–42; "Hadith an al-fara''ina," *Al-Hilal* 37 (June 1929), 929–32; "Thaqafat Misr 'ind al-arab," *Al-Hilal* 37 (February 1929): 426–8; "Misr asl hadarat al-alam," *Al-Majalla al-Jadida* 1 (December 1929): 195–98; "Al-wajh al-misri al-an wa 'ind ayyam al-fara'ina" *Al-Majalla al-Jadida* 3 (April 1934): 12–15; "Al-misriyyun wa al-Kaldaniyyun," *Al-Majalla al-Jadida* 1 (July 1930): 1065–67; "Turath qadim," *Al-Majalla al-Jadida* 1 (June 1930): 1007; "Al-misriyyun wa ikhtira'al-sufun" *Al-Majalla al-Jadida* 3 (February 1934): 21–25. Musa also published a series of articles in *Al-Balagh* in the 1930s that were installments of his book *Misr asl al-hidara*: "Dima' al-fara'ina tajri fi 'uruqina jami'an" *Al-Balagh* (18 October 1933): 1; "Nahnu al-misriyyun," *Al-Balagh* (8 October 1933): 3; "Qimat al-hadara al-misriyya," *Al-Balagh* (29 June 1935): 3; "Misr asl al-hadara wa al-ighriqiyya hiya al-mahd al-thani laha," *Al-Balagh* (15 June 1935): 3.

52. Musa, *Misr asl al-hadara*, 6–7.

53. Smith's proto-Egyptians were based on Giuseppe Sergi's *The Mediterranean Race*, which argued that the original primitive inhabitants of Europe were not Aryans but a dolichocephalic northern African "Hamitic" people. Unlike Sergi, who argued that the prehistoric or proto-Egyptians were of the same race (a Mediterranean stock of African origin) as the historic Egyptians, Smith developed an intricate theory of racial admixture and cultural diffusion. Musa addresses neither the crucial differences between Sergi and Smith, nor the rather negative implications of Smith's view of the historic (and thus also contemporary) Egyptians as the product of racial admixture and cultural regression.

54. Egger, *A Fabian in Egypt*, 132–39.

55. Egger, perhaps, overstates the case. In 1936 *Al-Muqtataf* issued a retrospective of articles on *Turath Misr al-qadima*, with contributions from Salama Musa, Mustafa Amer, Muharram Kamal, Sami Gabra, Jurji Subhi, and others.

56. Egger, *A Fabian in Egypt*, 136–37.

57. Musa, *Misr asl al-hadara*, 61.

58. L. Awad, ed., *The Literature of Ideas in Egypt*, 130.

59. The "East" for Husayn was India and the Far East (especially China and Japan).

60. Renan, "What Is a Nation?"

61. 'Abbas Mustafa 'Ammar, "The Physical, Ethnographic, Cultural and Economic Bases of the Unity," in Presidency of the Council of Ministers, *Unity of the Nile Valley*, 6–33.

62. Rieker, "Reading the Colonial Archive." See also Edward Said's discussion of the Napoleonic invasion and the *Description de l'Égypte* in his *Orientalism*.

63. Bernal, *Black Athena*.

64. Najib, "'Abbas Mustafa 'Ammar," in *A'lam Misr fi al-qarn al-'ishrin*, 289; *Al-rasa'il al-'ilmiyya li darajatay al-majistir wa al-dukturuh*.

65. Mustafa 'Amir, "Al-gughrafiyya al-haditha," *Al-Muqtataf* 90 (April 1937): 542–47. In this didactic piece on modern geography, 'Amir outlines the discipline of geography as a unique scientific endeavor concerned with the study of natural and human phenomena and their reciprocal relationhip with the environment. He notes that by 1937 the geography department had seventy students (of which one was preparing for a doctorate and six for a master's) and six professors and instructors (544).

66. Ibid., 547.

67. Najib, "Mustafa 'Amir," in *A'lam Misr fi al-qarn al-'ishrin*, 472; Reid, "The Egyptian Geographical Society," 560–61.

68. Najib, "Muhammad 'Awad Muhammad," in *A'lam Misr fi al-qarn al-'ishrin*, 433.

69. Reid, "The Egyptian Geographical Society," 560–62. Another notable figure in Egyptian geography was Sulayman Huzayyin, born in Khartoum in 1909. A graduate in the first class of the Egyptian University in 1929, Huzayyin completed his Master's degree at Liverpool in 1933, and his doctorate at Manchester, focusing on Egyptian prehistory. In England Huzayyin studied under P. M. Roxby and H. J.

Fleure. Huzayyin led the 1935 Egyptian University scientific expedition to southwestern Arabia, were he collected anthropometric and other data on the physical character of the Arabs. Huzayyin was a pivotal figure in the foundation of Asyut University in 1955, and was director of the Institut d'Egypt twice, in 1954 and 1974. In the late 1960s he became president of the RGS. See Huzayyin, "Egyptian University Scientific Expedition to S.W. Arabia"; Huzayyin, *Arabia and the Far East*; Najib, "Sulayman Huzayyin," in *A'lam Misr fi al-qarn 'al-'ishrin*, 240.

70. 'Ammar, "Ba'd nawahi al-gughrafiyya al-bashariyya li shibh jazirat Sina." 'Ammar later published another extensive study on the Sinai entitled "Al-madkhal al-sharqi li Misr" (*BSRGE* 21, no. 2 (1945): 140–228, and *BSRGE* 21, nos. 3–4 (1946): 371–492), in which he explored the Sinai as an eastern point of entry (or corridor) into Egypt. 'Ammar pointed out the importance of the peninsula as a means of transportation and a passageway for human migration, focusing on its geographical location, its military and commercial significance, and the development of travel routes.

71. 'Ammar, *The People of Sharqiya*, 1:viii.
72. Tilley, "Ambiguities of Racial Science in Colonial Africa."
73. 'Ammar, *The People of Sharqiya*, 1:1.
74. Ibid., 1:11.
75. 'Ammar relied heavily on the classical medieval and early modern texts of Arab history by authors such as Ibn Khaldun, al-Maqrizi, al-Isfahani, al-Hamdani, al-Waqidi, al-Qalqashandi, Ali Pasha Mubarak, and al-Jabarti.
76. Chatterjee, "The Disciplines in Colonial Bengal," 25.
77. Ludwig Hirszfeld and Hannah Hirszfeld, quoted in 'Ammar, *The People of Sharqiya*, I:46. For an exhaustive study on serology, see Schneider, "Blood Group Research in Great Britain, France and the United States Between the Wars."
78. 'Ammar, *The People of Sharqiya*, 1:63–64.
79. Ibid., 1:68, 74.
80. For discussions of serology and racial classification, see Schneider "Blood Group Research in Great Britain, France and the United States"; Mazumdar, "Blood and Soil;" Tapper, "Interrogating Bodies." 'Ammar cites the pinnacle studies by the Hirszfelds (physicians working on the Macedonian front during World War I) on "Serological differences between the blood of different races."
81. Sudipta Sen, *Distant Sovereignty*, chap. 5.
82. 'Ammar, *The People of Sharqiya*, 1: 87.
83. Ibid., 1: 146.
84. Ibid., 1:150, emphasis in original.
85. See Gershoni and Jankowski, *Redefining the Egyptian Nation*.
86. See, for example, Mohamed Mitwalli's comprehensive survey of the Egyptian oases, also an anthropometric and demographic study. Mohamed Mitwalli, "The Population of the Egyptian Oases," *BSRGE* 21, no. 2 (1945): 109–38 and *BSRGE* 21, nos. 3–4 (1946): 289–312.
87. Tilley, "Ambiguities of Racial Science," 268–69.
88. Stocking, *After Tylor*, 407.

89. Ibid., 420.

90. 'Ammar, *A Demographic Study of an Egyptian Province*. Not surprisingly, in this work 'Ammar touched on one of the theoretical and methodological debates raging at the time—that of the optimum population—concluding that a large number of writers had determined the standard of living itself to be equivalent to the problem of population. See my discussion in Chapter 5.

91. 'Ammar, *People of Sharqiya*, 1:284.

92. Ibid., 1:321.

93. Ibn Khaldun, *The Muqaddimah: an Introduction to History*.

94. Quoted in Ghurbal, "Introductory Note," in Egyptian Kingdom, *Unity of the Nile Valley*, 5.

95. Powell, "From Odyssey to Empire."

96. Ibid., 420.

97. Ibid., 424.

98. Powell, however, occasionally lapses into a conception of knowledge generated solely from the imperial center and "mimicked" by colonized subjects. To be fair, she modifies this view in her full-length text *A Different Shade of Colonialism*, in which she argues that "the [Egyptian] idea of colonialism was much more fluid, much less dependent on the European model" (112).

99. See ibid.

100. See Sharkey, *Living with Colonialism*.

101. Gershoni and Jankowski, *Egypt, Islam, and the Arabs*, 53.

102. Ibid., 53.

103. Al-Disuqi, *Misr fi al-harb al-'alamiyya al-thaniyya*, 300–11.

104. Ibid., 301–3.

105. Gershoni and Jankowski, *Redefining the Egyptian Nation*, 110–11.

106. Al-Disuqi, *Misr fi al-harb al-'alamiyya al-thaniyya*, 301–2.

107. Ibid.; Gershoni and Jankowski, *Redefining the Egyptian Nation*, 123–24.

108. Gershoni and Jankowski, *Redefining the Egyptian Nation*, 123–24.

109. Clearly, there were many more nuanced views on the Sudan, such as those of Ahmed Lutfi Al-Sayyid (not to mention those of Sudanese nationalists). On Lutfi Al-Sayyid's views see Powell, *A Different Shade of Colonialism*, 164–69; on Sudanese nationalists see Sharkey, *Living with Colonialism*. However, in this section I focus on the views of Egyptian nationalists who articulated claims in geographical and ethnographic terms.

110. Shafiq Ghurbal, "Introductory Note," in Presidency of the Council of Ministers, *The Unity of the Nile Valley*, 1.

111. For a discussion of this earlier period of Egyptian colonialism, see Jeppie, "Constructing a Colony on the Nile."

112. See Shafiq Ghurbal, "The Building-up of a Single Egyptian-Sudanese Fatherland," in Presidency of the Council of Ministers, *The Unity of the Nile Valley*, 61–63. Ghurbal likens Mehmed 'Ali's policy in the Sudan to the nineteenth-century movements of national consolidation—especially those of Germany, Italy, and the Slavonic peoples. See also Abdel Rahman Zaki "The Progress of the Sudan in the

Nineteenth Century" (also in *The Unity of the Nile Valley*, 76–98), in which he reviews developments in Sudanese agriculture, education, railways, postal system, Nile transport, and geographical explorations (e.g., the "reconnaissance" work of members of the RGS in their African expeditions), under Egyptian rule.

113. Ghurbal, "Introductory Note," 3.

114. Shafiq Ghurbal, "British Policy in Egypt and the Sudan," in Presidency of the Council of Ministers, *The Unity of the Nile Valley*, 64–75.

115. Ghurbal, "Introductory Note," 1–2.

116. See 'Ammar, "The Physical, Ethnographic, Cultural and Economic Bases of the Unity," and "The Transformation of the People of the Sudan into a Moslem Arabic-Speaking Nation," both in Presidency of the Council of Ministers, *The Unity of the Nile Valley*.

117. 'Ammar, "The Physical, Ethnographic, Cultural and Economic Bases of the Unity," 11.

118. Tilley, "Ambiguities of Racial Science in Colonial Africa."

119. 'Ammar, "The Physical, Ethnographic, Cultural and Economic Bases of the Unity," 24.

120. Ibid., 12.

121. Fleure, *The Races of England and Wales*, 72–73.

122. Fleure, "Racial Evolution and Archaeology," 19.

123. Fleure, *The Races of England and Wales*, 16. "The fully-fledged Nordic, Mediterranean or Semitic long-head is the *terminus ad quem*, i.e. the goal of a long-continued process of descent with modification in an area of characterisation rather than a type of untold antiquity and permanence" (ibid., 84).

124. 'Ammar, "The Physical, Ethnographic, Cultural and Economic Bases of the Unity," 13.

125. Stocking, *After Tylor*, 117–18. Among Seligman's well-known works were *Races of Africa*, *The Pagan Tribes of the Nilotic Sudan*, and *Egypt and Negro-Africa: A Study in Divine Kingship*.

126. Stocking, *After Tylor*, 117; Kuklick, *The Savage Within*, 50.

127. C.G. Seligman, "Some Aspects of the Hamitic Problem in the Anglo-Egyptian Sudan"; Seligman, "Physical Characters of the Arabs." Hamites were African peoples divided into two groups: northern Hamites (North African Berbers) and eastern Hamites (the ancient and modern Egyptians). Relying on cultural, linguistic, anthropometric, and archaeological evidence, Seligman argued that Northeastern and Eastern Africa retained affinities with ancient Egypt which could be traced back to an undifferentiated Hamitic culture layer. The least modified descendants of the Hamites were the Hamites of the Anglo-Egyptian Sudan, "physically identical to the pre-dynastic Egyptians," Seligman, "Hamitic Problem in the Anglo-Egyptian Sudan," 595.

128. 'Ammar, "The Physical, Ethnographic, Cultural and Economic Bases of the Unity," 16.

129. Ammar "The Physical, Ethnographic, Cultural and Economic Bases of the Unity," 16–17.

130. Charles Seligman, as quoted in Kuklick, *The Savage Within*, 268.
131. 'Ammar, "The Physical, Ethnographic, Cultural and Economic Bases of the Unity," 20.
132. Ibid., 22–23.
133. Ibid., 24.
134. Ibid., 26.
135. Ibid., 26.
136. Ibid., 26–28.
137. Ibid., 31–32.
138. Ibid., 33.
139. On the "Southern policy," see Holt and Daly, *A History of the Sudan*, 130–31.
140. Colla, "The Stuff of Egypt," 90.
141. T. Mitchell, *Rule of Experts*, 183. For another significant and critical theoretical view of nationalism and national identity, see Massad, *Colonial Effects*.
142. See for example, Rafael, *Contracting Colonialism*; Van der Veer, ed., *Conversions to Modernities*.
143. 'Ammar, *Ibn Khaldun's Prolegomena to History*, 178. I am grateful to Michael Hopper of Harvard University's Widener Library for making this manuscript available to me.
144. Ibid.
145. Ibid., 177.
146. Ibid., 2, 164–65.
147. See Kuklick, *The Savage Within*. Interestingly, three prominent colonial anthropologists served as professors of sociology in Egypt: E. E. Pritchard, 1930–33 at Fu'ad I University; A. M. Hocart, 1934–39, also at Fu'ad I University; and A. R. Radcliffe-Brown, 1947–49 at Faruq I University.
148. The case of postcolonial India provides an interesting contrast—there, social anthropology and sociology developed alongside one another, and retained the colonial fixation with caste as a social and cultural institution to be explained in social scientific terms (see Dirks, *Castes of Mind*).

Chapter 3. The Painting of Rural Life

1. Qutb, *A Child from the Village*.
2. Qutb wrote prolifically for the journal of the Ministry of Social Affairs (*Shu'un Ijtima'iyya*). I list here just a few representative examples of his output: "Daribat al-tatawwur," *Shu'un Ijtima'iyya* 1 (June 1940): 43–46; "'Alam Jadid," *Shu'un Ijtima'iyya* 2 (August 1941): 52–57; "Mashru' al-mabarrat al-ijtima'iyya," *Shu'un Ijtima'iyya* 3 (February 1942): 51–57. See also Roussillon, "Trajectoires Reformistes Sayyid Qutb et Sayyid 'Uways."
3. Schulze, "Colonization and Resistance," 182.
4. Chatterjee, *The Nation and Its Fragments*, 159.
5. Weber, *Peasants into Frenchmen*; Frierson, *Peasant Icons*; Palacios, "Post-

revolutionary Intellectuals, Rural Readings and the Shaping of the 'Peasant Problem' in Mexico."

6. See Clay, "Russian Ethnographers in the Service of Empire"; Frierson, *Peasant Icons*.

7. Esmeir, "The Work of Law in the Age of Empire," chaps. 3–4. Esmeir argues that the colonial state purified itself of the question of rural labor by relegating labor concerns to the domain of private property, as, for example, in the new realms of sovereignty exercised on the large private estates.

8. Cromer, *Modern Egypt*, 2: 198.

9. Esmeir, "The Work of Law in the Age of Empire," 196–204; Cromer, *Modern Egypt*, 2: 397–419, 456–65.

10. T. Mitchell, *Rule of Experts*.

11. Frierson, *Peasant Icons*.

12. On Algeria, See Fanon, *Wretched of the Earth*; on Vietnam, see Young, *The Vietnam Wars*, on Egypt, see Nasser, *Falsafat al-thawra*.

13. Wolf, *Peasant Wars of the Twentieth Century*; T. Mitchell, *Rule of Experts*, chap. 4. See also Brown, "The Ignorance and Inscrutability of the Egyptian Peasant."

14. T. Mitchell, *Rule of Experts*, chaps. 4–5; cf. Baer, *Studies in the Social History of Modern Egypt*, chap. 6.

15. The story of the establishment of British colonial domination over Egypt's economic, political, and social life has been told in detail elsewhere. On the British in Egypt see T. Mitchell, *Colonising Egypt*; Tignor, *Modernization and British Colonial Rule in Egypt*; Berque, *Egypt*; Marsot, *Egypt and Cromer*; Cromer, *Modern Egypt*.

16. Schulze, "Colonization and Resistance," 182.

17. Marsot, *A Short History of Modern Egypt*, 79.

18. Schulze, "Colonization and Resistance," 182–83.

19. Al-Daba', *Ruwayyit al-fellah, fellah al-ruwayya*, 31–32.

20. Gershoni and Jankowski, *Egypt, Islam, and the Arabs*, 84–85.

21. Goldschmidt, *Biographical Dictionary of Modern Egypt*, 234; Marsot, *A Short History of Modern Egypt*, 83.

22. Berque, *Egypt*. On Sa'd Zaghlul see Lashin, *Sa'd Zaghlul wa dawruhu fi al-siyasa al-misriyya*; on the Wafd party see Deeb, *Party Politics in Egypt*.

23. Deeb, *Party Politics in Egypt*; Botman, "The Liberal Age"; Tignor, *State, Private Enterprise, and Economic Change in Egypt*, 45–46.

24. Reinhard Schulze gives the estimate of 3,000 deaths—a figure that falls between the official Egyptian and British estimates (Schulze, "Colonization and Resistance," 189).

25. Goldberg, *Tinker, Tailor, and Textile Worker*, 64.

26. Abdel-Malek, *Egypt: Military Society*.

27. Abdel-Malek, *Egypt: Military Society*; Goldberg, *Tinker, Tailor, and Textile Worker*; Gershoni and Jankowski, *Egypt, Islam, and the Arabs*.

28. Schulze, "Colonization and Resistance."

29. Ibid., 172. Schulze uses the term "colonization" to refer to the "systematic restructuring of a regional economy, whereby the ultimate goal is to integrate it into a superimposed division of labor, hierarchized and centralized on the basis of capitalist production."

30. Brown, *Peasant Politics in Modern Egypt*, 23–27. See also Schulze, "Colonization and Resistance"; Baer, *A History of Landownership in Modern Egypt*. Arabic sources on the history of landownership are numerous: 'Amir, *Al-Ard wa al-fellah*; Barakat, *Tatawwur al-milkiyya al-zira'iyya fi Misr wa atharuh 'ala al-haraka al-siyasiyya*; al-Disuqi, *Kibar al-mullak al-aradi al-zira'iyya wa dawruhum fi al-mujtama' al-misri*; Hamid, *al-Nizam al-ijtima'i fi Misr fi zil al-milkiyya al-zira'iyya al-kibira*; and Hamid and al-Disuqi, *Kibar al-mullak wa al-fellahin fi Misr*.

31. Brown, *Peasant Politics in Modern Egypt*, 27–29. For a review and critique of the debates on the development of private property and landownership in eighteenth- and nineteenth-century Egypt, see Cuno, *The Pasha's Peasants*; T. Mitchell, *Rule of Experts*, chap. 2.

32. T. Mitchell, *Rule of Experts*, chap. 2.

33. Schulze, "Colonization and Resistance," 173, 179.

34. Ibid., 180.

35. Ibid., 181. The 'Urabi revolt was led by Colonel Ahmed 'Urabi, one of only four native Egyptian (rather than Turco-Circassian) officers in the army. It has been portrayed in many ways, ranging from an army mutiny, to an anticolonial proto-nationalist revolt, to a full-scale bourgeois-nationalist revolution. The events, in brief, were as follows. A group of dissatisfied Egyptian army officers called for the replacement of the Turco-Circassian minister of war with their own nominee, 'Urabi. 'Urabi was then arrested, and later freed by his own regiment. Calling for "Egypt for the Egyptians," the 'Urabists demanded a change in government, a new constitution, and an increase in the size of the army. Although he served briefly as minister of war in a revolutionary cabinet, 'Urabi would soon be declared a rebel. Indigenous civilian opposition to Khedive Tawfiq and to Anglo-French hegemony grew, as did support for 'Urabi, and tensions culminated with the British bombardment of Alexandria on June 11, 1882. The riots and rebellions that flared up in both urban and rural areas in response to the impending British invasion were seenby the British as an attack on the Ottoman-Egyptian and the European elite. Although 'Urabi was often portrayed as a rural figure, the view that the 'Urabi revolt was itself a peasant uprising has been dispelled (see Brown, *Peasant Politics in Modern Egypt*, 177–94). The literature on 'Urabi is vast, and interpretations of the revolt vary widely. A brief but insightful account of the 'Urabi revolt may be found in Reid, "The 'Urabi Revolution and the British Conquest." The most important English-language texts on the subject are Cole, *Colonialism and Revolution in the Middle East*; Schölch, *Egypt for the Egyptians!*; Ramadan, "Social Significance of the 'Urabi Revolt"; Mayer, *The Changing Past*. Key Arabic texts are 'Urabi, *Mudhakkirat 'urabi*; Al-Rafa'i, *Al-thawra al-'urabiyya wa al-ihtilal al-injlizi*; Salim, *Al-quwwa al-ijtima'iyya fi al thawra al-'urabiyya*.

36. Schulze, "Colonization and Resistance," 184–85. According to Nathan Brown, the impact of British policy on the Egyptian countryside during World War I was varied. The most negative effects resulted from the imposition of forced wartime labor—peasants were enlisted to work in the Labour Corps, Camel Corps, and other units devoted to military transportation and construction. Brown estimates that "by the end of the war, according to official British figures, the amount of labor enlisted in the war effort (calculated in working days) had reached and perhaps even passed the level of the corvée at its apex in the years before the 'Urabi revolt. It even exceeded the figures for laborers used in the digging of the Suez Canal." In addition, the British imposed restrictions on basic crops (mainly cotton) in order to requisition the crops and animals needed for the British army. Brown, *Peasant Politics in Modern Egypt*, 196–210.

37. In a similar vein and different historical context, Christopher Boyer argues, regarding the Mexican revolution in Michoacán, that *agrarismo* had different meanings for different participants—it was never simply associated with the cultural projects of postrevolutionary elites, as it often aligned with older cultural forms and peasant struggles, and villagers recast revolutionary ideology in their own terms (C. Boyer, "Old Loves, New Loyalties," 453–55).

38. Schulze, "Colonization and Resistance," 189.

39. Ibid., 186–92.

40. Ibid, 196–97.

41. Brown, *Peasant Politics in Modern Egypt*, 201; Goldberg, "Peasants in Revolt," 273.

42. The most insightful discussions of peasant insurgency are to be found in the literature on India. See, for example, Guha, *Elementary Aspects of Peasant Insurgency in Colonial India*; Chatterjee, *The Nation and Its Fragments*.

43. On the fear of Bolshevism in post-1919 Egypt, see Ashmawi, *Al-fellahun wa al-sulta*; Goldberg, "Peasants in Revolt," 274. On the colonial archive, particularly in reference to the comparative history of the colonial project in India and Egypt, see Rieker, "Reading the Colonial Archive."

44. Much attention has been devoted to literary and descriptive writings on the Egyptian peasant, so I outline in the broadest contours only some of the defining features and exemplars of this type of discourse.

45. On the study of the Egyptian character in colonial and Egyptian writings and on the influence of Gustave Le Bon's conception of the collective mind and of the crowd on Arabic writers, see T. Mitchell, *Colonising Egypt*, 104–8, 122–25. On Le Bon's influence on the writings of Father Ayrout, see T. Mitchell, *Rule of Experts*, 134–35.

46. Onofrio Abbate's voluminous corpus of writing on Egyptian ethnography is discussed in Chapter 2. See also Piot Bey, "Causerie ethnographique sur le fellah," *BSRGE* 5, no. 4 (1899): 201–48.

47. Edward Said discusses the citationary nature of Orientalism in his classic work *Orientalism*.

48. Piot Bey, "Causerie ethnographique sur le fellah."

49. Ibid., 232–33.
50. Ibid., 234–35.
51. Ibid., 244–46.
52. Ibid., 235–40.
53. Ibid., 248.
54. Ibid., 233.
55. The following paragraph is based on Nahas, *Situation économique et sociale due fellah égyptien*; see also Nahhas, *Al-Fellah*.
56. On the extraordinary resilience of stereotypes of the Egyptian peasant, see T. Mitchell, *Rule of Experts*, chap. 4.
57. John Alden Williams, "Foreword," in Ayrout, *The Egyptian Peasant*.
58. Ayrout, *The Fellaheen*, 18. Later editions of this work are *Fellahs d'Egypte* (1943); *Al-Fellahun* (1944); and *Fellahs d'Egypte* (1952).
59. Hambly, "Moeurs et coutumes des fellahs."
60. For more on Muhammad Ghallab see Chapter 1.
61. See the catalog compiled by Roel Meijer for the Tali'a al-'Ummal collection at the International Institute of Social History: http://www.iisg.nl/archives/en/files/t/10861732full.php.
62. Al-'Alim and Anis, *Fi al-thaqafa al-misriyya*; Selim, *The Novel and the Rural Imaginary in Egypt*; Gershoni and Jankowski, *Egypt, Islam, and the Arabs*; Marsot, *Egypt's Liberal Experiment*.
63. For instance, after Zaghlul's death in 1927, and the transfer of power to the relatively inept leadership of Mustafa al-Nahhas, the stage was set for upheavals and political machinations when in 1928–29 King Fu'ad dismissed Nahhas and appointed a liberal constitutionalist cabinet. This cabinet was headed by Muhammad Mahmud, who suspended parliament for three years and was succeeded in 1930 by Isma'il Pasha Sidqi; Sidqi was ousted in 1933. On the vicissitudes of political power during this turbulent period, see Deeb, *Party Politics in Egypt*.
64. Marsot, *A Short History of Modern Egypt*, 87, 90.
65. Ayrout, as quoted in Baer *Studies in the Social History of Modern Egypt*, 102.
66. Ayrout, *The Fellaheen*, chap. 1.
67. Ibid., 33.
68. Ibid., 77.
69. Ibid., 110.
70. Ibid., 95.
71. Ibid., 131.
72. Ibid., 132.
73. Ibid., 133. Repetition, memorization, and reproduction were the same characteristics that Abbate Pasha highlighted as being Arab or Oriental traits. See Abbate, "Prééminence des facultés mecaniques dans la race égyptienne," in *Aegyptiaca*, 147–56.
74. Ayrout, *The Fellaheen*, 136.
75. Ibid., 137.

76. Ibid., 139.
77. Ibid., 125–30.
78. Ibid., 139–40.
79. Selim, *The Novel and the Rural Imaginary in Egypt*, 2.

80. Selim traces the ambiguous figure of the fellah (as both authentic native and symbol of Egypt's stagnation) back to the late-nineteenth-century writings of 'Abdallah al-Nadim. She finds Ya'qub Sannu''s contemporaneous depiction of the peasant to be a far more articulate and incendiary figure.

81. See Selim, "Novels and Nations," in *The Novel and the Rural Imaginary in Egypt*; Gershoni and Jankowski, *Egypt, Islam, and the Arabs*, 191–227. My account is drawn from these two sources.

82. Al-Daba', *Ruwayyit al-fellah, fellah al-ruwayya*, 26.

83. Al-Daba', *Ruwayyit al-fellah, fellah al-ruwayya*. Examples he gives include Mahmud Tahir Haqqi's *Adhra' Dinshaway* (1906), Mahmud Khayrat's *Al-fatat al-rifi* and *Al-fatat al-rifiyya* (1903–1905), and Muhammad Husayn Haykal's *Zaynab* (1914).

84. For a fascinating study of Russian post-emancipation representations of the peasantry, both literary and publicistic, see Frierson, *Peasant Icons*. See also Gershoni and Jankowski, *Egypt, Islam, and the Arabs*.

85. *Zaynab* was first published in 1913, but it was with the second edition (1929) that the novel became more widely known and read. *Al-Ayyam* was first serialized in *Al-Hilal* from 1926 to 1927, and published in book form in 1929. Qutb's book was written in emulation of Taha Husayn's autobiography; there is no exact date for its publication. On Haykal and Husayn, see Selim *The Novel and the Rural Imaginary in Egypt*, 79–87; Gershoni and Jankowski, *Egypt, Islam, and the Arabs*, 221–23. On Qutb, see Abu-Rabi', *Intellectual Origins of Islamic Resurgence in the Modern Arab World*, 98–100.

86. Important early studies sponsored by other institutes included V. M. Mosséri and Ch. Audebeau, "Quelques mots sur l'histoire de l'ezbah égyptienne," *Bulletin de l'Institut d'Égypte* 3 (1920–21): 27–48; Mosséri and Audebeau, *Les constructions rurales en Égypte*.

87. Société Royale de Géographie d'Égypte, *Congrès de 1925, Comité d'organisation, Procès-Verbaux*, DWQ 'Abdin, al-jama'iyyat al-'ilmiyya, al-jama'iyya al-gughrafiyya, 1916–50, box 201. This folder contains a series of files related to the Congrès Internationale de Géographie.

88. Union Géographique Internationale, "Célébration du cinquantenaire de la Société Royale de Géographie d'Égypte," in *Congrès Internationale de Géographie*, I: 118–19.

89. Ibid., 1:118–20.

90. Union Géographique Internationale, "Voeux proposés et émis par le Congrès," in *Congrès Internationale de Géographie*, I: 138.

91. Freeman, "Geography from Congress to Congress," 203.

92. Demangeon, "De l'influence des régimes agraires sur les modes d'habitat dans l'Europe occidentale." See also his earlier critical piece "L'habitation rurale en

France." A posthumous collection of Demangeon's work was published as *Problèmes de Géographie Humaine*.

93. Claval, "L'habitat rural."

94. Ibid.

95. "Congrès de Géographie, Cambridge, 1928. L'Habitat Rural, 23-11-1927," DWQ '*Abdin, mu'tamarat*, 1925-29, box 59. The results of the Belgian study were published in Lefevre, *L'habitat rural en Belgique*.

96. Bernard, *Enquête sur l'habitation rurale des indigènes de l'Algérie*; Bernard, *Enquête sur l'habitation rurale des indigènes de la Tunisie*. See also Reid, "The Egyptian Geographical Society," 555.

97. Bernard, "La charrue en Afrique."

98. On this text see Claval, "Playing with Mirrors." According to Claval, Demangeon, by using the British rather than French empire, successfully undermined the beliefs of French imperialists in empire.

99. Ibid., 243.

100. Demangeon, as quoted in Claval, "Playing with Mirrors," 236.

101. See T. Mitchell, *Rule of Experts*, chap. 4.

102. Demangeon had written on rural habitat—see his "L'habitation rurale en France" and "La géographie de l'habitat rural."

103. Jean Lozach, "Enquête sur l'habitat rural en Égypte," *BSRGE* 15, no. 2-3 (1927): 117-18.

104. See Albert Demangeon, "Un questionnaire sur l'habitat rural."

105. "Séance tenue le 20 Janvier, 1927," *Procès-Verbaux des séances du Conseil d'administration de la Société Royale de Géographie d'Égypte*, DWQ, '*Abdin, al-jama'iyyat al-'ilmiyya, al-jama'iyya al-gughrafiyya*, 1895-1949, box 198, 1-2.

106. See for example, "Séance tenue le 5 Avril, 1928," *Procès-Verbaux des séances du Conseil d'administration de la Société Royale de Géographie d'Égypte*, DWQ, '*Abdin, al-jama'iyyat al-'ilmiyya, al-jama'iyya al-gughrafiyya*, 1895-1949, box 198, 3-4.

107. Lozach and Hug, *L'Habitat Rurale en Egypte*, xv.

108. Ibid., xv. Some respondents went so far as to provide additional information on their history and local customs.

109. Union Géographique Internationale: Comité Nationale d'Égypte, "Séance tenue le 24 Avril, 1929," DWQ, '*Abdin, al-jama'iyyat al-'ilmiyya, al-jama'iyya al-gughrafiyya*, 1895-1949, box 198, 1-2.

110. Ibid.

111. Lozach and Hug also published separate detailed studies on their geographical regions of specialization: Lozach, *La Delta du Nil*; Hug, *Le Fayoum et ses abords*.

112. Jean Lozach, "La géographie humaine, d'après l'ouvrage de J. Brunhes," *BSRGE* 14, no. 1 (1926): 35-40.

113. Brunhes, *Human Geography*.

114. Ibid., 569.

115. Ibid., 585.

116. See Edward Lane as quoted in Brunhes, *Human Geography*, 105, n.1. Lane's text was written in Egypt between 1833 and 1835.
117. Brunhes, *Human Geography*, 108.
118. Albert Demangeon, "Problèmes actuels et aspects nouveaux de la vie rurale en Égypt."
119. Georges Hug, "Mélanges. Albert Demangeon, Problèmes actuels et aspects nouveaux de la vie rurale en Égypte," *BSRGE* 14, nos. 3-4 (1927): 209-11.
120. Rabinow, *French Modern*, 196.
121. Ibid.
122. Ibid., 195-97.
123. On the contribution of Demangeon's methods to human geography, see Claval, "L'habitat rural," 135-37.
124. Lozach and Hug, *L'habitat rurale en Egypte*, 56.
125. "La Séance tenue le 27 Mars, 1930," in *Procès-Verbaux des séances du Conseil d'administration de la Société Royale de Géographie d'Égypte*, DWQ, 'Abdin, al-jama'iyyat al-'ilmiyya, al-jama'iyya al-gughrafiyya, 1895-1949, box 198. De Martonne was also in attendance at the 1925 Cairo Geographical Congress.
126. Lozach and Hug, *L'habitat rurale en Egypte*, 114-17.
127. This paragraph is based on Lozach and Hug, *L'habitat rurale en Egypte*, 180-206.
128. P. M. Roxby attended the 1925 conference and revisited Egypt as professor of geography in 1930 (Reid, "The Egyptian Geographical Society," 559-60).
129. Dr. Mansur Fahmi, director of Dar al-kutub, for instance, noted the francophone literature on the peasantry in his 1941 article "Al-Qarya al-misriyya," *Majallat al-Shu'un al-Ijtima'iyya wa al-Ta'wun* 2 (February 1941): 25-32. Elie Nassif, "L'Égypte est-elle surpeuplée?" *L'Égypte Contemporaine* 33, no. 208 (1942): 613-768, refers to the work as the authoritative text on rural habitat.
130. See Sayyid Karim, "Islah al-qarya: Bayn al-qarya al-namudhajiyya wa qaryat al-intiqal," *Al-'Imara* no. 2 (1941): 51-64.

Chapter 4. Rural Reconstruction

1. As quoted in Brown, *Peasant Politics in Modern Egypt*, 108. The Minister of Interior at the time Husayn wrote this (1950) was Fu'ad Siraj al-Din. Husayn, a graduate of the Law School of Cairo University, was the leader of the party Misr al-fatat (Young Egypt), which he had founded in 1933 with Fathi Radwan. Husayn changed the party's name to the Socialist Party in 1950. He was imprisoned on numerous occasions under the monarchy, notably in January of 1952 under suspicion for the burning of Cairo. On Young Egypt, see Jankowski, *Egypt's Young Rebels*; Deeb, *Party Politics in Egypt*, 372-78; Shalabi, *Misr al-fatat wa dawriha fi al-siyasa al-misriyya*. On Husayn, see Najib, "Ahmed Husayn," in *A'lam Misr fi al-qarn 'al-'ishrin*, 89-90. Ahmed Husayn (1911-82) is not to be confused with Dr. Ahmed Husayn (1902-84), the rural reformer.
2. Ashmawi, *Al-fellahun wa al-sulta*, 157-58, 181-83.

3. Ibid., 151; al-Babli, *Al-ijram fi Misr*, 193.

4. For a discussion of the significance of the peasantry to Egyptian nationalist discourse in the pre-1919 period, see Gasper, "Civilizing Peasants."

5. Mallon, *Peasant and Nation*; Vaughn, *Cultural Politics in Revolution*.

6. Palacios, "Postrevolutionary Intellectuals, Rural Readings and the Shaping of the 'Peasant Problem' in Mexico."

7. Boyer, "Old Loves, New Loyalties," 421.

8. Clark, "Racial Ideologies and the Quest for National Development."

9. Mahumd Shakir Ahmad (undersecretary of state for village amelioration), "Mashru'at wizarat al-siha al-'umumiyya li islah al-qarya al-misriyya wa rafa' mustawa ma'ishat al-fellah sahiyyan wa ijtima'iyyin" ["Projects for the Amelioration of the Egyptian Villages"], *Al-Majalla al-Tibiyya al-Misriyya* 20 (February 1937): 73–100, 55–58 (English synopsis of a lecture delivered at the Ninth Congress of the Egyptian Medical Association, Section of Medical and Sanitary Reforms, Cairo, 14–18 December 1936; Ahmad presided over this congress). The same lecture was delivered at the American University in Cairo (22 January 1937).

10. Ibid., 92.

11. Muhammad Husayn Haykal, "Hijrat al-rif 'ila al-mudun," *Shu'un Ijtima'iyya* 1 (June 1940): 11–14.

12. Selim, *The Novel and the Rural Imaginary in Egypt*; Johnson, *Reconstructing Rural Egypt*; Volait, *L'Architecture Moderne en Egypte et la revue al'Imara*; Chiffoleau, "La réforme sociale par l'hygiène."

13. This set of social and political processes I refer to as a "social welfare mode of regulation," and I develop the idea throughout the course of chapters 4–7.

14. The question of whether or not Egypt was overpopulated, and the "quality" of its population, is discussed in Part III.

15. I should note that my identification of a "crisis in the social reproduction of labor power" is distinct from Ellis Goldberg's discussion of (unfounded) narratives of a structurally embedded agricultural crisis in 1920s Egypt. My concern is not so much with the empirical state of agricultural production as it is with the social understanding of poverty, crime, and population, and its relationship to the maintenance of elite hegemony. See Goldberg, "The Historiography of Crisis in the Egyptian Political Economy."

16. Beinin, "Egypt: Society and Economy," 321.

17. Marsot, *A Short History of Modern Egypt*, 84; see also Abdallah, *The Student Movement and Nationalist Politics in Egypt*; Hamid, *Al-Haraka al-'ummaliyya fi Misr*; Hamid, *al-Haraka al-'ummaliyya fi Misr fi daw' al-watha'iq al-baritaniyya*; Beinin and Lockman, *Workers on the Nile*.

18. The high inflation during World War II was caused by the increased demand and purchasing power of the Allied troops stationed in Egypt and the curtailment of supplies, which was exacerbated by speculation, profiteering, and hoarding (see el-Barawy, *The Military Coup in Egypt*, 93). On the social and economic impact of World War II on Egyptian society see 'Asim al-Disuqi, *Misr fi al-harb al-'alamiyya al-thaniyya*; Hamid, *Jama'at al-nahda al-qawmiyya*, 22–23;

Abdel-Malek, *Egypt: Military Society*, 61. On the working-class struggle during the war, see Hamid, *Al-haraka al-'ummaliyya fi Misr*; Beinin and Lockman, *Workers on the Nile*.

19. As Nathan Brown observes, most peasant households combined various different forms of economic activities: subsistence farming, renting out land, sharecropping and so forth. There were however, three dominant economic systems in the countryside: the commercial estate system (*'izab*), the commercial smallholding system (the small plot of land, owned, rented, or both, and intensively cultivated by the peasant household), and the subsistence smallholding system (independently managed plots, owned or rented, and cultivated by family members). Neither large estates nor commercialized agriculture spread evenly throughout Egypt, although in general commercialization progressed and subsistence smallholding receded between 1882 and 1952 (see, Brown, *Peasant Politics in Modern Egypt*, 32–58).

20. Issawi, *Egypt at Mid-Century*, 128. Generally speaking, anyone owning less than 3 feddans of land would have to supplement their income either by renting themselves out as agricultural laborers for a portion of the year or by renting agricultural land from landowners. Charles Issawi notes that agricultural rents could be paid in cash, in kind, or combined cash and kind (i.e. the rent is fixed in cash, but the landlord gets a share of the crops), or through métayage. Métayage became more widespread during WWII. Thus as Issawi rightly points out—tenants were little better off than laborers, especially because of the inflation in agricultural rents caused by the war. Ibid., 127–28.

21. On Sidqi's ties to Egypt's business sector, and in particular the 'Abbud group, see Vitalis, *When Capitalists Collide*.

22. The capitulations were "grants of extraterritoriality given by Ottoman sultans from the sixteenth century to various European Powers, along with the right to trade in Ottoman territories. The grants allowed Europeans to station in the Ottoman empire consuls who would try any of their citizens who resided in the area for the infringement of their own national law." Many nationalists argued that the capitulations were abused by Europeans to avoid taxation and the law. Marsot, *A Short History of Modern Egypt*, 70.

23. There were splits in the Wafd, and a dispute over the Aswan Dam electrification scheme led Ahmad Mahir and Mahmud Fahmi Nuqrashi to splinter and form the Sa'dist party, representing the interest of indigenous capitalists. Makram 'Ubayd formed the Kutla bloc party, which furthered the "assault on foreign privilege" and become the emblem for this period's "more socially conscious and state-interventionist approach to economic questions" (Tignor, *State, Private Enterprise, and Economic Change in Egypt*, 149). Not even the Bank Misr crisis of 1939, in which economic nationalist Tal'at Harb resigned and was replaced by British sympathizers (Hafiz Afifi Pasha and 'Abdel Maqsud Ahmad), signaled the end of the attempt to build an indigenous Egyptian capitalism (ibid., 170).

24. Ibid., 150.

25. Brown, *Peasant Politics in Modern Egypt*; Al-Babli, *Al-ijram fi Misr*; Ashmawi, *Al-fellahun wa al-sulta*.

26. Haykal, "Hijrat al-rif 'ila al-mudun"; Abdel Hamid Ibrahim Salih, "Al-fellah, kayfa narqi?" *Shu'un Ijtima'iyya* 1 (April 1940): 92–96; Ibrahim Rashad Bey, "Mashakil al-rif al-ijtima'iyya," *Shu'un Ijtima'iyya* 1 (June 1940): 100–106; Fu'ad Abaza Pasha, "Al-rif wa al-fellah da'im," *Shu'un Ijtima'iyya* 3 (February 1942): 29–33.

27. Brown, *Peasant Politics in Modern Egypt*, 41–43; Schulze, "Colonization and Resistance," 170–202; T. Mitchell, *Rule of Experts*, chap. 2. See also Guha, *Elementary Aspects of Peasant Insurgency in Colonial India*.

28. Ashmawi, *Al-fellahun wa al-sulta*, chap. 1.

29. T. Mitchell, *Rule of Experts*, chap. 5.

30. Ashmawi, *Al-fellahun wa al-sulta*.

31. Ibid., 134.

32. Ibid., 189–98; Brown, *Peasant Politics in Modern Egypt*, 108–9.

33. Brown, *Peasant Politics in Modern Egypt*, 83.

34. Ibid., 88–98. Atomistic crimes in 1933 and 1936 were particularly violent.

35. Ibid., 83–85.

36. Ibid., 111.

37. Ibid., 111.

38. Ibid., 115–19.

39. Ibid., 119–26.

40. Muhammad Mustafa al-Qolali a noted lawyer, graduated from the Higher School of Law in Cairo in 1922. In 1929 he traveled to Paris to study criminal law at the Sorbonne, where he received his doctorate. He was subsequently appointed an instructor of criminal law in the Faculty of Law at Cairo University. Preferring to practice law rather than teach it, he left the university and was selected as an expert consultant for the International Court of Justice. In 1947 he won a national award for his book *Al-masu'liyya al-jina'iyya (Criminal Responsibility)* (Najib, *A'lam Misr*, 473).

41. Among the numerous other positions al-Babli held were deputy for the Supreme Court; judge for local courts; assistant magistrate; inspector for local courts; inspector at the Ministry of the Interior; deputy for the Administration of General Security; director of the Criminal Administration; a provincial director; and director of the Police Department and Administration. He also taught a criminology course in the Faculty of Law at Cairo University; his students suggested that he publish his lectures, which resulted in his book, *Al-ijram fi Misr* (Al-Babli, *Al-ijram fi Misr*, 7–8).

42. Brown, *Peasant Politics in Modern Egypt*, 59–82.

43. Al-Babli, *Al-ijram fi Misr*, 234.

44. Ibid., 74–78; Mahmud Bey Mahir, "Jara'im al-qura," *Al-Majalla al-Tibiyya al-Misriyya* 20 (March 1937): 163–69 (lecture given at the Ninth Congress of the Egyptian Medical Association, Section on Village Reform).

45. Al-Babli, *Al-ijram fi Misr*, 74–78.

46. Al-Babli, *Al-ijram fi Misr*, 185; Muhammad al-Qolali, "Al-ijram fi al-rif," *Shu'un Ijtima'iyya* 1 (July 1940): 20–29.

47. The violent nature of rural crime, al-Qolali argued, was illustrated by public-safety statistics collected from 1930 to 1937, which showed that murder or

attempted murder was an inordinately high percentage of all crimes committed in the rural (and especially southern) provinces (Al-Qolali, "Al-ijram fi al-rif," 22). The north–south divide was a crucial part of organizing statistical data. The Sa'id was known for the violent and cruel nature of its crime, partly attributed to the entrenched presence of *tha'r* in that area, whereas in the Delta crime was characterized by the use of terror and warning (e.g., arson, crop poisoning and destruction). See ibid., 24–25; Mahir, "Jara'im al-qura," 166.

48. Al-Qolali, "Al-ijram fi al-rif," 22
49. Mahir, "Jara'im al-qura," 164.
50. Al-Qolali, "Al-ijram fi al-rif," 28.
51. Morphine or opium addiction was thought to be on the increase in the rural provinces in the late 1930s. Of particular concern was the intravenous use of morphine, and subsequent septic infections as well as higher dependence and addiction. See Central Narcotics Intelligence Bureau, *Annual Report for the Year 1938* and *Annual Report for the Year 1939*.
52. Al-Babli, *Al-ijram fi Misr*, 223–28.
53. Central Narcotics Intelligence Bureau, "Adulterated Tea," in *Annual Report for the Year 1938*, 92.
54. Central Narcotics Intelligence Bureau, "Boiled tea," in *Annual Report for the Year 1939*, 104–5.The 1939 Annual Report also included a thirty-page report that had been produced in 1938 by Aziz Abaza Bey (the *mudir* of Fayum Province), in which "he emphasised the lamentable effect on the fellaheen of the continuous drinking of this black concoction produced by the repeated boiling of inferior and often adulterated tea."
55. L. Askren, "New Method of Taking Opium," in Central Narcotics Intelligence Bureau, *Annual Report for the Year 1938*, 95–99; Central Narcotics Intelligence Bureau, "Boiled tea," 104–5.
56. Askren, "New Method of Taking Opium," 98. Propaganda was viewed as an essential component of social reform, crucial to any form of pedagogical activism amongst the peasantry. In this, the Central Narcotics Intelligence Bureau was no different; the agency ran various projects such as "lantern lectures" (the use of a projecting lantern "for illustrating stories setting forth the evils of intemperance and drug addiction"), the distribution of leaflets at festivals (*mawalid*, sing. *mulid*) and on buses and trains, and informal talks to groups and individuals (Central Narcotics Intelligence Bureau, "Propaganda," in *Annual Report for the Year 1938*, 101). Figures for 1938 were as follows: 340 villages visited; 451 lantern lectures; estimated total audience of 156,142.
57. Al-Babli, *Al-ijram fi Misr*, 58–61; Ashmawi, *Al-fellahun wa al-sulta*, 162.
58. Al-Qolali, "Al-ijram fi al-rif," 29.
59. Bandits or brigands could be rented out for protection, to return stolen goods, or to commit specific crimes of revenge. Because no one would testify against such criminals, their use guaranteed immunity (al-Babli, *Al-ijram fi Misr*, 192–222; cf. Brown, *Peasant Politics in Modern Egypt*).
60. Al-Babli, *Al-ijram fi Misr*, 235–36.

61. Ibid., 77.
62. Ibid., 228.
63. Al-Qolali, "Al-ijram fi al-rif"; Mahir, "Jara'im al-qura"; al-Babli, *Al-ijram fi Misr*.
64. Al-Babli, *Al-ijram fi Misr*, 77.
65. Elie Nassif, "L'Égypte est-elle surpeuplée?" *L'Égypte Contemporaine* 33, no. 208 (1942): 703–4; cf. T. Mitchell, *Colonising Egypt*, 44.
66. Nassif, "L'Égypte est-elle surpeuplée?" 703–4.
67. Ibid., 704.
68. T. Mitchell, *Rule of Experts*, 66–70.
69. Lozach and Hug, *L'habitat rurale en Egypte*, 156–57.
70. T. Mitchell, *Rule of Experts*, chap. 2.
71. Ibid.; T. Mitchell, *Colonising Egypt*. See also Bonaudo and Sonzogni, "To Populate and to Discipline," for a discussion of the constitution of a rural labor market in Argentina in the second half of the nineteenth century under conditions of labor scarcity.
72. Even when rural reconstruction took place at the level of an entire village (rather than *'izba*), it still often served to reinforce the network of obligations between peasants and *'ayan* (notables). There were parliamentary deliberations in November and December, 1927, on the "*'izba* question" (Nassif, "L'Égypte est-elle surpeuplée?" 704).
73. This is abundantly clear in the Nasserist Mudiriyat Tahrir project discussed in Chapter 7
74. J. Scott, *Seeing Like a State*, 4.
75. Ibid.
76. Royal Society of Agriculture, *Improving the Lot of the Egyptian Fallah*, 1.
77. Royal Agricultural Society, "Notes sur le projet de reorganisation de la Société Royale d'Agriculture" (3 January 1923), and Royal Agricultural Society, "Mathaf al-qutn/Musee du coton" (1936), both DWQ, *Abdin, al-jama'iyyat al-'ilmiyya, al-jama'iyyat al-zira'iyya al-malakiyya, 1922–1944*, box 212; Royal Agricultural Society, "Al-jama'iyya al-zira'iyya al-malakiyya, mathaf Fuad al-awwal al-zira'iyya: taqrir 'an al-birnamij al-muqtarah li tamthil al-zira'a al-haditha bi mathaf al-hadara al-misriyya" (3 July 1939), DWQ, *Abdin, al-jama'iyyat al-'ilmiyya, al-jama'iyya al-sina'iyya, 1916–1944*, box 210.
78. Nassif, "L'Égypte est-elle surpeuplée?" 711–12.
79. Ibid., 712–13.
80. Ibid., 711. The categories were weighted: 42 points for construction and architecture, 50 points for hygiene, and 8 points for social institutions.
81. Fu'ad Abaza, "Al-rif al-misri wa turuq islahiha," *Shu'un Ijtima'iyya* 1 (May 1940):10–15.
82. Abaza, "Al-rif wa al-fellah da'im."
83. Fu'd Abaza, "Al-nashat al-ijtima'i fi Misr," *Shu'un Ijtima'iyya* 3 (January 1942): 33–35, (lecture presented at the Main Hall of the Bahtim Social Center, 2 December 1941, Prince Omar Tusun and the Minister of Social Affairs in attendance);

"Al-'izbatan al-namudhajitan: Al-jama'iyya al-zira'iyya al-malakiyya bi mazra'it bahtim bi mudiriyyat al-Qalyubiyya," *Al-Majalla al-Tibiyya al-Misriyya* 20 (October 1937): 833–35 (lecture presented at the Ninth Annual Medical Congress, Cairo, December 1936).

84. Nassif, "L'Égypte est-elle surpeuplée?" 708–9.

85. Ayrout, *The Fellaheen*, 147–49; cf. 'Abaza, "Al-rif al-misri wa turuq islahiha"; Nassif, "L'Égypte est-elle surpeuplée?" 708–9.

86. Fu'ad Abaza, "Al-rif al-misri wa turuq islahiha," 12–13; Nassif, "L'Égypte est-elle surpeuplée?" 709.

87. Fu'ad Abaza, "Al-rif al-misri wa turuq islahiha," 12.

88. Royal Society of Agriculture, *Improving the Lot of the Egyptian Fallah*. Fahmi was the first Egyptian employee in the Department of Architecture and Design of the Public Buildings Service, which he directed between 1921–1929. He also served as Palace architect and as minister of works, and taught in the engineering department at Cairo University and founded its architecture department. Among his designs are the buildings of the Engineering Society, the Agricultural Society, the Huda Sha'rawi Women's Society, and the Doctor's Syndicate, as well as Sa'd Zaghlul's mausoleum (Goldschmidt, "Mustafa Fahmi," in *Biographical Dictionary of Modern Egypt*, 52).

89. On the development of modern architecture in Egypt and the formation of the journal *al'Imara*, see Volait, *L'architecture moderne en Egypte et la revue al'Imara*.

90. Royal Society of Agriculture, *Improving the Lot of the Egyptian Fallah*, 4–5.

91. Ibid., 5.

92. Ayrout, *The Fellaheen*, 112.

93. Ahmad, "Mashru'at wizarat al-siha al-'umumiyya," 55. The image of animals and humans in the same house was a powerful one. 'Abd al-Wahid al-Wakil stated forcefully the need for separation: "It is not appropriate, sanitarily or socially, that animals be the neighbors of humans in their homes—if so the village will become a huge cattle pen as it is now. I hope you will agree with me on our duty of separating humans and animals, so that each may live the life ordained by nature" (A. W. al-Wakil, "Al-marafiq al-amma fi al-qarya al-misriyya," *Al-Majalla al-Tibiyya al-Misriyya* 20 (February 1937): 134).

94. Royal Society of Agriculture, *Improving the Lot of the Egyptian Fallah*, 6.

95. Abaza, "Al-nashat al-ijtima'i fi Misr."

96. The steering committee for the social center included Hafiz Afifi Pasha, Fua'd Abaza Pasha, Muhammad Tahir Pasha, and Uthman Muharam Pasha.

97. Hassan Fathy was born in Alexandria in 1900, to a middle-class landowning family. He was educated in British schools in Cairo, and subsequently studied agriculture and then architecture at the University of Cairo, obtaining his degree in 1926. He would later earn a degree from the École Supérieure des Beaux-Arts in Paris. Initially, Fathy taught at Cairo University and was employed by the Architecture section of the Municipal Affairs Department. Eventually Fathy went into

private practice (Goldschmidt, "Hasan Fathi," in *Biographical Dictionary of Modern Egypt*, 56).

98. Steele, *An Architecture for People*, 24.
99. Ibid., 16.
100. Ibid., 189–90.
101. Ibid., 24.
102. Fathy, *Architecture for the Poor*, 4–5.
103. This was an ongoing problem for Fathy. See his 1954 memorandums to the Ministry of Social Affairs concerning the rebuilding of the village of Mit al-Nasara in the province of Gharbiyya, for example, "Hassan Fathy to director-general of the Building Department, Ministry of Social Affairs, 17 July, 1954" (memo), Private Papers, Mit Al-Nasara File, project 54.02, Hassan Fathy Archives, Rare Books and Special Collections, American University in Cairo.
104. Steele, *An Architecture for People*, 91.
105. Fathy, *Architecture for the Poor*, 5–6.
106. Ibid., 6.
107. Steele, *An Architecture for People*, 190. Cf. J. Scott, *Seeing Like a State*.
108. Nassif, "L'Égypte est-elle surpeuplée?" 714–16.
109. Issues addressed in these works include cooling, heating, vaults, wind catches (*malkaf*), orienting rooms according to the position of the sun etc.
110. Hassan Fathy, marginal annotations in copy of *Ekistics: Review in the Problems and Science of Human Settlements* 12, no. 69 (July 1961), Private Papers, Journals Collection, Hassan Fathy Archives, Rare Books and Special Collections, American University in Cairo.
111. Fathy, *Architecture for the Poor*, 1.
112. Fathy, "Planning and Building in the Arab Tradition," 213; cf. Fathy, *Architecture for the Poor*.
113. See T. Mitchell, *Rule of Experts*, chap. 6.
114. Fathy, *Architecture for the Poor*, 149–82.
115. Ibid., 183–94.
116. Sachs, "Honoring a Visionary if Not His Vision."
117. Hassan Fathy, "Lajnat takhtit al-qarya," Private Papers, Ministries Collection, Hassan Fathy Archives, Rare Books and Special Collections, American University in Cairo.
118. Steele, *An Architecture for People*, 109–11.
119. Egyptian Association for Social Studies, *Taqrir majlis al-idara 'an sanat 1943*, 8.
120. "Madrasat al-khidma al-ijtima'iyya bil kahira," in DWQ, Abdin, *al-jama'iyyat, al-jam'iyyat al-ijtima'iyya, 1899–1952*, box 203, 1.
121. Ibid., 1.
122. Ibid., 6.
123. Ibid., 5.
124. Ibid., 2–3.
125. Ibid., 5.

126. Ibid., 4.

127. Shalaby, *An Experiment in Rural Reconstruction in Egypt*, 17. Mohamed Shalaby, a graduate of the Faculty of Commerce at Fu'ad I University, and of the CSSW, worked from the beginning of the project (1939) as a rural social worker for five years. Shalaby later received postgraduate training at the New York School of Social Work, Columbia University.

128. Ahmed Husayn, "Tajarib islah al-qarya fi Misr," *Shu'un Ijtima'iyya* 2 (July 1941): 61–67. Dr. Ahmed Husayn, who received his Ph.D. in agricultural economics from the University of Berlin, was the first director of Egypt's Fellah Department, served as minister of social affairs in 1950, and was a member of the EASS and an active rural reformer. Born in Helwan, Husayn began his official career in 1928 as a government inspector, and in 1953 served as the Egyptian ambassador to Washington under Nasser (Goldschmidt, *Biographical Dictionary of Modern Egypt*, 79–80). See A. Johnson, *Reconstructing Rural Egypt*, for a full-length biography of Husayn.

129. Husayn, "Tajarib islah al-qarya fi Misr"; Shalaby, *An Experiment in Rural Reconstruction in Egypt*, 17–18.

130. Husayn, "Tajarib islah al-qarya fi Misr"; Egyptian Association for Social Studies, *Taqrir majlis al-idara 'an sanat 1943*, 15.

131. Husayn, "Tajarib islah al-qarya fi misr."

132. Egyptian Association for Social Studies, *Taqrir majlis al-idara 'an sanat 1943*, 18–19.

133. Galal Husayn, "Al-islah al-ijtima'i fi al-rif," *Al-Majalla al-Tibiyya al-Misriyya* 20 (March 1937): 181–98; Shalaby, *An Experiment in Rural Reconstruction in Egypt*.

134. The Egyptian constitution of 1923 declared elementary education compulsory for all children, and a law was passed to that effect in 1925. By 1933 an act was passed authorizing the minister of education to enforce compliance when necessary. According to Mohamed Shalaby, the number of students receiving elementary education went from one-quarter of a million in 1920 to one million in 1945 (Shalaby, *An Experiment in Rural Reconstruction in Egypt*, 9).

135. Husayn, "Al-islah al-ijtima'i," 187–90.

136. Shalaby, *An Experiment in Rural Reconstruction in Egypt*, 26.

137. Ibid., 26.

138. Ibid., 26–27.

139. Shalaby, *Rural Reconstruction in Egypt*, 29–30.

140. Husayn, "Tajarib islah al-qarya fi misr"; Egyptian Association for Social Studies, *Taqrir majlis al-idara 'an sanat 1943*, 16.

141. Husayn, "Tajarib islah al-qarya fi misr."

142. Shalaby, *Rural Reconstruction in Egypt*, 33.

143. Marcel Vincenot, "Réflexions sociales sur le fellah," *La Revue du Caire* 4, no. 34 (September 1941): 437–50; Vincenot, *Une experience sociale dans un village d'Egypte*, 14–16.

144. Vincenot, "Réflexions sociales sur le fellah," 445–48; Husayn, "Al-islah al-ijtima'i fi al-rif"; Salih, "Al-fellah, kayfa narqi?"

145. Vincenot, *Une experience sociale*, 15.

146. Village projects such as those of the EASS were quite successful. Thus, upon reading the final yearly report of the EASS and its success in village work, Marcel Vincenot of the Crédit Foncier suggested that the bank fund a third experiment. The location chosen was the village of Al-Agaiza, 50 kilometers from Cairo in the Delta province of Menufiyya. The project at Al-Agaiza, viewed as a private initiative toward a solution to the national problem of an impoverished, abundant, and illiterate rural population, came on the heels of the relative success of the EASS's earlier projects. Begun in November of 1941, it entailed many of the same components as the other projects: a social center (with a social worker), a maternal and child welfare center, a health unit, a cooperative society, and a committee for religious reform. See Vincenot, *Une experience sociale* and Egyptian Association for Social Studies, *Taqrir majlis al-idara 'an sanat 1943*, 16–19.

147. Anonymous, "Ila al-masulin 'an al-fellah," *Shu'un Ijtima'iyya* 1 (March 1940): 93–95; Salih, "Al-fellah, kayfa narqi?"; Muhammad Abu Ta'ila, "Tajmil al-qarya al-misriyya," *Shu'un Ijtima'iyya* 1 (May 1940): 78–81; Mansur Fahmi, "Al-qarya al-misriyya," *Shu'un Ijtima'iyya* 2 (February 1941): 25–32; Sayyid Karim, "Islah al-qarya: Bayn al-qarya al-namudhajiyya wa qaryat al-intiqal," *Al-'Imara* (1941): 51–64.

148. Anonymous, "Ila al-masulin 'an al-fellah."

149. Ahmed Thabit Muwafa, "'Aqliyyat al-fellah," *Al-Majalla al-Tibiyya al-Misriyya* 20 (December 1937): 981–92 (lecture delivered at the Ninth Congress of the Egyptian Medical Association, Section of Medical and Sanitary Reforms, Cairo, 14–18 December 1936). The attempt to eradicate such antimodern superstitious practices has a long history in the Egyptian context. The concept of "survivals" itself had as its Islamic counterpart the idea of *bid'a*, or non-Islamic ideas and practices (or non-religious innovations). The critique of *bid'a* was a critical component of the Islamic revivalist tradition, and its most strident representatives in the modern (eighteenth- and nineteenth-century) reform movement were Muhammad Ibn 'Abd al-Wahhab, Muhammad Ibn 'Ali al-Shawkani, al-Sayyid Jamal al-Din al-Afghani, Muhammad 'Abduh, and Rashid Rida.

150. For instance, Shaykh Mahmud Shaltut, the inspector of religious and Arabic sciences at al-Azhar University, wrote an article criticizing funerary rituals, a commonly targeted set of practices. Shaltut noted the prevalence of funeral customs that were in direct conflict with religious tenets, including excessive sadness, the use of facial dyes, the sacrificing of animals, and the presence of women. He urged the Ministry of Social Affairs to take steps to prevent such moral corruption through the provision of religious guidance, which could be aimed at eradicating harmful practices, such as funeral customs and spirit exorcisms (*zar*), in the countryside; Shaykh Mahmud Shaltut, "Al-bida' al-sha'i'a fi al-janazat wa al-matam wa ziyarat al-maqabir," *Shu'un Ijtima'iyya* 2 (March 1941): 49–53. Shaltut was critical in the reforms of al-Azhar in the 1950s; see Zebiri, *Mahmud Shaltut and Islamic Modernism*. An early critique of indigenous curative practices is Abdel Rahman Isma'il's *Al-tibb al-rukka*; on Isma'il see T. Mitchell, *Colonising Egypt*, 99–100.

151. Ali Bey Fu'a'd, "Ra'iyyat al-umm wa al-tifl fi al-qura," *Al-Majalla al-Tibiyya al-Misriyya* 20 (April 1937): 241–48. Ali Bey Fu'ad was director of the Child Welfare Section of the Ministry of Public Health.

152. G. Husayn, "Al-islah al-ijtima'i fi al-rif," 191–93; Salih, "Al-fellah, kayfa narqi?"; Dr. Muhammad Abu Ta'ila, "Tajmil al-qarya al-misriyya."

153. Ahmad, "Mashru'at wizarat al-siha al-'umumiyya," 76.

154. The filling of *birkas*, or stagnant pools, which figured prominently in most schemes for village sanitation, was not uniformly agreed upon. In an address to the Egyptian Medical Association, M. Khalil Bey, a professor of parasitology and director of the research institute and endemic diseases hospital, argued against it. See his *"Birkas* and the Role They Play in the Spread of Diseases," *Al-Majalla al-Tibiyya al-Misriyya* 20 (1937): 59–61.

155. Ahmad, "Mashru'at wizarat al-siha al-'umumiyya," 94–95.

156. Ahmad, "Projects for the Amelioration of the Egyptian Villages," 58. Hassan Fathy conceptualizes a similar large-scale project of national rural reconstruction based on co-operative principles in his *Architecture for the Poor*, 134–48.

157. Gallagher, *Egypt's Other Wars*, 13; A. Johnson, *Reconstructing Rural Egypt*, 112.

158. A. Johnson, *Reconstructing Rural Egypt*, 111–14.

159. Al-Wakil, "Al-marafiq al-'amma fi al-qarya al-misriyya"; G. Husayn, "Al-islah al-ijtima'i fi al-rif."

160. Ahmad, "Mashru'at wizarat al-siha al-'umumiyya," 75.

161. Al-Wakil, "Al-marafiq al-'amma fi al-qarya al-misriyya," 129.

162. Ibid., 130–31.

163. The Ministry of Social Affairs (whose predecessor the Supreme Council for Social Reform was formed in 1936) was established in 1939 "in order to combat the backwardness which years of foreign imperialism and feudalism have imposed upon the people"; its emphasis was upon "guiding people towards the means of their own self-improvement and betterment." This ministry covered virtually all aspects of social services: prison and penitentiary reform; orphanages and charitable services for the poor or disabled; supervision of theaters, cinemas, clubs, and festivals; morality policing; maternal and child health care, eugenics, and other protections of childhood and the family; cooperative societies (for production and consumption); labor relations for the betterment of the conditions of the worker and the fellah; unemployment assistance; the organization of free-time; and the organization of lectures, sports events, and all activities related to guidance and propaganda. Although the Ministry of Social Affairs would later delegate many of these responsibilities to other ministries, such as the Ministry of Defense (prison reform), it retained, albeit in a slightly disaggregated fashion, the same general structure and function from its inception throughout the Nasser period. Wizarat al-shu'un al-ijtima'iyya, *Wizarat al-shu'un al-ijtima'iyya: nisha'atuha, tatawwuriha, wa khadamatuha*, 12–16; Wizarat al-shu'un al-ijtima'iyya, *Wizarat al-shu'un al-ijtima'iyya fi khamsa wa 'ishrin 'amm*, 15–18.

164. Ministry of Social Affairs, *Social Welfare in Egypt*, 11.

165. Ahmed Husayn, "Al-marakiz al-ijtima'iyya wa ma haqaqituha lil fellah," *Shu'un Ijtima'iyya* 3 (May 1942): 57–69.

166. Ministry of Social Affairs, *Social Welfare in Egypt*, 15.

167. Ministry of Social Affairs, *Annual Report on the Rural Welfare Centers*, 3; Ahmed Husayn, "Al-marakiz al-ijtima'iyya fi al-rif" *Shu'un Ijtima'iyya* 1 (April 1940): 68–71.

168. Ministry of Social Affairs, *Annual Report on the Rural Welfare Centers*, 3.

169. See Husseini, "The Reconstruction of Siriakous Village."

170. Ministry of Social Affairs, *Annual Report on the Rural Welfare Centers*, 3–8; Husayn, "Al-marakiz al-ijtima'iyya wa ma haqaqituha lil fellah." These centers were later to become the "combined units" of the Nasser period, which were also multidimensional projects aimed at satisfying the needs (agricultural, industrial, educational, social) of the rural population (see Combined Rural Centres, *A New Development in Rural Welfare Programmes*).

171. Ministry of Social Affairs, *Annual Report on the Rural Welfare Centers*, 11–12.

172. An account of the 1942 malaria invasion and its effect upon the agricultural laboring population of Upper Egypt may be found in Gallagher, *Egypt's Other Wars*, and T. Mitchell, "Can the Mosquito Speak?" in *Rule of Experts*.

173. Gallagher, *Egypt's Other Wars*. According to Gallagher there was an incidence rate of between 50% and 90% in Upper Egypt, an estimated 750,000 cases of *falciparum malaria*.

174. Prior to the malaria epidemic, however, there was another concern that preoccupied elite reformers—the problem of population. Part III of this book addresses this concern in debates on the political economy of poverty and the problem of the quality of the population.

175. 'Abd al-Rahman (Bint al-Shati'), "Fi janat al-rif," (reprinted from *al-Ahram*, 29 August 1935), in *Al-rif al-misri*; cf. Muhammad Abd Al-Karim, "Yawm fi Bahtim," *Shu'un Ijtima'iyya* 4 (May 1943): 48–54.

Chapter 5. Barren Land and Fecund Bodies

1. Wendell Cleland, "The Necessity of Restricting Population Growth in Egypt," *Al-Majalla al-Tibiyya al-Misriyya* 20, no. 7 (1937): 279.

2. See the July 1937 issue of *Al-Majalla al-Tibiyya al-Misriyya*, which was dedicated to population issues (vol. 20, no. 7); Rizk, "Population Policies in Egypt," 38; Shanawany, "Stages in the Development of a Population Control Program," 193.

3. The quotation is from Mustafa Fahmi, "Hal min al-khiyr li Misr fi zurufiha al-haliyya wa fi nitaq hajatuha al-harbiyya in tu'amim fiqrat tahdid al-nasl?!," *Al-Majalla al-Tibiyya al-Misriyya* 20, no.7 (1937): 113.

4. See Horn, *Social Bodies*; Anagnost, *National Past-times*, 117–37. Recent works in Middle East studies, which have addressed the historical and contemporary construction of population are: Ali, *Planning the Family in Egypt*; Kanaaneh, *Birthing the Nation*. Timothy Mitchell's "The Object of Development," in *Rule of*

Experts provides a cogent critique of contemporary development discourse and the construction of a population problem in Egypt.

5. Cuno and Reimer, "The Census Registers of Nineteenth-Century Egypt."

6. See, for example, Owen, "The Population Census of 1917 and Its Relationship to Egypt's Three 19th Century Statistical Regimes."

7. T. Mitchell, *Rule of Experts*, 246.

8. See, for example, Ali Bey Fu'ad, "Tahdid al-nasl," *Al-Majalla al-Tibiyya al-Misriyya* 20, no. 7 (1937): 48–56; Abdel Hakim al-Rifa'i, "Mushkilat al-sukkan fi Misr," *Al-Majalla al-Tibiyya al-Misriyya* 20, no. 7 (1937): 135–49; Fahmi, "Hal min al-khiyr li Misr?"

9. I borrow the term "total social fact" from Mauss, *The Gift*.

10. I thank one of the anonymous reviewers of the International Journal of Middle East Studies for bringing this point to my attention.

11. The most important actors in these debates throughout the nationalist period were Egyptians who wrote in Arabic, with the sole and noteworthy exception of Wendell Cleland, an American.

12. As Rayna Rapp and Faye Ginsburg have argued, women's centrality to reproduction has often been effaced from social practices through state or patriarchal structures. It has been no different in the case of Egypt, where women remained objects of population discourse, effectively excluded from the public discourse on birth control, until the middle of the century (Rapp and Ginsburg, "Introduction").

13. On the omission of discussions of distribution from population debates in contemporary development discourse, see T. Mitchell, *Rule of Experts*, chap. 7.

14. The pinnacle and defining feature of the Nasserist discourse on population, however, was land reclamation. Under Nasser, land reclamation projects were begun to address the slow rate of expansion of cultivated land area in relation to rapid population growth. Efforts were to be made both toward reducing population growth, through the nascent family planning programs, and toward expanding horizontally to reclaim land. Yet the distinctive and positive content of the revolutionary regime was contingent upon a conception of social welfare as the telos of government. Later, after *infitah* (economic liberalization), as Egypt's population agenda became yoked to international development agendas and a liberal-capitalist regime, population increasingly came to be viewed in terms of economic development. In brief, population agendas shifted from a notion of birth control or family planning as embedded within a social welfare model of the state (1930s to 1960s) to a more economistic model in which population control was isolated and disaggregated as a component of economic development (after *infitah*) (see El Shakry, *Reproducing the Family*).

15. See Adams, ed., *The Wellborn Science*; Mazower, *Dark Continent*; Stoler, *Race and the Education of Desire*.

16. Goldscheid, "Discussion."

17. See *Al-Majalla al-Tibiyya al-Misriyya* 20, no.7 (1937).

18. Cuno and Reimer, "The Census Registers of Nineteenth-Century Egypt," 213.

19. Ibid., 197.

20. J. I. Craig, as quoted in 'Ammar, *The People of Sharqiya*, 1: 215.

21. See J. I. Craig, "The Census of Egypt," *L'Égypte Contemporaine* 8, no. 32 (1917): 209–34; J. I. Craig, "The Census of Egypt," *L'Égypte Contemporaine* 17, no. 96 (1926): 434–55; J. I. Craig, "Statistics," *L'Égypte Contemporaine* 26, nos. 153–4 (1935): 115–45.

22. The following paragraph relies on 'Abbas 'Ammar's discussion of the unreliability of the modern Egyptian censuses; see 'Ammar, *The People of Sharqiya*, 1: 213–18. See also Owen, "The Population Census of 1917."

23. 'Ammar, *The People of Sharqiya*, 1: 216.

24. Ibid.

25. Ibid., 1: 217.

26. T. Mitchell, *Rule of Experts*, chap. 3 (quotation, 105).

27. Asad, "Ethnographic Representation, Statistics and Modern Power," 76–7. See also Hacking, "Biopower and the Avalanche of Printed Numbers"; Hacking, *The Taming of Chance*.

28. Craig, "Statistics," 115.

29. Craig, "The Census of Egypt" (1917), 210.

30. Craig, "The Census of Egypt" (1926), 449.

31. Ibid., 448–54.

32. Craig, "The Census of Egypt" (1926), 450.

33. Owen, "The Population Census of 1917," 469.

34. Ibid.

35. Ibid.

36. On Mustafa 'Amir, see Chapter 2.

37. Amer, "Some Problems of the Population of Egypt."

38. Ibid., 19.

39. My use of the term "homogeneous mass" refers to the process by which population comes to be viewed as a uniform, and national, entity, and resonates with Benedict Anderson's use of Walter Benjamin's concept of "homogeneous, empty time" to refer to the conception of temporality within the modern nation-state. See Anderson, *Imagined Communities*, 24.

40. Cleland held various posts related to the Middle East before his arrival in Cairo, such as in the Syria and Palestine Relief Fund. The book grew out of his Ph.D. thesis, which he wrote in Columbia University's department of Sociology. See also Wendell Cleland, "Egypt's Population Problem," *L'Égypte Contemporaine* 28, no. 167 (1937): 67–87;Wendell Cleland, "A Population Plan for Egypt," *L'Égypte Contemporaine* 30, no. 185 (1939): 461–84.

41. Roussillon, "Sociology in Egypt and Morocco," 457.

42. It would be grossly erroneous to think of Malthusianism as the product (or "master paradigm") of a bygone era,transformed from theodicy into a secular platitude. Indeed, one can argue that throughout the twentieth century Malthusianism became ever more linked to the idea of the national economy as a self-contained structure. On the modern transformation of the idea of the economy, see T. Mitchell, *Rule of Experts*, chap. 3.

43. Hasan al-Sa'ati, "Tatawur al-madrasa al-fikriyya li 'ilm al-ijtima' fi Misr," *Al-Majallat al-Ijtima'iyyah al-Qawmiyya / The National Review of Social Sciences*, National Centre for Sociological and Criminological Research, January 1964, 21–34.

44. Cleland's text was favorably reviewed by *al-Muqtataf*, which situated it as part of a broader set of discussions on population and birth control that had flourished in 1936 and 1937. See "Mushkilat al-sukkan fi Misr," *Al-Muqtataf* (May 1937): 646–47.

45. Cleland, *The Population Problem in Egypt*, 90.

46. Ibid., 32.

47. Ibid., 36.

48. Wendell Cleland, "Discussion of Prof. Bentley's Paper: Fertility and Overpopulation in Egypt," *Al-Majalla al-Tibiyya al-Misriyya* 20, no. 7 (1937): 296–303.

49. Cleland, "Egypt's Population Problem," 67–68.

50. For a critique of Malthusian thought from a Marxist perspective, see Meek, *Marx and Engels on the Population Bomb*. On the postwar use of Malthusian arguments linking poverty to overpopulation, and in turn rationalizing development policies (such as the replacement of peasant agriculture with commercial agriculture and the widescale support of population programs in the third world and its relation to the cold-war), see E. Ross, *The Malthus Factor*.

51. There is an extensive literature historicizing and critiquing Thomas Robert Malthus's theory of population, both empirically and theoretically. Two excellent collections, one of historical discussions and one of more recent writings, are, respectively: Gilbert, ed., *Malthus: Critical Responses*; and Cunningham, *Thomas Robert Malthus: Critical Assessments*.

52. Cleland, "Egypt's Population Problem," 82. However, Cleland cautioned, once these diseases were eradicated and the peasants possessed more energy, "the stage will be set for a first class revolution. . . . It might be the part of wisdom for the Egyptian upper classes to think some decades ahead and prevent these troubles by helping the now-too-numerous fellaheen to achieve more abundant experience of the good things of life before they decide to take it for themselves." Cleland, "The Necessity of Restricting Population Growth in Egypt," 285–86.

53. A. W. al-Wakil, "Al-marafiq al'amma fi al-qarya al-misriyya," *Al-Majalla al-Tibiyya al-Misriyya* 20, no. 2 (1937): 129–48.

54. On al-Wakil, see T. Mitchell, *Rule of Experts*, 32, 39; Gallagher, *Egypt's Other Wars*.

55. The conference proceedings were published as *Al-Majalla al-Tibiyya al-Misriyya* 20, no. 7 (1937).

56. Mustafa Fahmi, "Hal min al-khiyr li Misr?" *Al-Majalla al-Tibiyya al-Misriyya* 20, no. 7 (1937): 96–117; Muhammad 'Awad Muhammad, "Al-nawahi al-ijtima'iyya al-khasa bi tanzim al-nasl," *Al-Majalla al-Tibiyya al-Misriyya* 20, no. 7 (1937): 57–75.

57. Muhammad, "Al-nawahi al-ijtima'iyya," 66. Muhammad, along with his student 'Abbas 'Ammar, later became a member of the 1953 National Commission

for Population Problems, the first official body established in Egypt to deal with the population problem.

58. Mustafa Fahmi, "Hal min al-khiyr li Misr?" 110.

59. Hamid El-Sayed Azmi, "The Growth of Population as Related to Some Aspects of Egypt's National Development," *L'Égypte Contemporaine* 28, no. 168 (1937): 267–303.

60. See Ghali, *The Policy of Tomorrow*; 'Abd al-Rahman, *Al-rif al-misri*, a collection of articles printed in *al-Ahram* in 1935.

61. See Hamid, *Jama'at al-nahda al-qawmiyya*.

62. Najib, "Mirrit Butrus Ghali," in *A'lam Misr fi al-qarn al-'ishrin*, 467.

63. Ghali, *The Policy of Tomorrow*, 49. Within a few years Ghali would radicalize his arguments, making the redistribution of national wealth the pivot of Egypt's national regeneration, particularly with the 1945 publication of his landmark text *Al-islah al-zira'i*, in which he argued for the redistribution of land, proposing a 100-feddan limit on the acquisition of new landholdings and the generalization and preservation of small holdings.

64. Salama Musa, "Dabt al-tanasul wa man' al-haml," in *Salama Musa: Al-mu'allafat al-kamila*, 2: 217–36.

65. Cleland, *The Population Problem in Egypt*, 110.

66. The assumption that standards of living and population growth were inversely related may be traced back to Malthus. For a critique see Sowell, "Malthus and the Utilitarians."

67. It was in the development of "a psychological attitude, the 'desires,' for fewer and more cultured children, that the peasantry can be made to curb their own growth. . . . In more primitive circumstances, such as surround the fellaheen . . . the chief source of recreation is sex, and that raises the birth rate. . . . Our aim then would be to do everything possible to sublimate the emotions and attention of the fellaheen while trying to raise their standards" (Cleland, "A Population Plan for Egypt," 477–78). Such assertions were loosely derived from older nineteenth-century views, such as those of Herbert Spencer, that the fecundity of the civilized races and classes was lower than that of the uncivilized because of their level of moral and material progress and their preoccupation with matters of the intellect or spirit.

68. Cleland, "A Population Plan for Egypt," 479.

69. At the core of debates on Malthus's theory of population is the question of the origin of poverty, its relationship to progress, and the perfectibility of man and society. See Bonar, "Population"; Sowell, "Malthus and the Utilitarians"; Harvey, "Population, Resources and the Ideology of Science"; Santurri, "Theodicy and Social Policy in Malthus' Thought."

70. Cleland, *The Population Problem in Egypt*, 109–10.

71. 'Awad Muhammad, "Al-nawahi al-ijtima'iyya," 61.

72. Kamal al-Din Effendi Fahmi, "Tanzim al-nasl fi ba'd al-aqtar—khatina fi Misr," *Al-Majalla al-Tibiyya al-Misriyya* 20, no. 7 (1937): 118–29.

73. Cleland, *The Population Problem in Egypt*, 59.

74. Cleland, "A Population Plan for Egypt," 470–71.

75. The phrase is from Elie Nassif, "L'Égypte est-elle surpeuplée?" *L'Égypte Contemporaine* 33, no. 208 (1942): 641. An Arabic synopsis of this article appeared in the same issue (pp. 775–91), with the title "Hal tashku Misr min al-izdiham bi al-sukkan?"

76. Nassif, "L'Égypte est-elle surpeuplée?" According to Galal Amin, training in political economy from 1920 to 1945 was subsumed under other branches, most notably law, and the Faculty of Law in Cairo was one of the principal locales where economics could be studied and taught. See Amin, "Seventy-five Years of Economic Thought in Egypt." Nassif was also a member of the Royal Society of Political Economy, Statistics and Legislation, which was founded in 1909, and which published the journal *L'Égypte Contemporaine*.

77. Gini, "The Cyclical Rise and Fall of Population," 4.

78. Elie Nassif, "Les critères de l'optimum démographique," in "L'Égypte est-elle surpeuplée?" 621–38; here Nassif surveys, reviews, and critiques the main trends of thought on the demographic optimum.

79. The "Anglo-Saxon doctrinaires" Nassif was referring to were numerous, and included William Beveridge, Allyn Young, A. M. Carr-Saunders, Edwin Cannan, Hugh Dalton, and Lionel Robbins. For an overview see Penrose, *Population Theories with Special Reference to Japan*, 49–55; Elie Nassif, "L'Égypte est-elle surpeuplée?" 621–38; Robbins, "The Optimum Theory of Population"; Dalton, "The Theory of Population"; Carr-Saunders, *World Population*, 320–21.

80. Gini, "Some Considerations of the Optimum Density of a Population"; Nassif, "L'Égypte est-elle surpeuplée?" 629.

81. Nassif, "Hal tashku Misr min al-izdiham bi al-sukkan?" 777–78.

82. Nassif, "L'Égypte est-elle surpeuplée?", 635–36. Nassif noted the examples of the U.S.S.R., Italy, Germany, and the United States, all of which possessed central organizations for the preparation and implementation of long-term programs for raising the moral and material level of the population. Nassif would later write a book evaluating the alternatives of capitalism and collectivism, *Capitalisme ou Collectivisme*.

83. Muhammad Hasan, "Mushkilat al-nasl fi Misr," *Al-Majalla al-Tibiyya al-Misriyya* 20, no. 7 (1937): 183–86; Hasan al-Banna, "Ra'y fi tahdid al-nasl min al-wajha al-islamiyya," *Al-Majalla al-Tibiyya al-Misriyya* 20, no. 7 (1937): 217–22.

84. Hasan, "Mushkilat al-nasl fi Misr," 185–86.

85. Abd al-Majid Nafi'a, "Al-dawa' ila tahdid al-nasl: Jarima qawmiyya la darura ijtima'iyya," *Shu'un Ijtima'iyya* 2, no. 5 (1941): 34–39.

86. Owen, "The Ideology of Economic Nationalism in its Egyptian Context"; Wahba, *The Role of the State in the Egyptian Economy*; Tignor, *State, Private Enterprise, and Economic Change in Egypt*.

87. Nassif, "L'Égypte est-elle surpeuplée?" 617–18.

88. See E. F. Penrose, *Population Theories and Their Application: With Special Reference to Japan*, 72–91.

89. Nassif, "L'Égypte est-elle surpeuplée?" 636–37.

90. Ibid., 639. The Arabic terms for the criteria are *al-had al-marghub lil-sukkan* (optimum population), *mawarid al-hayat* (resources), and *ma'yar al-hayat* (standards of living).

91. Ibid., 639.

92. Ibid., 720.

93. Ibid., 767. Nassif was indeed prescient. A policy of population redistribution through land reclamation and resettlement would become the cornerstone of the Nasserist population program. See Wizarat al-istislah al-aradi, *Takwin wa tanmiyat al-mujtama'at al-jadida fi aradi al-mustasliha*; M. Hasanayn, *Al-Sahara'*.

94. Nassif, "L'Égypte est-elle surpeuplée?" 768.

95. Polanyi, *The Great Transformation*, 125–26.

96. For a brief overview of Malthus's influence on economic theories and their relation to biological theories of multiplication, see Bonar, "Population," 162–69.

97. Beinin, "Egypt: Society and Economy," 321. Between 1928 and 1938, agricultural production declined 32 percent, wages declined 40 percent, and rents declined 35 percent; the cotton crop lost ⅔ of its nominal value in 1931–33 compared to the late 1920s. On the reorganization of Egyptian polity and society along the lines of social welfare and etatism in the post-1952 period, see Chapter 7.

98. See Brown, *Peasant Politics in Modern Egypt*; Hamid, *Al-haraka al-'ummaliyya fi Misr, 1899–1952*; Hamid, *Al-haraka al-'ummaliyya fi Misr fi daw' al-watha'iq al-baritaniyya*; Beinin and Lockman, *Workers on the Nile*; Abdallah, *The Student Movement and Nationalist Politics in Egypt*.

Chapter 6. Body Politics

1. Najib Mahfuz Bey was trained as a surgeon at Qasr al-'Ayni Medical School and Hospital, graduating in 1902. He began his career in Suez in 1903, but was soon transferred to Qasr al-'Ayni. In 1930 he received a masters in surgery from Cairo University. By 1935 he was a professor of obstetrics and gynecology at Cairo University, and he became director-general of Qasr al-'Ayni in 1939. Mahfuz received numerous awards and honorary degrees throughout his lifetime for his pioneering work in gynecology; wrote several gynecological textbooks and a history of medical education in Egypt; and established a Museum of Gynecology and Obstetrics at Qasr al-'Ayni. Mahfuz's autobiography, *The Life of an Egyptian Doctor*, provides a wealth of information on the practice of medicine in Egypt in the first half of the century. On Muhammad 'Awad Muhammad, see Chapter 2. Hasan al-Banna is discussed in depth below.

2. Foucault, *The History of Sexuality*, 139. As Foucault has taught us so well, power over life is the fundamental site for the deployment of modern power. What is at stake in biopolitics is the optimization of the strength of the population and its constituent subjects, while simultaneously rendering them more governable. My analysis of population politics is informed largely by the Foucaultian elaboration of governmentality, biopower and the political investment of the individual body and the body politic. See Michel Foucault's analysis of biopower as found in his *History*

of Sexuality and "Governmentality." See also Giorgio Agamben's refinement of the concept of biopolitics as the defining feature of modern politics in *Homo Sacer*.

3. Duben and Behar, *Istanbul households*, chap. 7.
4. Ibid., 226–38.
5. Mazower, *Dark Continent*, 87. See his fascinating chapter on "Healthy Bodies, Sick Bodies" for a discussion of European welfare states, social policy, and public health.
6. Asad, *Formations of the Secular*, chap. 7.
7. Pollard, "The Family Politics of Colonizing and Liberating Egypt," 50.
8. Booth, *May Her Likes Be Multiplied*.
9. Kholoussy, "Talking about a Revolution."
10. See Doumani, *Family History in the Middle East*; Baron, *Egypt as a Woman*.
11. For a social history of a similar process in Turkey, see Duben and Behar, *Istanbul Households*.
12. For a discussion of similar processes in Iran, see Schayegh, "Hygiene, Eugenics, Genetics, and the Perception of Demographic Crisis in Iran."
13. See Asad, *Formations of the Secular*, chap. 7.
14. Other key terms in Arabic in this field include *sukkan* (population; root "s-k-n"—to live, dwell, inhabit); *khusuba* (fertility of soil or bodies; root "kh-s-b"—to be fertile, to make fertile, fructify); *ifrat al-tanasul, ifrat al-nasl* (excess reproduction or offspring, the usual expression for over-population); *intilaq al-tanasul* (unrestrained reproduction); *kuthrat al-nasl, kuthrat al-sukkan* (excess population); and even *fawdat al-tanasul* (chaotic reproduction). In contrast to the English use of the term reproduction, the Arabic term (*tanasul*) does not connote a process of duplication (as in photocopying), nor does it apply to all biological entities; rather, it refers quite specifically to human procreation. Further, the root "n-s-l" has no resonance in the world of agricultural or industrial production, which does not mean that biological reproduction could not be subsumed as a category into the general world of production. The roots "k-th-r" (to increase, augment, multiply, grow) and "n-t-j" (to bear, bring forth a young one, produce, manufacture) are used to refer to agricultural production, and to animal or industrial production, respectively. The root "w-l-d" (to give birth, beget, generate, or produce, to engender or cause) is closer to the English concept of generation. See Wehr, *A Dictionary of Modern Written Arabic*; on the English origins of the term "reproduction" see Jordanova, "Interrogating the Concept of Reproduction in the Eighteenth Century."
15. It would not be until the early 1960s that the term and concept of family planning (*tanzim al-usra*) gained widespread acceptance and usage. The first instances I have come across of the use of the term are from May 1962, when the Egyptian Medical Association held a conference entitled Family Planning. By the middle of the 1960s, numerous institutional and governmental establishments were using the term—for example, the Supreme Council for Family Planning was established by Nasser in 1965. By the 1970s the term had become dominant. On population politics in twentieth century Egypt, including the postrevolutionary period, see El Shakry, *Reproducing the Family*.

16. Mustafa Fahmi, "Hal min al-khiyr li Misr fi zurufiha al-haliyya wa fi nitaq hajatuha al-harbiyya in tu'amim fiqrat tahdid al-nasl?!," *Al-Majalla al-Tibiyya al-Misriyya* 20, no. 7 (1937): 116–17.

17. Kamal al-Din Effendi Fahmi, "Tanzim al-nasl fi ba'd al-aqtar—khatina fi Misr," *Al-Majalla al-Tibiyya al-Misriyya* 20, no. 7 (1937): 118.

18. See Omran, *Family Planning in the Legacy of Islam*.

19. Muhammad 'Awad Muhammad, "Al-nawahi al-ijtima'iyya al-khasa bi tanzim al-nasl," *Al-Majalla al-Tibiyya al-Misriyya* 20, no. 7 (1937): 62. Muhammad later became a member of the 1953 National Commission for Population Problems, the first official body established in Egypt to deal with the population issue.

20. Muhammad, "Al-nawahi al-ijtima'iyya," 59.

21. Ibid., 62.

22. M. Fahmi, "Hal min al-khiyr li Misr?" 113.

23. Filib Shidyaq, "Hal yajib in yu'di tanzim al-nasl fi al-qutr al-misri ila tahdidu am ila tahsinu?" *Al-Majalla al-Tibiyya al-Misriyya* 20, no. 7 (July 1937): 178–82.

24. See, for example, Abd al-Aziz Hilmi Bey, "Tanzim al-nasl," *Al-Majalla al-Tibiyya al-Misriyya* 20, no. 7 (July 1937): 167–77.

25. Ann Anagnost has discussed the shift from quantity to quality in Chinese population discourse following the 1978 one-child policy. According to her, the Chinese notion of population quality is multivocal and covers a broad range: birth control, child rearing, sanitation, education, technology, law, and eugenics. Although post-Mao population discourse resonated with earlier 1920s eugenics discourse, it moved far beyond the concerns of a small elite, to include themes such as blaming national backwardness on poor population quality, characterization of the rural masses as backward and peripheral by the urban and intellectual elites, and the coupling of "raising the quality of the people" with the building of socialist civilization (Anagnost, *National Past-Times*, 118–28). David Horn has discussed the goals of fascist demographic politics: "rather than purification, the goals . . . were social defense and multiplication, rather than selective breeding and sterilization, its means were improved hygiene, diet and education." Thus, although the emphasis was on quantity in the Italian case, quality mattered at least in preventive terms, a process Horn refers to as "euthenics," by which he means positive eugenics—pronatalist social hygiene (Horn, *Social Bodies*, 60). See also Schneider, *Quality and Quantity*, for a discussion of similar processes in early-twentieth-century France.

26. There is a vast and rich literature on the development of the eugenics movement, which has gone far in debunking various myths portraying eugenics as solely an Anglo-American phenomenon, as a pseudoscience, as predominantly Mendelian, and as right wing (See Adams, "Toward a Comparative History of Eugenics").

27. Broadly, Egyptian ideas on eugenics were only vaguely biological in orientation, and were more concerned with social reform, public health, and sanitation. Most of those writing on the subject were either members of the medical profession or social reformers. If any particular scientific traditions are to be singled out as exerting the most influence on population writings, it would be neo-Lamarckian and social Darwinian; Mendelian genetics had not yet made serious inroads into

discussions of population. The neo-Lamarckian strains are noticeable in discussions surrounding the importance of improving the physical and social environment of the working poor, as well as in the general concern for puericulture, hygiene, and sanitation. And although there were those who insisted on sterilization, at least in cases where the genetic basis of disease transmission had been proven beyond a doubt, few argued for it on Mendelian grounds. The social-Darwinian approach could be discerned in the few instances where natural selection and elimination were discussed, but its usage was often imprecise. A key figure in debates on biology was Shibli Shumayyil, whose social Darwinism drew from Huxley, Spencer, Haeckel, and Büchner. In fact, Shumayyil had translated Büchner's commentary on Darwin into Arabic. Salama Musa was influential in the transmission of Lamarckian ideas into Arabic scholarship. On Shumayyil, see Hourani, *Arabic Thought in the Liberal Age*, 245–53. On Musa, see Egger, *A Fabian in Egypt*. On Darwinism in Egypt and Greater Syria, see Elshakry, "Darwin's Legacy in the Arab East." On the persistence of neo-Lamarckism in France and Brazil see, Schneider, "The Eugenics Movement in France," Stepan, "Eugenics in Brazil"; Stepan, *"The Hour of Eugenics."*

28. "Tahsin al-nasl: Itijah ijtima'i jadid," *Shu'un Ijtima'iyya* 2 (June 1941): 101–3. The article cites Husayn al-Ibyari's *Al-Wiratha wa tahsin al-nasl* as a sourcebook for contemporary work on eugenics.

29. Fu'ad, "Tahdid al-nasl"; M. Fahmi, "Hal min al-khiyr li Misr?"; K. Fahmi, "Tanzim al-nasl fi ba'd al-aqtar."

30. Fu'ad, "Tahdid al-nasl," 51; K. Fahmi, "Tanzim al-nasl fi ba'd al-aqtar," 126.

31. Fu'ad, "Tahdid al-nasl," 49, 51.

32. Abd al-Hakim al-Rifa'i, "Mushkilat al-sukkan fi Misr," *Al-Majalla al-Tibiyya al-Misriyya* 20, no. 7 (July 1937): 135–49. Al-Rifa'i, originally from Gharbiyya Province, was a political economist trained in Paris. After receiving his doctorate in political economy and law in 1929, he began his teaching career at the Faculty of Law, Cairo University, and held various governmental posts, including undersecretary of the Ministry of Finance, from 1948 to 1952, and executive officer of the Board of Directors of the Crédit Agricole Foncier in 1952 (Najib, "Abdel-Hakim al-Rifa'i," in *A'lam Misr fi al-qarn al-'ishrin*, 292).

33. These are the categories defined in the abortion law passed in Germany on July 14, 1933.

34. Al-Rifa'i, "Mushkilat al-sukkan fi Misr," 146.

35. Ibid., 147.

36. Ibid., 148.

37. Ibid., 147–48.

38. M. Fahmi, "Hal min al-khiyr li Misr?" 108. The concepts of reproductive selection and elimination as related to the quality of a population are discussed in Carr-Saunders, *Population*, 103–11.

39. M. Fahmi, "Hal min al-khiyr li Misr?" 109.

40. Ibid., 109.

41. Ibid., 109–10.

42. Shidyaq, "Hal yajib in yu'di tanzim al-nasl fi al-qutr al-misri ila tahdidu am ila tahsinu?"

43. Ibid., 180.

44. "Taqyid al-nasl am intikhabu," *Al-Hilal* 41 (November 1932), 84–90. The article was a synoptic translation of the ideas of an American eugenicist named Osborne.

45. "Dabt al-tanasul: Haraka ijtima'iyya khatira tu'am al-'alam al-mutamadin al-yawm," *Al-Hilal* 33 (June 1925), 938–40; Amir Buqtur, "Ifa al-tanasul wal ighraq fihi: Bahth ijtima'i wa iqtisadi wa sihi," *Al-Hilal* 38 (August 1930), 1201–6; "Al-shakawi min izdiyad sukkan al-alam," *Al-Hilal* 39 (April 1931), 868–72; "Taqyid al-nasl wal tahakum bi adad al-mawalid," *Al-Hilal* 39 (July 1931), 1393–96; "Hal nu'amid ila tahdid al-nasl?" *Al-Hilal* 40 (December 1931), 234–38; "Taqyid al-nasl am intikhabu," *Al-Hilal* 41 (November 1932), 84–90; "Tahdid al-nasl: Wa atharu al-sahiyya wa al-ijtima''iyya wa al-dawliyya," *Al-Muqtataf* 90 (March 1937), 261–67; "Tahdid al-nasl wa mushkilat al-sukkan," *Al-Muqtataf* 94 (January 1939), 283–9; "Tahdid al-nasl fil mizan," *Al-Muqtataf* 95 (June 1939), 41–45.

46. "Hal nu'amid ila tahdid al-nasl?" 236–37.

47. S.Q., "Sihhat al-nasl: Aham manab'a al-tharwa al-qawmiyya," *Shu'un Ijtima'iyya* 2 (April 1941): 88–93. Although this article was signed just "S.Q.," all indications point to the authorship of Sayyid Qutb, who was a regular contributor to the journal. On Sayyid Qutb's writings regarding social reform, see Roussillon, "Trajectoires Reformistes Sayyid Qutb et Sayyid 'Uways."

48. S.Q., "Sihhat al-nasl," 90. The anonymous article "Tahsin al-nasl: Itijah ijtima'i jadid," *Shu'un Ijtima'iyya* also called for the medicalization of marriage licenses.

49. Anagnost, "A Surfeit of Bodies," 31.

50. For discussions of motherhood and the nation in Egypt, see Baron, "Mothers, Morality and Nationalism in Pre-1919 Egypt"; Baron, "The Construction of National Honor in Egypt"; Baron, *The Women's Awakening in Egypt*; Ahmed, *Women, Gender and Islam*, chaps. 7–10; Philipp, "Feminism and Nationalist Politics in Egypt." On Bengal, see Borthwick, *The Changing Role of Women in Bengal*; Bose, "Sons of the Nation"; Chakrabarty, "The Difference-Deferral of a Colonial Modernity"; Samita Sen, "Motherhood and Mothercraft."

51. For a discussion of the importance of *tarbiya* and the cultivation of new types of children "acclimated to physical, mental, and moral work" in Egyptian nationalist and Islamist writings on motherhood and child rearing between 1890 and 1920, see El Shakry, "Schooled Mothers and Structured Play." A similar process in Iran is documented in Najmabadi, *Women with Mustaches and Men Without Beards*, chap.7.

52. It would be wrong, however, to presume that anticolonial nationalist discourses on motherhood, and in particular those of the Islamists, were merely parasitic upon colonial or European discourses. Crucial to the discourse of *tarbiya* was the indigenous concept of *adab*, which involved a complex of valued dispositions (intellectual, moral, and social), appropriate norms of behavior, comportment, and bodily habitus. Islamist reformers drew upon resources indigenous to the Islamic

discursive tradition that emphasized the proper pedagogy for children, the cultivation of the body, and the moral education of the self as essential for the constitution of a rightly guided Islamic community. Such norms of pedagogy were complementary, not antithetical, to the modernist disciplinization of the body and rationalization of the household.

53. Chatterjee, *The Nation and Its Fragments*, 134.

54. Ibid., 117.

55. On the history of maternalist processes in Europe and their relationship to imperialism, nationalism, and the welfare state, see Bock and Thane, *Maternity and Gender Policies*; Davin, "Imperialism and Motherhood;" de Grazia, *How Fascism Ruled Women*, chap. 3; Frevert, "The Civilizing Tendency of Hygiene"; Horn, *Social Bodies*; Koven and Michel, *Mothers of a New World*. On areas outside Europe, see the fascinating study by Nancy Rose Hunt, *A Colonial Lexicon of Birth Ritual, Medicalization, and Mobility in the Congo*; and Lavrin, *Women, Feminism, and Social Change in Argentina, Chile, and Uruguay*, chaps. 3, 5.

56. See El Shakry, "Schooled Mothers and Structured Play."

57. Ministry of Finance, *Almanac for the Year 1935*, 286.

58. An official Egyptian delegation was sent to the 1925 First General Congress on Child Welfare. At the Congrès Quinzaine Sociale Internationale, held in Paris in 1928, Sayyid Effendi 'Arif, an administrative inspector, was sent to the conference's Congrès International de la Protection de l'Enfance. See DWQ, *Abdin, mu'tamarat, 1925–29*, box 59. See also Paul-Valentin, "La protection de l'enfance: Comment elle devrait être organisée en Egypte," 20ème Congrès International de Bruxelles, *L'Egypte Contemporaine* 14 (April 1923): 371–97; Paul-Valentin, "Une étape nouvelle dans l'organisation scientifique de la protection de l'enfance," *L'Egypte Contemporaine* 14 (January 1923): 10–41.

59. DWQ, *Abdin, al-jama'iyyat, al-jama'iyyat al-ijtima'iyya, 1899–1952*, box 203; "Report from the Egyptian Official Delegation," First General Congress on Child Welfare (Geneva, August 1925), 4, in DWQ, *Abdin, mu'tamarat, 1925–29*, box 59. See also Istiphan, *Directory of Social Agencies in Cairo*.

60. "Report from the Egyptian Official Delegation," First General Congress on Child Welfare, 3–4. According to this report, since the 1915 opening of schools for midwives, 1,511 midwives had finished their training and settled down to practice. Each midwife in training was required to attend a minimum of twenty labor classes, and to follow a course of lectures in midwifery and hygiene. The pupil was also asked to assist for at least one month in a children's dispensary. According to Wendell Cleland's estimates, by 1933 there were twenty such schools for training midwives, with 264 licensed women graduating, bringing the total number of licensed and practicing midwives to 438 out of a total of 5,744 (Cleland, *The Population Problem in Egypt*, 59–60).

61. "Report from the Egyptian Official Delegation," First General Congress on Child Welfare, 3–4.

62. "Report from the Egyptian Official Delegation," First General Congress on Child Welfare, 2.

63. Mahfuz, *The History of Medical Education in Egypt*, 88. Nancy Gallagher discusses the establishment and development of the Department of Public Health in "Introduction," *Egypt's Other Wars*.

64. Ministry of Finance, *Almanac for the Year 1929*, 160.

65. Cleland, *The Population Problem in Egypt*, 59.

66. On Egypt's philanthropic movement, see Abdel Kader, *Egyptian Women in a Changing Society*, 97–99; Arafa, *The Social Activities of the Egyptian Feminist Union*, 25–37; Badran, *Feminists, Islam, and Nation*, 48–52, 111–23; Baron, *The Women's Awakening in Egypt*, 169–75; Gallagher, *Egypt's Other Wars*, 40–55. Day-care centers for working mothers had been called for as early as the 1920s, and eventually the Egyptian Feminist Union opened its own centers in 1946.

67. The EFU began rural activities in the late 1930s (previously the organization had targeted urban poor women), with agitation for the moral and material improvement of the peasantry. To be sure, the extension of health and education was not sufficient, and members of the EFU "insisted that medical services should include basic instruction in health and hygiene, and in new techniques of childbirth and child care" (Badran, *Feminists, Islam, and Nation*, 120).

68. See Levy, *Other Women*; Poovey, *Uneven Developments*.

69. Arafa, *The Social Activities of the Egyptian Feminist Union*, 34; Nabarawi, 1932, quoted in Badran, *Feminists, Islam, and Nation*, 100, 112.

70. Arafa, *The Social Activities of the Egyptian Feminist Union*, 25, 28–29.

71. "Société Internationale pour la Protection de l'Enfance" (18 December 1940), in DWQ, *Abdin, al-jama'iyyat, al-jama'iyyat al-ijtima'iyya, 1899–1952*, box 203.

72. Ibid.

73. "Red Crescent Society, Fédération Royale des Associations Internationales d'Assistance Publique en Egypte," in DWQ, *Abdin, al-jama'iyyat, al-jama'iyyat al-ijtima'iyya, 1902–1949*, box 204.

74. "Jama'iyyat al-khidma al-ijtima'iyya bi Misr al-jadida wa dawahiha, muthakira talkhisiyya 'an 'amal al-jama'iyya munthu ta'sisiha," n.d. (c. 1942) in DWQ, *Abdin, al-jama'iyyat, al-jama'iyyat al-ijtima'iyya, 1899–1952*, box 203.

75. Ibid., 1.

76. Ibid., 4.

77. Ibid., 2.

78. K. Fahmi, "Tanzim al-nasl fi ba'd al-aqtar," 129.

79. 'Abbas 'Ammar, "Al-nahya al-insaniyya fi mawdu' tanzim al-nasl," *Al-Majalla al-Tibiyya al-Misriyya* 20, no. 7 (1937): 209–11.

80. Declining birth rates were mobilized in arguments against population policy—see Hilmi Bey, "Tanzim al-nasl," 168.

81. Muhammad, "Al-nawahi al-ijtima'iyya," 63–64; M. Fahmi, "Hal min al-khiyr li Misr?" 114.

82. To prove the absurdity of comparing nations by numbers, Muhammad cited the pointed example of a colony and colonial power, India and England, in which the former would appear to be eight times as great (in sheer numbers) as the latter despite the average life expectancy of twenty-four years in India and fifty-six

in England. Birth control, therefore, also meant improving a population's labor productivity (Muhammad, "Al-nawahi al-ijtima'iyya," 65–66).

83. M. Fahmi, "Hal min al-khiyr li Misr?" 101–3. See also al-Rifa'i, "Mushkilat al-sukkan fi Misr," 141–42.

84. Owen, "The Ideology of Economic Nationalism in Its Egyptian Context"; Wahba, *The Role of the State in the Egyptian Economy*; Tignor, *State, Private Enterprise, and Economic Change in Egypt*. For a more detailed discussion of economic nationalism and etatism, see Chapter 7.

85. "Report from the Egyptian Official Delegation," First General Congress on Child Welfare, 2. According to Mustafa Fahmi, 65 percent of deaths in Egypt were children under the age of ten ("Hal min al-khiyr li Misr?" 110). See also al-Rifa'i, "Mushkilat al-sukkan fi Misr," 140; Cleland, *The Population Problem in Egypt*, 55–58.

86. M. Fahmi, "Hal min al-khiyr li Misr?" 111.

87. 'Ammar, "Al-nahya al-insaniyya," 201–3.

88. M. Fahmi, "Hal min al-khiyr li Misr?" 107, 111.

89. Muhammad, "Al-nawahi al-ijtima'iyya." See also M. Fahmi, "Hal min al-khiyr li Misr?" 112.

90. Muhammad, "Al-nawahi al-ijtima'iyya," 61.

91. Ibid. (Muhammad gives the quotation from the Indian census in English).

92. M. Fahmi, "Hal min al-khiyr li Misr?" 101.

93. Of course, there were those who pointed out that Egypt's situation was nowhere near comparable to those of the pronatalist nations. Italy and the fascist nations had colonial ambitions, and France needed to compensate for the losses it had sustained during the war. Egypt did not have any such justifications. See 'Ammar, "Al-nahya al-insaniyya," 210–11.

94. "Mashru' Itali li targhib al-nas fi al-zawaj wa al-tanasul," in Hilmi Bey, "Tanzim al-nasl," 167. On Italian pronatalism, see Horn, *Social Bodies*; and de Grazia, *How Fascism Ruled Women*.

95. Abd al-Majid Nafi'a, "Al-da'wa ila tahdid al-nasl: Jarima qawmiyya la darura ijtima'iyya," *Shu'un Ijtima'iyya* 2 (May 1941): 34–39.

96. Issa 'Abduh, "Ra'y fi tahdid al-nasl wa tanzimuhu: Bahth min al-nahyatin al-Islamiyya wal iqtisadiyya," *Al-Majalla al-Tibiyya al-Misriyya* 20 (July 1937): 155–65.

97. Ibid., 164.

98. Ibid., 162–64.

99. See Pedersen, "Regulating Abortion and Birth Control" for a discussion of the French debates on abortion and birth control leading up to the infamous law of 1920.

100. For a discussion of the crisis of paternity and the reestablishment of paternalistic privilege in post–World War I Syria and Lebanon, see Elizabeth Thompson's fine study *Colonial Citizens*.

101. Hacking, *The Taming of Chance*, 22.

102. For a review of this literature, see Connelly, "Population Control Is History."

103. On 'Ammar, see Chapter 2.

104. 'Ammar, "Al-nahya al-insaniyya."

105. Ibid., 192–94.

106. For Fu'ad this meant that the urban working classes should organize their births. He thus encouraged the creation of state clinics, as in Britain, where each family's economic, social, and health conditions could be studied and where birth control would be dispensed (Fu'ad, "Tahdid al-nasl," 52–3). Muhammad 'Awad tried to refute the assumption that birth control should become an urban phenomenon. Upon closer inspection, he noted, the excess of inhabitants and the appearance of crowdedness in the city was an effect of the recent influx of rural migrants. Such a high migration indicated the limited nature of resources (notably, land) in the countryside, yet the migration of peasants into the city ended only in poverty (Muhammad, "Al-nawahi al-ijtima'iyya," 72–73). Only a decade earlier, rural-urban migration had been considered virtually nonexistent by geographer Mustafa Amer ("Some Problems of the Population of Egypt," 23).

107. Hasan al-Banna, "Ra'y fi tahdid al-nasl min al-wajha al-Islamiyya," *Al-Majalla al-Tibiyya al-Misriyya* 20 (July 1937): 217–22.

108. Muhammad Mahmud Hasan, "Mushkilat al-nasl fi Misr," *Al-Majalla al-Tibiyya al-Misriyya* 20 (July 1937): 183–86.

109. 'Ammar, "Al-nahya al-insaniyya," 195.

110. Ibid., 197.

111. Al-Banna, "Ra'y fi tahdid al-nasl," 222.

112. 'Ammar, "Al-nahya al-insaniyya," 197–98.

113. Ibid., 194.

114. *Al-Majalla al-Tibiyya al-Misriyya* 20 (July 1937): 55; translated in Omran, *Family Planning in the Legacy of Islam*, 250; reprinted in Wizarat al-awqaf, *Mawqif al-islam min tanzim al-usra*, 81–82. I have amended the translation where necessary from the original text. Note that this is representative of the *Hanafite* school of jurisprudence. In the Muslim tradition children are considered to be "gifted with souls" after the first 120 days of gestation.

115. Al-Ghazali, *Ihya' 'ulum al-din*. On the history of birth control in Islamic jurisprudence see Omran, *Family Planning in the Legacy of Islam*, chap. 8. See also Musallam, *Sex and Society in Islam*.

116. Omran, *Family Planning in the Legacy of Islam*, 168–69. Reasons that al-Ghazali regarded as ill-intentioned (*niyya fasida*) were the avoidance of female children and the avoidance of maternity in general out of an exaggerated sense of cleanliness.

117. For a more extensive discussion of transformations in twentieth-century Islamic religious discourse on birth control and planning, see El Shakry, "Reproducing the Family."

118. R. Mitchell, *The Society of the Muslim Brothers*.

119. As al-Banna became increasingly militant, he came to be perceived as a threat by government officials; he was murdered, presumably by the political police, on February 12, 1949. This was a few months after the assassination of Prime

Minister Mahmud Fahmi al-Nuqrashi by a Muslim Brother in December 1948, after Nuqrashi had banned the Brothers' organization. The Muslim Brothers (along with Young Egypt and various Marxist communist organizations) represented a vital counterhegemonic social and political force in opposition to secularist government politics. On al-Banna and the Muslim Brothers, see R. Mitchell, *The Society of the Muslim Brothers*; Wendell, *Five Tracts of Hasan al-Banna;* Saʿid, *Hasan al-Banna*; Goldschmidt, *Biographical Dictionary of Modern Egypt*, 34–35.

120. Al-Banna, "Ra'y fi tahdid al-nasl," 217.

121. Ibid., 217.

122. Ibid., 218. In this article, al-Banna quotes *ahadith* (sayings of the Prophet Muhammad) in support of his argument in favor of procreation as the goal of marriage. One recounts a man who approached the Prophet stating that he loved a woman who was of noble birth and rank, and of wealth, but who could not conceive. He then asked the Prophet, "Should I marry her?" The Prophet said no. The man returned two more times. On the third occasion, the Prophet stated: "Marry those that are dear and fertile (*al-wudud al-wulud*) for I shall make a display of you before other nations."

123. Al-Banna was fully aware of the contentious nature of his claim, recognizing that as with other issues, religious opinions on birth control varied widely, as did the evidence used to support the varying claims. There were those who declared *al-ʿazl* (coitus interruptus) completely forbidden; those who declared it *mabah* (either absolutely or with *qaraha*), asserting that it did not occlude God's will in any way; and those who declared it *mabah* so long as the wife's consent was obtained (including the taking of medicine as birth control or reduction).

124. ʿAbduh, "Ra'y fi tahdid al-nasl wa tanzimuhu," 164–66.

125. Ibid., 156. This is a much-quoted verse from *al-Isra '* (The Night Journey), Sura 17:31.

126. Hasan, "Mushkilat al-nasl fi Misr," 184–85.

127. ʿAbduh, "Ra'y fi tahdid al-nasl wa tanzimuhu," 156.

128. Ibid., 157–59.

129. Ibid., 160.

130. R. Mitchell, *The Society of the Muslim Brothers*.

131. Al-Banna, "Ra'y fi tahdid al-nasl," 220–21.

132. Ibid., 221; ʿAbduh, "Ra'y fi tahdid al-nasl wa tanzimuhu," 166.

133. Al-Banna noted the distinction between Egyptian territorial nationalism and pan-Islamism: "The point of contention between us and them is that we define the limits of patriotism in terms of creed, while they define it according to territorial borders and geographical boundaries. For every region in which there is a Muslim . . . is a homeland for us, having its own inviolability and sanctity. . . . All Muslims in these geographical regions are our people and our brothers. . . . The advocates of patriotism alone are not like this, since nothing matters to them except the affairs of that specific, narrowly delimited region of the earth" (quoted in Gershoni and Jankowski, *Redefining the Egyptian Nation*, 82). For a fuller discussion of al-Banna and of Egyptian Islamic nationalism, see ibid., 79–96.

134. A. M. Anous, "The Dangers of Frequent Child-Bearing and Necessity of Birth-Control" (in English), *Al-Majalla al-Tibiyya al-Misriyya* 20 (July 1937): 273.

135. These included "harmful and known methods such as applying concentrated salt solution, aloes, and even faecal material" (ibid., 277). See also Muhammad, "Al-nawahi al-ijtima'iyya," 69–70; Fu'ad, "Tahdid al-nasl," 50.

136. 'Ammar, "Al-nahya al-insaniyya," 208–9.

137. For a discussion of bachelorhood and its relation to the "marriage crisis" in pre-1919 Egypt, see Kholoussy "Talking about a Revolution."

138. Fu'ad, "Tahdid al-nasl," 50, 52; Anous, "The Dangers of Frequent Child-Bearing," 273; Muhammad, "Al-nawahi al-ijtima'iyya," 70–71; 'Ammar, "Al-nahya al-insaniyya," 205.

139. Muhammad, "Al-nawahi al-ijtima'iyya," 68.

140. Anous, "The Dangers of Frequent Child-Bearing," 273. 'Abbas 'Ammar underscored the dangers of prolonged bachelorhood and the necessity of advocating not celibacy, but earlier marriage with birth control ('Ammar, "Al-nahya al-insaniyya," 205–7).

141. Hilmi Bey, "Tanzim al-nasl," 169–70.

142. Rapp and Ginsburg, "Introduction," in *Conceiving the New World Order*.

143. In 1944 Marzuq, then administrative director of the benevolent societies of the Ministry of Social Affairs, along with Muhammad Sa'id Amin, conducted a study on Alexandria that was published in 1947 as *Al-hala al-ijtima'iyya li sukkan al-iskindiriyya: Bahth wa ihsa wa tahlil*. Al-Sa'ati, "Tatawur al-madrasa al-fikriyya li 'ilm al-ijtima' fi Misr."

144. Zahya Marzuq, "Kilmat lil mar'a fi tanzim al-nasl," *Al-Majalla al-Tibiyya al-Misriyya* 20 (July 1937): 150–54.

145. The idea that the status of women was inextricably tied to the retrogression or progress of nations gained wide currency in Egypt at the turn of the century (see El Shakry, "Schooled Mothers and Structured Play").

146. Ibid., 203–4.

147. Al-Rifa'i, "Mushkilat al-sukkan fi Misr," 149.

148. Ibid., 145.

149. Ahmad Khayri Sa'id, "Tahdid al-nasl fi al-mizan," *Al-Majalla al-Tibiyya al-Misriyya* 20 (July 1937): 132.

150. Ibid., 134.

151. Ibid., 132–33. 'Abbas 'Ammar referred to the necessary reform process as "the re-creation of Egyptian society" (*khalq hatha al-mujtama' al-misri min jadid*) ('Ammar, "Al-nahya al-insaniyya," 188).

Chapter 7. Etatism

1. "Al-safir al-Yugoslavi ya qul: Mudiriyat al-tahrir min 'azam al-tajarib al-ijtima'iyya fi al-'alam," *Al-Sahara'* 1, no. 12 (1957): 17; "Ma' al-nuwwab fi mudiriyat al-Tahrir," *Al-Sahara'* 2, no., 20 (1957).

2. Warriner, *Agrarian Reform and Community Development in the U.A.R.*, 54.

3. Institute of National Planning, *Research Report on Employment Problems in Rural Areas of the United Arab Republic*, 34.

4. Ibid.

5. Egypt's so-called "liberal experiment" (1919–1952) has been the subject of recent revisionist scholarly attention; see Goldschmidt et.al., *Re-Envisioning Egypt*.

6. The idea of a social-welfare mode of regulation is my own. A mode of regulation refers to the most efficient approach for creating a population of governable subjects and citizens. Subjects, that is, who are self-regulating individuals—physically and mentally sound, economically productive, and socially adapted to a particular phase of capitalist production. Multiple agents and forces (such as international, state, and private agencies, members of the intelligentsia, educators, the religious establishment, etc.), interact in complex, often unconscious ways, consonant with the reproduction of the national economy, polity, and society, to maintain the status quo. It is the materialization of the mode of regulation (in the "form of norms, habits, laws, regulating networks. . . . [a] body of interiorized rules and social processes" [Lipietz, "New Tendencies in the International Division of Labour," 19]) that defines a particular era, as well as the structures and conditions of possibility that exist within it. I draw here on the theory of the French regulation school, which attempts to disaggregate Marx's concept of a mode of production, and was pioneered by Michel Aglietta's (1979) *A Theory of Capitalist Regulation*; this school is familiar to most through the popularization of the concepts of Taylorism, Fordism, and Post-Fordism. Two useful introductions are R. Boyer, *The Regulation School*; Harvey, *The Condition of Postmodernity*. For the use of regulation theory in the context of post-1960 Egypt, see Toth, *Rural Labor Movements and Their Impact on the State*.

7. Polanyi, *The Great Transformation*.

8. Ibid.

9. Gramsci's term is "hegemonic deputies of the state"; Althusser called it the ideological state apparatus; and Foucault has referred to the process of the "governmentalization" of the state. See Gramsci, *Selections from the Prison Notebooks of Antonio Gramsci*; Althusser, "Ideology and Ideological State Apparatuses (Notes towards an Investigation)," in *Lenin and Philosophy and Other Essays*; Foucault, "Governmentality."

10. For an interesting discussion that problematizes the imprecise usage of populism in the Latin American context, see Knight, "Populism and Neo-Populism in Latin America." While Knight confines the usage of populism to a particular rhetorical style, and an invocation of "the people," he retains the category as useful for a taxonomy of political systems. I am more interested in mapping out the historical specificity of Nasserism rather than generating abstract models of political styles, or systems, to be applied to the Middle East generally.

11. Wahba, *The Role of the State in the Egyptian Economy*, 18.

12. Ibid., 24.

13. Ibid., 15.

14. Ibid., 28.

15. Ibid., 32–33. See also Monciaud, "Le projet de la piastre et Jeune Egypte"; Tignor, *State, Private Enterprise, and Economic Change in Egypt*; Vitalis, *When Capitalists Collide*.

16. Wahba, *The Role of the State in the Egyptian Economy*; al-Disuqi, *Misr fi al-harb al-'alamiyya al-thaniyya*.

17. Wahba, *The Role of the State in the Egyptian Economy*, 43.

18. Ali, *Planning the Family in Egypt*, 27–28.

19. Baer, *A History of Landownership in Modern Egypt*, 201.

20. Ibid., 202–3.

21. Ibid., 203–4. As Baer correctly notes, writers such as Mirrit Butrus Ghali and Ahmed Sadiq Sa'd explicitly connected the domestic hardships endured during the war to the call for agrarian reform.

22. Ashmawi, *Al-fellahun wa al-sulta*.

23. Ibid., 92; Baer, *A History of Landownership in Modern Egypt*, 201–19; Wahba, *The Role of the State in the Egyptian Economy*, 37–38; Tignor, *State, Private Enterprise, and Economic Change in Egypt*, 234–35. Many books were published in the late 1930s that dealt with the peasantry but did not address the political issue of land distribution. These include Aisha 'Abd al-Rahman's *Al-rif al-misri* and *Qadiyyat al-fellah*; Hafiz Afifi Pasha's *'Ala hamish al-siyasa*, and even Mirrit Butrus Ghali's earlier work, *Siyasat al-ghad*. Texts that tackled distribution included the writings of Ghali (who radicalized his earlier 1938 argument and published his *Islah al-Zira'i* in 1945); Ahmed Sadiq Sa'd, *Mushkilat al-fellah*; the 1950 *Al-ard al-Tayyiba* (a critique of colonialism and capitalism) by Ahmed Husayn, head of the group Misr al-fatat; the 1945 second edition of Rashid al-Barrawi and Muhammad Ulaysh's *Al-tatawwur al-iqtisadi fi Misr*, which added a new chapter calling for a limit on landholdings; and Islamist Khalid Muhammad Khalid's *Min huna' nabda'* (1950) which called for a directed economy along the lines of France and Britain. The postrevolutionary period brought the writings of what Anouar Abdel-Malek called the Marxist Historical School: Ibrahim 'Amir's 1957 study *Al-ard wa al-fellah*; Ahmed Rushdi Salih's *Al-adab al-sha'abi* (1954); Fawzi Girgis's *Dirasat fi tarikh Misr al-siyasi* (1958); and Shuhdi Attiyya al-Shafa'i's *Tatawwur al-haraka al-wataniyya al-misriyya* (1957). On this body of writings see Abdel-Malek, *Egypt: Military Society*.

24. Chatterjee, *The Nation and Its Fragments*, 212. Chatterjee's argument is noteworthy in that he shifts the usual terms of debate regarding non-Western nationalisms. Here, reversing Gramsci's thesis, he argues that passive revolution has in fact been the norm in the twentieth century. Gramsci's treatment of the "blocked dialectic" of passive revolution as an exception to the paradigmatic case of bourgeois revolution (Jacobinism), Chatterjee argues, is misguided. As Samira Haj points out, this makes the vital point that "the non-Western model of the modern nation-state is, empirically speaking, the "norm" and not the aberration" (Haj, *The Making of Iraq*).

25. Jamal 'Abd al-Nasir, *Falsafat al-thawra*; Lenin, "Preliminary Draft Theses on the National and the Colonial Questions."

26. Chatterjee, *The Nation and Its Fragments*, 212.

27. Ibid.

28. Abdel-Malek, ed., *Contemporary Arab Political Thought*.

29. Historiographically, two broad approaches to the development of capitalism in Egypt may be delineated: modernization theory (and its later manifestations in statist approaches), and international political economy (world-systems and Marxist). Both approaches take as their point of departure a narrative of failed, aborted, or blocked transition to capitalism. For modernization theorists, Egypt's historical trajectory is problematically inserted within progressivist narratives of socioeconomic development, democratization, and economic liberalization. Taking Egypt as a self-contained unit of analysis following a discrete pathway, they tend to foreground the state as a free-standing agent, thereby occluding the larger global historical and political context—i.e., colonialism and global capitalism. The 1952 revolution figures into their narrative as emblematic of the failure of the national bourgeoisie to "capture the state." The Nasser regime, characterized by an authoritarian military regime, a charismatic strong leader, state-led growth, and aggressive developmentalist strategies, is seen to have, in effect, aborted a natural teleology towards socioeconomic development, a privatized market, and democracy. International political-economy approaches, by contrast, foreground the historically constituted relations between local and international capitalist forces and relations of production. These accounts have tried to make sense of the structural constraints within which the development of Egyptian capitalism has operated, i.e., an agrarian and industrial bourgeoisie pursuing a "backward" colonial capitalism in forced (structurally constrained) alliance with foreign and comprador capital, blocking indigenous capital accumulation and viewed in terms of a "failed national-bourgeois revolution." The Marxist and neo-Marxist literature is quite rich, and includes Abdel-Malek, *Egypt: Military Society*; Beinin and Lockman, *Workers on the Nile*; M. Hussein, *Class Conflict in Egypt*; and Zaalouk, *Power, Class, and Foreign Capital in Egypt*. A revisionist thesis is Vitalis, *When Capitalists Collide*, which argues against narratives of colonial exceptionalism—that is, against the view of the 1952 revolution as the necessary outcome of a failed national bourgeois project, constrained by the conditions of colonial capitalist development. My own argument is also meant to address the unwarranted emphasis on external influences on the economic, political, and ideological origins of the Egyptian postcolonial nation-state building project.

The following interpretation is based primarily on the following sources: Abdel-Malek, *Egypt: Military Society*; Hussein, *Class Conflict in Egypt*; Zaalouk, *Power, Class, and Foreign Capital in Egypt*; Abdel-Fadil, *Development, Income Distribution, and Social Change in Rural Egypt*.

30. Zaalouk, *Power, Class, and Foreign Capital in Egypt*, 30. Or, as Mahmoud Hussein put it, the state sector which was to launch Egypt's political economic development emerged not out of radical socialist transformation, but was "growing within the framework that had existed in the past-the political and economic apparatus created by the imperialists and traditional bourgeoisie." M. Hussein, as quoted in Zaalouk, *Power, Class and Foreign Capital in Egypt*, 33.

31. On India, see Chatterjee, *The Nation and Its Fragments*, chap. 10; on Turkey, see Mehmet, "Turkey in Crisis."

32. See Posusney, *Labor and the State in Egypt*.

33. See Bianchi, *Unruly Corporatism*.

34. My analysis bears some resemblance to recent writings on the Nasser era, but it differs in important ways. Amira Sonbol's *The New Mamluks* (among the most creative historical interpretations of Egyptian modernity) views Nasserism as the continuation of older patterns of feudalism and patronage, in combination with modern socialism. Thus, the state functioned as the "grand seigneur, offering protection and services in return for political allegiance and labor" (xxxix). Roel Meijer's account (*The Quest for Modernity*) looks to pre-1952 liberal secular ideologies and their co-optation by the revolutionary elite, but relies on a notion of authoritarian modernism. Other important texts include Joel Gordon's *Nasser's Blessed Movement*, a political history of the early years of the revolution, illustrating the regime's initial tenuous hold on power and the importance of pragmatic power politics in the Revolutionary Command Council and later Nasser's consolidation of power; Kirk Beattie's *Egypt During the Nasser Years*, which explores the importance of ideology in the building of a stable hegemonic bloc within civil society; and *Rethinking Nasserism*, a collection of essays edited by Elie Podeh and Onn Winckler that revives the idea of populism and authoritarian modernization to discuss the appeal of Nasserism in the wake of postmonarchical anomie. All of these accounts rely on some notion of authoritarianism in political agendas or developmentalism at the level of economic policy. In contrast, I try to show an underlying coherence in the historical bloc spanning the 1930s to the 1960s, evidenced in new modes of governance, expertise, and social knowledge. Such a bloc may be distinguished by a common discourse of social improvement and welfare.

35. For a critique of "failure" and "lack" as analytic rubrics for understanding Indian history, see Chakrabarty *Provincializing Europe*, chap. 1.

36. As will become clear, my intent is not to argue that the Nasserist state actually succeeded in winning "hearts and minds," but rather to explore the techniques and strategies through which it attempted to fabricate its ideological hegemony. For a discussion of the former, see Tawfiq al-Hakim's *The Return of Consciousness*, in which he discusses the era of Nasserism as one characterized by enthusiasm, love, pride, and the loss of consciousness.

37. Chatterjee, *The Nation and Its Fragments*, 202–8.

38. See, for example, United Arab Republic, *The U.A.R. Yearbook 1960*, 202–3.

39. United Arab Republic, *The U.A.R. Yearbook 1960*, 437; al-Abd, "Land Reclamation and Resettlement in Egypt," 95.

40. Johnson et. al., *Egypt: The Egyptian Rural Improvement Service*, 1.

41. Al-Abd, "Land Reclamation and Resettlement in Egypt," 93.

42. Institute of National Planning, *Research Report on Employment Problems in Rural Areas of the United Arab Republic*, 22.

43. United Arab Republic, *The U.A.R. Yearbook 1960*, 439.

44. M. Hasanayn, *Al-Sahara'*.

45. M. Hasanayn as quoted in Warriner, *Land Reform and Development in the Middle East*, 49.
46. M. Hasanayn, *Al-Sahara'*, 103.
47. Al-Abd, "Land Reclamation and Resettlement in Egypt," 94.
48. Bassiouni, "Mudiriyat al-Tahrir kanamudhaj lil mujtama'at al-mukhatata," 179–87.
49. Warriner, *Land Reform and Development in the Middle East*, 51, emphasis added. Zaki was a key figure in the social development of the province. His ideas on social development in general, and planned communities specifically, may be found in Zaki, "Some Sociological Aspects of Planned Communities," *Al-Majallat al-Ijtima'iyyah al-Qawmiyya / The National Review of Social Sciences* 1, no. 1, (January 1964): 149–62. See also Zaki, *Tanzim wa tanmiyat al-mujtama'a*.
50. Bassiouni, "Mudiriyat al-tahrir," 183.
51. "Masana' al-salb al-bashari zo al-farayn," *Al-Sahara'*, 1, no.1 (February 1956): 16–18.
52. Ibid., 17.
53. Abu Zayd, *Al-takayyuf al-ijtima'i*, 54–67; Ahmed El-Hammami, interview with author, Spectra Physics, Cairo, May 1, 1999.
54. Bassiouni, "Mudiriyat al-Tahrir," 179–87.
55. "Masana' al-salb al-bashari zo al-farayn," 18.
56. Ibid.
57. Warriner, *Land Reform and Development in the Middle East*, 51.
58. Wizarat al-Istislah al-Aradi, *Takwin wa tanmiyat al-mujtama'at al-jadida*, 34–70; Abu Zayd *Al-takayyuf al-ijtima'i*, 54–67; El-Hammami, interview.
59. El Hammami 1999.
60. Abu-Zayd, *Al-takayyuf al-ijtima'i*, 61–62.
61. El-Hammami, interview.
62. Abu-Zayd, *Al-takayyuf al-ijtima'i*, 62.
63. Springborg, "Patrimonialism and Policy Making in Egypt"; El-Hammami, interview.
64. El-Hammami, interview. Shortly after the project was taken over by Marei, however, the pro-Leftist faction of the regime (Ali Sabri and Abdel Muhsin Abuel Nur) successfully challenged Marei's leadership and regained control of the province in 1961 under Abuel Nur's direction, following a Soviet state-farm model, and emboldened by Nikita Khrushchev's May 1964 visit to the province. After Nasser's death, Sadat purged the pro-Leftist faction of the regime and began to experiment with various reclamation models (including land grants to agricultural engineering graduates). EAUDRL was dissolved in 1976, however, and independent private sector companies such as the South Tahrir Company were established in its place to oversee land reclamation. There were suggestions of simply selling the land to joint venture agribusinesses, and indeed one such venture, FAAB (First Arabian Agribusiness), located itself on 10,000 *feddans* in southern Tahrir. By the late 1970s the land reclaimed by the government had begun to be parceled off and sold in five- to twenty-five-feddan blocs at subsidized prices, and eventually to sole or joint

ventures such as Coca Cola, which leased large tracts for agribusiness-style farms. Thus, the emphasis during the Infitah period shifted from public to private ownership of land;more significantly, it moved away from a holistic model of building a community of settlers to reclaim land and toward simply expanding cultivation to larger tracts of land via capital-intensive projects. For accounts of the later history of Tahrir Province, see Springborg, "Patrimonialism and Policy Making in Egypt"; Voll, "Egyptian Land Reclamation since the Revolution"; Hinnebusch, *Egyptian Politics under Sadat*, 143; Hopkins et al., *Participation and Community in the Egyptian New Lands*.

65. Wizarat al-istislah al-aradi, *Takwin wa tanmiyat al-mujtama'at al-jadida*, 7–8.

66. Ibid., 24.

67. I develop this argument in El Shakry, "Cairo as Capital of Socialist Revolution."

68. The memorandum was titled "The Population Situation in Egypt and the Necessity of Planning Population Policy for the Country" ('Ammar "The Population Situation in Egypt").

69. Ibid., 13, 15.

70. Ibid., 15–16.

71. Rizk, "Population Policies in Egypt," 40.

72. Husayn al-Shafa'i, as quoted in Rizk, "Population Policies in Egypt," 39–40.

73. Gamal Abdel-Nasser, as quoted in Shanawany, "Stages in the Development of a Population Control Program," 197.

74. Wizarat al-shu'un al-ijtima'iyya, *Wizarat al-shu'un al-ijtima'iyya fi khamsa wa 'ishrin 'amm*, 49.

75. Quoted in Rizk, "Population Policies in Egypt," 105; see aso Shanawany, "Stages in the Development of a Population Control Program," 202; Omran and el-Nomrossey, "The Family Planning Effort in Egypt," 224.

76. Omran and el-Nomrossey, "The Family Planning Effort in Egypt," 222.

77. Shanawany, "Stages in the Development of a Population Control Program," 205.

78. Ibid., 204–5. Some of the groundwork for training in statistics had been laid previously. In 1951 a statistics training workshop sponsored by the United Nations and the World Health Organization was held in Cairo (see "Training Centre on Vital Statistics and Health Statistics for the Eastern Mediterranean," *L'Egypte Contemporaine* 42 (1951): 95–99).

79. Gamal Abdel-Nasser, as quoted in Shanawany, "Stages in the Development of a Population Control Program," 207.

80. Shanawany, "Stages in the Development of a Population Control Program," 207.

81. Omran and el-Nomrossey, "The Family Planning Effort in Egypt," 225–26.

82. Khalid Muhammad Khalid (1950), as quoted in Rizk, "Population Policies in Egypt," 39.

83. Wizarat al-awqaf, "Mawqif al-islam min tanzim al-usra," 143.
84. As quoted in Omran, *Family Planning in the Legacy of Islam*, 253–54.
85. Vaclav Havel, quoted in J. Scott, *Seeing Like a State*, 85.
86. This assertion begs the question of how a social-welfare mode of regulation may be distinguished from socioeconomic development. After the economic liberalization policies of Sadat (*Infitah*) in the mid-1970s, a global shift occurred in which local and international agents (such as the representatives of the state bourgeoisie and landowning interests in the state apparatus, led by Anwar Sadat; global multinational corporations with local liaisons; and USAID) actively incorporated Egypt into a neoliberal capitalist regime in which socioeconomic development became the state's primary object of governance. This led to the demonization of "the people," understood now as principally a population threat to be curbed (or redistributed to uninhabited parts of Egypt) rather than as a resource to be cultivated. In sum, although the type of individual subject sought in social-welfare and neo-liberal regimes may be rational, healthy, and modern; the type of collective national subject sought is different (in the former, a unified "happy family made of workers and peasants" inculcated with communitarian and socialist ethics; and in the latter, autonomous individuals who seek to maximize their own economic well-being). The means for attaining this goal are also altogether different. The social-welfare mode of regulation is integrated and characterized by comprehensive and holistic social schemes—addressing psychological, social, and economic issues all at once; whereas the neoliberal mode is disaggregated, with separate projects for health care, population control, economic development (community "income generating" projects are a classic example), and social services.

Conclusion

1. Guha, "On Some Aspects of the Historiography of Colonial India."
2. O'Hanlon, "Recovering the Subject."
3. Asad, *Genealogies of Religion*, 13–19. A recent anthropological attempt to critique liberal humanist notions of agentival subjectivity is Saba Mahmood's *The Politics of Piety*.
4. On this shift, see Gyan Prakash's thoughtful review essay, "Subaltern Studies as Postcolonial criticism."
5. Take, for example, a volume of the Subaltern Studies collective published in 1999. In the words of its editors, "we have always conceived the presence and pressure of subalternity to extend beyond subaltern groups; nothing—not elite practices, state policies, academic disciplines, literary texts, archival sources, language—was exempt from effects of subalternity. . . . The articles . . . deal with the intractable presence of subalternity in dominant formations and representations" (Bhadra et. al., *Subaltern Studies X*, v).
6. See Asad, "Ethnographic Representation, Statistics and Modern Power."
7. The entire corpus of the Subaltern Studies collective demonstrates this point; see, for instance, Guha, ed., *Subaltern Studies*.

8. Asad, *Genealogies of Religion*, 13.

9. Guha, "Dominance without Hegemony"; Asad, "Introduction," in *Genealogies of Religion*.

10. 'Ammar, "Ibn Khaldun's Prolegomena to History," 7. My understanding of unilinear progressive time is informed by Koselleck, *Futures Past*, 231–88.

11. Cf. Asad, *Formations of the Secular*, 222.

12. The verb *tatawarra* (to develop), according to Stetkevych, does not constitute a modern derivation. It was already used by al-Tawhidi (d. AH 414). The verb's original meaning was "to disguise oneself." Its modern meaning, "to develop or to change from state to state," was thus a modern semantic extension (Stetkevych, *The Modern Arabic Literary Language*, 42).

13. 'Ammar, "Ibn Khaldun's Prolegomena to History," 211–12.

14. These themes are pervasive in the works of Freud and Nietzsche; see, for example, Freud's *Totem and Taboo* and his *The Psychopathology of Everyday Life*, and Nietzsche's *Beyond Good and Evil* and *Thus Spoke Zarathustra*.

15. I draw here on Samah Selim's discussion of the rural imaginary, in which she discusses the affinitive, expansive time of rural life as a mode of narrativity that is epistemologically and geographically distinct from that of the bourgeois nationalist project. See Selim, *The Novel and the Rural Imaginary in Egypt*, especially chaps. 6–8.

Bibliography

Primary and secondary source books, articles, and dissertations in Arabic, English, and French are listed in one list (under "Other Sources"), to facilitate cross-referencing. Archives and primary-source periodicals published in Egypt are cited in full in the Notes.

Archives and Periodicals

Archives

Dar al-Watha'iq al-Qawmiyya (Egyptian National Archives)
    Al-Archif al-Urubi
        'Ahd Isma'il
    'Abdin 1906–55
        Al-jama'iyyat
        Mu'tamarat
    Majlis al-wuzara
        Al-fatra ba'd 1923
        Sharikat wa jama'iyyat
The American University in Cairo: Rare Books and Special Collections
    Hassan Fathy Archives
        Private Papers, Bahtim File
        Private Papers, Journals Collection
        Private Papers, Ministries Collection
        Private Papers, Mit Al-Nasara File

Periodicals

Al-Balagh
Bulletin de la Société de Géographie de Égypte (BSGE)

Bulletin de la Société Khédiviale de Géographie d'Égypte (BSKGE)
Bulletin de la Société Royale de Géographie d'Égypte (BSRGE)
Bulletin de la Société Sultanieh de Géographie d'Égypte (BSSGE)
Bulletin de l'Institut d'Egypte
L'Égypte Contemporaine
Al-Hilal
Al-'Imara
Al-Majalla al-Jadida
Al-Majalla al-Tibiyya al-Misriyya
Al-Majallat al-ijtima'iyyah al-qawmiyya / The National Review of Social Sciences
Majallat al-Shu'un al-Ijtima'iyya wa al-Ta'wun (Shu'un Ijtima'iyya)
Al-Mujtama' al-Jadid
Al-Muqtataf
La Revue du Caire
Al-Sahara'

Government Publications

Central Narcotics Intelligence Bureau (Egypt). *Annual Report for the Year 1938.* Cairo: Government Press, Bulaq, 1939.

———. *Annual Report for the Year 1939.* Cairo: Government Press, Bulaq, 1940.

Combined Rural Centres (Egypt). *A New Development in Rural Welfare Programmes.* Cairo, 1957.

Institute of National Planning (United Arab Republic). *Research Report on Employment Problems in Rural Areas of the United Arab Republic: Report B: Migration in the U.A.R.* Cairo: Institute of National Planning, 1965.

Ministry of Finance (Egypt). *Almanac for the Year 1929.* Cairo: Government Press, 1929.

———. *Almanac for the Year 1935.* Cairo: Government Press, 1935.

Ministry of Social Affairs (Egypt). *Social Welfare in Egypt.* Cairo: Government Press, 1950.

———. Fellah Department. *Annual Report on the Rural Welfare Centers.* Cairo: Ministry of Social Affairs, 1942.

Presidency of the Council of Ministers (Egypt). *The Unity of the Nile Valley: Its Geographical Bases and Its Manifestations in History.* Cairo: Government Press, 1947.

United Arab Republic. *The U.A.R. Yearbook 1960.* Cairo: Information Department, 1960.

Wizarat al-awqaf wa wizarat al-a'lam. *Mawqif al-islam min tanzim al-usra.* Cairo: State Information Service/Information, Education and Communication Center, 1991.

Wizarat al-istislah al-aradi, al-mu'assassa al-'amma lil istighlal wa al-tanmiya lil aradi al-mustasliha. *Takwin wa tanmiyat al-mujtama'at al-jadida fil aradi al-mustasliha.* Cairo: Ministry of Land Reclamation, 1969.

Wizarat al-shu'un al-ijtima'iyya. *Wizarat al-shu'un al-ijtima'iyya: nisha'atuha, tatawwuriha, wa khadamatuha.* Cairo: Information Department, Ministry of Social Affairs, 1955.

———. *Wizarat al-shu'un al-ijtima'iyya fi khamsa wa 'ishrin 'amm.* Cairo: Information Department, Ministry of Social Affairs, 1964.

Other Sources

Abbate, Onofrio. *Aegyptiaca.* Cairo: El-Madbouli, 1909.

al-Abd, Salah. "Land Reclamation and Resettlement in Egypt." In *Human Settlement on New Lands: Their Design and Development,* edited by Laila El-Hamamsy, 91–113. Cairo: Social Research Center/American University in Cairo Press, 1979.

Abdallah, Ahmed. *The Student Movement and Nationalist Politics in Egypt.* London: Saqi, 1985.

'Abd al-Rahman, 'Aisha [Bint al-Shati']. *Qadiyyat al-fellah.* Cairo: Makatabat al-nahda al-misriyya, 1939.

———. *Al-rif al-misri.* Cairo: Al-matba'a al-rahmaniyya, 1936.

Abdel-Fadil, Mahmoud. *Development, Income Distribution, and Social Change in Rural Egypt (1952–1970), A Study in the Political Economy of Agrarian Transition.* Cambridge: Cambridge University Press, 1975.

Abdel Kader, Soha. *Egyptian Women in a Changing Society, 1899–1987.* Boulder, CO: Lynne Rienner Publishers, 1987.

Abdel-Malek, Anouar. *Egypt: Military Society. The Army Regime, the Left and Social Change under Nasser.* Translated by Charles Lam Markmann. New York: Vintage, 1968.

———. *Idéologie et Renaissance Nationale: L'Egypte Moderne.* Paris: Anthropos, 1969.

———, ed. *Contemporary Arabic Political Thought.* Translated by Michael Pallis. London: Zed, 1983.

Abu-Rabi', Ibrahim M. *Intellectual Origins of Islamic Resurgence in the Modern Arab World.* Albany: State University of New York Press, 1996.

Abu Zayd, Hekmat. *Al-takayyuf al-ijtima'i fi al-rif al-misri al-jadid.* Cairo: Maktabat al-anglo al-misriyya, n.d.

Adams, Mark. "Toward a Comparative History of Eugenics." In Adams, *The Wellborn Science,* 217–31.

———, ed. *The Wellborn Science: Eugenics in Germany, France, Brazil, and Russia.* Oxford: Oxford University Press, 1990.

Afifi, Hafiz. *'Ala hamish al-siyasa: Ba'd masa'ilna al-qawmiyya.* Cairo: Matba'at dar al-kutub al-misriyya, 1938.

Agamben, Giorgio. *Homo Sacer: Sovereign Power and Bare Life.* Stanford, CA: Stanford University Press, 1998.

Ahmed, Leila. *Women, Gender and Islam.* New Haven, CT: Yale University Press, 1992.

Ali, Kamran Asdar. *Planning the Family in Egypt: New Bodies, New Selves*. Austin: University of Texas Press, 2002.

al-'Alim, Mahmud Amin. *Al-fikr al-'arabi bayn al-khususiyya wa al-kawniyya*. Cairo: Dar al-mustaqbal al-'arabi, 1996.

———. *Al-ibda' wa al-dalala: Muqarna nazariyya wa tatbiyqiyya*. Cairo: Dar al-mustaqbal al-'arabi, 1997.

al-'Alim, Mahmud Amin, and 'Abd al-Azim Anis. *Fi al-thaqafa al-misriyya*. Beirut: Dar al-fikr al-jadid, 1955.

Althusser, Louis. *Lenin and Philosophy and Other Essays*. Translated by Ben Brewster. New York: Monthly Review Press, 1971.

Amer ['Amir], Mustafa. "Some Problems of the Population of Egypt." In *Annexes of the Report of the Egyptian Delegates to the International Geographical Congress*. Cambridge, 1928. Reprint, Cairo: Al-ma'arif Printing Office, 1929.

Amin, Ahmed. *Qamus al-'adat wa al-taqalid wa al-ta'bir al-misriyya*. Cairo: Matba'at lajnat al-ta'alif wa al-tarjama wa al-nashr, 1953.

Amin, Galal. "Seventy-five Years of Economic Thought in Egypt." In *The Development of Social Science in Egypt: Economics, History and Sociology*, 2–17. Cairo Papers in Social Science, vol. 18, monograph 3. Cairo: American University in Cairo Press, 1996.

'Amir, Ibrahim. *Al-Ard wa al-fellah: al-masala al-zira'iyya fi Misr*. Cairo: Matba'at al-dar al-misriyya, 1958.

'Ammar, 'Abbas Mustafa. "Ba'd nawahi al-gughrafiyya al-bashariyya li shibh jazirat Sina." Master's thesis, Cairo University, 1936.

———. *A Demographic Study of an Egyptian Province (Sharqiya)*. London School of Economics, Monographs on Social Anthropology, no. 8. London: Percy Lund, Humphries & Co., 1942. Reprint Oxford and New York: BERG, 2004.

———. "Ibn Khaldun's Prolegomena to History: The Views of a Muslim Thinker of the 14th Century on the Development of Human Society and the Rise and Fall of States." Unpublished manuscript. Department of Geography and Anthropology, University of Manchester (c. 1941).

———. *The People of Sharqiya: Their Racial History, Serology, Physical Characters, Demography and Conditions of Life*, 2 vols. Cairo: Société de Géographie de Égypte, 1944.

———. "The Population Situation in Egypt and the Necessity for Planning a Population Policy for the Country." In *The Egyptian Association for Population Studies*, 5–17. Cairo: Imprimerie Misr S.A.E., 1960.

Anagnost, Ann. *National Past-Times: Narrative, Representation, and Power in Modern China*. Durham, NC: Duke University Press, 1997.

———. "A Surfeit of Bodies: Population and the Rationality of the State in Post-Mao China." In Ginsburg and Rapp, *Conceiving the New World Order*, 22–41.

al-Andalusi, Abu Qasim Sa'd bin Ahmed. *Tabaqat al-umam*. Cairo: Matba'at Muhammad Muhammad Mutran, n.d.

Anderson, Benedict. *Imagined Communities: Reflections on the Origins and Spread of Nationalism*. London: Verso, 1991.
Arafa, Bahiga. *The Social Activities of the Egyptian Feminist Union*. Cairo: Elias Modern Press, 1973.
Artin, Yacoub. *Contes populaires inedits de la Vallée du Nil, traduit de l'Arabe parlé*. Paris: Maisonneuve, 1895.
Asad, Talal. "Conscripts of Western Civilization." In *Civilization in Crisis*, edited by Christine Ward Gailey, 333–52. Gainesville: University Press of Florida, 1992.
———. "Ethnographic Representation, Statistics and Modern Power." *Social Research* 61, no. 1 (1994): 55–88.
———. *Formations of the Secular: Christianity, Islam, Modernity*. Stanford, CA: Stanford University Press, 2003.
———. *Genealogies of Religion: Discipline and Reasons of Power in Christianity and Islam*. Baltimore, MD: Johns Hopkins University Press, 1993.
———. "The Idea of An Anthropology of Islam." Occasional Papers Series. Washington, DC: Georgetown University Center for Contemporary Arab Studies, 1986.
———, ed. *Anthropology and the Colonial Encounter*. New York: Humanities Press, 1973.
Ashmawi, Sayyid. *Al-fellahun wa al-sulta: 'Ala daw' al-harakat al-fellahiyya al-misriyya (1919–1999)*. Cairo: Mirit, 2001.
Awad, Hassân. *La Société Royale de Géographie d'Égypte (1875–1950) Son Histoire—Ses Activités*. Cairo: Al Maaref, 1950.
Awad, Louis, ed. *The Literature of Ideas in Egypt*. Atlanta, GA: Scholars Press, 1986.
Ayrout, Henry Habib. *The Egyptian Peasant*. Cairo: American University in Cairo, 2005.
———. *The Fellaheen*. Translated by Hilary Wayment, foreword by M. Taher Pasha. Cairo: R. Schindler, 1945.
———. *Fellahs d'Egypte*. Forward by Fu'ad Abaza Pasha. Cairo: Horus, 1943.
———. *Fellahs d'Egypte*. Forward by Muhammad Ghallab. Cairo: Editions du Sphynx, 1952.
———. *Al-Fellahun*. Translated and annotated by Muhammad Ghallab. Cairo, 1944.
———. *Moeurs et coutumes des fellahs*. Forward by Andre Allix. Paris: Payot, 1938.
al-Babli, Muhammad. *Al-ijram fi Misr: Asbabuh wa turuq 'ilajiha*. Cairo: Dar al-kutub al-misriyya, 1941.
Badran, Margot. *Feminists, Islam, and Nation: Gender and the Making of Modern Egypt*. Princeton, NJ: Princeton University Press, 1995.
Baer, Gabriel. *A History of Landownership in Modern Egypt 1800–1950*. London: Oxford University Press, 1962.

———. *Studies in the Social History of Modern Egypt*. Chicago: University of Chicago Press, 1969.
Balibar, Etienne. "Fichte and the Internal Border: On *Addresses to the German Nation*." In *Masses, Classes, Ideas: Studies on Politics and Philosophy before and after Marx*, 61–85. Translated by James Swenson. London: Routledge, 1994.
Balibar, Etienne, and Immanuel Wallerstein. *Race, Nation, Class: Ambiguous Identities*. New York: Verso, 1991.
Barakat, 'Ali. *Tatawwur al-milkiyya al-zira'iyya fi Misr wa atharuh 'ala al-haraka al-siyasiyya 1813–1924*. Cairo: Dar al-thaqafa al-jadida, 1977.
el-Barawy [al-Barrawi], Rashed. *The Military Coup in Egypt: An Analytic Study*. Cairo: Renaissance Bookshop, 1952.
Barnett, Clive. "Impure and Worldly Geography: The Africanist Discourse of the Royal Geographical Society, 1831–1879." *Transactions of the Institute of British Geographers* New Series vol. 23, no. 2 (1998): 239–51.
Baron, Beth. "The Construction of National Honor in Egypt." *Gender and History* 5, no.2 (1993): 244–55.
———. *Egypt as a Woman: Nationalism, Gender, and Politics*. Berkeley: University of California Press, 2005.
———. "Mothers, Morality and Nationalism in Pre-1919 Egypt." In *The Origins of Arab Nationalism*, edited by Rashid Khalidi et.al., 271–88. New York: Columbia University Press, 1991.
———. *The Women's Awakening in Egypt: Culture, Society, and the Press*. New Haven, CT: Yale University Press, 1994.
al-Barrawi, Rashid, and Muhammad 'Ulaysh. *Al-tatawwur al-iqtisadi fi Misr fi al-asr al-hadith*. 5th edition. Cairo: Maktabat al-nahdah al-misriyyah, 1954.
Barshay, Andrew. "The Social Sciences in Japan." In Porter and Ross, *The Cambridge History of Science*, 513–35.
———. *The Social Sciences in Modern Japan: The Marxian and Modernist Traditions (Twentieth Century Japan: The Emergence of a World Power)*. Berkeley: University of California, 2004.
Bassiouni, Mohammed Salah Abdel-Meguid. "Mudiriyat al-Tahrir kanamudhaj lil mujtama'at al-mukhatata (Planned Communities: A Case Study of the Tahrir Province Community as a Pattern)." Master's thesis, Ayn Shams University, 1972.
Beattie, Kirk. *Egypt During the Nasser Years: Ideology, Politics and Civil Society*. Boulder, CO: Westview Press, 1994.
Beinin, Joel. "Egypt: Society and Economy, 1923–1952." In *The Cambridge History of Modern Egypt, Modern Egypt from 1517 to the End of the Twentieth Century*, vol. 2, edited by M. W. Daly, 309–33. Cambridge: Cambridge University Press, 1998.
Beinin, Joel, and Zachary Lockman. *Workers on the Nile: Nationalism, Communism, Islam and the Egyptian Working Class, 1882–1954*. Princeton, NJ: Princeton University Press, 1987.

Bernal, Martin. *Black Athena: The Afroasiatic Roots of Classical Civilization*, 2 vols. London: Free Association Books, 1987.
Bernard, Augustin. "La charrue en Afrique." In Union Géographique Internationale, *Congrès Internationale de Géographie*, vol. 4, 283–293.
———. *Enquête sur l'habitation rurale des indigènes de l'Algérie*. Algiers, 1921.
———. *Enquête sur l'habitation rurale des indigènes de la Tunisie*. Tunis, 1924.
Berque, Jacques. *Egypt: Imperialism and Revolution*. Translated by Jean Stewart. New York: Praeger, 1972.
Bhadra, Gautam, Gyan Prakash, and Susie Tharu, eds. *Subaltern Studies X: Writings on South Asian History and Society*. Oxford: Oxford University Press, 1999.
Bianchi, Robert. *Unruly Corporatism: Associational Life in Twentieth-Century Egypt*. Oxford: Oxford University Press, 1989.
Blackman, Winifred. "Ancient Egyptian Custom Illustrated by a Modern Survival." *Man* 25, no. 38 (1925): 65–67.
———. *The Fellāhīn of Upper Egypt: Their Religious, Social and Industrial Life To-Day with Special Reference to Survivals from Ancient Times*. London: George G. Harrap, 1927.
Bock, Gisela, and Pat Thane. *Maternity and Gender Policies: Women and the Rise of the European Welfare States, 1880s–1950s*. London: Routledge, 1991.
Bonar, J. "Population: Economic Theory." In *Palgrave's Dictionary of Political Economy*, ed. Robert Harry Inglis Palgrave, 2nd ed. (ed. Henry Higgs), vol. 3, 162–69. London: Macmillan, 1926.
Bonaudo, Marta, and Elida Sonzogni. "To Populate and to Discipline: Labor Market Construction in the Province of Santa Fe, Argentina, 1850–1890." Translated by Andrew Klatt. *Latin American Perspectives* 26, no. 1 (1999): 65–91.
Booth, Marilyn. *May Her Likes Be Multiplied: Biography and Gender Politics in Egypt*. Berkeley: University of California Press, 2001.
———. "Talal Asad, *Formations of the Secular: Christianity, Islam, Modernity*" (book review). *Bryn Mawr Review of Comparative Literature* 4, no. 2 (Spring 2004): n.p. http://www.brynmawr.edu/bmrcl/ Summer2004/Asad.html.
Borthwick, Meredith. *The Changing Role of Women in Bengal 1849–1905*. Princeton, NJ: Princeton University Press, 1984.
Bose, Pradip Kumar. "Sons of the Nation: Child Rearing in the New Family." In Chatterjee, *Texts of Power*, 118–44.
Botman, Selma. "The Liberal Age, 1923–1952." In Daly, *The Cambridge History of Modern Egypt*, 285–308.
Bovier-Lapierre, Paul. "L'Égypte Préhistorique." In *Précis de l'Histoire d'Égypte par diverse historiens et archéologues*, vol. 1, 1–50. Cairo: Institut Français d'Archaéologie Orientale du Caire, 1932.
Boyer, Christopher. "Old Loves, New Loyalties: Agrarismo in Michoacán, 1920–1928." *Hispanic American Historical Review* 78, no. 3 (1998): 419–55.
Boyer, Robert. *The Regulation School: A Critical Introduction*. Translated by Craig Charney. New York: Columbia University Press, 1990.

Brown, Nathan. "The Ignorance and Inscrutability of the Egyptian Peasant." In *Peasants and Politics in the Modern Middle East*, edited by John Waterbury and Farhad Kazemi, 203–21. Miami: Florida International Press, 1991.

———. *Peasant Politics in Modern Egypt: The Struggle Against the State*. New Haven, CT: Yale University Press, 1990.

Brunhes, Jean. *Human Geography: An Attempt at a Positive Classification*. Translated by I. C. Le Compte, edited by I. Bowman and R. E. Dodge. New York: Rand McNally, 1920.

Burton, Richard. *Personal Narrative of a Pilgrimage to al-Madinah and Meccah*. New York: Dover, 1964 [1893].

Cabrera, Miguel A. "The Crisis of the Social and Post-social History." *The European Legacy* 10, no.6 (2005): 611–20.

Carr-Saunders, Alexander Morris. *Population*. London: Oxford University Press, 1925.

———. *World Population: Past Growth and Present Trends*. Oxford: Oxford University Press, 1936.

Çelik, Zeynap. *Displaying the Orient: Architecture of Islam at Nineteenth Century World's Fairs*. Berkeley and Los Angeles: University of California Press, 1992.

Césaire, Aimé. *Discourse on Colonialism*. Translated by Joan Pinkham. New York: Monthly Review Press, 2000.

Chakrabarty, Dipesh. "The Difference-Deferral of a Colonial Modernity: Public Debates on Domesticity in British Bengal." In *Subaltern Studies* 8, edited by David Arnold and David Hardiman, 50–88. Delhi: Oxford University Press, 1994.

———. *Provincializing Europe: Postcolonial Thought and Historical Difference*. Princeton, NJ: Princeton University Press, 2000.

Chalcraft, John. *The Striking Cabbies of Cairo and Other Stories: Crafts and Guilds in Egypt, 1863–1914*. Albany: State University of New York Press, 2004.

Chatterjee, Partha. "The Disciplines in Colonial Bengal." In Chatterjee, *Texts of Power*, 1–29.

———. "A Modern Science of Politics for the Colonized." In Chatterjee, *Texts of Power*, 93–117.

———. *The Nation and Its Fragments: Colonial and Postcolonial Histories*. Princeton, NJ: Princeton University Press, 1993.

———. *Nationalist Thought and the Colonial World: A Derivative Discourse*. Minneapolis: University of Minnesota Press, 1986.

———, ed. *Texts of Power: Emerging Disciplines in Colonial Bengal*. Minneapolis: University of Minnesota Press, 1995.

Chiffoleau, Sylvie. "La réforme sociale par l'hygiène: Une formule pour médicaliser les campagnes." In Roussillon, *Entre reforme sociale et mouvement national*, 421–41.

Clark, A. Kim. "Racial Ideologies and the Quest for National Development: Debating the Agrarian Problem in Ecuador (1930–1950)." *Journal of Latin American Studies* 30, no. 2 (1998): 373–93.

Claval, Paul. "L'habitat rural." In Union Géographique Internationale—Commission Histoire de la Pensée Géographique, *La géographie à travers un siècle de congrès internationaux*, 131–45.

———. "Playing with Mirrors: The British Empire According to Albert Demangeon." In Godlewska and Smith, *Geography and Empire*, 228–43.

Clay, Catherine. "Russian Ethnographers in the Service of Empire, 1856–1862." *Slavic Review* 54, no.1 (1995): 45–61.

Cleland, Wendell. *The Population Problem in Egypt*. Lancaster: Science Press, 1936.

Clifford, James. *The Predicament of Culture: Twentieth-Century Ethnography, Literature, and Art*. Cambridge, MA: Harvard University Press, 1988.

Clifford, James, and George E. Marcus, eds. *Writing Culture: The Poetics and Politics of Ethnography*. Berkeley: University of California Press, 1986.

Cohn, Bernard. *Colonialism and Its Forms of Knowledge: The British in India*. Princeton, NJ: Princeton University Press, 1996.

Cohn, Bernard, and Nicholas Dirks. "Beyond the Fringe: The Nation-State, Colonialism, and Technologies of Power." *Journal of Historical Sociology* 1, no. 2 (1988): 224–29.

Cole, Juan. *Colonialism and Revolution in the Middle East: Social and Cultural Origins of Egypt's 'Urabi Movement*. Princeton, NJ: Princeton University Press, 1993.

Colla, Elliott. "The Stuff of Egypt: The Nation, the State, and Their Proper Objects." *New Formations* 45 (Winter 2001–02): 72–90.

Conklin, Alice. *A Mission to Civilize: The Republican Idea of Empire in France and West Africa, 1895–1930*. Stanford, CA: Stanford University Press, 1997.

Connelly, Matthew. "Population Control Is History: New Perspectives on the International Campaign to Limit Population Growth." *Comparative Studies in Society and History* 45, no.1 (2003): 122–47.

Cooper, Frederick. *Colonialism in Question: Theory, Knowledge, History*. Berkeley: University of California Press, 2005.

Cooper, Frederick, and Ann Stoler, eds. *Tensions of Empire: Colonial Cultures in a Bourgeois World*. Berkeley: University of California Press, 1997.

Craib, Raymond B. "A National Metaphysics: State Fixations, National Maps, and the Geo-Historical Imagination in Nineteenth-Century Mexico." *Hispanic American Historical Review* 82, no.1 (2002): 33–86.

Cromer, Earl of. *Modern Egypt*. 2 vols. New York: Macmillan, 1908.

Cunningham, John Wood, ed. *Thomas Robert Malthus: Critical Assessments*. 4 vols. London: Croom Helm, 1986.

Cuno, Kenneth M. *The Pasha's Peasants: Land, Society, and Economy in Lower Egypt, 1740–1858*. Cambridge: Cambridge University Press, 1992.

Cuno, Kenneth M., and Michael J. Reimer. "The Census Registers of Nineteenth-Century Egypt: A New Source for Social Historians." *British Journal of Middle Eastern Studies* 24, no. 2 (1997): 193–216.

al-Dabaʿ, Mustafa. *Ruwayyit al-fellah, fellah al-ruwayya*. Cairo: Al-hay'a al-misriyya al-ʿamma lil kitab, 1998.

Dale, Stephen Frederic. "Ibn Khaldun: The Last Greek and the First *Annaliste* Historian." *International Journal of Middle East Studies* 38, no.3 (2006): 431–51.

Dalton, Hugh. "The Theory of Population," *Economica* 8 (March 1928): 28–50.

Daly, M. W. *Empire on the Nile: The Anglo-Egyptian Sudan, 1898–1934*. Cambridge: Cambridge University Press, 1986.

———. *Imperial Sudan: The Anglo-Egyptian Condominium, 1934–1956*. Cambridge: Cambridge University Press, 1991.

———, ed. *The Cambridge History of Modern Egypt*. Vol. 2, *Modern Egypt, from 1517 to the End of the Twentieth Century*. Cambridge: Cambridge University Press, 1998.

Davin, Anna. "Imperialism and Motherhood." *History Workshop* 5 (1978): 9–65.

Deeb, Marius. *Party Politics in Egypt: The Wafd and Its Rivals 1919–1939*. St. Anthony's Middle East Monographs No.9. London: Ithaca Press, 1979.

de Grazia, Victoria. *How Fascism Ruled Women: Italy, 1922–1945*. Berkeley: University of California Press, 1992.

Demangeon, Albert. "De l'influence des régimes agraires sur les modes d'habitat dans l'Europe occidentale." In Union Géographique Internationale, *Congrès Internationale de Géographie*, 4: 92–97.

———. "La géographie de l'habitat rural." *Annales de Géographie* 36 (1927): 1–23, 97–114.

———. "L'habitation rurale en France." *Annales de Géographie* 29 (1920): 352–75, pl. 9–12.

———. "Problèmes actuels et aspects nouveaux de la vie rurale en Égypt." *Annales de Géographie* 35 (1926): 155–73.

———. *Problèmes de géographie humaine*. Paris: Armand Colin, 1947.

———. "Un questionnaire sur l'habitat rural." *Annales de Géographie* 35 (1926): 289–92.

Deringil, Selim. *The Well-Protected Domains: Ideology and the Legitimation of Power in the Ottoman Empire, 1876–1909*. London: I.B. Tauris, 1998.

Dirks, Nicholas. *Castes of Mind: Colonialism and the Making of Modern India*. Princeton, NJ: Princeton University Press, 2001.

al-Disuqi, 'Asim. *Kibar al-mullak al-aradi al-zira'iyya wa dawruhum fi al-mujtama' al-misri, 1914–1952*. Cairo: Dar al-thaqafa al-jadida, 1975.

———. *Misr fi al-harb al-'alamiyya al-thaniyya, 1939–1945*. Cairo: Jami'at al-duwwal al-'arabiyya, Al-munazzama al-'arabiyya lil tarbiya wa al-thaqafa wa al-'ulum, Ma'had al-buhuth wa al-dirasat al-arabiyya, 1976.

Douin, Georges. *Histoire du règne du Khédive Ismail*. Vol. 3a, *L'empire africaine (1874–1876)*. Cairo: Société Royale de Géographie d'Égypte, 1941.

Doumani, Beshara, ed. *Family History in the Middle East: Household, Property, and Gender*. Albany: State University of New York Press, 2003.

Driver, Felix. *Geography Militant: Cultures of Exploration and Empire*. Oxford: Blackwell, 2001.

Duben, Alan, and Cem Behar. *Istanbul Households: Marriage, Family and Fertility, 1880–1940*. Cambridge: Cambridge University Press, 1991.

Edison, Paul N. "Conquest Unrequited: French Expeditionary Science in Mexico, 1864–1867." *French Historical Studies* 26, no.3 (2003): 459–95.

Egger, Vernon. *A Fabian in Egypt: Salamah Musa and the Rise of the Professional Classes in Egypt, 1909–1939*. Lanham, MD: University Press of America, 1986.

Egyptian Association for Social Studies (Al-jamaʿiyya al-misriyya lil dirasat al-ijtimaʿiyya). *Taqrir majlis al-idara ʿan sanat 1943*. Cairo: Matbaʿat al-ʿatimad, 1944.

Elshakry, Marwa. "Darwin's Legacy in the Arab East: Science, Religion and Politics, 1870–1914." Ph.D. diss., Princeton University, 2003.

Esmeir, Samera. "The Work of Law in the Age of Empire: Production of Humanity in Colonial Egypt." Ph.D. diss., New York University, 2005.

Eze, Emmanuel Chukwudi. *Race and the Enlightenment: A Reader*. Cambridge, MA: Blackwell, 1997.

Fabian, Johannes. *Out of Our Minds: Reason and Madness in the Exploration of Central Africa*. Berkeley: University of California Press, 2000.

———. *Time and the Other: How Anthropology Makes Its Object*. New York: Columbia University Press, 1983.

Fahmy, Khaled. *All the Pasha's Men: Mehmed Ali, His Army and the Making of Modern Egypt*. Cambridge: Cambridge University Press, 1998.

Fanon, Frantz. *Wretched of the Earth*. Translated by Richard Philcox. New York: Grove, 2004.

Fathy, Hassan. *Architecture for the Poor: An Experiment in Rural Egypt*. Cairo: American University in Cairo, 1989 [1969].

———. *Natural Energy and Vernacular Architecture: Principles and Examples with Reference to Hot Arid Climates*. Chicago: University of Chicago Press, 1986.

———. "Planning and Building in the Arab Tradition: The Village Experiment at Gourna." In *The New Metropolis in the Arab World*, edited by Morroe Berger, 211–29. New York: Octagon, 1974.

Fleure, Herbert John. *The Races of England and Wales: A Survey of Recent Research*. London: Benn Brothers, 1923.

———. "Racial Evolution and Archaeology." Huxley Memorial Lecture. *Journal of the Royal Anthropological Institute* 67 (1937): 1–25.

Foucart, George. *Histoire des religions et méthode comparative*. Paris: A. Picard, 1912.

———. *Introductory Questions on African Ethnology*. Cairo: Printing Office of the French Institute of Oriental Archaeology, 1919.

Foucart, George, and Adolphe Cattaui Bey. *La Société Sultanieh de Géographie du Caire: Son ouevre, 1875–1921*. Cairo: Imprimerie de l'Institut Français d'Archéologie Orientale, 1921.

Foucault, Michel. *The Archaeology of Knowledge*. Translated by A. M. Sheridan Smith. London: Tavistock, 1972.

———. "Governmentality." In *The Foucault Effect*, edited by Graham Burchell, Colin Gordon, and Peter Miller, 87–104. Chicago: University of Chicago Press, 1991.

———. *History of Sexuality*. Vol. 1, *An Introduction*. Translated by Robert Hurley. New York: Vintage, 1990.
Freeman, Walter. "Geography from Congress to Congress." In Union Géographique Internationale—Commission Histoire de la Pensée Géographique, *La géographie à travers un siècle*, 197–209.
Freud, Sigmund. *Totem and Taboo: Resemblances Between the Psychic Life of Savages and Neurotics*. Translated by A. A. Brill. London: Routledge, 1919.
———. *The Psychopathology of Everyday Life*. In *The Basic Writings of Sigmund Freud*, translated and edited by A. A. Brill. New York: Modern Library, 1938.
Frevert, Ute. "The Civilizing Tendency of Hygiene." In *German Women in the Nineteenth Century: A Social History*, edited by John Fout, 320–44. New York: Holmes and Meier, 1984.
Frierson, Cathy. *Peasant Icons: Representations of Rural People in Late Nineteenth-Century Russia*. New York: Oxford University Press, 1993.
Gadamer, Hans-Georg. *Truth and Method*. 2nd revised edition, translation revised by Joel Weinsheimer and Donald Marshall. New York: Continuum, 1994.
Gallagher, Nancy Elizabeth. *Egypt's Other Wars: Epidemics and the Politics of Public Health*. Syracuse, NY: Syracuse University Press, 1990.
Galton, Francis. "Identification Offices in India and Egypt." *Nineteenth Century* 48 (1900): 118–26.
Gasper, Michael. "Civilizing Peasants: The Public Sphere, Islamic Reform and the Generation of Political Modernity in Egypt, 1875–1919." Ph.D. diss., New York University, 2004.
Gershoni, Israel. "The Theory of Crisis and the Crisis in a Theory: Intellectual History in Twentieth-Century Middle Eastern Studies." In Gershoni et. al., *Middle East Historiographies*, 131–82.
Gershoni, Israel, and James Jankowski. *Egypt, Islam, and the Arabs: The Search for Egyptian Nationhood, 1900–1930*. New York: Oxford University Press, 1987.
———. *Redefining the Egyptian Nation, 1930–1945*. Cambridge Middle East Studies 2. Cambridge: Cambridge University Press, 1995.
Gershoni, Israel, Amy Singer, and Y. Hakan Erdem, eds. *Middle East Historiographies: Narrating the Twentieth Century*. Seattle: University of Washington Press, 2006.
Ghali, Mirrit Butrus. *Al-islah al-zira'i: Al-milkiyya, al-ijar, al-'amal*. Cairo: Jama'at al-nahda al-qawmiyya, 1945.
———. *The Policy of Tomorrow*. Translated by Ismail el Faruqi. Washington, D.C.: American Council of Learned Societies, 1953 [1938].
Ghallab, Mohammed. *Les survivances de l'Égypte antique dans le folklore égyptien moderne*. Paris: Librairie Orientaliste, 1929.
al-Ghazali, Abu Hamid Muhammad. *Ihya' 'ulum al-din*. Cairo: Matba'at al-istiqama, 1965.
Ghosh, Kaushik. "A Market for Aboriginality: Primitivism and Race Classification in the Indentured Labour Market of Colonial India." In Bhadra, Prakash, and Tharu, *Subaltern Studies X*, 8–48.

Gilbert, Geoffrey, ed. *Malthus: Critical Responses*. 4 vols. London and New York: Routledge, 1998.
Gini, Corrado. "The Cyclical Rise and Fall of Population." In *Population: Lectures on the Harris Foundation 1929*, 1–140. Chicago: University of Chicago Press, 1930.
———. "Some Considerations of the Optimum Density of a Population." In Sanger, *Proceedings of the World Population Conference*, 118–22.
Ginsburg, Faye, and Rayna Rapp, eds. *Conceiving the New World Order: The Global Politics of Reproduction*. Berkeleys: University of California Press, 1995.
Girgis, Fawzi. *Dirasat fi tarikh Misr al-siyasi munzu' al-asr al-mamluki*. Cairo: Matba'at al-dar al-misriyya lil tiba'a wa-al-nashr wa-al-tawzi'a, 1958.
Glassman, Jonathan. "Slower than a Massacre: The Multiple Sources of Racial Thought in Colonial Africa." *American Historical Review* 109, no. 3 (2004): 720–54.
Godlewska, Anne. "Map, Text and Image: The Mentality of Enlightened Conquerors. A New Look at the *Description de l'Egypte*." *Transactions of the Institute of British Geographers* New Series, vol. 20, no. 1 (1995): 5–28.
———. "Napoleon's Geographers (1797–1815): Imperialists and Soldiers of Modernity." In Godlewska and Smith, *Geography and Empire*, 31–53.
Godlewska, Anne, and Neil Smith, eds. *Geography and Empire*. Oxford: Blackwell, 1994.
Goldberg, Ellis. "The Historiography of Crisis in the Egyptian Political Economy." In Gershoni et. al. *Middle East Historiographies*, 183–207.
———. "Peasants in Revolt—1919." *International Journal of Middle East Studies* 24, no. 2 (May 1992), 261–80.
———. *Tinker, Tailor, and Textile Worker: Class and Politics in Egypt, 1930–1952*. Berkeley: University of California Press, 1986.
Goldscheid, R. "Discussion." In Sanger, *Proceedings of the World Population Conference*, 104–5.
Goldschmidt, Arthur Jr. *Biographical Dictionary of Modern Egypt*. Cairo: American University in Cairo Press, 2000.
Goldschmidt, Arthur Jr., Amy Johnson, and Barak Salmoni, eds. *Re-Envisioning Egypt, 1919–1952*. Cairo: American University in Cairo Press, 2005.
Goldstein, Jan. *Console and Classify: The French Psychiatric Profession in the Nineteenth Century*. Cambridge: Cambridge University Press, 1988.
Gordon, Joel. *Nasser's Blessed Movement: Egypt's Free Officers and the July Revolution*. Oxford: Oxford University Press, 1992.
Gorman, Anthony. "Anarchists in Education: The Free Popular University (1901)." *Middle Eastern Studies* 41, no. 3 (2005): 303–20.
Goswami, Manu. *Producing India: From Colonial Economy to National Space*. Chicago: University of Chicago Press, 2004.
Gramsci, Antonio. *Selections from the Prison Notebooks of Antonio Gramsci*. Translated and edited by Quintin Hoare and Geoffrey Nowell Smith. New York: International Publishers, 1971.

Gran, Peter. *Beyond Eurocentrism: A New View of Modern World History*. Syracuse, NY: Syracuse University Press, 1996.

Gregory, Derek. "Between the Book and the Lamp: Imaginative Geographies of Egypt, 1849–50." *Transactions of the Institute of British Geographers* New Series, vol. 20, no. 1 (1995): 29–57.

Guha, Ranajit. "Dominance Without Hegemony and its Historiography." In Guha, *Subaltern Studies*, vol. 6, 210–309.

———. *Elementary Aspects of Peasant Insurgency in Colonial India*. Delhi: Oxford University Press, 1983.

———. "On Some Aspects of the Historiography of Colonial India." In Guha, *Subaltern Studies*, vol. 1, 1–7.

———, ed. *Subaltern Studies*. 6 vols. Delhi: Oxford University Press, 1982–89.

Hacking, Ian. "Biopower and the Avalanche of Printed Numbers." *Humanities in Society* 5 (1982): 279–95.

———. *The Taming of Chance*. Cambridge: Cambridge University Press, 1990.

Haddon, A. C. *Reports of the Cambridge Anthropological Expedition to Torres Straits*. Vol. 2, *Physiology and Psychology*. Cambridge: Cambridge University Press, 1901–03.

Haj, Samira. *The Making of Iraq 1900–1963: Capital, Power and Ideology*. Syracuse, NY: Syracuse University Press, 1997.

———. "Reconfiguring Tradition: Islamic Reform, Rationality and Modernity." Unpublished ms.

al-Hakim, Tawfiq. *The Return of Consciousness*. Translated by Bayly Winder. London: Macmillan, 1985.

Hambly, Wilfred Dyson. "Moeurs et coutumes des fellahs." *American Sociological Review* 5, no. 2 (April 1940): 276–77.

Hamid, Ra'uf 'Abbas. *Al-haraka al-'ummaliyya fi Misr, 1899–1952*. Cairo: Dar al-katib al-'arabi lil-tiba'ah wa-al-nashr, 1967.

———. *Al-haraka al-'ummaliyya fi Misr fi daw' al-watha'iq al-baritaniyya, 1924–1937*. Cairo: 'Alam al-kutub, 1975.

———. *Jama'at al-nahda al-qawmiyya*. Cairo: Dar al-fikr lil dirasat wa-al-nashr wa-al-tawzi'a, 1986.

———. *Al-nizam al-ijtima'i fi Misr fi zil al-milkiyya al-zira'iyya al-kibira 1837–1914*. Cairo: Dar al-katib al-'arabi lil-tiba'ah wa-al-nashr, 1973.

Hamid, Ra'uf 'Abbas, and Asim al-Disuqi. *Kibar al-mullak wa al-fellahin fi Misr 1837–1952*. Cairo: Dar qiba lil-tiba'ah wa-al-nashr wa-al-tawzi'a, 1998.

Hannaford, Ivan. *Race: The History of an Idea in the West*. Baltimore, MD: Johns Hopkins University Press, 1996.

Harvey, David. *The Condition of Postmodernity: An Enquiry into the Origins of Cultural Change*. Oxford: Blackwell, 1989.

———. "Population, Resources and the Ideology of Science." In Cunningham, *Thomas Robert Malthus*, vol. 1, 308–35.

Hasanayn, Ali Fu'ad. *Qasasuna al-sha'bi*. Cairo: Dar al-fikr al-'arabi, 1947.

Hasanayn, Magdi. *Al-Sahara': Al-thawra wa al-tharwa—Qissat mudiriyat al-Tahrir*. Cairo:Al-Hay'a al-misriyya al-'amma lil-kitab, 1975.
Herzfeld, Michael. *Ours Once More: Folklore, Ideology and the Making of Modern Greece*. Austin: University of Texas Press, 1982.
Heyworth-Dunne, J. *An Introduction to the History of Education in Modern Egypt*. London: Luzac, 1939.
Hinnebusch, Raymond. *Egyptian Politics under Sadat*. Cambridge: Cambridge University Press, 1985.
Hochschild, Adam. *King Leopold's Ghost: A Story of Greed, Terror, and Heroism in Colonial Africa*. Boston: Mariner, 1999.
Hodgen, Margaret T. *The Doctrine of Survivals: A Chapter in the History of Scientific Method in the Study of Man*. London: Allenson, 1936.
Holt, P. M., and M. W. Daly. *A History of the Sudan: From the Coming of Islam to the Present day*. 5th edition. Harlow, UK: Pearson Education, 2000.
Hopkins, Nicholas, et. al. *Participation and Community in the Egyptian New Lands: The Case of South Tahrir*. Cairo Papers in Social Science, vol. 11, monograph 1. Cairo: American University in Cairo Press, 1988.
Horn, David. *Social Bodies: Science, Reproduction and Italian Modernity*. Princeton, NJ: Princeton University Press, 1994.
Horne, Janet R. *A Social Laboratory for Modern France: The Musée Social and the Rise of the Welfare State*. Durham, NC: Duke University Press, 2002.
Hourani, Albert. *Arabic Thought in the Liberal Age, 1798–1939*. Cambridge: Cambridge University Press, 1983.
Howland, Douglas. "Society Reified: Herbert Spencer and Political Theory in Early Meiji Japan." *Comparative Studies in Society and History* 42, no.1 (2000): 67–86.
Hug, Georges. *Le Fayoum et ses abords: Etude de geographie physique, économique, et humaine*. Cairo: Publications de la Société Royale de Géographie d'Égypte, n.d.
Hunt, Nancy Rose. *A Colonial Lexicon of Birth Ritual, Medicalization, and Mobility in the Congo*. Durham, NC: Duke University Press, 1999.
Husayn, Ahmed. *Al-ard al-tayyiba*. Cairo, 1950.
Husayn, Taha. *Falsafat Ibn Khaldun al-ijtima'iyya: tahlil wa naqd*. Translated by 'Abd Allah 'Inan. Cairo: Matba'at al-'itimad, 1925.
———. *Mustaqbal al-thaqafa fi Misr*. Cairo: Matba'at al-ma'arif, 1938.
Hussein, Mahmoud. *Class Conflict in Egypt (1945–1971)*. New York: Monthly Review Press, 1978.
Hussein [Husayn], Taha. *The Days: His Autobiography in Three Parts*. Translated by E. H. Paxton, Hilary Wayment, and Kenneth Cragg. Cairo: American University in Cairo Press, 1997.
Husseini, Samira. "The Reconstruction of Siriakous Village." Bachelor's thesis, American University in Cairo, 1951.
Huzayyin, Sulayman A. S. *Arabia and the Far East: Their Commercial and Cultural*

Relations in Graeco-Roman Times and Irano-Arabian Times. Cairo: Publications de la Société Royale de Géographie d'Égypte, 1942.

———. "Egyptian University Scientific Expedition to S.W. Arabia," *Nature* 140 (September 18, 1937): 513–14.

Ibn Khaldun, *The Muqaddimah: An Introduction to History.* Translated by Franz Rosenthal. Princeton, NJ: Princeton University Press, 1967.

Ibrahim, Hassan Ahmed. "The Egyptian Empire, 1805–1885," In Daly, *The Cambridge History of Modern Egypt*, 198–216.

Ilbert, Robert, and Ilios Yannakakis, eds., with Jacques Hassoun. *Alexandria 1860–1960: The Brief Life of a Cosmopolitan Community.* Translated by Colin Clement. Alexandria, Egypt: Harpocrates, 1997.

Isma'il, Abdel Rahman. *Al-tibb al-rukka.* Partially translated by John Walker as *Folk Medicine in Modern Egypt, Being the Relevant Parts of the Tibb Al-Rukka or Old Wives Medicine of 'Abd Al-Rahman Isma'il.* London: Luzac, 1934.

Issawi, Charles. *Egypt at Mid-Century, An Economic Survey.* London: Oxford University Press, 1954.

Istiphan, Isis. *Directory of Social Agencies in Cairo.* Cairo: Social Research Center/American University in Cairo, 1956.

al-Jabarti, Abd al-Rahman. *Napoleon in Egypt: Al-Jabarti's Chronicle of the First Seven Months of the French Occupation of Egypt, 1798.* Translated by Shmuel Moreh. Princeton, NJ: Markus Weiner, 1993.

Jankowski, James. *Egypt's Young Rebels, "Young Egypt": 1932–1952.* Stanford, CA: Hoover Institution Press, 1975.

Jasanoff, Maya. *The Edge of Empire: Lives, Culture, and Conquest in the East, 1750–1850.* New York: Vintage, 2006.

Jeppie, Shamil. "Constructing a Colony on the Nile, c. 1820–1870." Ph.D. diss., Princeton University, 1997.

Johnson, Amy. *Reconstructing Rural Egypt: Ahmed Hussein and the History of Egyptian Development.* Syracuse, NY: Syracuse University Press, 2004.

Johnson, Pamela, et. al. *Egypt: The Egyptian Rural Improvement Service, A Point Four Project, 1952–1963*, AID Project Impact Evaluation Report no. 43. Cairo: USAID/Egypt, 1983.

Jordanova, Ludmilla. "Interrogating the Concept of Reproduction in the Eighteenth Century." In Ginsburg and Rapp, *Conceiving the New World Order*, 369–86.

Kamal, Muharram. *Athar hadarat al-fara'inah fi hayatuna al-haliyah.* Cairo: Dar al-hilal, 1956.

Kanaaneh, Rhoda Ann. *Birthing the Nation: Strategies of Palestinian Women in Israel.* Berkeley: University of California Press, 2002.

Kearns, Gerry. "The Imperial Subject: Geography and Travel in the Work of Mary Kingsley and Halford Mackinder." *Transactions of the Institute of British Geographers* New Series, vol. 22, no. 4 (1997): 450–72.

Khalid, Khalid Muhammad. *Min huna' nabda'.* Cairo: Mu'assasat al-khanji, 1958.

Khanna, Ranjana. *Dark Continents: Psychoanalysis and Colonialism*. Durham, NC: Duke University Press, 2003.
Kholoussy, Hanan. "Talking about a Revolution: Gender and the Politics of Marriage in Early Twentieth-Century Egypt." *Journal for the Arts, Sciences, and Technology* 1 (2): 2003, 25–34.
Kincaid, Harold. "Positivism in the Social Sciences." In *Routledge Encyclopedia of Philosophy*, Version 1.0 (CD-ROM). London: Routledge, 1998.
Kinney, Leila, and Zeynap Çelik. "Ethnography and Exhibitionism at the Expositions Universelles." *Assemblages* 13 (December 1990): 35–59.
Knight, Alan. "Populism and Neo-Populism in Latin America, Especially Mexico." *Journal of Latin American Studies* 30, no. 2 (1998): 223–48.
El-Kolaly [al-Qolali], Muhammad. *Essai sur les causes de la criminalité en Egypte*. Paris: Librarie de la Droit et de Jurisprudence, 1939.
Koselleck, Reinhart. *Futures Past: On the Semantics of Historical Time*. Translated by Keith Tribe. Cambridge, MA: MIT Press, 1985.
Koven, Seth, and Sonya Michel, eds. *Mothers of a New World: Maternalist Politics and the Origins of Welfare States*. London: Routledge, 1993.
Kremer-Marietti, Angèle. "Comte, Isidore-Auguste-Marie-Francois-Xavier (1798–1857)." In *Routledge Encyclopedia of Philosophy*, Version 1.0 (CD-ROM). London: Routledge, 1998.
Kuklick, Henrika. *The Savage Within. The Social History of British Anthropology, 1885–1945*. Cambridge: Cambridge University Press, 1991.
Lane, Edward William. *An Account of the Manners and Customs of the Modern Egyptians*. 5th ed, facsimile of the 1860 edition. Edited by Edward Stanley Poole. New York: Dover, 1973.
Laroui, Abdallah .*The Crisis of the Arab Intellectual*. Berkeley: University of California Press, 1976.
Lashin, 'Abd al-Khaliq. *Sa'd Zaghlul wa dawruhu fi al-siyasa al-misriyya hata sanat 1914*. Cairo and Beirut: Dar al-ma'arif, 1975.
Lavrin, Asunción. *Women, Feminism, and Social Change in Argentina, Chile, and Uruguay, 1890–1940*. Lincoln: University of Nebraska Press, 1995.
Lefevre, M. A. *L'habitat rural en Belgique: Etude de geographie humaine*. Liège, Belgium: H. Vaillant-Carmanne, 1926.
Legrain, Georges. *Louqsor sans les pharaons: Legendes et chansons populaires de la Haute-Egypte*. Paris and Brussels: Vromant, 1914.
Lenin, Vladimir I. "Preliminary Draft Theses on the National and the Colonial Questions for the Second Congress of the Communist International." In V.I. Lenin, Collected Works, 4th English edition. Moscow: Progress Publishers, 1966, v. 31, 144–51.
Levy, Anita. *Other Women: The Writing of Class, Race, and Gender, 1832–1898*. Princeton, NJ: Princeton University Press, 1991.
Lipietz, Alain. "New Tendencies in the International Division of Labour: Regimes of Accumulation and Modes of Regulation." In *Production, Work, Territory:*

The Geographical Anatomy of Industrial Capitalism, edited by M. Storper and A. J. Scott, 16–40. Boston: Allen and Unwin, 1986.

Lozach, Jean. *La Delta du Nil: Une étude de géographie humaine*. Cairo: E. R. Schindler, 1935.

Lozach, Jean, and Georges Hug. *L'Habitat rurale en Egypte*. Cairo: Publications de la Société Royale de Géographie d'Égypte, 1930.

MacIntyre, Alasdair. *After Virtue: A Study In Moral Theory*. 2nd ed. Notre Dame, IN: University of Notre Dame Press, 1984.

———. *Three Rival Versions of Moral Enquiry: Encyclopaedia, Genealogy and Tradition: Being Gifford Lectures Delivered at the University of Edinburgh in 1988*. Notre Dame, Indiana: University of Notre Dame Press, 1990.

Madkur, Ibrahim. *Ma'jam al-'ulum al-ijtima'iyya*. Cairo: Al-Hay'a al-misriyya al-'amma lil-kitab, 1975.

Mahfuz, Najib Bey. *The History of Medical Education in Egypt*. Cairo: Government Press, 1935.

———. *The Life of an Egyptian Doctor*. Edinburgh and London: E. & S. Livingstone, 1966.

Mahmood, Saba. *The Politics of Piety: The Islamic Revival and the Feminist Subject*. Princeton, NJ: Princeton University Press, 2004.

Mahmoudi, Abdelrashid. *Tāhā Husain's Education: From the Azhar to the Sorbonne*. London: Curzon, 1998.

Makdisi, Ussama. "Ottoman Orientalism." *American Historical Review* 107, no. 3 (2002): 768–96.

Mallon, Florencia. *Peasant and Nation: The Making of Postcolonial Mexico and Peru*. Berkeley: University of California Press, 1995.

Mani, Lata. "Contentious Traditions: The Debate on Sati in Colonial India." In *Recasting Women: Essays in Colonial History*, edited by Kumkum Sangari and Sudesh Vaid, 88–126. New Delhi: Kali for Women, 1989.

Marsot, Afaf Lutfi al-Sayyid. *Egypt and Cromer*. New York: Praeger, 1969.

———. *Egypt's Liberal Experiment*. Berkeley: University of California Press, 1977.

———. *A Short History of Modern Egypt*. Cambridge: Cambridge University Press, 1985.

Maspero, Gaston. *Causeries d'Égypte*. Paris: E. Guilmoto, 1907.

———. *Les contes populaires de l'Égypte ancienne*. Paris: E. Guilmoto, 1905.

———. *Du genre épistolaire chez les égyptiens de l'époque pharaonique*. Paris: A. Franck (F. Vieweg), 1872.

Massad, Joseph. *Colonial Effects: The Making of National Identity in Jordan*. New York: Columbia University Press, 2001.

Mauss, Marcel. *The Gift: The Form and Reason for Exchange in Archaic Societies*. New York: W. W. Norton, 1990 [1925].

Mayer, Thomas. *The Changing Past: Egyptian Historiography of the Urabi Revolt, 1882–1983*. University of Florida Monographs in Social Sciences, no. 73. Gainesville: University of Florida Press, 1988.

Mazower, Mark. *Dark Continent: Europe's Twentieth Century.* New York: Vintage, 1998.
Mazumdar, Pauline. "Blood and Soil: The Serology of the Aryan Racial State." *Bulletin of the History of Medicine* 64 (1990):187–219.
McEwan, Cheryl. "Cutting Power Lines Within the Palace? Countering Paternity and Eurocentrism Within the Geographical Tradition." *Transactions of the Institute of British Geographers* New Series, vol. 23, no. 3 (1998): 371–84.
Meek, Ronald, ed. *Marx and Engels on the Population Bomb: Selections from the Writings of Marx and Engels Dealing with the Theories of Thomas Robert Malthus.* Berkeley: Ramparts, 1971.
Mehmet, Özay. "Turkey in Crisis: Some Contradictions in the Kemalist Development Strategy." *International Journal of Middle East Studies* 15 (1983): 47–66.
Meijer, Roel. *Cosmopolitanism, Identity and Authenticity in the Middle East.* London: Curzon, 1999.
———. *The Quest for Modernity. Secular Liberal and Left-Wing Political Thought in Egypt, 1945–1958.* London: RoutledgeCurzon, 2002.
Mitchell, Richard P. *The Society of the Muslim Brothers.* New York: Oxford University Press, 1993.
Mitchell, Timothy. *Colonising Egypt.* Cambridge: Cambridge University Press, 1988.
———. *Rule of Experts: Egypt, Techno-politics, Modernity.* Berkeley: University of California Press, 2002.
———. "The Stage of Modernity." In Mitchell, *Questions of Modernity*, 1–34.
———, ed. *Questions of Modernity.* Minneapolis: University of Minnesota Press, 2000.
Monciaud, Didier. "Le projet de la piastre et Jeune Egypte: Entre réforme et conscience économique nationaliste." In Roussillon, *Entre reforme sociale et mouvement national*, 113–27.
Mosséri, V. M., and Ch. Audebeau. *Les constructions rurales en Égypte.* Cairo: Société Sultanienne d'Agriculture, 1921.
al-Muqtataf. *Turath Misr al-qadima.* Cairo: Dar al-muqtataf, 1936.
Musa, Salama. *The Education of Salama Musa.* Translated by L. O. Schuman. Leiden: E. J. Brill, 1961.
———. *Misr asl al-hadara.* Cairo: Matba'at al-majalla al-jadida, n.d. (c.1935).
———. *Nazariyyat al-tatawwur wa asl al-insan.* 3rd ed. Cairo: Salama Musa lil nashr wa al-tawzi'a, 1958.
———. *Salama Musa: Al-mu'allafat al-kamila.* Vol. 2: *'Ulum al-ijtima'.* Cairo: Salama Musa lil nashr wa al-tawzi'a, 2002.
Musallam, Basim. *Sex and Society in Islam: Birth Control Before the Nineteenth Century.* Cambridge: Cambridge University Press, 1983.
Nahas, Joseph F. *Situation économique et sociale du fellah égyptien.* Paris: Arthur Rousseau, 1901.
Nahhas, Yusuf Bey. *Al-fellah.* Cairo: Matba'at al-muqtataf wa al-muqattam, 1926.

Najib, Mustafa. *A'lam Misr fi al-qarn 'al-'ishrin*. Qalyub, Egypt: Al-Ahram, 1996.

Najmabadi, Afsaneh. *Women with Mustaches and Men Without Beards: Gender and Sexual Anxieties of Iranian Modernity*. Berkeley: University of California Press, 2005.

Nasir [Nasser], Jamal Abd al. *Falsafat al-thawra*. Cairo: Wizarat al-'alam, 1953.

Nassif, Elie. *Capitalisme ou collectivisme: L'alternative presente*. Cairo: Les Lettres Françaises, 1946.

Nietzsche, Friedrich. *Beyond Good and Evil: Prelude to a Philosophy of the Future*. Translated by Walter Kaufmann. New York: Vintage, 1966.

———. *Thus Spoke Zarathustra: A Book for All and None*. Translated by Walter Kaufmann. New York: Penguin, 1978.

Nye, Robert. *Crime, Madness, and Politics in Modern France. The Medical Concept of National Decline*. Princeton, NJ: Princeton University Press, 1984.

O'Hanlon, Rosalind. "Recovering the Subject: *Subaltern Studies* and Histories of Resistance in Colonial South Asia." In *Mapping Subaltern Studies and the Postcolonial*, edited by Vinayak Chaturvedi, 72–115. London: Verso, 2000.

Omran, Abdel Rahim, ed. *Egypt: Population Problems and Prospects*. Chapel Hill: Carolina Population Center, University of North Carolina at Chapel Hill, 1973.

———. *Family Planning in the Legacy of Islam*. London and New York: Routledge, 1992.

Omran, Abdel Rahim, and Malek el-Nomrossey. "The Family Planning Effort in Egypt: A Descriptive Sketch." In Omran, *Egypt: Population Problems and Prospects*, 219–253.

Owen, Roger. "The Ideology of Economic Nationalism in Its Egyptian Context: 1919–1939." In *Intellectual Life in the Arab East, 1890–1939*, edited by Marwan Buheiry, 1–9. Beirut: American University in Beirut Press, 1981.

———. *Lord Cromer: Victorian Imperialist, Edwardian Proconsul*. Oxford: Oxford University Press, 2005.

———. "The Population Census of 1917 and Its Relationship to Egypt's Three 19th Century Statistical Regimes." *Journal of Historical Sociology* 9, no. 4 (December 1996): 457–72.

Palacios, Guillermo. "Postrevolutionary Intellectuals, Rural Readings and the Shaping of the 'Peasant Problem' in Mexico: *El Maestro Rural*, 1924–34." *Journal of Latin American Studies* 30, no. 2: 309–39.

Pedersen, Jean Elisabeth. "Regulating Abortion and Birth Control: Gender, Medicine and Republican Politics in France, 1870–1920." *French Historical Studies* 19, no. 3 (1996): 673–98.

Pels, Peter. "The Rise and Fall of the Indian Aborigines: Orientalism, Anglicism, and the Emergence of an Ethnology of India, 1833–1869." In Pels and Salemink, *Colonial Subjects*, 82–116.

Pels, Peter, and Oscar Salemink, eds. *Colonial Subjects: Essays on the Practical History of Anthropology*. Ann Arbor: University of Michigan Press, 1999.

Penrose, E. F. *Population Theories and Their Application: With Special Reference to Japan*. Stanford, CA: Food Research Institute, Stanford University, 1934.
Petrie, W. M. F. *Amulets: Illustrated by the Egyptian Collection at University College*. London: Constable, 1914.
Philipp, Thomas. "Feminism and Nationalist Politics in Egypt." In *Women in the Muslim World*, edited by Lois Beck and Nikkie Keddie, 277–94. Cambridge, MA: Harvard University Press, 1978.
Pick, Daniel. *The Faces of Degeneration: A European Disorder, c. 1848–c.1918*. Cambridge: Cambridge University Press, 1989.
Podeh, Elie, and Onn Winckler, eds. *Rethinking Nasserism: Revolution and Historical Memory in Modern Egypt*. Florida: University of Florida Press, 2004.
Polanyi, Karl. *The Great Transformation: The Political and Economic Origins of Our Times*. Boston: Beacon Press, 1944.
Pollard, Lisa. "The Family Politics of Colonizing and Liberating Egypt, 1882–1919." *Social Politics* 7, no. 1 (2000): 47–79.
———. *Nurturing the Nation: The Family Politics of Modernizing, Colonizing, and Liberating Egypt (1805–1923)*. Berkeley: University of California Press, 2005.
Poovey, Mary. *A History of the Modern Fact: Problems of Knowledge in the Sciences of Wealth and Society*. Chicago: University of Chicago Press, 1998.
———. *Making a Social Body: British Cultural Formations, 1830–1864*. Chicago: University of Chicago Press, 1995.
———. *Uneven Developments: The Ideological Work of Gender in Mid-Victorian England*. Chicago: University of Chicago Press, 1988.
Porter, Theodore, and Dorothy Ross, eds. *The Cambridge History of Science*. Vol. 7, *The Modern Social Sciences*. Cambridge: Cambridge University Press, 2003.
Posusney, Marsha Pripstein. *Labor and the State in Egypt: Workers, Unions and Economic Restructuring*. New York: Columbia University Press, 1997.
Powell, Eve Troutt. *A Different Shade of Colonialism: Egypt, Great Britain, and the Mastery of the Sudan*. Berkeley: University of California Press, 2003.
———. "From Odyssey to Empire: Mapping Sudan Through Egyptian Literature in the mid-19th Century." *International Journal of Middle East Studies* 31 (1999): 401–27.
Prakash, Gyan. *Another Reason: Science and the Imagination of Modern India*. Princeton, NJ: Princeton University Press, 1999.
———. "Subaltern Studies as Postcolonial Criticism." *American Historical Review* 99, no. 5 (1994): 1475–90.
Qutb, Sayyid. *Al-'adalat al ijtima'iyya fi al-islam*. Beirut: Dar al-shuruq, 1975.
———. *A Child from the Village*. Edited and translated by John Calvert and William Shepard. Syracuse, NY: Syracuse University Press, 2004.
———. *Khasa'is al-tasawwur al-islami wa muqawimatuhu*. Beirut: Dar ihya al-kutub al-'arabiyya, 1962.
———. *Ma'rakat al-islam wa al-ra'smaliyya*. Jiddah: Al-Dar al-sa'udiyah, 1969.

Rabinbach, Anson. *The Human Motor: Energy, Fatigue, and the Origins of Modernity*. Berkeley: University of California Press, 1992.

Rabinow, Paul. *French Modern: Norms and Forms of the Social Environment*. Chicago: University of Chicago Press, 1989.

Rafael, Vicente. *Contracting Colonialism: Translation and Christian Conversion in Tagalog Society under Early Spanish Rule*. Manila: Ateneo de Manila University Press, 1988.

al-Rafa'i, 'Abd al-Rahman. *Al-thawra al-'urabiyya wa al-ihtilal al-injlizi*. Cairo: Maktabat al-nahda al-misriyya, 1939.

Ramadan, Abd el-Azim. "Social Significance of the 'Urabi Revolt." In Groupe de Recherches et d'Etudes sur le Proche Orient, *L'Egypte au XIXe siècle*, 187–96. Paris: Centre National de la Recherche Scientifique, 1982.

Rapp, Rayna, and Faye Ginsburg. "Introduction." In Ginsburg and Rapp, *Conceiving the New World Order*, 1–17.

Al-Rasa'il al-'ilmiyya li darajatay al-majistir wa al-dukturuh. Cairo: Matba'at jami'at al-Qahira, 1958.

Reid, Donald M. *Cairo University and the Making of Modern Egypt*. Cambridge: Cambridge University Press, 1990.

———. "The Egyptian Geographical Society: From Foreign Laymen's Association to Indigenous Professional Association." *Poetics Today* 14, no. 3 (Fall 1993): 538–72.

———. "The 'Urabi Revolution and the British Conquest, 1879–1882." In Daly, *The Cambridge History of Egypt*, 217–38.

———. *Whose Pharaohs? Archaeology, Museums, and Egyptian National Identity From Napoleon to World War I*. Berkeley: University of California Press, 2002.

Renan, Ernest. "What Is a Nation?" In *Nation and Narration*, edited by Homi Bhabha. New York: Routledge, 1990.

Rhodes, Dr. "S.E. LE Dr. Onofrio Abbate Pasha." In Abbate, *Aegyptiaca*, 661–64.

Rieker, Martina. "Reading the Colonial Archive." In *New Frontiers in the Social History of the Middle East*, edited by Enid Hill, 134–61. Cairo Papers in Social Science, vol. 23, no. 2. Cairo: American University in Cairo Press, 2000.

Rizk, Hanna. "Population Policies in Egypt." In *The Fifth International Conference on Planned Parenthood, Report of the Proceedings 24–29 October 1955, Tokyo, Japan*. London: International Planned Parenthood, 1955.

Robbins, Lionel. "The Optimum Theory of Population." In *London Essays in Economics: In Honour of Edwin Cannan*, edited by T. E. Gregory and H. Dalton, 103–34. London: George Routledge & Sons, 1927.

Robic, Marie-Claire. "Geography." In Porter and Ross, *The Cambridge History of Science*, 379–90.

Rogaski, Ruth. *Hygienic Modernity: Meanings of Disease and Health in Treaty-Port China*. Berkeley: University of California Press, 2004.

"Romanticism." In *Dictionary of Philosophy*, edited by Dagobert D. Runes, 272–73. 15th edition. New York: Philosophical Library, 1960.

Ross, Dorothy. *The Origins of American Social Science*. Cambridge: Cambridge University Press, 1991.
Ross, Eric. *The Malthus Factor: Population, Poverty and Politics in Capitalist Development*. London: Zed, 1998.
Roussillon, Alain, ed. *Entre reforme sociale et mouvement national: Identité et modernization en Egypte (1882–1962)*. Cairo: CEDEJ, 1995.
———. "Sociology in Egypt and Morocco." In Porter and Ross, *The Cambridge History of Science*, 450–65.
———. "Trajectoires reformistes Sayyid Qutb et Sayyid 'Uways: Figures modernes de l'intellectuel en Egypte." In *Egypte/Monde Arabe* 6 (1991): 91–139.
Royal Society of Agriculture, Agricultural Research Section. *Improving the Lot of the Egyptian Fallah: The Model Village at Bahtim*. Cairo: Société Royale d'Agriculture, n.d.
Sachs, Susan. "Honoring a Visionary if Not His Vision: Egyptian's Reputation Outlives His Designs." *New York Times*, April 4, 2000, E1–E2.
Sa'd, Ahmed Sadiq. *Mushkilat al-fellah*. Cairo: Dar al-qirn al-'ishrin, 1945.
Said, Edward. *Culture and Imperialism*. New York: Vintage, 1993.
———. *Orientalism*. New York: Random House, 1978.
Sa'id, Rifa't. *Hasan al-Banna': Kayfa wa li matha?* Cairo: Dar al-thaqafa al-jadida, 1984.
Salih, Ahmed Rushdi. *Al-adab al-sha'abi*. Cairo: Maktabat al-nahda al-misriyya, 1955.
———. *Al-funun al-sha'abiyya*. Cairo: Dar al-qalam, 1961.
Salim, Latifa Muhammad. *Al-quwwa al-ijtima'iyya fi al thawra al-'urabiyya*. Cairo: Al-Hay'a al-misriyya al-'amma lil-kitab, 1981.
Sanger, Margaret, ed. *Proceedings of the World Population Conference, 29 August–3 September, Geneva*. London: Edward Arnold, 1927.
Santurri, E. N. "Theodicy and Social Policy in Malthus' Thought." In Cunningham, *Thomas Robert Malthus*, vol. 1, 402–18.
Schayegh, Cyrus. "Hygiene, Eugenics, Genetics, and the Perception of Demographic Crisis in Iran, 1910s–1940s." *Critique: Critical Middle Eastern Studies* 13, no. 3 (2004): 335–61.
Schneider, William H. "Blood Group Research in Great Britain, France and the United States Between the Wars." *American Journal of Physical Anthropology* 38, no. S21 (1995): 87–114.
———. "The Eugenics Movement in France, 1890–1940." In Adams, *The Wellborn Science*, 69–109.
———. *Quality and Quantity: The Quest for Biological Regeneration in Twentieth-Century France*. Cambridge: Cambridge University Press, 1990.
Schölch, Alexander. *Egypt for the Egyptians! The Sociopolitical Crisis in Egypt, 1878–1882*. London: Ithaca Press for The Middle East Centre, St. Antony's College, Oxford, 1981.
Schreier, Joshua. "Napoleon's Long Shadow: Morality, Civilization, and Jews in

France and Algeria, 1808–1870." *French Historical Studies* 30, no. 1 (2007): 77–103.

Schulze, Reinhard. "Colonization and Resistance: The Egyptian Peasant Rebellion, 1919." In *Peasants and Politics in the Modern Middle East*, edited by John Waterbury and Farhad Kazemi, 170–202. Miami: Florida International Press, 1991.

Schweinfurth, Georg August. *The Heart of Africa. Three Years' Travels and Adventures in the Unexplored Regions of Central Africa. From 1868 to 1871*, 2 vols. Translated by Ellen Frewer. New York: Harper and Brothers, 1874.

Scott, David. "Colonial Governmentality." *Social Text* 43 (Autumn, 1995): 191–220.

———. *Conscripts of Modernity: The Tragedy of Colonial Enlightenment*. Durham, NC: Duke University Press, 2004.

———. *Refashioning Futures: Criticism after Postcoloniality*. Princeton, NJ: Princeton University Press, 1999.

Scott, James C. *Seeing Like a State: How Certain Schemes to Improve the Human Condition Have Failed*. New Haven, CT: Yale University Press, 1998.

Seligman, Charles. *Egypt and Negro-Africa: A Study in Divine Kingship*. London: G. Routledge and Sons, 1934.

———. *The Pagan Tribes of the Nilotic Sudan*. London: Routledge and Sons, 1932.

———. "Physical Characters of the Arabs." *Journal of the Royal Anthropological Institute of Great Britain and Ireland* 47 (1917): 214–37.

———. *Races of Africa*. London: T. Butterworth, 1930.

———. "Some Aspects of the Hamitic Problem in the Anglo-Egyptian Sudan." *Journal of the Royal Anthropological Institute of Great Britain and Ireland* 33 (1913): 593–705.

Selim, Samah. *The Novel and the Rural Imaginary in Egypt 1880–1985*. New York: RoutledgeCurzon, 2004.

Sen, Samita. "Motherhood and Mothercraft: Gender and Nationalism in Bengal." *Gender and History* 5, no. 2 (Summer 1993): 231–43.

Sen, Sudipta. *Distant Sovereignty: National Imperialism and the Origins of British India*. New York: Routledge, 2002.

Senghor, Léopold Sédar. *The Collected Poetry*. Translated by Melvin Dixon. Charlottesville: University Press of Virginia, 1991.

Sergi, Giuseppe. *The Mediterranean Race: A Study of the Origin of European Peoples*. London: W. Scott, 1901.

al-Shafa'i, Shuhdi Attiyya. *Tatawwur al-haraka al-wataniyya al-misriyya 1882–1956*. Cairo: Matba'at al-dar al-misriyya lil tiba' wa al-nashr wa al-tawzi'a, 1957.

El Shakry, Omnia. "Barren Land and Fecund Bodies: The Emergence of Population Discourse in Interwar Egypt," *International Journal of Middle East Studie* 37, no. 3 (2005), 351–72.

———. "Cairo as Capital of Socialist Revolution?" In *Cairo Cosmopolitan: Politics, Culture, and Urban Space in the New Globalized Middle East*, edited by

Diane Singerman and Paul Amar, 73–98. Cairo: American University in Cairo Press, 2006.

———. "The Great Social Laboratory: Reformers and Utopians in Twentieth Century Egypt." Ph.D. diss., Princeton University, 2002.

———. "Reproducing the Family: Bio-Politics in Twentieth Century Egypt." Master's Thesis, New York University, 1995.

———. "Schooled Mothers and Structured Play: Child Rearing in Turn-of-the-Century Egypt." In *Remaking Women: Feminism and Modernity in the Middle East*, edited by Lila Abu-Lughod, 126–70. Princeton, NJ: Princeton University Press, 1998.

Shalabi, 'Ali. *Misr al-fatat wa dawriha fi al-siyasa al-misriyya 1933–1941*. Cairo: Dar al-kitab al-jami'i, 1982.

Shalaby, Mohamed. *An Experiment in Rural Reconstruction in Egypt*. Cairo: Egyptian Association for Social Studies, 1950.

Shanawany, Haifa. "Stages in the Development of a Population Control Program." In Omran, *Egypt*, 189–217.

Sharkey, Heather. *Living with Colonialism: Nationalism and Culture in the Anglo-Egyptian Sudan*. Berkeley: University of California Press, 2003.

Sheehi, Stephen. *Foundations of Modern Arab Identity*. Gainesville: University of Florida Press, 2004.

Sherman, Daniel. "'Peoples Ethnographic': Objects, Museums, and the Colonial Inheritance of French Ethnology." *French Historical Studies* 27, no. 3 (2004): 669–703.

Smith, Grafton Elliot. *The Ancient Egyptians and Their Influence upon the Civilization of Europe*. London: Harper and Brothers, 1911.

———. *The Ancient Egyptians and the Origin of Civilization*. Rev. ed. London: Harper and Brothers, 1923.

———. *The Diffusion of Culture*. London: Watts, 1933.

———. *Elephants and Ethnologists*. London: Kegan Paul, 1924.

———. *The Evolution of the Dragon*. Manchester, UK: Manchester University Press, 1919.

———. *Human History*. New York: W.W. Norton, 1929.

———. *The Influence of Ancient Egyptian Civilization in the East and in America*. Manchester, UK: Manchester University Press, 1916.

———. *In the Beginning: the Origin of Civilization*. London: Howe, 1928.

———. *The Migrations of Early Culture: A Study of the Significance of the Geographical Distribution of the Practice of Mummification as Evidence of the Migration of Peoples and the Spread of Certain Customs and Beliefs*. Manchester, UK: Manchester University Press, 1915.

———. *Ships as Evidence of the Migrations of Early Culture*. Manchester, UK: Manchester University Press, 1917.

Sonbol, Amira El-Azhary. *The New Mamluks: Egyptian Society and Modern Feudalism*. Syracuse, NY: Syracuse University Press, 2000.

Sowell, T. "Malthus and the Utilitarians." In Cunningham, *Thomas Robert Malthus*, vol. 1, 210–16.

Spivak, Gayatri Chakravorty. "Acting Bits / Identity Talk." In *Identities*, edited by Kwame Anthony Appiah and Henry Louis Gates Jr., 147–80. Chicago: University of Chicago Press, 1995.

———. *Outside in the Teaching Machine*. London: Routledge, 1993.

Springborg, Robert. "Patrimonialism and Policy Making in Egypt: Nasser and Sadat and the Tenure Policy for Reclaimed Lands." *Middle Eastern Studies* 15, no. 1 (1979): 48–69.

Stanley, Henry Morton. *In Darkest Africa or the Quest, Rescue, and Retreat of Emin Governor of Equatoria*. 2 vols. New York: Charles Scribner's Sons, 1890.

Steele, James. *An Architecture for People: The Complete Works of Hassan Fathy*. New York: Whitney Library of Design, 1997.

Steinmetz, George. *Regulating the Social: The Welfare State and Local Politics in Imperial Germany*. Princeton, NC: Princeton University Press, 1993.

———, ed. *The Politics of Method in the Human Sciences: Positivism and Its Epistemological Others*. Durham, NC: Duke University Press, 2005.

Stepan, Nancy Leys, *"The Hour of Eugenics": Race, Gender, and Nation in Latin America*. Ithaca, NY: Cornell University Press, 1991.

———. "Eugenics in Brazil, 1917–1940." In Adams, *The Wellborn Science*, 110–52.

Stetkevych, Jaroslav. *The Modern Arabic Literary Language: Lexical and Stylistic Developments*. Chicago: University of Chicago Press, 1970.

Stocking, George W. Jr. *After Tylor: British Social Anthropology, 1888–1951*. Madison: University of Wisconsin Press, 1995.

———. *The Ethnographer's Magic and Other Essays in the History of Anthropology*. Madison: University of Wisconsin Press, 1992.

———. *Race, Culture, and Evolution: Essays in the History of Anthropology*. New York: Free Press, 1968.

———. *Victorian Anthropology*. New York: Free Press, 1987.

Stoler, Ann Laura. *Carnal Knowledge and Imperial Power: Race and the Intimate in Colonial Rule*. Berkeley: University of California Press, 2002.

———. *Race and the Education of Desire: Foucault's History of Sexuality and the Colonial Order of Things*. Durham, NC: Duke University Press, 1995.

Tapper, Melbourne. "Interrogating Bodies: Medico-Racial Knowledge, Politics and the Study of a Disease." *Comparative Studies in Society and History* 37, no. 1 (1995): 76–93.

Thompson, Elizabeth. *Colonial Citizens: Republican Rights, Paternal Privilege, and Gender in French Syria and Lebanon*. New York: Columbia University Press, 2000.

Tignor, Robert L. *Modernization and British Colonial Rule in Egypt, 1882–1914*. Princeton, NJ: Princeton University Press, 1966.

———. *State, Private Enterprise, and Economic Change in Egypt, 1918–1952*. Princeton, NJ: Princeton University Press, 1984.

Tilley, Helen. "Ambiguities of Racial Science in Colonial Africa: The African Re-

search Survey and the Fields of Eugenics, Social Anthropology and Biomedicine, 1920–1940." In *Science Across the European Empires, 1800–1950*, edited by Benedikt Stuchtey, 245–87. Oxford: Oxford University Press, 2005.
Toth, James. *Rural Labor Movements and Their Impact on the State, 1961–1992*. Gainesville: University Press of Florida, 1999.
Trillo, Mauricio Tenorio. *Mexico's Presence at World's Fairs: Crafting a Modern Nation*. Berkeley: University of California Press, 1996.
———. "Stereophonic Scientific Modernisms: Social Science Between Mexico and the United States, 1880s–1930s." *Journal of American History* 86, no.3 (1999): 1156–87.
'Umar, Muhammad. *Hadir al-misriyyin aw sirr ta'khuruhim*. Cairo: Dar Misr al-mahrusa 2002 [1902].
Union Géographique Internationale. *Congrès Internationale de Géographie*. 5 vols. Cairo: Imprimerie de l'Institut Français d'Archéologie Orientale du Caire, 1925.
Union Géographique Internationale—Commission Histoire de la Pensée Géographique / International Geographical Union—Commission on the History of Geographical Thought. *La géographie à travers un siècle de congrès internationaux (Geography Through a Century of International Conferences)*. Paris: UNESCO, 1972.
'Urabi, Ahmed. *Mudhakkirat 'urabi: kashf al-sitar an sirr al-asrar fi al-nahda al-misriyya al-mashhura bi al-thawra al-'urabiyya*. Cairo: Dar al-Hilal, 1989.
Van der Veer, Peter, ed. *Conversions to Modernities: The Globalization of Christianity*. London: Routledge, 1996.
Vaughn, Mary Kay. *Cultural Politics in Revolution: Teachers, Peasants, and Schools in Mexico, 1930–1940*. Tucson: University of Arizona Press, 1997.
Vincenot, Marcel. *Une experience sociale dans un village d'Egypte*. Cairo: Imprimerie de l'Institut Français d'archéologie orientale du Caire, 1946.
Vitalis, Robert. *When Capitalists Collide: Business Conflict and the End of Empire in Egypt*. Berkeley: University of California Press, 1995.
Volait, Mercedes. *L'architecture moderne en Egypte et la revue al'Imara, 1939–1959*. Cairo: CEDEJ, 1988.
Voll, Sara. "Egyptian Land Reclamation since the Revolution." *Middle East Journal* 34, no. 2 (1980): 127–48.
Wafi, Ali Abd al-Wahid. *Al-Falsafa al-ijtima'iyya li Ibn Khaldun wa Auguste Comte*. Cairo: Matba'at lajnat al-bayan al-'arabi, 1951.
Wagner, Richard. "Judaism in Music." In *Richard Wagner's Prose Works*, vol. 3, *The Theatre*, translated by William Ashton Ellis. New York: Broude Brothers, 1894.
Wahba, Mourad Magdi. *The Role of the State in the Egyptian Economy: 1945–1981*. Reading, UK: Ithaca Press, 1994.
Warriner, Doreen. *Agrarian Reform and Community Development in the U.A.R.* Cairo: Dar al-Ta'wun, 1961.
———. *Land Reform and Development in the Middle East: A Study of Egypt, Syria and Iraq*. London: Royal Institute of International Affairs, 1957.

Watenpaugh, Keith David. *Being Modern in the Middle East: Revolution, Nationalism, Colonialism, and the Arab Middle Class*. Princeton, NJ: Princeton University Press, 2005.

Weber, Eugen. *Peasants into Frenchmen: The Modernization of Rural France, 1870–1914*. Stanford: Stanford University Press, 1976.

Wehr, Hans. *A Dictionary of Modern Written Arabic*. Edited by Milton Cowan. 3rd ed. New York: Spoken Language Services, 1976.

Wendell, Charles. *Five Tracts of Hasan al-Banna' (1906–1949)*. Berkeley: University of California Press, 1978.

Wheeler, George. *Report upon the Third International Geographical Congress and Exhibition at Venice, Italy, 1881, Accompanied by Data Concerning the Principal Government Land and Marine Surveys of the World*. Washington, DC: Government Off Print, 1885.

Wolf, Eric R. *Peasant Wars of the Twentieth Century*. New York: Harper and Row, 1969.

Wright, Gwendolyn. *The Politics of Design in French Colonial Urbanism*. Chicago: University of Chicago Press, 1989.

Young, Marilyn B. *The Vietnam Wars, 1945–1990*. New York: HarperCollins, 1991.

Zaalouk, Malak. *Power, Class, and Foreign Capital in Egypt: The Rise of the New Bourgeoisie*. London: Zed, 1989.

Zaki, Gamal. *Tanzim wa tanmiyat al-mujtamaʿa*. Cairo: Dar al-thaqafa wa al-ʿulum lil tibaʿ wal nashr, n.d.

Zayed, Ahmed. "Al-nazariyya al-ijtimaʿiyya al-muʿasira wa al-waqiʿ al-ʿarabi," *Al-Mustaqbal al-ʿarabi* 189 (November 1994): 90–111.

———. "Seventy Years of Sociology in Egypt." In *The Development of Social Science in Egypt: Economics, History and Sociology*, 41–71. Cairo Papers in Social Science, Fifth Annual Symposium, vol. 18, monograph 3. Cairo: American University in Cairo Press, 1996.

Zebiri, K. *Mahmud Shaltut and Islamic Modernism*. Oxford: Clarendon, 1993.

Index

Abaza, Fu'ad, 99, 126–128
Abbate, Onofrio, 26–28, 30–41, 52, 97, 101
'Abbas Helmi II, Khedive, 15, 27
Abdel-Malek, Anouar, 12, 116, 204
'Abd al-Rahman, A'isha, 96, 142, 155
'Abduh, Issa, 183–84, 188–89; and jihad, 188
'Abduh, Muhammad, 161, 166
Abdülaziz, Sultan, 24
Abou-Zeid, Ahmed, 86
Abu-Zayd, Hekmat, 211
Abyssinia, 27–29
Afifi, Hafiz, 42, 117, 147
Africa: Egyptian colonial ambitions towards, 3, 26–27, 29, 53, 74–83, 246n112; ethnographic study of, 27–29, 45. See also 'Ammar, 'Abbas Mustafa; Sudan
agriculture, 6, 63, 94, 107–110, 125–126, 154, 161–162, 181, 192, 200, 205, 256n15. See also Estates, agricultural; Land; Peasantry; Royal Agricultural Society
Ahmad, Mahmud Shakir, 115, 137
'Alam, Muhammad Sabri Abu, 202
'Ali, Mehmed, 3, 9, 15, 23, 26, 28, 74–75, 77, 94, 109–110, 123–124, 126, 146, 150
al-'Alim, Mahmud Amin, 12
Allenby, E.H.H., 93
Althusser, Louis, 197, 283n9
Amin, Ahmad, 16
'Amir [Amer], Mustafa, 16, 29, 67–68, 110, 147, 153, 244n65
'Ammar, 'Abbas Mustafa, 16–17, 56, 66–86, 102, 110, 221–22, 245n70; and birth control, 180, 184–86, 190–91, 213; and critiques of British views of the Sudan, 80–83; understandings of race, 77–79; and the uniqueness of the Egyptian nation, 69, 84; and the unity of the Nile Valley, 76–83
Anagnost, Ann, 146, 179, 274n25
al-Andalusi, Sa'd, 55, 59
Annals history, 10, 223n5
Anous, A. M., 165, 190
anthropology, 55–86. See also Abbate, Onofrio; 'Ammar, 'Abbas Mustafa; Arabism; Ethnography; Musa, Salama; Nationalism; Pharaonicism; Survivals; Race
anthropometry, 18, 34, 60–61, 70–72, 74

al-'Aqqad, 'Abbas Mahmud, 63, 99
Arabism, 7, 56–57, 67, 70–71, 79–84
Artin, Yacoub, 49
Asad, Talal, 152, 166, 220
Ashmawi, Sayyid, 118
Aswan dam, 130, 153
Awad, Louis, 65
Ayrout, Henry Habib, 96, 98–101, 111, 127–28
Azmi, Hamid El-Sayed, 155–56, 200

al-Babli, Muhammad, 120, 122–123, 258n41
Bachatly, Charles, 45–47, 53
backwardness, allegations of, 5–6, 13, 56, 90–91, 136, 207, 210, 219, 221
Baer, Gabriel, 201
Bahtim village, 126–132, 142
al-Banna, Hasan, 117, 160, 165, 185–89, 280n119, 281n122, 281n123, 281n133; and jihad, 188
Baring, Sir Evelyn (Earl of Cromer), 4, 14, 90–91
Barnett, Clive, 44
Barshay, Andrew, 2
Bayoumi, Abbas, 46–47, 53
Bernard, Augustin, 43, 104
Berque, Jacques, 93
Blackman, Winifred, 47–49, 52–53, 86
Blumenbach, Johann Friedrich, 34
de la Boétie, Étienne, 98
Bonaparte, Napoleon, 3, 30, 41; invasion by, 109–110
Bonola, Frédéric, 27, 29
Booth, Marilyn, 166
Bovier-Lapierre, Paul, 45
Boyer, Christopher, 114, 251n37
British colonial rule: in Egypt, 3, 26, 75–77, 90–95, 117, 141, 150–151, 166; in Sudan, 75–77, 80–82
Brown, Nathan, 95–96, 118, 120, 251n36, 257n19
Brunhes, Jean, 106–107
Burton, Richard Francis, 25, 27, 42

Cairo School of Social Work (CSSW), 132–134. *See also* Egyptian Association for Social Studies
capitalism, 91, 94–95, 116–119, 198–207, 220, 285n29. *See also* Etatism; Socialism
Carr-Saunders, Alexander Morris, 73, 168–69
Çelik, Zeynep, 24, 30
Chakrabarty, Dipesh, 7, 9
Chantre, Ernest, 74
Chatterjee, Partha, 2, 4–5, 12, 70, 89, 113, 174, 202–203, 206, 228n65, 284n24
Chiffoleau, Sylvie, 115
childhood, 175–77, 191, 276n51
civilization, ideas of, 4, 29, 33, 41, 55–56, 150, 158, 183; decline of Egyptian civilization, 97; Elliot Smith's theories of cultural diffusion, 55, 64–65; origins of Egyptian civilization, 50–52, 55–56, 66–67; and reproduction, 167–169, 191, 270n67. *See also* Modernity; Progress, idea of
Clark, Kim, 114
class, 18; divergence of peasant and *effendiyya* interests, 94–96; emergence of an urban working class, 148; as a factor in population policy, 159–162, 184–86; and nationalism, 92–96; and revolution of 1952, 201–206. *See also* Capitalism; Etatism; *Effendiyya*; Socialism; Peasantry
Claval, Paul, 104
Cleland, Wendell, 133, 145, 153–60, 162–63
Clerget, Marcel, 110
Clot Bey, Antoine-Barthélemy, 124
Colla, Elliott, 83
colonialism, 2, 4–8, 25, 30–31, 104–105, 219–222
Comte, Auguste, 1, 7, 10, 169, 227n55

communism, 95–96, 118, 122, 140–41, 201, 203, 220; Communist International, Second Congress, 203
Conference on Birth Control (Cairo, 1937), 69, 155, 157, 160, 165–170, 181, 184, 191
Coon, Carleton, 74
Craig, James Ireland, 147, 151–153
criminology, 119–124, 140; and the difference between urban and rural crime, 120–123
Crouchley, A. E., 200
Cuno, Kenneth, 150
Cuvier, Georges, 35, 234n64

al-Daba', Mustafa, 102
Dar Fur, 27–29
Darwinism, social, 35, 38, 156, 163, 173, 274n27
Davies, Elwyn, 69
Dayf, Ahmad, 102
Demangeon, Albert, 104–105, 107–109, 254n98
demography, 147, 149, 159, 165, 180, 182–84, 192–93; demographic mass; 96, 101, 152–53, 164, 198, 218, 268n39; demographic optimum, 159–61, 169, 192, 246n90
Derengil, Selim, 2
Dinshaway, "incident" of 1906, 91–92
Dirault, Edouard, 43
Dirks, Nicholas, 31, 225n28, 248n148
Douin, Georges, 43
Durkheim, Emile, 1, 7, 48–50

effendiyya, 16, 89, 91–92, 94–95, 114. See also Intelligentsia, Egyptian
Egger, Vernon, 63, 65
Egyptian Association for Social Studies (EASS), 110, 132–137, 153, 155, 157, 191
Egyptian Feminist Union (EFU), 175, 177–78
Egyptian Medical Association, 145, 147. See also Conference on Birth Control (1937)
Egyptian National Commission on Rural Habitat, 105
Egyptian University, 7, 14–17, 43, 153; subjects taught, 15, 67–69
Egyptology, 46–48, 50, 62. See also Survivals; Pharaonicism
Enlightenment, 4, 34, 222
Esmeir, Samera, 90, 249n7
estates, agricultural ('izba), 94–95, 105, 107–10, 119, 124–28. See also Agriculture; Land; Peasantry
etatism, 164, 197–218; definition of, 199–202; and economic planning, 198–200, 204–207, 213, 221
ethnography, 2, 42–47; of Egypt, 43–47, 52–53; and ethnological uniqueness, 55–57, 68–72, 74, 84; of the peasantry, 96–101. See also Arabism; Hamites; Nationalism; Pharaonicism; Semites; Survivals; *and Individual ethnographers*
eugenics (*tahsin al-nasl*), 149, 157, 160, 165, 168, 170–74, 274nn26, 27
Europeans, in Ottoman-Egyptian service, 33, 43. See also Abbate, Onofrio
Evans-Pritchard, 15, 79
Exposition Universelle (1867), 23–24

Fabian, Johannes, 53
Fahmi, 'Abd al-Aziz, 92
Fahmi, Kamal al-Din, 157, 168, 171
Fahmi, Mansur, 1, 16
Fahmi, Mustafa, 127, 155, 168–69, 171–72, 181
al-Falaki, Mahmud, 28, 236n101
family, as a site of intervention, 18, 75, 158, 166–67, 170, 179, 181–86, 190, 212–17; and religious discourse, 186–89
Faruq, King, 117
fascism, 149–150, 182
Fathy [Fathi], Hassan, 127–132, 261n97

Fellahin. *See* Peasantry
fertility, 73, 97, 146, 154, 157, 160, 164, 170, 180, 182; and civilization, 168–169, 172, 270n67; and class, 184–185; and magical practices, 46, 48. *See also* Demography; Peasantry; Population; Women
Fichte, Johann, 34
Firth, Raymond, 72
Fleure, Herbert John, 69, 78–79, 85
folk, the, 49, 53.
folklore, 11, 46–52. *See also* Ethnography; Magic; Survivals
Foucart, George, 47, 110
Foucault, Michel, 272n2, 283n9
Frazer, James George 49, 243n45
Free Officers, 204, 209
Freud, Sigmund, 222
Fu'ad I, King, 14, 42–43, 103–104, 117
Fu'ad, Ali, 171, 185, 190

Gaillardot, Bey, 23
Galton, Francis, 25, 232n21
gender, 166–167. *See also* Women
geography, 2, 33, 42–43, 67–69; French tradition of, 103–110; human, 18, 73, 103–111. *See also* Royal Geographic Society; Ibn Khaldun
Gershoni, Israel, 52, 75–76, 189
Ghali, Mirrit Butrus, 92, 117, 147, 155–57, 202, 270n63
Ghallab, Muhammad, 49–53, 99, 241n30
al-Ghazali, Abu Hamid Muhammad, 187
Ghurbal, Shafiq, 15, 76–77, 246n112
Gini, Corrado, 159
Ginsberg, Faye, 191, 267n12
Glassman, Jonathan, 57
Godlewska, Anne, 31
Goethe, Johann Wolfgang von, 36, 68
Goldberg, Ellis, 95–96, 256n15
Gordon, Charles, 27–28

governance, discourses of, 2–3, 5–6, 19, 118, 146, 150, 166, 198, 219
Gramsci, Antonio, 14, 17, 219, 283n9
"great social laboratory," 8
Guha, Ranajit, 221

Hacking, Ian, 184
Haddon, Alfred Cort, 32
al-Hakim, Tawfiq, 62, 93, 99, 122
El-Hammami, Ahmed, 211
Hamites, 79–80, 244n53, 247n127
Hamza, 'Abd al-Qadir, 63, 242n43
Hannaford, Ivan, 34–35
Happy Family Society, the, 145
Haqqi, Yahya, 92
Harb, Tal'at, 161
Hasan, Muhammad, 160–61, 185
Hasanayn, Ahmad, 42, 52, 103
Hasanayn, Magdi, 209, 211–12. *See also* Tahrir Province project
Havel, Vaclav, 218
Haykal, Muhammad Husayn, 50, 61–62, 96, 99, 102, 115, 202
Heliopolis Social Service Association, 178–79
von Helmholtz, Hermann, 35–36
al-Hilali, Najib, 156
Hilmi, Bey, 183, 190–91
Hobbes, Thomas, 34
Horn, David, 146, 274n25
Hrdlička, Aleš, 74
Hug, Georges, 105–110, 124. *See also* Jean Lozach
human difference, notions of, 55–61, 64. *See also* Ethnography; Nationalism; Race
Hume, David, 34
Hume, W. F., 110
Husayn Kamil I, 125
Husayn, Ahmed, 62, 76, 113, 255n1
Husayn, Ahmad, Dr., 117, 133, 138, 255n1, 263n128. *See also* Ministry of Social Affairs, Fellah Department

Husayn [Hussein], Taha, 1, 16, 56, 63, 65, 99, 102–103
Huzayyin, Sulayman, 76, 244n69

Ibn Khaldun, 1, 7, 53, 71, 73, 84–85, 221–22
identity, discourses of, 12–14, 18, 219. *See also* Arabism; Pharaonicism; Nationalism; Race, taxonomies of
India, 2, 4, 41, 174, 182, 204
intelligentsia, Egyptian 5–6, 10–19, 220–22. *See also* Social sciences, Egyptian *and Individual intellectuals*
International Geographical Union, 104–105
Isma'il, Khedive, 15, 23–28, 30, 32, 42, 52, 77, 110
'izba. *See* Estates, agricultural

al-Jabarti, Abd al-Rahman, 7
James, William, 49
Jankowski, James, 52, 75–76, 189
Jawish, 'Abd al-'Aziz, 92
Johnson, Amy, 115

Kamal, Ahmad, 62
Kamil, Mustafa, 92
Kant, Immanuel, 34, 37
Karim, Sayyid, 132
Keane, A.H., 60
Keith, Arthur, 59
Kemal, Mustafa (Atatürk), 193, 204
Khalid, Khalid Muhammad, 216
Khattab, Muhammad, 202
Kholoussy, Hanan, 166
knowledge production, 1–10, 17–18, 23–25, 68–69, 90
Koselleck, Reinhart, 53
Kutla bloc, 117

Lamarck, Jean-Baptiste, 35, 234n64, 274n27
land: availability of, 154–56, 161–64; and 1919 revolution, 94–96; reclamation, 162, 197, 207–12; reform and redistribution, 148, 162, 201–202, 204–212, 287n64. *See also* Agriculture; Estates, agricultural; Peasantry; Population
Lane, Edward, 39, 50, 96
Le Bon, Gustave, 96, 251n45
Leclerc, Georges-Louis (Comte de Buffon), 34
de Lesseps, Ferdinand, 25, 28, 32
Lévy-Bruhl, Lucien, 1, 2
Liberal Constitutionalist Party, 93
Linneaus, Carolus, 34
Lozach, Jean, 105–110. *See also* Georges Hug

Mabarrat Muhammad 'Ali, 141, 175
Madhist revolt, 27
magic: study of, 32, 39–41, 46, 48–49, 51, 97; peasant use of, 89, 102, 136, 264nn149, 150
Maher, Mustafa, 44–45, 105
Mahfuz, Najib, 62, 92–93
Mahfuz, Najib, Dr., 165, 272n1
Mahir, Ali, 117
Makdisi, Ussama, 2
malaria, 141, 201
Malinowski, Bronislaw, 72
Mallon, Florencia, 114
Malthus, Thomas Robert, 154–55, 163, 268n42, 269nn50, 51, 270n69. *See also* Neo-Malthusianism; Population; Women
Ma'mun, Hassan, 217
Marei, Sayed, 212
Marey, Jules, 36
Marett, Robert Ranulph, 48–49, 53
marriage, 166, 173, 185–190
Mariette, August, 24–25
de Martonne, Emmanuel, 109
Marx, Karl, 7
Marzuq, Zahya, 191
Maspero, Gaston, 15, 47, 49
Massignon, Louis, 15

al-Mazini, Ibrahim, 63
Mazower, Mark, 166
Ministry of Agriculture, 125, 133, 208
Ministry of Public Health, 137–140
Ministry of Social Affairs, 125, 133, 136, 138, 145, 149, 265n163; Fellah Department, 123, 125, 138–139
al-Misri, Ibrahim, 102
Mitchell, Timothy, 8, 23, 31, 57, 84, 91, 118, 124, 141, 146, 151–152
modernity, 4–10, 12–13, 63, 150, 207, 219–22, 229n69
modernism: Arab, 4–5, 8, 11–14, 17, 19, 91, 228nn61, 63; architectural, 115, 140 (*see also* Fathy, Hassan); Islamist, 13–14. See also Intelligentsia, Egyptian; Nationalism
Montesquieu, 34, 37
Montreaux Convention, 117
de Morgan, J. 38
motherhood, 136, 139–140, 147, 174–79, 183, 190–92, 276n51, 276n52. *See also* Women
Mubarak, 'Ali, 15
Muhammad, 'Awad Muhammad, 16, 67–69, 110, 155, 157, 180, 182, 190
Mukhtar, Muhammad, 42
Müller, Max, 58
Munier, Henri, 106
Musa, Salama, 55–56, 60, 83, 102, 156, 240n2, 242nn36, 38, 244n53; biography of, 62; and pharaonicism, 62–66; as proponent of Westernization, 62–63, 65
Muslim Brotherhood, 13–14, 117, 141, 203; and social welfare, 183. *See also* al-Banna, Hasan; Population, and religious discourse
Myers, Charles, 74

Nabarawi, Saiza, 177
Nafi'a, 'Abd al-Majid, 161, 183
al-Nahhas, Mustafa, 161
Nahhas, Yusuf, 98, 117

Nasser, Gamal Abdel, 13, 17, 125, 148–49, 197–98, 203–207, 208, 212–18, 286n34. *See also* Etatism; Socialism
Nassif, Elie, 159–163
National Charter, 214–215
national literature, Egyptian, 101–102
National Population Commission, 1953, 69
National Renaissance Society (*Jama'at al-nahda al-qawmiyya*), 117, 156
national popular, postcolonial, 203, 206–207
nationalism, 2, 6–7, 55–57, 83–86, 219–221; and anthropology, 49–53; anti-colonial, 5–7, 57, 174, 202–203, 219, 221; economic, 117, 161–62, 180–81, 200, 204; and Islamism, 183–84; and motherhood, 174–79; and national identity, 219, 239n155; and the peasantry, 89–96, 101–102, 111, 114–115, 139–140, 219–220; and population policy, 148–150, 159–163, 173, 183, 185; territorial, 76, 93, 241n27, 281n133; and use of Arabic sources, 1, 7, 46, 53, 59, 67, 70, 84–85, 245n75, 276n52 (*see also* Ibn Khaldun). *See also* 'Ammar, 'Abbas Mustafa; Arabism; Etatism; Musa, Salama; Pharaonicism, Revolution of 1919; Revolution of 1952
Nehru, Jawaharlal, 204
Neo-Malthusianism, 115, 140, 147, 156–157, 160–61, 163, 219. *See also* Cleland, Wendell; Gini, Corrado; Mathus, Thomas Robert Malthus; Population; Women
Nietzsche, Friedrich, 222
Nile Valley, ethnographic study of, 43, 45–46, 67–68; unity of, 74–83, 85–86, 102. *See also* 'Ammar, 'Abbas Mustafa; Ghallab, Muhammad
Nubia, 29, 153

Ondaatje, Michael, 42
Orientalism, 30–31. *See also* Edward Lane
Osman, Osman Ahmed, 130
Ottoman Empire, 2–3, 30, 41, 150
Owen, Roger, 153, 161

Palacios, Guillermo, 114
pan-Islamism, 189
peasant studies, 89–91, 111, 114–15, 220
peasantry, 6, 17–19, 36–39, 89–142, 219–221;
    agricultural practices, 94–95, 107, 109–110, 162 ;
    crime, 113, 115, 119–123, 141–142, 220, 258n47, 259n59;
    discipline, 96, 116–19, 124, 140, 181, 197;
    educability, 17, 98, 107–108, 114, 136, 259n56;
    education, 134–137, 210–11, 263n134;
    expert guidance, 132–40, 199, 211;
    housing, 103–111, 125–132, 137–140, 162, 261n93;
    hygiene, 127–129, 134–135, 137–142, 155, 162;
    mentalité, 11, 18, 96–102, 120, 122, 135–36, 138, 155;
    mobility, 120, 123;
    model villages, 123–132, 138, 142, 148–49, 158, 264n146;
    nationalism, 89–96, 101–102, 111, 114–115, 139–140, 219–220;
    the "new Egyptian," 125, 140, 197–98, 208, 210–12;
    Orientalist depictions of, 96–102, 106–107
    pharaonicism, 65;
    poverty, 73, 99–100, 115–17, 162–64, 181, 200–202, 257n20;
    relations with landowners 90, 94, 113–114, 116, 201, 204–206;
    relations with urban classes, 90, 93–94, 108–109, 114;
    reproduction, 184–89, 192–94;
    rural reform, 113–142, 148;
    social uplift of, 89, 91, 110–11, 113–142, 147, 157–58, 169, 170, 197;
    violence in the countryside, 91–95, 100, 113–114, 116–119, 125, 140, 164, 201.
    See also Agriculture; Bahtim village; Egyptian Association for Social Studies; Estates, agricultural; Ethnography, of Egypt; Geography, human; Land; Royal Agricultural Society; Sharqiya; Social welfare; Tahrir Province project
Pels, Peter, 30–31
Penrose, E. F., 161
People's Party, 93
pharaonicism, 47, 50, 55–57, 61–66, 71–72, 83, 102, 241n27. *See also* Musa, Salama
Pick, Daniel, 35
Piot Bey, 97, 101
Ploetz, Alfred, 181
Polanyi, Karl, 163, 198–99
Pollard, Lisa, 166
population, 2, 5, 10–11, 17–19, 145–194, 219–221;
    birth and death rates, 153–158, 170–71, 176, 180–81;
    birth control, 146, 149, 155, 157, 159–62, 165–173, 179–184, 208, 214–217;
    census, 150–153;
    class, 183–86;
    comparisons with Europe, 2, 146, 159–160, 180, 182, 184;
    comparisons with India and China, 146, 160, 182;
    debates (over- vs. under-population), 146–150, 153–156, 159–164, 170–73, 184, 200, 207–208;
    diversity, 152–53;

emergence of the "problem of population", 115, 145–150, 163–164, 198, 201;
labor productivity, 89, 155, 163, 180, 185, 201;
motherhood, 174–79;
nation building, 148–50, 156, 159–63, 167;
population policy, 73, 145–146, 162, 213–216;
regulation of the peasantry, 147–148, 220;
regulation of women, 147–148, 220;
religious discourse, 183–89, 215–17;
reproductive politics, 167–173;
rural poverty, 73, 148, 155, 164, 201–2, 269n52;
rural reform, 192–93;
species body, 165–194;
standard of living, 153–162, 164, 170, 180, 201;
state planning, 206–207, 213–218, 267n14.
See also Eugenics; Fertility; Geography; Land; Neo-Malthusianism; Peasantry; Progress; Reproduction; Women
population studies, 149
positivism, 10–11, 91, 129, 227n55.
See also Geography, human
postcoloniality, 198, 212, 219–22
Powell, Eve Troutt, 57, 74–75, 246n98
Prakash, Gyan, 8
primitive, idea of the, 52–53. See also Peasantry
progress, idea of, 5, 30, 41, 98, 108–109, 146, 158, 169, 200, 219–222. See also Civilization

al-Qolali, Muhammad, 120–122, 258n40
Qutb, Sayyyid, 13, 90, 102

Rabinbach, Anson, 10, 35

Rabinow, Paul, 8, 107
race: and colonialism, 2, 5–6, 18; indigenous discourse of, 17, 55–61 (see also 'Ammar, 'Abbas Mustafa; Musa, Salama; nationalism, anti-colonial); and national identity, 57, 61, 63; and population growth, 159–162; scientific study of, 32, 34–39, 55–86, 234nn55, 64; taxonomies of, 5, 18, 32, 34–39, 58–61. See also Anthropometry; Arabism; Pharaonicism; Serology; Sharqiya
Rapp, Rayna, 191, 267n12
al-Rifa'i, 'Abd al-Hakim, 171, 192, 275n32
Ramzi, Ahmed, 76
Red Crescent Society, 141, 178
Reid, Donald, 27, 42, 110
Reimer, Michael, 150
Renan, Ernest, 66
reproduction, modernization of, 146, 166–179, 181, 187, 193–94, 220. See also Population; Women
revolution, of 1919, 49–50, 52, 61, 91–96, 101, 119, 123, 220; of 1952, 156, 197–218; of 1952, as "passive revolution," 202–204
Rivers, W.H.R., 79
Rockefeller Foundation, 141
romanticism, 10–11, 18, 91, 129, 227n55
Rommel, Erwin, 141
Roxby, P. M., 110
Royal Agricultural Society (RAS), 90, 110, 125–129, 142
Royal Geographic Society of Egypt (RGS), 23–30, 32, 42–47, 103–111; International Geographical Congress, 1925, 103–104, 153; museum of geography and ethnography, 27–30; 42–43, 45–46, 53

Sabri, Ahmad, 62,
Sa'd, Ahmed Sadiq, 202

Sa'dist Party, 117
Sadiq, Muhammad, 28, 42,
Sa'id, Ahmad Khayri, 178, 193
Sa'id, Khedive 15, 27-28, 32-33, 41
Said, Edward, 30-31
Saint Simon, 10
Salaman, Brenda, 79
Salim, 'Abd al-Majid, 145, 186-87
Sammarco, Angelo, 43
Sanger, Margaret, 149
al-Sayyid, Ahmed Lufti, 103
Schweinfurth, Georg August, 25, 28
Schopenhauer, Arthur, 38
Schulze, Reinhard, 94-95
Scott, James, 125, 130
Seligman, Charles, 74, 79-80, 247n127
Selim, Samah, 101, 115, 290n15
semicolonialism, 3
Semites, 70-71
serology, 70-71, 74, 245n80
al-Sha'arawi, Ali, 92
Shadi, Ahmed Abu, 62
al-Shafa'i, Husayn, 214
Shalabi, Mohamed, 135
Shaltut, Mahmud, 216-17
al-Sharqawi, 'Abd al-Rahman, 102
Sharqiya, 69-73
Shawqi, Ahmed, 62-63, 92, 99
Shidyaq, Filib, 169, 172
Sidqi, Isma'il, 117
Simaika, Marcus, 62
Simmel, Georg, 1, 151-152
Siwa oasis, 42, 44-45
Smith, Grafton Elliot, 55, 60, 63-64, 243n51
social engineering, 4, 11, 17, 111, 218
socialism, 156, 198-199, 202-208, 211-218, 274n25, 285n30, 286n34, 289n86. *See also* Capitalism; Etatism
social sciences, colonial, 2, 4-8; colonial anthropology, 18, 32, 66, 72, 79, 234n55
social sciences, Egyptian, 1, 3-8, 18-19. *See also* Anthropology; Geography; Intelligentsia, Egyptian; Peasantry; Population; *and Individual intellectuals*
social sciences, European, 1-2, 7, 10, 15, 18, 30-41. *See also* Geography, French tradition of; *and Individual intellectuals*
social welfare, 6; and anthropological studies, 45, 69; as a mode of regulation, 113-142, 183, 197-218, 230n83, 289n86; definition of, 198-99, 283n6. *See also* Etatism; Peasantry; Population; Socialism; Tahrir Province project
Société Internationale pour la Protection de l'Enfance (S.I.P.E.), 178
Sorbonne, 1, 43, 104, 109
Spencer, Herbert, 38, 163, 169
Stack, Lee, 99
Stanley, Henry Morton, 25, 231n17
Steele, James, 129
Stoler, Ann, 35
Subaltern Studies Group, 219-220
subalternity, 219-220
Sudan, 3, 26-27, 29, 32, 74-86, 99, 246n109, 246n112. *See also* Africa, Egyptian colonial ambitions towards
Suez Canal, 24, 28, 103, 117
Supreme Council for Rural Welfare, 139
survivals, doctrine of, 46-52, 264n149; nationalist underpinnings, 52

Tahrir Province project, 198, 208-212
al-Tahtawi, Rifa'a Rafi', 15, 66, 74
Taussig, Michael, 118
Tawfiq, Khedive, 15, 27, 32
tea, misuse of, 121-22, 192
Tervuren Museum, 43, 237n109
Third International Geographical Congress and Exhibition at Venice (1881), 26-27
Tignor, Robert, 117
Tilley, Helen, 77
temporality, 53, 221-22

Torres Straits expedition, 79, 234n55
translation, 6–10, 66, 221–222, 226n50, 273n14, 290n12; concepts of race, 56, 60–61; reproductive politics, 167–68, 170
Trillo, Mauricio Tenorio, 24
Tusun, Umar 117
Tutankhamun, 62; tomb of, 61–62
Tyler, E.B., 58

'Umar, Muhammad, 119–120
'Urabi revolt, 119, 151, 250n35

Vaughn, Mary Kay, 114
Verdi, 24
Vidal de la Blanche, Paul, 107–110
violence, 6, 84, 198. *See also* Peasantry; Social welfare, as a mode of regulation
Volait, Mercedes, 115

Wafd Party, 92–94, 99, 117, 141, 202
Wahba, Mourad Magdi, 199–200
Wainwright, G.A., 45
al-Wakil, 'Abd al-Wahid, 117, 138, 155, 173
Warriner, Doreen, 197, 209
Wayment, Hilary, 99
Weber, Max, 7
Westernization, 65
Wingate, Francis Reginald, 92–93
women, 6, 12–13, 18–19, 37–39, 219–221;
    birth control, 167–73, 179–81, 184–94;
    domesticity, 174–77, 179;
    health, 134;
    feminism, 174–75, 183, 191;
    Islamist discourse, 174, 186–89;
    maternal-child welfare programs, 157–58, 170, 174–76, 280n106;
    motherhood, 136, 139–140, 147, 174–79, 183, 190–92, 276nn51, 52;
    pregnancy, 140;
    reproductive insanity, 189–191;
    reproductive politics, 145, 149, 155, 157, 160, 165–194, 213–218;
    social uplift of, 18, 147, 149, 177, 191–92, 211.
    See also Eugenics; Egyptian Feminist Union (EFU); Motherhood; Nationalism; Population; Tahrir Province project
Workers' Vanguard, 99
World Population Conference (Geneva, 1927), 149

Young Egypt, 76, 117, 141, 255n1

Zaalouk, Malak, 204
Zaghlul, Ahmed Fathi, 92
Zaghlul, Sa'd, 51–52, 92–93, 99, 161
Zaki, Abd al-Rahman, 76
Zaki, Gamal, 209–209
Zaydan, Émile, 62
Zaydan, Jurji, 58–59

The authorized representative in the EU for product safety and compliance is:
Mare Nostrum Group
B.V Doelen 72
4831 GR Breda
The Netherlands

www.ingramcontent.com/pod-product-compliance
Lightning Source LLC
Chambersburg PA
CBHW021801220426
43662CB00006B/145